PSYCHOLOGICAL
EXPERIMENTS
on the
INTERNET

PSYCHOLOGICAL EXPERIMENTS

on the

INTERNET

Edited by

Michael H. Birnbaum

Department of Psychology
California State University, Fullerton
and Decision Research Center
Fullerton, California 92834

ACADEMIC PRESS

A Harcourt Science and Technology Company

San Diego   San Francisco   New York   Boston   London   Sydney   Tokyo

Academic Press
A Harcourt Science and Technology Company
525 B Street, Suite 1900, San Diego, California 92101-4495, USA
http://www.apnet.com

Academic Press
24-28 Oval Road, London NW1 7DX, UK
http://www.hbuk.co.uk/ap/

Library of Congress Catalog Card Number: 99-68195

International Standard Book Number: 0-12-099980-3

PRINTED IN THE UNITED STATES OF AMERICA
00   01   02   03   04   05   ML   9   8   7   6   5   4   3   2   1

CONTENTS

SECTION I
GENERAL ISSUES

CHAPTER 1
Decision Making in the Lab and on the Web
Michael H. Birnbaum

CHAPTER 2
Validity of Web-Based Psychological Research
John H. Krantz and Reeshad Dalal

CHAPTER 3
A Brief History of Web Experimenting
Jochen Musch and Ulf-Dietrich Reips

CHAPTER 4
The Web Experiment Method: Advantages, Disadvantages, and Solutions
Ulf-Dietrich Reips

SECTION II
INDIVIDUAL DIFFERENCES AND CROSS-CULTURAL STUDIES

CHAPTER 5
Potential of the Internet for Personality Research
Tom Buchanan

CHAPTER 6
Human Sexual Behavior:
A Comparison of College and Internet Surveys

Robert D. Bailey, Winona E. Foote, and Barbara Throckmorton

CHAPTER 7
An Intercultural Examination of
Facial Features Communicating Surprise
Donatella Pagani and Luigi Lombardi

CHAPTER 8
What Are Computing Experiences Good For?:
A Case Study in Online Research
John H. Mueller, D. Michele Jacobsen, and Ralf Schwarzer

SECTION III
COMPUTER TECHNIQUES FOR
INTERNET EXPERIMENTATION

CHAPTER 9
PsychExps: An Online Psychology Laboratory
Kenneth O. McGraw, Mark D. Tew, and John E. Williams

CHAPTER 10
Techniques for Creating and Using
Web Questionnaires in Research and Teaching
Jonathan Baron and Michael Siepmann

CHAPTER 11
The Cognitive Psychology Online Laboratory

Gregory Francis, Ian Neath, and Aimee Surprenant

CHAPTER 12
The Server Side of Psychology
Web Experiments
William C. Schmidt

CONTRIBUTORS

Numbers in parentheses indicate the pages on which the authors' contributions begin.

Robert D. Bailey (141), Department of Psychology, California State University, Fullerton, Fullerton, California 92834

Jonathan Baron (235), Department of Psychology, University of Pennsylvania, Philadelphia, Pennsylvania 19104

Michael H. Birnbaum (xv, 3), Department of Psychology, California State University, Fullerton, and Decision Research Center, Fullerton, California 92834

Tom Buchanan (121), Department of Psychology, University of Westminster, London Wir 8AL, United Kingdom

Reeshad Dalal (35), Hanover College, Hanover, Indiana 47243

Winona E. Foote (141), Department of Psychology, California State University, Fullerton, Fullerton, California 92834

Gregory Francis (267), Department of Psychological Sciences, Purdue University, West Lafayette, Indiana 47904

D. Michele Jacobsen (195), EDPS Department, University of Calgary, Calgary, Alberta T2N 1N4, Canada

John H. Krantz (35), Hanover College, Hanover, Indiana 47243

Luigi Lombardi (169), Department of Social and Developmental Psychology, University of Padua, 35131 Padova, Italy

Kenneth O. McGraw (219), Department of Psychology, University of Mississippi, University, Mississippi 38677

John H. Mueller (195), EDPS Department, University of Calgary, Calgary, Alberta T2N 1N4, Canada

Jochen Musch (61), Psychological Institute, University of Bonn, D-53117 Bonn, Germany

Ian Neath (267), Department of Psychological Sciences, Purdue University, West Lafayette, Indiana 47904

Donatella Pagani (169), Department of Social and Developmental Psychology, University of Padua, 35131 Padova, Italy

Ulf-Dietrich Reips (61, 89), Experimental and Developmental Psychology, University of Zürich, CH-8032 Zürich, Switzerland

William C. Schmidt (285), Department of Psychology, University at Buffalo, The State University of New York, Buffalo, New York 14260

Ralf Schwarzer (195), Institute of Psychology, Freie University of Berlin, Habelschwerdter Allee 45, Berlin 14195, Germany

Michael Siepmann (235), University of Pennsylvania, Philadelphia, Pennsylvania 19104

Aimee Surprenant (267), Department of Psychological Sciences, Purdue University, West Lafayette, Indiana 47904

Mark D. Tew (219), Department of Electrical Engineering, University of Mississippi, University, Mississippi 38677

Barbara Throckmorton (141), Department of Psychology, California State University, Fullerton, Fullerton, California 92834

John E. Williams (219), Department of Psychology, University of Mississippi, University, Mississippi 38677

INTRODUCTION TO PSYCHOLOGICAL EXPERIMENTS ON THE INTERNET

Michael H. Birnbaum

In the past few years, it has become possible to conduct meaningful behavioral research via the Internet. As of June 17, 1998, there were 35 Internet experiments in the American Psychological Society's (APS) list of Psychological Research on the Net, maintained by John Krantz (URL http://psych.hanover.edu/APS/exponnet.html). By May 11, 1999, this figure had grown to 65, suggesting a growth rate of about 100% per year. I expect that this book and others like it will accelerate this growth. Of the experiments listed on the APS Web site, 24 were in social psychology, 13 in cognitive psychology, 8 in sensation–perception, 5 in health psychology, 4 in developmental psychology, 3 in clinical psychology, 3 in personality and industrial–organizational psychology, 2 in biological psychology, 2 in emotions, and 1 in general psychology. Although this list does not include all experiments, it gives a proportional estimate that indicates the growth of research conducted via the Web.

Early "pioneers" of Internet research soon learned that it was not only possible to conduct research this way, but also feasible to collect large samples of high-quality data in a short period of time. This book is intended for psychologists who are interested in learning from the experiences of those who have been engaged in this type of research. There is a great deal of good advice given in these pages from those who have learned the hard way.

In reading this book, you should follow suggested links on your computer, which should be your window to the Web and your study companion. One advantage of Web-based research is the ease with which another can see exactly what the participants experienced and also learn how the experimenter carried it out. To save space (and trees), the authors have made a great deal of information available to you electronically via the Internet. Terms used in this book unique to this type of research (e.g., HTTP, HTML, FTP) are defined in a glossary at the end of the book.

The book has three sections. The first deals with general questions such as: Do the results of Web experiments agree with those of laboratory experiments? Who are the people who volunteer to participate via the Internet? What were the developments that led to the first Web studies and what did the early Web researchers experience? What are the methodological considerations in doing research by "remote control"? The second section considers studies of individual differences and cultural differences. Because the Internet provides a means of reaching large and diverse samples, it seems ideally suited to use for these purposes. The third section covers advanced computer techniques that allow for greater control of Internet experiments. These include the dynamic creation and display of graphics, randomization, and timing in experiments such as those in cognitive experimental psychology. In addition, methods for scoring and feedback on surveys or tests, tracking of participants, security, and saving of data on the server are discussed.

GENERAL ISSUES

The first chapter provides a preview of several of the issues and questions that are themes of this book: (1) how to conduct Internet research; (2) recruitment of special populations; (3) how Internet samples differ demographically from college subject pools; (4) how results of Internet and lab experiments compare. The chapter also describes a program of research in decision making. The Appendix to Chapter 1 illustrates how experiments that might be done by paper-and-pencil methods can be easily conducted using the technique of forms available in hypertext markup language (HTML; see glossary). The chapter reviews experiments on decision making that were done with three samples, one conducted with undergraduates in the laboratory, one recruited from experts in judgment and decision making, and another recruited through Web sites that advertise games and drawings with prizes. The decision-making experiments of this chapter can be viewed at URLs http://psych.fullerton.edu/mbirnbaum/exp2a.htm and http://psych.fullerton.edu/mbirnbaum/exp2b.htm.

Krantz and Dalal review studies that test the validity of Web experiments. Whereas laboratory studies typically use a small, homogeneous sample tested under controlled conditions, the Internet study typically uses a large, heterogeneous sample tested under less well controlled conditions. Krantz and Dalal define *validity* in terms of the correspondence of results between experiments conducted via the Web and those done in the laboratory. The trend emerging from the early research on this problem is that Internet studies yield the same conclusions as studies done in the lab. The skeptic may argue that the number of research issues studied so far is limited, so the issue of Internet versus laboratory research will remain an active one until more topics have been studied.

Musch and Reips review the brief history of experimentation on the World Wide Web (WWW). In 1995, several developments (Java, JavaScript, HTML 2 with forms) combined to facilitate Web research. Musch and Reips have surveyed those who conducted the first Web experiments and report their results in their chapter. Most of those who responded to the survey concluded that their research projects were successful and planned to continue research via the Web.

The chapter by Reips considers methodological issues in Internet research. Reips reverses the definition of validity given by Krantz and Dalal, arguing that one should be more skeptical of traditional laboratory research than of Web-based research, because of certain problems of traditional research. For instance, because large and diverse samples are obtained from the Web, one can separately analyze a research question in each demographic subsample to ensure that conclusions that are found with 19-year-old college students also hold in other demographic groups. The chapter reviews pros and cons of Web research, concluding that the advantages of Internet research outweigh the disadvantages. Reips also describes techniques for dealing with potential problems, illustrating certain issues with data from his Web Experimental Psychology Lab (URL http://www.genpsylab.unizh.ch). This site, first established at Tübingen, is now in Zurich. The site contains a number of Web experiments, an archive of past experiments, and commentaries on the Web experiment method.

INDIVIDUAL DIFFERENCES AND CROSS-CULTURAL STUDIES

The second section includes chapters that deal with individual and cross-cultural differences. The chapter by Buchanan reviews the psychometric properties of tests given via the Internet. An important approach to validity is the use of criterion groups. For example, a test of mental illness should distinguish people who are patients in mental institutions from those who work there. Buchanan uses natural criterion groups existing in the form of subscribers to contrasting newsgroups. People who choose to join different groups should differ systematically in specific aspects of their personalities. Illustration of a personality test given by Internet is available at URL http://www.mailbase.ac.uk/lists/psy-net-research/files/tbdemo1.htm. From that site, one can also follow links to join the psy-net-research list (for Internet researchers).

The chapter by Bailey, Foote, and Throckmorton reports a survey of human sexual behavior and attitudes (URL http://psych.fullerton.edu/throck). The chapter considers several difficult issues in sex surveys. Are people honest and unbiased when they answer the questions? Would people be more honest with a computer than they would be with paper-and-pencil surveys or face-to-face interviews? The chapter compares data obtained by requesting university students to complete the survey in class and those obtained by passive recruitment from the Internet. How do such samples differ, and are these differences correlated with sexual attitudes, knowledge, and behavior? Since 1995, over 10,000 people have already responded to a questionnaire of over 400 items.

The Internet makes an experiment available to people from all parts of the world. Pagani and Lombardi take advantage of this new opportunity to conduct a cross-cultural examination of perceptions of the expression of surprise depicted in schematic faces. To experience the experiment, visit the Padua online laboratory (URL http://www.psy.unipd.it/personal/laboratorio/surprise/htmltesi/first3.html). By manipulating features in schematic faces, they are able to change judgments of the degree of surprise. For people of all cultures, a general expansion of the features of the upper face produces higher judgments of degree of surprise. Interestingly, there are differences in judgment that are correlated with the culture or region of the participants. North Americans and Northern Europeans give very similar judgments, but these differ from the judgments of Asians, who appear to give relatively more weight to the eyes than to the eyebrows. Southern Europeans give results that are intermediate between those of Asians and Northern Europeans.

The chapter by Mueller, Jacobsen, and Schwarzer asks if experiences in controlling a computer are correlated with greater self-efficacy. Perhaps people who learn that by following a scheme they can control a computer also learn that they can control other aspects of their lives. The Internet seems a good place to recruit people who either have or have not learned to program. The Internet also allows one to collect large samples in which small correlations can be detected. The survey can be experienced by visiting URL http://www.acs.ucalgary.ca/~mueller/tai-consent.html.

COMPUTER TECHNIQUES FOR
INTERNET EXPERIMENTATION

The third section of the book reviews techniques that allow greater control of an Internet experiment than is afforded by simple HTML. Each technique has certain advantages and potential difficulties compared with other techniques that might accomplish the same goals. These various techniques are discussed in different chapters.

McGraw, Tew, and Williams discuss the use of Shockwave and Authorware to develop their online psychology laboratory, PsychExps. Shockwave, now known as the Authorware Web Player, is a plug-in that plays experiments created by Authorware. The plug-in is available free from http:// www.macromedia.com or via links at http://www.olemiss.edu/ PsychExps, the PsychExps site. Authorware is a Macromedia product that McGraw and his colleagues have found to be an excellent tool for developing computer-controlled psychology experiments. They believe that Authorware is easy enough to learn that a person without programming experience can develop sophisticated experiments. They hope that PsychExps will become a collaborative site developed through the mutual efforts of psychology instructors who will share Authorware experiments and provide data gathering opportunities for students and colleagues. In their chapter, they present this vision and an overview of the technology that makes it possible.

Baron and Siepmann describe how one can use JavaScript to randomize and control Web questionnaires. JavaScript is a scripting language that is distinct from the Java language. JavaScript code can be included as source code on a Web page. Advantages of including the source code on the Web page include the openness of research to the scientific community and the generally fast loading times of such pages. Examples illustrating the techniques described in their chapter can be viewed at URL http://www.psych.upenn.edu/ ~baron/examples/.

The Cognitive Psychology OnLine Laboratory of Purdue is described in the chapter by Francis, Neath, and Surprenant (URL http://coglab. psych.purdue.edu/coglab/). This Web site includes many classic cognitive psychology experiments, with good introductions on the theories behind the experiments. The chapter by Francis et al. discusses advantages and considerations of the Java programming language for implementation of cognitive psychology experiments. Java programs, or classes, are created and compiled by their developers. The compiled code for the applet is then sent along with Web pages as byte codes, which can be interpreted by different browsers on different computers. Like JavaScript, Java applets run on the client's (the visitor's) computer, but they usually take longer to load. A Web page of resources for learning more about Java, including a sample program, can be found at URL `http://coglab.psych.purdue.edu/coglab/java.html`.

Finally, Schmidt discusses ways in which programs on the server can be used to help control Internet experiments. The server is the computer that delivers (or "serves") Web pages to be viewed on the client's (the visitor's) browser. Although some functions such as error checking or question randomization can be carried out using JavaScript, using server programs provides a universal solution guaranteed to work even if JavaScript is not installed on the browser. Other functions such as tracking participants, summarizing group data, password and security control, or the saving of data require server programming. Schmidt has written software that eliminates the need to program when administering Web surveys and tests; it creates both the Web page and the server-side script. This software can be accessed from URL `http://survey.psy.buffalo.edu`.

ACKNOWLEDGMENTS

My efforts in editing this book and writing my chapter were supported by Grant SBR-9410572 from the National Science Foundation. I also thank Juan Navarrete, J. Nicole Patton, Melissa Lott, and Dana Storm for assistance, and Chris Cozby, who administers our department's Web server.

This book owes a debt of gratitude to those who generously gave their time to review one or more chapters. Thanks are due to Robert Bailey, John Bancroft, Jonathan Baron, Tom Buchanan, Douglas L. Chute, Gregory Francis, Dietmar Janetzko, Mark Johnston, John Krantz, Kenneth McGraw, John Mueller, Jochen Musch, Ian Neath, Ulf-Dietrich Reips, William Schmidt, Michael Siepmann, Mark Tew, Connie Varnhagen, and three anonymous reviewers. Many of the definitions for the glossary were suggested by the chapter authors.

WEB SITE

Links for this book will be maintained at the following URL:
`http://psych.fullerton.edu/mbirnbaum/web/Introweb.htm`

SECTION I

General Issues

CHAPTER 1

Decision Making in the Lab and on the Web

Michael H. Birnbaum
Department of Psychology
California State University, Fullerton
and Decision Research Center
Fullerton, California 92834

INTRODUCTION

Psychologists in different fields seem to have different individual characteristics. Clinical psychologists are noted for their odd personalities and mental problems. Developmental psychologists often do not have children of their own. Those in perception usually wear glasses or a hearing aid. Mathematical psychologists seem to have trouble when it comes to simple computations with numbers.

Those of us in decision making have our quirks, too. When you go to a conference, try going out to dinner with a group of decision scientists. First, there will be a long process deciding what time to meet. Then, it will take another hour to decide where to meet. When the time arrives and not everyone is there (at least one of us will be in the hotel room deciding what to wear), there will be a lengthy discussion of whether to wait or go to the restaurant. If we go, should we leave a message saying where we have gone? If so, with whom should we leave the message? Should one person stay behind to wait? Who? Where should we go? When there is disagreement about choosing the French, Italian, or Thai restaurant, how will we decide? Should we have each person give rank-order preferences, or should we use ratings of strength of preference? How should we aggregate the separate opinions? How should we get there? When we get there, how will the bill be divided? One person remarks that if the bill is to be divided equally, he would like to buy the restaurant; everyone then asks for separate checks. And so on, and on, and on.

The problem behavioral decision scientists have is that we recognize that all of our actions are decisions, and we worry whether we are making the right choices. We are aware that people do not always make good decisions, and we know that there is disagreement over what a rational person should do. We know that every action, or failure to act, may have infinite consequences. We realize that different individuals have different values or utilities and that if a group must make a decision, some individuals will come off better than others will. We are cognizant of theories of fairness that dictate how a group should make a decision to maximize both the utility of the members and the perception of fairness. We understand the problems in trying to compare or measure utilities between people, so we are aware that we cannot yet solve important problems we need to solve in order to make good decisions. It makes deciding very hard.

One of the things that we decision scientists have not yet decided is how to represent the processes by which individuals make decisions when confronted with the simplest kinds of choices involving risk or uncertainty. These simple choices are decisions between gambles for cash in which the consequences are amounts of money and the probabilities are stated explicitly. Would you rather have a 50–50 chance of winning $100 or $0 or be given $49 in cash? Typical college students will answer quickly that they prefer $49 in cash to the gamble, even though they know that the gamble has a higher average, or expected value, of $50.

The attraction of studying choices between gambles is that the experimenter can vary consequences and probabilities cleanly. If we asked people about whether they would prefer to order the fish or the chicken at a new restaurant, the decision is complicated by the fact that each person has a different subjective probability distribution for consequences and different utilities for those consequences. Perhaps the person likes well-prepared fish better than well-prepared chicken, but knows that if the fish is not fresh or the cook unskilled, then the chicken would taste better than the fish. Then also, the person may have just eaten chicken yesterday, and that person might have tastes that depend on sequential and temporal effects. These individual differences in utilities of the consequences, subjective probabilities concerning the tastes of food, and other complicating factors make such real-life decisions harder to study than choices between gambles.

Over the years, descriptive models of individual decision making have grown more and more complicated, to reconcile theory with empirical data for even these simple choices. Another trend is that definitions of rationality have changed, to accommodate empirical choices that people insist are rational, even if they violate old definitions of rationality. There are three solid principles of rationality, however, that have rarely been disputed, and this chapter will discuss cases where empirical choices in laboratory studies have violated implications deduced from these principles. These three principles are transitivity, consequence monotonicity, and coalescing. They are assumed not only by models considered normative, but also by theories that attempt to describe empirical choices.

TRANSITIVITY, MONOTONICITY, AND COALESCING

Suppose A, B, and C are gambles. Let $\succ$ represent the preference relation, and let $\sim$ represent indifference. *Transitivity* asserts that if $B \succ C$ and $A \succ B$ (one prefers B to C and A to B), then $A \succ C$. If a person persisted in violating transitivity, he or she could be made into a "money pump." That person would presumably pay a premium to get B instead of C, pay to get A instead of B, pay to get C instead of A, pay again to get B instead of C, and so on forever.

Let $G = (x, p; y, q; z, r)$ represent a gamble to win x with probability p, y with probability q, and z with probability $r = 1 - p - q$. *Consequence monotonicity* says that if we increased x, y, or z, holding everything else constant, the gamble with the higher consequence should be preferred. In other words, $G+ = (x^+, p; y, q; z, r) \succ G$, where $x^+ > x$. For example, if $G+ = (\$100, .5; \$1, .5)$, you should prefer $G+$ to $G = (\$25, .5; \$1, .5)$. $G+$ is the same as G, except you might win \$100 instead of \$25, so if you satisfy consequence monotonicity (you prefer more money to less), you should prefer $G+$.

Coalescing says that if two events in a gamble produce equal consequences, they can be combined by adding their probabilities, and this combination should not affect one's preferences. Suppose $GS = (x, p; x, q; z, r)$. Then $GS \sim G = (x, p + q; z, r)$. I will call GS the *split* version of the gamble, G the *coalesced* version of the same gamble. For example, if $G = (\$100, .5; \$0, .5)$ and $GS = (\$100, .3; \$100, .2; \$0, .5)$, coalescing asserts that one should be indifferent between G and GS. Coalescing and transitivity together imply that $G \succ H$ if and only if $GS \succ HS$. Because GS is really the same gamble as G and HS is really the same gamble as H, it seems quite rational that one's preference should not depend on how the gambles are described. If this combination is violated (e.g., if $G \succ H$ and $GS \prec HS$), this violation is called an *event-splitting effect*. Starmer and Sugden (1993) and Humphrey (1995) reported event-splitting effects.

These three properties (transitivity, monotonicity, and coalescing) taken together imply *stochastic dominance*, a property that has been considered both rational and descriptive. Stochastic dominance is implied by current descriptive models of decision making, such as rank-dependent expected utility (RDU) theory (Quiggin, 1982, 1985, 1993), rank- and sign-dependent utility (RSDU) theory (Luce, 1990; Luce & Fishburn, 1991, 1995; von Winterfeldt, 1997), and cumulative prospect theory (CPT Tversky & Kahneman, 1992; Wakker & Tversky, 1993; Tversky & Wakker, 1995; Wu & Gonzalez, 1996). Stochastic dominance has also been assumed in other descriptive theories (Becker & Sarin, 1987; Machina, 1982). Although RDU and configural weight models have in common that weights may be affected by rank (Birnbaum, 1974; Weber, 1994), certain configural weight models predict that stochastic dominance will be violated in certain circumstances (Birnbaum, 1997, 1999a; Birnbaum & Navarrete, 1998), contrary to RDU.

STOCHASTIC DOMINANCE

Consider two nonidentical gambles, $G+$ and $G-$, where the probability to win x or more in gamble $G+$ is greater than or equal to the probability of winning x or more in gamble $G-$ for all x. Gamble $G+$ stochastically dominates $G-$. If choices satisfy stochastic dominance, then $G+$ should be preferred to $G-$; that is, $G+ \succ G-$.

Consider $G+ = (\$2, .05; \$4, .05; \$96, .9)$ and $G- = (\$2, .1; \$90, .05; \$96, .85)$, which might be presented to people as follows:

Would you prefer to play Gamble A or B?			
A:	.05 probability to win \$2	B:	.10 probability to win \$2
	.05 probability to win \$4		.05 probability to win \$90
	.90 probability to win \$96		.85 probability to win \$96

I proposed this choice (Birnbaum, 1997) as a test between the class of RSDU/RDU/CPT theories, which satisfy stochastic dominance, and the class of configural weight models that my colleagues and I had published (e.g., Birnbaum, 1974; Birnbaum & Chavez, 1997; Birnbaum & Stegner, 1979), which can violate stochastic dominance.

According to the configural weight models of Birnbaum and McIntosh (1996) and Birnbaum and Chavez (1997), with parameters estimated from choices of college students, the value of $G-$ exceeds the value of $G+$. If such a model and its parameters have any generality, one should be able to predict from one experiment to the next, so college students tested under comparable conditions should systematically violate stochastic dominance on this choice. However, no RSDU/RDU/CPT model can violate stochastic dominance, except by chance response error.[1]

It is instructive to show that transitivity, consequence monotonicity, and coalescing imply $G+ \succ G-$. Note that $G+ = (\$2, .05; \$4, .05; \$96, .9) \succ GS = (\$2, .05; \$2, .05; \$96, .9)$ by consequence monotonicity. By coalescing, $GS \sim G = (\$2, .1; \$96, .9) \sim GS' = (\$2, .1; \$96, .05; \$96, .85)$. By consequence monotonicity, $GS' \succ G- = (\$2, .1; \$90, .05; \$96, .85)$. We now have $G+ \succ GS \sim G \sim GS' \succ G-$; by transitivity, $G+ \succ G-$.

Birnbaum and Navarrete (1998) included 4 variations of this recipe (testing stochastic dominance) among over 100 other choices between gambles. They found that about 70% of 100 college undergraduates violated stochastic dominance by choosing $G-$ over $G+$ in these tests. Birnbaum, Patton, and Lott (1999) found similar rates of violation of stochastic dominance with a new group of 110 students and 5 new variations, also tested in the lab.

Because these violations are inconsistent with both rational principles and a wide class of descriptive theory, it is important to know if these violations are limited to the particular methods used in the laboratory studies. Do these results generalize from the lab to the so-called real world where real people who have completed their educations make decisions for real money?

EXPERIMENTAL PROCEDURES

One of the things that decision scientists cannot decide, or at least agree upon, is how to do a decision-making study. Some investigators like to give out questionnaires with one or two decision problems and ask a classroom full of students to respond to these as they might to a quiz. Others like to collect many decisions from each decision maker. Whereas most psychologists are content to collect judgments and decisions from people about hypothetical situations, some investigators argue that only when decisions have real consequences should we take the responses seriously.

The studies by Birnbaum and Navarrete (1998) and Birnbaum et al. (1999), like any experiments in any field of science, can be questioned for their procedures. Those studies did not use real financial incentives; maybe people would conform to stochastic dominance if there were real consequences to their decisions. In those studies, judges were requested to make over 100

---

[1]To compute predictions for CPT and the configural weight, TAX models, use a Netscape to visit the following on-line calculator in URL http://psych.fullerton.edu/mbirnbaum/taxcalculator.htm

decisions. Perhaps with so many trials, judges become bored or fatigued. The judges were college students; perhaps college students are uneducated with respect to the value of money and the laws of probability. Perhaps the particular format for presentation of the gambles is crucial to the findings. Perhaps the particular instructions are crucial to the results.

Decision-making experiments in my lab typically require judges to evaluate differences between gambles; they are asked not only to choose between gambles, but also to judge how much they would pay to get their preferred gamble rather than the other gamble in each pair. This procedure has been used in several studies in an attempt to get more information from each trial (Birnbaum & McIntosh, 1996; Birnbaum & Chavez, 1997; Birnbaum & Navarrete, 1998; Birnbaum et al., 1999). Perhaps the task of evaluating differences affects how people choose; if so, then these studies, which have found evidence troublesome to RSDU/RDU/CPT theories, might not predict the results of studies in which people just choose between gambles.

Teresa Martin and I tested three variations of experimental procedure with college students to address these procedural questions (Birnbaum & Martin, 1999); those studies form a prelude to those that are the focus of this chapter. In two of those studies, students were asked only to choose (they did not also judge strength of preference). Two different formats for displaying the choices were also investigated. Two studies used real cash incentives (with possible prizes as high as $220). There were also a few other procedural variations to address concerns raised by reviewers, who seemed stunned by the high rates of violation of stochastic dominance observed by Birnbaum and Navarrete (1998) and Birnbaum et al. (1999).

One of the variations was to reduce the number of choices from over 100 to 14. This allowed all of the choices to be printed on the same page, so that people could see any inconsistency among their choices without even having to turn the page.

I must tell you that short experiments are not really my cup of tea. However, the Internet experiments I will be reviewing in this chapter are short experiments. They were made short in hopes of recruiting well-educated, busy people to complete the task. Therefore, I need to explain as clearly as I can the connections between the long and the short of experiments.

ADVANTAGES OF LONGER EXPERIMENTS

The advantage of a longer experiment in the lab is that we can collect enough data to test theories at the level of the individual. If we have enough data, we can fit the model to each person, allowing different parameters in the model to represent individual differences among people. In a longer experiment, one has the luxury to manipulate components of the gambles that will enable the study to create proper tests for each individual.

This last point deserves emphasis. One should not construct an experimental design by throwing together some choices between gambles and then hope to study violations of a property or the fit of a model. Instead, one should design the experiment based on everything that is known in advance and show that the experiment will actually test between two or more theories under investigation, given the numerical results that have been observed in prior experiments with similar conditions.

Some people, who are otherwise very good scientists, sometimes lose sight of the consequences of numerical parameter values in psychological research. As noted above, we mathematical psychologists do not really like working with actual numbers. The ancient Greeks distinguished between abstract mathematics, consisting of elegant theorems and proofs, and mere "reckoning" or "accounting," referring to computation with numbers. Well, we mathematical psychologists enjoy working with abstract entities, but we sometimes forget that numbers can be real.

The way I think an experiment should be designed is as follows: Calculate predictions from rival models that have been fitted in previous experiments for the proposed design, and show that the proposed experiment will test between them. If the parameters estimated are "real" and if the theory is right, then we should be able to predict the results of a new experiment.

Thus, to design an experiment, show in advance that the experimental design distinguishes two or more theories based on the parameters estimated from the application of those theories to previous data.

Next, investigate the model to see what would happen if the parameters estimated from previous experiments are "off" a bit or if individuals were to have values that differ from the average. For example, to study violations of stochastic dominance, it would not work to just throw together pairs of gambles and then see how often people violate stochastic dominance for a random mix of gambles. Instead, use a theory that predicts violations to figure out where the violations can be found. The theory does not *always* predict violations, but it does for some pairs of gambles. Calculate the predictions under the model, and devise choices that should violate it according to the model and parameters.

If you would like to try a calculator to compute predictions according to two models, use Netscape to visit the JavaScript calculator at URL `http://psych.fullerton.edu/mbirnbaum/taxcalculator.htm` and calculate the values of the $G-$ and $G+$ gambles in the preceding example. Use the default parameters, and you will find that the transfer of attention exchange (TAX) model predicts that $G-$ is calculated to have a cash value of

$59.36, which is higher than the value of $G+$, which is $39.72. You can change the parameters over the range of values reported in the literature, and you will find that the configural weight TAX model that is implemented in that calculator continues to predict a violation of stochastic dominance for this choice for parameter values published in the literature.

The other class of theories (RSDU/RDU/CPT and others satisfying stochastic dominance) can tolerate no violations beyond those produced by random error. For example, in the calculator, you will find that CPT never predicts a violation, no matter what parameters you try. For that property, one need not calculate or reckon, because it can be proved mathematically (Birnbaum & Navarrete, 1998; Luce, 1998).

Therefore, we have a contrast between a model that can violate stochastic dominance for *certain choices* over a wide range of parameters and a class of theories that cannot violate the property for any set of choices under any parameters.

Suppose $G+ = (\$2, .05; \$40, .05; \$96, .9)$ and $G- = (\$2, .10; \$50, .05; \$96, .85)$. If you plug these values in to the online calculator, you will find that both models predict satisfaction of stochastic dominance. Only with parameter values that deviate considerably from typical values reported in the literature would the configural weight model predict systematic violations. Thus, this pair of gambles would not be fruitful, by itself, in a test between these models.

Similarly, if $G+ = (\$2, .05; \$50, .05; \$96, .9)$ and $G- = (\$2, .05; \$40, .05; \$96, .9)$, then neither model predicts a violation. This last comparison is an example of what is called *transparent* dominance, in which the probabilities are the same and the consequences differ or the consequences are the same and the probabilities of higher consequences are higher in one gamble. Both models also predict satisfaction of stochastic dominance in these cases.

One can think of an experimental design as a fishnet and think of violations of behavioral properties by different individuals as fish. If the gaps between lines are large, fish might swim through the holes. If the net is small, the fish might swim over, under, left, or right of the net. The larger and tighter the net, the more likely one is to "catch" the phenomena that the experiment is designed to find. If a person used a small net and caught no fish, it would not be correct to conclude that there are no fish in the lake. Another application of this philosophy of design is described in Birnbaum and McIntosh (1996), for the case of violations of branch independence.

For these reasons, I prefer large designs, which means fairly long experiments.

However, in the lab, my colleagues and I have now conducted these (relatively) long experiments and have fitted the data to models. If the theory is correct, then these models (and their estimated parameters) should predict the results in shorter experiments, unless the procedures, length, participants, or context of the experiment itself is crucial to the results.

Therefore, it was a relief to me that we could replicate the violations of stochastic dominance with a small design, financial incentives, and other variations in procedure (Birnbaum & Martin, 1999). In one condition of our study, undergraduates were tested in the laboratory with HTML forms displayed by computers. If that study had not replicated results found previously with paper and pencil in longer experiments, much additional work in the lab would have been required to pin down the effects of different procedures. We would need to determine if the choice process had changed or if merely parameters of the model were affected by changes in procedure. The replication in the new situation meant that I could put a short experiment on the Web, with some foreknowledge of what to expect.

WHY STUDY DECISION MAKING ON THE INTERNET?

Because violations of stochastic dominance, coalescing, and other properties potentially refute an important class of descriptive theories, I needed to find out if laboratory studies hold up outside the lab with people other than college students who have the chance to win real money. I decided to recruit members of the Society for Judgment and Decision Making (SJDM) and the Society for Mathematical Psychology. These groups consist primarily of university professors and graduate students who have expertise in this area. Most of them have studied theories of decision making and are aware of various phenomena that have been labeled as "biases or fallacies" of human decisions. Members of these groups are motivated not only by money, but also by a desire not to be caught behaving badly with respect to rational principles of decision making. Nobody wants to be called "biased."

Internet A was recruited by e-mail sent to all subscribers of these two societies, inviting their participation (Birnbaum, 1999b). I also wanted to recruit other denizens of the Web and to test in the laboratory a sample of undergraduates from the subject pool. I recruited the *Internet B* sample primarily by posting notices in sites that list contests with prizes, to see the effects of the recruitment method on the sample. However, the first study started a snowball effect that continued to bring friends of friends of the Internet A participants to the study.

This chapter features Internet B, but I will also review the results of Birnbaum (1999b), which compares a laboratory sample with Internet A. That study investigated not only the properties of consequence monotonicity, stochastic dominance, and event splitting, which are the focus of this chapter, but also properties known as lower cumulative independence, upper cumulative independence, and branch independence. Those tests are discussed in Birnbaum (1999b) and will not be reviewed here.

INTERNET AND LAB STUDIES

Participants completed the experiments online by visiting the Web site, which can be viewed at `http://psych.fullerton.edu/mbirnbaum /exp2b.htm`. Internet A's experiment can be viewed at `http:// psych.fullerton.edu/mbirnbaum/exp2a.htm`, which is also re-tired. A brief explanation of the HTML in the site is given in the Appendix.

The Web site instructed visitors that they might win some money by choosing between gambles. For example, would you rather play A—50–50 chance of winning either \$100 or \$0 (nothing)—OR B—50–50 chance of winning either \$25 or \$35?

> Think of probability as the number of tickets in a bag containing 100 tickets, divided by 100. Gamble A has 50 tickets that say \$100 and 50 that say \$0, so the probability to win \$100 is .50 and the probability to get \$0 is .50. If someone reaches in bag A, half the time they might win \$0 and half the time \$100. But in this study, you only get to play a gamble once, so the prize will be either \$0 or \$100. Gamble B's bag has 100 tickets also, but 50 of them say \$25 and 50 of them say \$35. Bag B thus guarantees at least \$25, but the most you can win is \$35.
>
> For each choice below, click the button beside the gamble you would rather play. ...after people have finished their choices... [1% of participants] will be selected randomly to play one gamble for real money. One trial will be selected randomly from the 20 trials, and if you were one of the lucky winners, you will get to play the gamble you chose on the trial selected. You might win as much as \$110. Any one of the 20 choices might be the one you get to play, so choose carefully.

By random devices (10- and 20-sided dice), 19 participants were selected and prizes were awarded as promised; 11 winners received \$90 or more.

STIMULI

Gambles were displayed as in the following example:

⊙1. Which do you choose?
        ○A: .50 probability to win \$0
             .50 probability to win \$100
   OR
        ○B: .50 probability to win \$25
             .50 probability to win \$35

There were 20 choices between gambles in each study. In Internet A (Birnbaum, 1999b) these were designed to include two tests of stochastic dominance, event-splitting, consequence monotonicity, upper cumulative independence, lower cumulative independence, and branch independence, with position of the gambles counterbalanced. For Internet A, the 20 choices were selected on the basis of prior research to be ones that should show violations, on the basis of models fitted to laboratory data of college students (Birnbaum, 1997, 1999a). In addition, there were tests of risk seeking versus risk aversion and indirect tests of consequence monotonicity. In Internet B, 8 of the choices were the same as those in Internet A, and 12 of the choices were different. The 8 choices common to both studies are listed in Table 1. The other choices in Internet B were tests of the Allais common ratio and common consequence paradoxes (Allais & Hagen, 1979), using cash amounts less than $111.

The forms also requested each participant's e-mail address, country, age, gender, and education. Subjects were also asked, "Have you ever read a scientific paper (i.e., a journal article or book) on the theory of decision making or the psychology of decision making? (Yes or No)." Comments were also invited, with a text box provided for that purpose.

RECRUITMENT OF LAB AND INTERNET SAMPLES

Lab Sample

The lab sample consisted of 124 undergraduates from the subject pool who signed up in the usual way and served as one option toward an assignment in introductory psychology. They were directed to a computer lab, where the experimental Web page was already displayed on several computers. Experimenters checked that participants knew how to use the mouse to click and to scroll through the page. After completing the form and clicking the "submit" button, each lab participant was asked to repeat the same task on a fresh page. The lab data thus permit assessment of reliability. The mean number of agreements between the first and second repetitions of the task was 16.4 (82% agreement).

Internet Samples

The Internet A sample consisted of 1224 people who completed Experiment A online within 4 months of its inauguration. The Internet B sample consisted of 737 people who completed Experiment B during the following 6 weeks.

Demographic Characteristics of the Samples

I was impressed by the speed with which the Internet data came in. Over 150 people participated within 2 days of the site's inauguration. Most of these first participants were members of SJDM who apparently clicked the link in the e-mail and immediately did the experiment. Within 12 days, 318 had participated, 77% of whom had some post-graduate education, including 69 with doctoral degrees. Only 14% of the first 318 were less than 23 years old.

A comparison of demographic characteristics of the three samples is presented in Table 2. The lab sample was composed of young college students; 91% were 22 and under, with the oldest being 28. On education, 91% of the lab sample had 3 years or less of college (none had degrees). Because I sought to recruit a highly educated sample, I was glad to see that in Internet A, 60% had college diplomas, including 333 who had taken postgraduate studies, among whom 134 had doctoral degrees. Whereas the lab sample was 73% female, Internet A was 56% female. Of the lab sample, 13% indicated having read a scientific work on decision making, compared to 31% of the Internet A sample. The Internet B sample is intermediate between the lab and Internet A with respect to education and experience.

All lab subjects were from the United States, whereas the Internet samples represented 49 different nations. One of the exciting things about doing Internet research is watching data come in from faraway lands. Countries that were represented by 8 or more people were Australia (34), Canada (110), Germany (57), Netherlands (70), Norway (14), Spain (8), United Kingdom (46), and United States (1502). Other nations represented were Afghanistan, Austria, Belgium, Brazil, Bulgaria, Chile, China, Colombia, Cyprus, Denmark, Finland, France, Greece, Hong Kong, Hungary, India, Indonesia, Ireland, Israel, Italy, Japan, Jordan, Korea, Lebanon, Malaysia, Mexico, New Zealand, Pakistan, Panama, Peru, Philippines, Poland, Puerto Rico, Singapore, Slovenia, South Africa, Sri Lanka, Sweden, Switzerland, Turkey, and United Arab Emirates. Internet A and B samples had 896 (73%) and 606 (82%) from the United States, respectively.

RESULTS

Comparison of Choice Percentages

The correlation between the 20 choice proportions for Internet A and lab samples was .94. Table 1 shows the choice percentages (% choice for the

Table 1

**Choices Used to Test Stochastic Dominance and Other Properties,
Common to All Three Samples**

Choice no.	Type			Choice			%Choice Internet A	B	Lab
1			A:	.50 to win $0 .50 to win $100	B:	.50 to win $25 .50 to win $35	48	52	58
2			C:	.50 to win $0 .50 to win $100	D:	.50 to win $45 .50 to win $50	60	63	69
3			E:	.50 to win $4 .30 to win $96 .20 to win $100	F:	.50 to win $4 .30 to win $12 .20 to win $100	6	9	8
4			G:	.40 to win $2 .50 to win $12 .10 to win $108	H:	.40 to win $2 .50 to win $96 .10 to win $108	96	97	94
5	$G+$	$G-$	I:	.05 to win $12 .05 to win $14 .90 to win $96	J:	.10 to win $12 .05 to win $90 .85 to win $96	58	64	73
7	$G-$	$G+$	M:	.06 to win $6 .03 to win $96 .91 to win $99	N:	.03 to win $6 .03 to win $8 .94 to win $99	54	46	36
11	$GS+$	$GS-$	U:	.05 to win $12 .05 to win $14 .05 to win $96 .85 to win $96	V:	.05 to win $12 .05 to win $12 .05 to win $90 .85 to win $96	10	14	15
13	$GS-$	$GS+$	Y:	.03 to win $6 .03 to win $6 .03 to win $96 .91 to win $99	Z	.03 to win $6 .03 to win $8 .03 to win $99 .91 to win $99	95	95	92

Note: Choice types are described in the Introduction. Percentages show choices for the gamble printed on the right in the table. Choices 1 and 2 assess risk aversion; Choices 3 and 4 test consequence monotonicity ("transparent" dominance).

gamble printed on the right in Table 1) for the 8 choice problems common to all 3 samples.

The term *risk aversion* refers to preference for safer gambles over riskier ones with the same or higher expected value (EV). If a person prefers a gamble to the expected value of the gamble or more, the person is described as *risk seeking*. If a person always chooses the gamble with the higher EV, that person is described as *risk neutral*. Consistent with previous findings, 60, 63, and 69% of the Internet A, Internet B, and lab samples chose a 50–50 gamble to win $45 or $50 over a 50–50 gamble to win $0 or $100, showing that the majority of each group exhibits risk aversion (Choice 2 in Table 1).

Table 2

Demographic Characteristics of the Samples (Percentages)

Characteristic	Internet A ($n = 1,224$)	Internet B ($n = 737$)	Lab ($n = 124$)
Age 22 years and under	20	22	91
Older than 40 years	20	24	0
College graduate	60	47	0
Doctorates	11	3	0
Read scientific paper on decision making	31	19	13
Female	56	61	73
Violations of stochastic dominance	52	59	68
Violations of consequence monotonicity	7	8	11

Note: Violations of stochastic dominance and consequence monotonicity are averaged over Choices 5 and 7 and Choices 11 and 13, respectively.

Similarly, 74 and 68% of the Internet A and lab samples preferred $96 for sure over a gamble with a .99 probability of winning $100, otherwise $0. These choices indicate that the majority of both groups are risk averse for medium and high probabilities. However, 58 and 55% of these groups showed evidence of risk seeking as well, since they preferred a .01 probability of winning $100, otherwise nothing over $1 for sure. This pattern of risk aversion for medium and high probabilities of winning and risk seeking for small probabilities of winning is consistent with previous results (e.g., Tversky & Kahneman, 1992).

MONOTONICITY

Consequence monotonicity requires that if two gambles are identical except for the value of one (or more) consequence(s), then the gamble with the higher consequence(s) should be preferred. There were four direct tests of consequence monotonicity. In two of the tests (Choices 3 and 4 in Table 1), both gambles were the same, except one consequence was higher in one of the gambles. In two tests (Choices 11 and 13), there were four consequences, two of which were better in the dominant gamble. The average rates of violation in direct tests of monotonicity were 6.0, 7.9, and 9.3% for Internet A, Internet B, and lab samples, respectively.

There were also six choices that indirectly tested monotonicity in the Internet A and lab samples. For example, suppose a person prefers $1 for sure to the gamble with a .01 chance of winning $100, otherwise $0. That same

Table 3

Violations of Stochastic Dominance and Event-Splitting Effects in Internet B ($n = 737$) and Lab Samples ($n = 124$, Two Replicates), Respectively

Internet sample B				Lab sample			
	Choice 11				Choice 11		
Choice 5	GS +	GS −		Choice 5	GS +	GS −	
G +	31.5	4.5	36.0	G +	21.8	4.8	26.6
G −	**54.3***	9.2	**63.5**	G −	**62.5***	9.7	**72.2**
	86.0	10.5			**84.3**	14.5	
	Choice 13				Choice 13		
Choice 7	GS +	GS −		Choice 7	GS +	GS −	
G +	43.3	2.6	45.9	G +	33.1	2.8	35.9
G −	**51.2***	2.6	**54.0**	G −	**58.5***	5.6	**64.1**
	94.6	5.2			**91.6**	8.4	

Note: Percentages sum to less than 100, due to a few who did not respond to all items.

person should also prefer \$3 for sure to the same gamble; if not, the person violated a combination of transitivity and consequence monotonicity. The average rates of violation of indirect monotonicity were 1.6 and 2.8% for Internet A and lab samples, respectively. There was one such test in Internet B, with 1.2% violations.

If we take consequence monotonicity as an index of the quality of the data, then the Internet data would be judged higher in quality than the lab data, because the Internet data have lower rates of violation. However, in longer lab experiments (e.g., Birnbaum & Navarrete, 1998), violations of consequence monotonicity are still lower.

STOCHASTIC DOMINANCE AND EVENT SPLITTING

Table 3 shows results of two tests of stochastic dominance and event splitting for Internet B (on the left) and laboratory (on the right) samples. Entries are percentages of each combination of preferences in Choices 5 and 11 and in 7 and 13 of Table 1. If everyone satisfied stochastic dominance, then 100% would have chosen $G +$ and $GS +$. Instead, half or more of choice combinations of Choices 5 and 11 were $G −$ and $GS +$ (shown in bold type). Note that whereas 86 and 84.3% of the Internet B and lab samples satisfied stochastic dominance by choosing $GS +$ over $GS −$ on Choice 11, 63.5 and 72.2% of these respective samples violated stochastic dominance by choosing

$G-$ over $G+$ on Choice 5. Results for Internet A were comparable to those of Internet B, as shown in Table 1.

To compare the choice probabilities of $G+ \succ G-$ and $GS+ \succ GS-$, one can use the test of correlated proportions. This test compares entries in the off-diagonals, that is, $G-$ and $GS+$ against $G+$ and $GS-$. If there were no difference in choice proportions, the two off-diagonal entries would be equal, except for error. The binomial sign test with $p = 1/2$ is the null hypothesis. For example, in Internet B, 400 people violated stochastic dominance by choosing $G- \succ G+$ on Choice 5 *and* switched preferences by choosing $GS+ \succ GS-$ on Choice 11, compared to only 33 who showed the opposite combination of preferences. In this case, the binomial has a mean of 216.5 with a standard deviation of 10.4; therefore, $z = 17.6^*$. Because the critical value of z with $\alpha = .05$ is 1.96, this result is significant. Asterisks in text or tables denote statistical significance.

One can also separately test the (very conservative) hypothesis that 50% or more of the people satisfied stochastic dominance by computing the binomial sign test on the split of the 468 (63.5%) who chose $G-$ over $G+$ against the 265 who chose $G+$ over $G-$ on Choice 5, $z = 7.5^*$. The percentage of violations on Choice 7 was lower (54%), but still significantly greater than $1/2$, $z = 2.21^*$.

Significantly more than half of the lab sample violated stochastic dominance in both tests, with an average of 68.3% violations. The lab sample also showed significant event-splitting effects in both tests. The lab sample had a higher percentage of violations of stochastic dominance (68.3%) than Internet A (51.7%) or Internet B (58.8%), a finding discussed in the next section.

DEMOGRAPHIC CORRELATIONS IN THE INTERNET SAMPLES

Because the Internet samples are relatively large, it is possible to subdivide them by gender, education level, experience reading a scientific work on decision making, and nationality. These divisions still leave enough data to conduct a meaningful analysis within each group. The data were then analyzed as previously described, within each of these divisions. Each of these subdivisions led to essentially the same conclusions with respect to properties that refute RSDU/RDU/CPT models; that is, the evidence within each group violated these rank-dependent models.

However, the incidence of violations of stochastic dominance correlates with education and gender. For example, of the 686 females in Internet A, 414 (60.3%) violated stochastic dominance on Choice 5, and 378 (55.1%) violated

Table 4

Violations of Stochastic Dominance and Monotonicity Related to Gender and Education in Internet Samples A and B, and Lab Sample

Sex	Education (years)	Stochastic dominance (%) $G- \succ G+$			Monotonicity (%) $GS- \succ GS+$			Number of subjects		
		A	B	Lab	A	B	Lab	A	B	Lab
F	< 16	60.2	66.1	70.4	9.6	11.3	11.8	318	248	91
F	16	61.9	56.8		10.0	8.1		206	148	0
F	17–19	44.9	58.5		7.4	13.4		108	41	0
F	20	41.7	54.5		1.9	9.1		54	11	0
M	< 16	53.1	56.0	62.9	6.4	7.8	10.6	163	141	33
M	16	42.6	55.6		6.4	10.2		195	98	0
M	17–19	36.4	56.3		2.3	3.1		88	32	0
M	20	37.5	57.1		6.2	7.1		80	14	0

Notes: Education < 16 indicates less than bachelor's degree; 16 = bachelor's degree; 17–19 = postgraduate studies; 20 = doctorate. Percentages indicate percentage of violations of stochastic dominance and consequence monotonicity, averaged over two choices.

stochastic dominance on Choice 7. Of the 526 males, 281 (53.4%) and 182 (34.6%) violated stochastic dominance on these choices, respectively.

Table 4 shows the relationship between violations of stochastic dominance (averaged over Choices 5 and 7), consequence monotonicity (averaged over Choices 11 and 13), education, and gender. Violations of stochastic dominance are less frequent among the highly educated than among those with less education. Females without college degrees have 60 and 66% violations in Internet A and B, respectively, and males without degrees have only 53 and 56% violations. The effect of education is more pronounced in Internet A (where education was more often in the specific field of decision making) than in Internet B. Data for the lab sample are shown in Table 4 for their appropriate gender and level of education. Note that even after gender and educational level are partialled out, there is a difference between the Internet and lab samples. Perhaps the Internet participants are brighter or better educated than people of the same age and with the same years of education recruited to our labs.

Violations of stochastic dominance were also more frequent among those who had not read a scientific work on decision making. For example, of the 837 people in Internet A who had not read a paper, 59.9% violated stochastic dominance on Choice 5; among the 382 who had read such a paper, there were 52.6% violations on Choice 5 ($\chi(1) = 5.41^*$).

The recruitment method brought in 95 participants in Internet A who had read a scientific paper on decision making and also held doctoral degrees; most of these were members of the Society for Judgment and Decision Making. This *expert* group had 50% violations of stochastic dominance on Choice 5. There were 46* with the preference combination $G - GS +$ against only 7 with the combination, $G + GS -$, $z = 5.36$. Thus, even within this expert group, violations of stochastic dominance were significantly more frequent than violations of consequence monotonicity. Nevertheless, the expert group had "only" 41.6% violations, averaged over the two tests, compared to 68.3% among undergraduates in the lab sample.

The 328 subjects in Internet A from nations outside the United States were more highly educated on average than those from the United States; for example, there were 62 with doctoral degrees in this group. The data of foreign subjects were similar to those of Americans, once their higher levels of education were taken into account. Correlations with gender and education (as in Table 4) were also observed in this group. For example, for the 59 foreign women with bachelor's degrees in Internet A, 66% violated stochastic dominance on Choice 5, compared to 64% for the American women. For the 64 foreign men with bachelor's degrees, 44% violated dominance on Choice 5, compared to 56% for the American men.

ALLAIS PARADOXES IN INTERNET B

Early criticisms of the Allais paradoxes were that they might apply only with hypothetical, large cash prizes used in the early demonstrations (Allais and Hagen, 1979). Internet B included a replication of the classic Allais paradoxes with real cash consequences less than or equal to $100.

The first two rows in Table 5 test common ratio independence. Choice 16 offers a choice that is the same as Choice 9, except the probabilities of prizes are four times larger in Choice 16. According to expected utility (EU) theory, $S = (x, p; 0; 1 - p) \succ R = (y, q; 0; 1 - q)$ if and only if $S_a = (x, ap; 0, 1 - ap) \succ R_a = (y, aq; 0, 1 - aq)$, where $a(a > 0)$ is the common ratio. Instead, 264 chose $R = (\$0, .8; \$80, .2) \succ S = (\$0, .75; \$60, .25)$ and $S_4 = \$60 \succ R_4 = (\$0, .2; \$80, .8)$ against 22 who had the opposite switch in preferences, $z = 14.3*$. This pattern is consistent with typical results in the literature.

Choices 15 and 18 test the common consequence paradox, which is a combination of branch independence and coalescing. Choices 15 and 18 are the same, except a common branch of .85 to win $0 in Choice 15 has been changed to $C = .85$ to win $40 in Choice 18, and equal consequences have been coalesced. The data show significant shifts in the direction observed in

Table 5

**Choices Used to Test Allais Common Ratio and Common Consequence
Paradoxes in Internet *B***

Choice no.	Choice type			Choice			%Choice Internet B ($n = 737$)
9	S	R	Q:	.75 to win \$0 .25 to win \$60	R:	.80 to win \$0 .20 to win \$80	43
16	S_4	R_4	e:	\$60 for sure	f:	.20 to win \$0 .80 to win \$80	10
15	S^*	R^*	c:	.85 to win \$0 .15 to win \$40	d:	.90 to win \$0 .10 to win \$100	70
18	$S^* + C$	$R^* + C$	i:	\$40 for sure	j:	.05 to win \$0 .85 to win \$40 .10 to win \$100	50
14	R'	S'	a:	.95 to win \$0 .05 to win \$96	b:	.93 to win \$0 .07 to win \$80	61
17	$R' + C_1$	$S' + C_1$	g:	.45 to win \$0 .50 to win \$80 .05 to win \$96	h:	.43 to win \$0 .57 to win \$80	44
8	$R' + C_2$	$S' + C_2$	o:	.07 to win \$0 .88 to win \$80 .05 to win \$96	p:	.05 to win \$0 .95 to win \$80	60
19	$R' + C_3$	$S' + C_4$	k:	.02 to win \$0 .93 to win \$80 .05 to win \$96	l:	\$80 for sure	70

Note: Percentages show preferences for the gamble printed on the right in the table.

previous tests; namely, improving the common consequence to convert the Safe gamble to a sure thing increases the choice proportion for the Safe gamble. In this case, 264 preferred $R^* \succ S^*$ and $S^* + C \succ R^* + C$, against only 66 who had the opposite switch in preferences ($z = 8.9^*$).

Choices 14, 17, 8, and 19 replicate a pattern reported by Wu and Gonzalez (1996). However, this study used smaller, real consequences. Notice that Choices 14, 17, and 8 do not involve certainty. All choices in this series involve $R' = (\$96, .05; \$0)$ versus $S' = (\$80, .07; \$0)$; however, each successive row of Table 5 adds a common branch of $C_1 = .5$ to win \$80, $C_2 = .88$ to win \$80, or $C_3 = .93$ to win \$80, respectively. Again, equal consequences are coalesced.

As found by Wu and Gonzalez (1996), the overall percentage choosing the "risky" (R') gamble shows an inverse-U as a function of the probability of the common branch (Table 5 shows the choice percentages for the S' gamble in this case). Each difference in choice percentage is significant by the test of correlated proportions, except the difference between Choices 14 and 8. All four choices are available for 727 of 737 subjects (10 left one or more choices unanswered). The notation *SRSS* denotes the following preference pattern: $S' \succ R'$ in choice 14, $R' + C_1 \succ S' + C_1$ in Choice 17, $S' + C_2 \succ R' + C_2$ in Choice 9, and $S' + C_3 \succ R' + C_3$ in Choice 19, respectively. Examining individual patterns, 191 of 727 showed inverse-U patterns of *SRSS, SRRS*, or *SSRS*, compared to 57 who showed opposite-U patterns (*RSSR, RRSR*, and *RSRR*). There were 166 who showed the patterns *RRRS, RRSS*, and *RSSS*; 85 who showed patterns *SRRR, SSRR*, and *SSSR*; 175 who showed no shifts of preference; and 53 who showed alternating patterns.

COMPARISON OF CPT AND CONFIGURAL WEIGHT MODELS

All of the models compared here assume transitivity and consequence monotonicity. However, they disagree on coalescing. All of the models assume that the gamble with the higher computed value should be chosen. All of the models are special cases of a fairly general model that allows the configural weight of a consequence to depend on its relations to other consequences in the same gamble.

The configurally weighted utility (CWU) of a gamble can be written as

$$\text{CWU}(G) = \sum_{i=1}^{n} w(x_i, G) u(x_i), \tag{1}$$

where $G = (x_1, p_1; x_2, p_2; \ldots; x_i, p_i; \ldots x_n, p_n)$ is a gamble with n distinct positive consequences, ranked such that $0 < x_1 < x_2 < \cdots < x_i < \cdots < x_n$; $\sum_{i=1}^{n} p_i = 1$; $u(x_i)$ is the utility of the consequence and $w(x_i, G)$ is its weight. All models discussed here (RSDU, RDU, CPT, RAM, TAX, EU, and EV) are special cases of Equation 1, with different assumptions about the weights.

For positive consequences, RSDU or CPT reduce to RDU. RDU assumes that weights can be written as

$$w(x_i, G) = W\left(\sum_{j=i}^{n} p_j\right) - W\left(\sum_{j=i+1}^{n} p_j\right), \tag{2}$$

where $W(P)$ is the strictly monotonic, decumulative weighting function that assigns decumulative weight to decumulative probability, $P_i = \sum_{j=i}^{n} p_j$, where $W(0) = 0$ and $W(1) = 1$. The model consisting of Equations 1 and 2 implies stochastic dominance (Quiggin, 1985, 1993; Tversky & Kahneman, 1992; Luce,

1998), coalescing, and cumulative independence (Birnbaum & Navarrete, 1998). If $W(P) = P$, this model reduces to EU.

The model used in CPT (Tversky & Wakker, 1995) further assumes that the weighting function in Equation 2 is given by

$$W(P) = \frac{cP^{\gamma}}{cP^{\gamma} + (1 - P)^{\gamma}}, \qquad (3)$$

where c is a parameter of risk aversion, and γ is a parameter that can create an inverse-S weighting function when $\gamma < 1$ and an S-shaped weighting function when $\gamma > 1$. Tversky and Kahneman (1992) also assumed that $u(x) = x^{\beta}$, where β was estimated to be .88.

The configural weighting model known as the transfer of attention exchange (TAX) model is also a special case of Equation 1. This model assumes that weights are transferred among branches according to the judge's point of view. Point of view can be manipulated by instructions to identify with the buyer or seller of a gamble, a neutral judge (who estimates "fair price"), or a person who gets to choose between gambles. In the seller's viewpoint, weight can be transferred from branches with lower consequences to those with higher ones, and in the buyer's viewpoint, weight is transferred from higher to lower branches.

When lower consequences are more important than higher ones, the tax rate is negative, $\rho < 0$ (lower valued items "tax" weight from higher valued items); in this case, relative weight is given by the expression

$$w(x_i, G) = \frac{S(p_i) + \rho \Sigma_{j=1}^{i-1} S(p_i) - \rho \Sigma_{j=i+1}^{n} S(p_j)}{\Sigma_{j=1}^{n} S(p_j)}, \qquad (4)$$

where $S(p_i)$ is a function of the probability of consequence x_i; and the weight given up by this branch is $\rho \Sigma_{j=1}^{i-1} S(p_i)$, indicating that this branch gives up weight to all branches with consequences lower in value than x_i (recall $\rho < 0$). Weight is gained by consequence x_i as a function of the probabilities of consequences that are higher, and x_i in turn gives up weight from its probability to lower branches.

Birnbaum and Chavez (1997) assumed that $\rho = \delta/(n + 1)$, and $S(p) = p^{\gamma}$. This simplified TAX model, like the CPT model, uses two parameters for the configural weighting of probabilities. If $\rho = 0$ and $\gamma = 1$, this model reduces to EU.

Research with configural weighting models has shown that one can fit the data fairly well with the simplifying assumption that $u(x) = x$, for $0 < x < \$150$. I do not really think that the psychological value of money is proportional to money. I believe that the subjective value of \$2 million differs less from $1 million than $1 million differs from $0. I also think that $1 million means less to Bill Gates (who has $billions) than it would to me. But for small amounts of cash (pocket money), the assumption that the value of money is proportional to face value seems reasonable. This approximation also makes it easier to interpret and compare parameters.

Subjectively weighted utility (SWU) theory (Edwards, 1954) is the nonconfigural, special case of Equation 1 in which $w(x_i, G) = w(p_i)$, so $SWU(G) = \sum_{i=1}^{n} w(p_i)u(x_i)$. Expected utility (EU) theory is the special case of SWU in which $w(p_i) = p_i$; $EU(G) = \sum_{i=1}^{n} p_i u(x_i)$. Expected value is the special case of EU in which $u(x_i) = x_i$; $EV(G) = \sum_{i=1}^{n} p_i x_i$. Although EV and EU theories have been rejected in previous studies (Kahneman & Tversky, 1979; Tversky & Kahneman, 1992; Luce, 1990; Birnbaum, 1999; Birnbaum & Beeghley, 1997; Wu & Gonzalez, 1996), they provide benchmarks for assessing the more complex models, of which they are special cases.

Birnbaum (1999b) reported fits of TAX, CPT, EU, and EV models to the data of Internet A and the lab data to compare the relative accuracy of the models in describing individual data. Each person's data were fitted to the models by methods described in Birnbaum and Chavez (1997). After a model was fitted to a person's data, it was checked for each choice. The computer program checked if the person indeed picked the gamble with the higher computed utility according to that model and its parameters, and the program counted the number of correct predictions (out of 20 choices).

The TAX model was fitted with $u(x) = x$. In Internet A, median estimates of γ and δ for the TAX model are .791 and $-.333$, respectively. This model correctly predicted 15 or more choices (75% correct or better) by 67% of the individuals, including perfect scores for 66 people.

The CPT model cannot explain violations of stochastic dominance, event-splitting effects, or violations of cumulative independence. For Internet A, median estimates of γ and c were .743 and .597, respectively. In the Internet sample, 58.5% had 15 or more choices predicted correctly, including 34 with perfect scores. The mean number of choices correctly predicted was significantly higher for the TAX model (15.53) than for CPT (14.91), $t(1223) = 8.05*$. The TAX model predicted more choices correctly for 614* people; 414 had more predicted correctly by CPT, and 196 were even.

For the EU model, utility was estimated as a power function of monetary value, $u(x) = x^\beta$. For Internet A, median estimate of $\beta = .611$. EU correctly predicted an average of 13.55 choices in Internet A, and it correctly predicted 15 or more choices for only 36.9% of the judges, including 28 with perfect scores. EU theory cannot explain violations of RDU, because it is a special case of RDU, nor can it explain violations of the Allais paradoxes.

No individual had data that were perfectly consistent with EV. This seemed a bit surprising because a number of people from Internet A with doctorates sent comments that they simply chose the gamble with the higher EV. One person even wrote that anyone who did not choose according to EV (in Internet A) would have to be "insane." However, no one wrote that they actually computed EV, and apparently no one did. For Internet A, EV correctly predicts 15 or more choices for only 16.8% of the judges with a mean of 12.4 correct predictions.

Similar results were obtained in model fits to the lab samples (Birnbaum, 1999b). In sum, the TAX model is more accurate in predicting choices than CPT, and both of these models are more accurate than EU or EV.

DISCUSSION

Systematic violations of stochastic dominance and event-splitting effects are observed in both Internet and lab samples. These phenomena contradict the implications of several models of decision making, but they are consistent with configural weight theories. Although there are differences between Internet and lab samples, both sets of results would lead to the same conclusions concerning the models. A comparison of fit showed that the configural weight TAX model fits better than the CPT model that has the same number of estimated parameters. Both of these models fit better than EU, which fit better than EV.

The procedures used in this study differ from those used by Birnbaum and Navarrete (1998) and Birnbaum et al. (1999). There were fewer trials, a different format for presentation of choices, a computer Web form instead of paper and pencil, real financial incentives instead of hypothetical financial incentives, and other differences. Results confirmed previous findings, suggesting that previous results were not fragile with respect to these changes in procedure.

Internet and lab samples yield similar conclusions, indicating that the findings are not unique to college students, tested in laboratories. Internet B replicates the findings of other investigators with variations of the Allais paradoxes (Allais & Hagen, 1979; Wu & Gonzalez, 1996), showing that these paradoxes can be replicated with smaller cash consequences and real incentives.

These studies demonstrate the feasibility of using the Internet to check results with a large, diverse sample. Compared to my usual research, which typically takes 6 months to collect data for 100 college students, it was quite pleasant to collect 1224 sets of data in 4 months and 737 in the next 6 weeks. It may not always be as easy as it was in 1998 to recruit participants on the Web. As more people put their experiments on the Web, there may develop more competition for people willing to take part in tests and experiments. On the other hand, more and more people surf the Net each day, so it is difficult to forecast whether the number of experiments or the number of willing participants will grow at a faster rate.

Internet research has two potential problems that are obvious to those who venture there: sampling and control. With lab studies, one can control the conditions. For example, we can ensure that laboratory subjects do not use calculators to compute expected value. Alternately, we could require them to do so. With an Internet study, we have very little control over the conditions. In these studies, there were no instructions one way or the other concerning the use of calculators. When people began sending me e-mail saying that they thought everyone would just choose the gamble with the higher EV, I wondered if perhaps I should have given an instruction concerning calculators. But that very instruction might have given the idea to people who might otherwise not have thought of it. And if I gave such an instruction, how would I know for certain if it was followed?

We could ask people to follow instructions, and we could ask them if they did. One might hope that variations of conditions would simply introduce random error that would average out with large samples. Ultimately, we must rely on the subject's honesty, on indirect checks, or on the hope that deviations of protocol do not matter to the case at hand. In this study, it seems unlikely that people used calculators because not even one person was perfectly consistent with EV. But this issue illustrates one of many possible aspects of control that would not be issues in lab experiments.

I think it would be an oversimplification to talk of the university subject pool and the Internet as if they referred to two *populations*. I do not think that the Internet is really a single population, but instead may be regarded as many different subpopulations tangled together. Nor are the samples found by these methods going to be constant over time. The Internet is ever changing, and as equipment becomes cheaper and easier to use, we can expect changes in the landscape and the travelers on this highway. In the past few years, the percentage of females on the Internet has increased sharply. Notice that both Internet A and B samples have more females than males. Subject pools have also changed over time, as a greater percentage of the general population enrolls in college and as an even greater percentage of females have elected to attend college and to enroll in psychology.

Slight changes in methods used to recruit participants in an experiment could potentially have great effects. This study used methods intended to reach a highly educated population, especially in the field of decision making. The fact that 95 people with doctorates were recruited who have read a scholarly work on decision making suggests that the method of recruitment succeeded in reaching its target audience.

Although one can use methods intended to reach certain groups, Internet experimenters do not have complete control of recruitment. For example, in an Internet study of sexual behavior, an Abuse Web site cross-listed the sex survey reported in the chapter by Bailey, Foote, and Throckmorton (chap. 6, this volume). This placing of a "link" by another well-meaning person recruited many people with histories of abuse to the sexual survey. If the purpose of the survey had been to estimate prevalence of abuse in the population, this link placed by another person might have altered the conclusions.

If demographic or other individual difference variables affect the behavior in question, then one can measure these and study their correlations with the results. The Internet certainly affords greater opportunities for recruiting a very heterogeneous sample. In the studies reviewed here, the Internet samples were much more diverse with respect to age and education than the sample recruited from the subject pool. Rates of violation of stochastic dominance were correlated with gender, education, and experience reading a scholarly work on decision making. The Internet sample was less likely to violate stochastic dominance than the lab sample, and the Internet sample also differed from the lab sample by having a lower percentage of females and a higher percentage of people who are highly educated, older, and more likely to have read a paper on decision making. Thus, the difference between Internet and lab results appears to be what one would expect from the demographic differences between the groups.

Education, which correlated with incidence of violations of stochastic dominance, is probably also correlated with variables not measured that might be causal agents. For example, those with more education are probably also higher in intelligence and wealth than those with less education. Therefore, lower incidence of stochastic dominance among the highly educated might be due to higher intelligence, for example, rather than to the effects of education per se. Experiments with random assignment to different types of education could determine if specific training would reduce violations of stochastic dominance.

In sum, Internet research confirms phenomena that violate the RSDU/RDU/CPT theories of decision making. Results are more compatible with Birnbaum's (1999a; 1999b) configural weight TAX model, which implies systematic violations of stochastic dominance and event-splitting effects. At the same time, Internet data reveal correlations between these violations and demographic variables. In this case, Internet data both reinforced the results of laboratory research and revealed variables that may moderate the generalization from lab research with undergraduates to research with other populations.

APPENDIX: ADDITIONAL DETAILS
OF EXPERIMENT

This appendix gives more detail on the HTML page and recruitment methods. The Web site was announced by an e-mail message sent to all members of the Society for Judgment and Decision Making and the Society for Mathematical Psychology. It was suggested to major search engines, announced in Web sites that list contests and games with prizes, and described by Meta tags within in the Web page (these help search engines locate the page). Links to the site were established (among others) in the American Psychological Society's list of online experiments, maintained by John Krantz, in the European Web Lab, maintained by Ulf Reips, and in Jonathan Baron's lab site (see the chapters by Baron, by Krantz and Dalal, and by Reips in this volume).

The HTML given in Table 6 shows the key features of the Web page to conduct an experiment on choices between gambles. Portions of the instructions and many of the trials are omitted, leaving the parts essential to explaining how the page works. Every HTML page has the ⟨HTML⟩ and ⟨/HTML⟩ tags, which identify the beginning and end of the page. Material between the ⟨HEAD⟩ and ⟨/HEAD⟩ contains the head of the page, and the ⟨BODY⟩⟨/BODY⟩ tags identify the beginning and end of the body of the page. In the head are the TITLE and META tags. Some search engines use the content in META tags to find key words and descriptions of the pages. The TITLE appears at the top of the page in the browser's display of the page.

The ⟨H3⟩⟨/H3⟩ tags identify a size 3 heading, which is fairly large. ⟨P⟩ tags identify paragraphs and, unlike most tags, do not require a closing ⟨/P⟩ tag.

The ⟨FORM⟩ tag identifies the next material as a form and shows where the data will be sent when the user pushes the "submit" button. The ACTION of a form sends the data to a URL that contains a Common Gateway Interface (CGI) script that decodes and organizes the data, places them in a file, and sends the browser to a page that displays a thank-you message. The URL listed in Table 6 refers to a real script, but not the one actually used in the study. Each variable name is preceded by a sequential number from 00 to 29, which determines the order by which the CGI script will organize the data in the data file. The ⟨/FORM⟩ tag signals the end of the form.

The first two variables created by ⟨INPUT TYPE="hidden"...⟩ are hidden variables, the date and time, available from the CGI script. They are "hidden" because they are not displayed in the page, but they are placed into the data file. These variables uniquely identify each data record, and it can be helpful to be able to look up a participant's record by time and date.

The ⟨PRE⟩ and ⟨/PRE⟩ tags instruct the browser to display everything between those tags in "preformatted text." Browsers typically use an equally spaced font (such as Courier) to display preformatted text. Line returns, tabs, and so forth are preserved in preformatted text. In this case, I chose preformatted text to make it easy to make all of the trials uniform in appearance without having to use tables or other tricks to align the text.

The line that reads

```
⟨input type="text" name="02Name"
                  size=60 maxlength=60⟩
```

illustrates use of text-type input. This tag creates a text box that is 60 characters wide, where the person was instructed to type his or her e-mail address. If the maxlength had been larger than 60, then someone could have continued to type after 60 columns until the maximum was reached. I think it is often best to make the size and maxlength equal, so the person has an idea of how much space is available for their comment, or whatever. Sometimes, you might want to allow a little extra room for the last few words. In the age box, I allowed an extra digit, because if anyone over 100 participated, I would certainly want to know about it. After a person types in his or her e-mail address in this box, that typing will appear in the data file as the third variable, after date and time. (Sometimes, if a person types in commas, it may create problems for data analysis. A comma-stripping routine is included in the study by Bailey et al. in this volume.) The request for age also uses the same method, as does the input field for education, and later in the form, the text box for comments.

The key to this study is the use of the radio buttons. The properties of radio buttons seem perfectly suited for choice experiments. The question about sex (male or female) uses radio buttons, as do the main 20 choices in the experiment. (I have edited out most of the questions and have removed most of the instructions).

Each button requires its own ⟨INPUT TYPE="radio"...⟩ tag. Notice that for the sex question, there are three tags, all with the same NAME. There is only one selected (blackened) dot for each set of radio buttons, which are defined (connected) by the same NAME. Thus, clicking one of the empty buttons darkens that button (selects it) and simultaneously deselects the previously selected button. Although one could request sex with two radio buttons (no pun intended), I strongly advise against it. The reason I use three radio buttons for gender and for decision problems is as follows: With only two choices, one will be selected before the person responds. That way, everyone (both you and the subject) may become confused whether the subject

Table 6

HTML (Abbreviated) for the Decision Experiment

```
〈HTML〉 〈HEAD〉
〈META NAME="keywords" CONTENT="Gamble, decision making, experiment, science, win money"〉
〈META NAME="description" CONTENT="Choose between gambles, without risk, and help science by participating
as a subject in decision making experiment. You might win money."〉
〈TITLE〉Decision Experiment〈/TITLE〉
〈/HEAD〉 〈BODY〉
〈H3〉Decision-Making Experiment: Choices between Gambles〈/H3〉
〈P〉This is a study of decision making ...Decide first if you want to participate.
You must be over 18, and each person can participate only once. Scroll down and look over the questionnaire.
It usually takes about 10 minutes. Also note: Study ends and prizes awarded 9 / 15 / 98.〈P〉
〈FORM METHOD="POST" ACTION="http://psych.fullerton.edu/cgi-win/polyform.exe/generic"〉
〈input type="hidden" name="00Date" value="pfDate"〉
〈input type="hidden" name="01Time" value="pfTime"〉
〈PRE〉
Email address: 〈input type="text" name="02Name" size=60 maxlength=60〉
We will notify you by email if you are a winner.
Country: 〈INPUT TYPE=TEXT NAME=03Con SIZE=20 maxlength=25〉
Age: 〈INPUT TYPE=TEXT NAME=04Age SIZE=2 maxlength=3〉 You must be over 18 years to participate.
〈input type="radio" name="05sex" value="0" checked〉Are you Male or Female?
                  〈input type="radio" name="05sex" value="F"〉Female
     OR
                  〈input type="radio" name="05sex" value="M"〉Male
Education (in years).
  If you are a college graduate, put 16.
  If you have a Ph.D., put 20.
Education: 〈INPUT TYPE=TEXT NAME=06Ed SIZE=2 maxlength=2〉 Years.
```

Now, look at the first choice, No. 1, below...

Think of probability as the number of tickets in a bag containing 100 tickets, divided by 100. Gamble A has 50 tickets that say $100 and 50 that say $0, so the probability to win $100 is .50 and the probability to get $0 is .50.

...**(more instructions were here)**

⟨input type="radio" name="07v1" value="0" checked⟩1. Which do you choose?

    ⟨input type="radio" name="07v1" value="-1"⟩A: .50 probability to win $0
      .50 probability to win $100

    OR

    ⟨input type="radio" name="07v1" value="1"⟩B: .50 probability to win $25
      .50 probability to win $35

⟨input type="radio" name="08v2" value="0" checked⟩2. Which do you choose?

    ⟨input type="radio" name="08v2" value="-1"⟩C: .50 probability to win $0
      .50 probability to win $100

    OR

    ⟨input type="radio" name="08v2" value="1"⟩D: .50 probability to win $35
      .50 probability to win $45

...**(more trials were here)**...

⟨input type="radio" name="27v21" value="0" checked⟩21. Have you ever read a scientific paper (i.e., a journal article or book) on the theory of decision making or on the psychology of decision making?

    ⟨input type="radio" name="27v21" value="No"⟩No. Never.

    OR

    ⟨input type="radio" name="27v21" value="Yes"⟩Yes, I have.

⟨P⟩

COMMENTS: ⟨INPUT TYPE="text" NAME="28COMS" size=65 maxlength=65⟩

Please check to make sure that you have answered all of the Questions.

⟨input type="hidden" name="29Exp2" value="exp2b"⟩

When you are finished, push this button to send your data:

⟨INPUT TYPE="submit" VALUE="I'm finished."⟩

⟨/PRE⟩⟨/FORM⟩⟨/BODY⟩⟨/HTML⟩

selected that choice or if perhaps it was that way to start. When we request choices between gambles, if one choice is selected in advance, the subject may be reluctant to switch to the other choice or may forget that he or she did not select that choice.

For these reasons, I use three radio buttons for each two-alternative choice. Note that the "nothing" button is preselected. This button is placed before the trial number, in the left margin. These buttons in the margin serve two purposes. First, they keep track of nonresponse and, second, they make it easy for the participant to see if each trial has been completed. Note that the nonresponse is assigned the value "0". It could also have been assigned a null value, "". However, I thought ahead to data analysis, and it occurred to me that a blank field of data might get lost if this file were saved as formatted text and then imported to a statistics program, using freefield. Because the values of male and female are assigned M and F, a "0" is clearly a nonresponse, so there is no confusion when it is time to analyze the data, and it holds the place of the variable.

Each of the choices in the decision experiment was handled in the same way. I used three radio buttons for each choice, with the third button holding the nonresponse. A person can scroll down the list of questions and note if any of the buttons in the left margin are still filled. Nonresponse was assigned the value 0, choice of the left was -1, and choice of the right was assigned the value 1. This numerical assignment means that the mean of this variable will indicate if the majority chose the gamble on the left or right.

The last items are of types already discussed. The last "hidden" variable allows me to make note of when conditions have changed (I can change to Exp2a, Exp2b, Exp3a, etc.) and it also provides a variable that is easy to align during data analysis. When the data have been read into Excel or SPSS, if the last variable is not "exp2b," then something is amiss in the importing of the data.

The ⟨INPUT TYPE="submit" VALUE="I'm finished"⟩ creates a button with the words "I'm finished" printed on it. When the subject pushes this button, the data are sent to the script to be placed in the data file, and the subject sees a thank-you message on the screen.

If you would like to check how the page works and to see sample data, you can first go to URL http://psych.fullerton.edu/mbirnbaum/exp2a.htm. Then, when you have completed the experiment, use your FTP program to download the file *data.csv*. You need the following to reach the FTP site, which only supports downloading:

Host: *psych.fullerton.edu*
User ID: *guest*
Password: *guest99*
Directory: (you should leave this blank).

The file *data.csv* will contain your data, including the time and date that you participated. You are welcome to use the generic script, to try out these principles, which will send data to this file, from which you can retrieve your data by FTP. Your HTML page can be on diskette, which you can load directly into your browser, or it can be on your local server. As long as you use the script address shown, the data will go to this data file.

The file *data.csv* will be erased from time to time when it gets large, so you should not leave anything there of any value. Also, because that file will be public to all who read this chapter, I advise you not to put anything personal or sensitive there.

In the long run, you will need to get access to a server and put your own scripts in place to allow you to collect data on your own computer. You can also change the ACTION in the FORM tag to read ACTION= "mailto:user@address.ext", where *user@address.ext* is your e-mail address. That method can get you data by e-mail, which allows you to check an experiment, but it is not practical for large projects to receive so many e-mail messages.

ACKNOWLEDGMENTS

Support was received from National Science Foundation Grant SBR-9410572. I thank John Krantz, Jochen Musch, and Ulf Reips for comments on an earlier draft.

REFERENCES

Allais, M., & Hagen, O. (Eds.). (1979). *Expected utility hypothesis and the Allais paradox.* Dordrecht, The Netherlands: Reidel.

Becker, J., & Sarin, R. (1987). Lottery dependent utility. *Management Science, 33,* 1367–1382.

Birnbaum, M. H. (1974). The nonadditivity of personality impressions. *Journal of Experimental Psychology, 102,* 543–561.

Birnbaum, M. H. (1997). Violations of monotonicity in judgment and decision making. In A. A. J. Marley (Ed.), *Choice, decision, and measurement: Essays in honor of R. Duncan Luce* (pp. 73–100). Mahwah, NJ: Erlbaum.

Birnbaum, M. H. (1999a). Paradoxes of Allais, stochastic dominance, and decision weights. In J. Shanteau, B. A. Mellers, & D. A. Schum (Eds.), *Decision science and technology: Reflections on the contributions of Ward Edwards* (pp. 27–52). Norwell, MA: Kluwer Academic.

Birnbaum, M. H. (1999b). Testing critical properties of decision making on the Internet. *Psychological Science, 10,* 399–407.

Birnbaum, M. H., & Beeghley, D. (1997). Violations of branch independence in judgments of the value of gambles. *Psychological Science, 8,* 87–94.

Birnbaum, M. H., & Chavez, A. (1997). Tests of theories of decision making: Violations of branch independence and distribution independence. *Organizational Behavior and Human Decision Processes, 71*(2), 161–194.

Birnbaum, M. H., & Martin, T. (1999). *Violations of stochastic dominance and event-splitting effects by financially motivated decision makers.* Manuscript submitted for publication.

Birnbaum, M. H., & McIntosh, W. R. (1996). Violations of branch independence in choices between gambles. *Organizational Behavior and Human Decision Processes, 67,* 91–110.

Birnbaum, M. H., & Navarrete, J. (1998). Testing descriptive utility theories: Violations of stochastic dominance and cumulative independence. *Journal of Risk and Uncertainty, 17,* 49–78.

Birnbaum, M. H., Patton, J. N., & Lott, M. K. (1999). Evidence against rank-dependent utility theories: Violations of cumulative independence, interval independence, stochastic dominance, and transitivity. *Organizational Behavior and Human Decision Processes, 77,* 44–83.

Birnbaum, M. H., & Stegner, S. E. (1979). Source credibility in social judgment: Bias, expertise, and the judge's point of view. *Journal of Personality and Social Psychology, 37,* 48–74.

Humphrey, S. J. (1995). Regret aversion or event-splitting effects? More evidence under risk and uncertainty. *Journal of Risk and Uncertainty, 11,* 263–274.

Kahneman, D., & Tversky, A. (1979). Prospect theory: An analysis of decision under risk. *Econometrica, 47,* 263–291.

Luce, R. D. (1990). Rational versus plausible accounting equivalences in preference judgments. *Psychological Science, 1,* 225–234.

Luce, R. D. (1998). Coalescing, event commutativity, and theories of utility. *Journal of Risk and Uncertainty, 16,* 87–113.

Luce, R. D., & Fishburn, P. C. (1991). Rank- and sign-dependent linear utility models for finite first order gambles. *Journal of Risk and Uncertainty, 4,* 29–59.

Luce, R. D., & Fishburn, P. C. (1995). A note on deriving rank-dependent utility using additive joint receipts. *Journal of Risk and Uncertainty, 11,* 5–16.

Machina, M. J. (1982). Expected utility analysis without the independence axiom. *Econometrica, 50,* 277–323.

Quiggin, J. (1982). A theory of anticipated utility. *Journal of Economic Behavior and Organization, 3,* 324–345.

Quiggin, J. (1985). Subjective utility, anticipated utility, and the Allais paradox. *Organizational Behavior and Human Decision Processes, 35,* 94–101.

Quiggin, J. (1993). *Generalized expected utility theory: The rank-dependent model.* Boston: Kluwer.

Starmer, C., & Sugden, R. (1993). Testing for juxtaposition and event-splitting effects. *Journal of Risk and Uncertainty, 6,* 235–254.

Tversky, A., & Kahneman, D. (1992). Advances in prospect theory: Cumulative representation of uncertainty. *Journal of Risk and Uncertainty, 5,* 297–323.

Tversky, A., & Wakker, P. (1995). Risk attitudes and decision weights. *Econometrica, 63,* 1255–1280.

von Winterfeldt, D. (1997). Empirical tests of Luce's rank- and sign-dependent utility theory. In A. A. J. Marley (Ed.), *Choice, decision, and measurement: Essays in honor of R. Duncan Luce* (pp. 25–44). Mahwah, NJ: Erlbaum.

Wakker, P., & Tversky, A. (1993). An axiomatization of cumulative prospect theory. *Journal of Risk and Uncertainty, 7,* 147–176.

Weber, E. U. (1994). From subjective probabilities to decision weights: The effects of asymmetric loss functions on the evaluation of uncertain outcomes and events. *Psychological Bulletin, 114,* 228–242.

Wu, G., & Gonzalez, R. (1996). Curvature of the probability weighting function. *Management Science, 42,* 1676–1690.

CHAPTER 2

Validity of Web-Based
Psychological Research

John H. Krantz
Hanover College
Hanover, Indiana 47243

Reeshad Dalal
Hanover College
Hanover, Indiana 47243

The World Wide Web represents a new advance as a method of conducting psychological research. As with any technological innovation, the Web needs to be assessed to determine if results from this innovation are valid, or, basically, meaningful. More than 20 studies to date have been conducted either on the Web or in other environments that nevertheless provide us insight into this question. The studies include surveys and correlational and experimental designs. In addition, a wide range of variables have been studied, including person variables such as self-monitoring and cognitive variables relating to decision making. Across this wide range of designs and variables, there is remarkable congruence between laboratory and Web-based results. There are a few differences, which, in some cases, are interesting and illuminating.

VALIDITY OF WEB-BASED
PSYCHOLOGICAL RESEARCH

With each new technological advance comes a change in the methods and environments of doing psychological research. Some of the profound breakthroughs in psychology that owe much to technological development as well as sound methodology and insight are: (1) Skinner's development of the operant conditioning chamber and the subsequent discovery of the schedules of

Psychological Experiments on the Internet

reinforcement; (2) Kuffler's (1953) recording from the ganglion cells of the retina and the discovery of receptive fields (which was dependent on the development of microelectrodes); (3) Ainsworth and Bell's (1970) discovery of attachment types (which depended on videotaping to allow the development of a reliable and standard scoring technique). In one sense, the World Wide Web is simply another technological advance that offers the possibility of advancing research methods.

The Internet-based study adds a new tool for collecting subjects that goes well beyond using introductory psychology students, phone and mail surveys, and the exhausting effort of soliciting subjects from the community. The benefits to research may come in several guises. One reason that many researchers look forward to the use of the Web is to collect samples that are broader cross-sections of the population at large. This issue is especially vital at smaller institutions where the student body is often more homogeneous and less representative of the national (not to mention global) population. Another reason Web research may represent a breakthrough is that we may be able to better verify several variables that are thought to be relevant to many psychological phenomena. By its very nature, the Web makes it easy to collect large samples; it will therefore allow more efficient examinations of person variables such as gender, ethnicity, and so on. In addition, the Web will facilitate the examination of issues such as reliability by having multiple sites of entrance and comparing the results across these sites.

With each innovation comes the requirement to ensure that the methods reveal what they claim they do. This question is often referred to as establishing the validity of the method. For Web research, there seem to be two primary ways to establish validity: (1) compare results from a Web-based study to a laboratory based study and (2) examine the research to see if the results follow theoretically predicted trends.

The first method is a type of convergent validity where different methods are used to see if they obtain the same results. Of course, this method of testing the validity of Web studies relies on the validity of the laboratory method. Disagreement between the Web results and laboratory results do not, *ipso facto*, demonstrate the lack of validity of Web studies. Just as there are threats to the validity of Web-based studies, there are threats to the validity of laboratory methods. A discussion of these latter threats is beyond the scope of this article but is covered in many books on research methods in the behavioral sciences. In this article, we will attempt to use only those studies in which the validity of the laboratory-based studies seems reasonable.

The second method of verifying the validity of Web-based research might be considered a type of construct validity to see if the findings follow the behavior of a hypothesized psychological construct. Usually construct validity is thought of as a way of testing whether a measure of a theoretical construct works as expected, and, in some sense, whether the theoretical construct is useful. However, in the former sense, we use established predictions and expectations to test a method that is in some ways analogous to the testing of construct measures. This method works if the theory is well validated such that the predictions made are well established in the literature. Because most predictions are methodologically dependent, it is often easier to simply do matched studies where the laboratory- and Web-based methods can be made more similar.

The methods of validity testing have emphasized what might be termed internal validity. This term is usually reserved for experiments, to indicate that the requirements for making a causal conclusion have been met. However, there is a broader issue of validity (external validity) that deals with the issue of the generalizability of the results. One major determinant of the generalizability of a finding is the nature of the sample. Thus, for findings where the characteristics of the sample significantly affect the data, the results of Web and laboratory studies may differ and, provided this is the only area in which the two studies differ, the greater external validity may well lie with the Web-based studies. This conclusion is made because Web-based samples tend to be more diverse than most laboratory samples as will be discussed in this chapter.

Some studies have examined this issue using a variety of methods and measuring a variety of variables. In an attempt to increase the database of studies using the Web, research on the Web can be considered an extension of research over a network and the Internet. Even given this extension, this research does not go back very far temporally. One of the early studies of the use of a network as a means of distributing a survey dates back only to 1986 (Kiesler & Sproull, 1986). In this study, the authors studied how e-mail compared to regular mail as a means for distributing surveys. Until the advent of the World Wide Web, distributing surveys was about the best that could be done using a network or the Internet.

However, with the development of Mosaic and the changes in the Web by the National Center for Supercomputing Applications (NCSA), the Web became capable of supporting multimedia (Levy, 1995). This capability was quickly exploited in the first published paper that referred to data collection using the World Wide Web (Welch & Krantz, 1996). Welch and Krantz (1996) could not really be called a study carried out over the Web, as these data collection enterprises were really attached to tutorials in auditory perception and these data collection elements were really canned laboratories in nature. Yet, these studies demonstrated the power of the Web as both a research medium and an experimental medium. Sound stimuli were transported to subjects around the world to collect some simple psychophysical data on some classic auditory phenomena.

It was not long before real experiments came online. Krantz, Ballard, and Scher (1997), Reips (1995), Schmidt (1997), and Smith and Leigh (1997) all represent attempts to collect data using the World Wide Web. Since then the pace of data collection has increased. To get a better sense of this, consider the American Psychological Society's (APS) Web page containing a listing of studies being run over the Web (Krantz, 1998b; Musch & Reips, chap. 3, this volume). It started in 1996 with fewer than 10 studies. As of the summer of 1998, a little over 2 years later, there were more than 45 links to sites that collect data. Some of these sites each contained several studies being run simultaneously, bringing the total number of studies to well over 50.

However, the World Wide Web and the Internet are somewhat unique as technological changes in that they are both not only research tools, but also objects of research. This latter aspect of research on the Web can be seen in the research of Schiano (1997), who investigated online communities, and Bonnenburg and Gosling (1998), who investigated the personality of Internet users. Another aspect of research that examines the Web is exemplified by the human factors study of Chen, Wang, Proctor, and Salvendy (1997). Thus, the World Wide Web has affected and will affect psychological research in many ways.

With respect to issues of validity, Web-based research is even more complex than most methods. The Web allows basically any type of research design that is possible using computers as equipment and humans as subjects, including surveys, psychological tests, correlational designs, and experimental methods. In addition, the validity of Web-based research may vary for the different psychological variables studied. This chapter will summarize these results in an effort to determine whether the Internet (in general) and the World Wide Web (in particular) are valid or invalid media for conducting research. To conveniently organize the discussion, the studies will be grouped according to the basic type of design employed: survey, correlational, or experimental.

THE VALIDITY OF RESEARCH ON THE WORLD WIDE WEB

SURVEYS

One of the simplest uses of the World Wide Web for research is to post a survey or psychological test instrument on a Web page and see who "hits" this page. Approximately half of the studies listed on the APS list of psychological studies fall into this category (Krantz, 1998b). Surveys raise many questions about how people choose their responses. With all the changes from most traditional formats to the Web–computer environment, the manner in which people could respond might change. Not many studies have examined the response differences between the Web surveys and traditional surveys but a few have looked at e-mail surveys versus mail surveys and can therefore enable comparisons. E-mail has many of the characteristics of the Web: the apparent anonymity of being at a remote computer, the use of a computer, the speed of feedback. Yet, there are differences—for instance, the interfaces differ because the use of forms is easier on the Web—but no studies comparing Web and traditional mail surveys exist.

Two studies nearly a decade apart attempted to determine the validity of e-mail surveys by directly comparing the same survey when mailed using both the traditional and electronic mail delivery (Kiesler & Sproull, 1986; Mehta & Sivadas, 1995). Kiesler and Sproull (1986) sent the survey both to employees at a company and to students at a university. Mehta and Sivadas (1995) compared both methods of delivering surveys with respect to whether the subjects were solicited to participate or whether they received the survey unsolicited. In both studies, the surveys were basic opinion surveys and the content was not discussed much in either paper. However, both studies found that the response rates for both methods of delivering of surveys were equivalent. This finding about response rate agrees with some reports (Bachmann, Elfrink, & Vazzana, 1996; Weible & Wallace, 1998) but not others (Kittleson, 1995; Schuldt & Totten, 1994). It appears that there may be many other variables involved than just whether the survey is electronic or paper that determine response rate. Both Kiesler and Sproull (1986) and Mehta and Sivadas (1995) also found that the mean and range on Likert type responses were similar for both survey types. The differences between the two delivery formats showed up in features like faster response times and less expense (no printing and mailing) for Internet surveys.

To investigate whether the type of survey differed with respect to how subjects presented themselves, Kiesler and Sproull (1986) used items from Marlowe and Crowne's (1964) Need for Approval scale. This included items such as "When I don't know something I don't at all mind admitting it." The e-mail respondents did not agree as often with such items as did those who received the survey in the mail. Kiesler and Sproull (1986) interpreted these results as indicating that e-mail survey respondents had a lower level of social desirability.

The one difference in the findings of the two studies involved the responses to open-ended questions. Kiesler and Sproull (1986) reported that there were no differences in either the quality or quantity of the responses to these questions. However, Mehta and Sivadas (1995) reported that the respondents to the electronic surveys wrote more and the writing was more complex than for the handwritten answers. The difference may lie in the change in e-mail editors over the intervening years. By the early 1990s, e-mail editors were much more sophisticated than those of the early 1980s. Thus, the typing may have become much easier so that people would be more willing to write more complex responses. These studies seem to indicate that Internet surveys are comparable in most respects to paper surveys and might even be a step forward, because Internet respondents seem to not be as prone to social desirability and because they give richer comments in the more recent of the two studies. Certainly the lack of expense and the increased speed of response is an advantage of these forms of surveys.

The methods of obtaining subjects for a survey is an interesting issue that can affect the validity of Internet research. Kiesler and Sproull obtained e-mail addresses at a college and developed a random sample. Mehta and Sivadas used membership in newsgroups either to send surveys or to ask for participation depending on their condition. E-mail lists are easy to obtain these days but the increasing frequency of junk e-mail may alter the willingness of subjects to participate in e-mail studies. These participation rates will need to be examined over time as the uses of e-mail change.

Although these studies of e-mail surveys are a good first step in examining whether online surveys and questionnaires could be valid, they only examined surveys and only determined if two formats were comparable. Nor were these surveys explicit psychological inventories, where much of the psychological use of the survey format is found. Two more recent studies have directly examined the reliability and validity of psychological inventories (Buchanan & Smith, 1999; Pasveer & Ellard, 1998). These studies are reviewed in detail in the next section of this chapter. Suffice it to say here that a remarkable congruence between Web and laboratory studies was the main finding in both studies. Although replications and extensions of this finding are needed, the consistent correspondence between the two media (Internet and lab) is astounding.

CORRELATIONAL DESIGNS

Table 1 shows a list of correlational studies that have or allow an examination of their validity. This list currently represents three different research efforts and two basically different types of correlational designs. Two of the efforts (Buchanan, 1998; Buchanan, chap. 5, this volume; Buchanan and Smith, 1999) deal directly with one of the primary tools of correlational research, the psychological test. Buchanan and Smith (1999) were interested in the general issue of putting a psychological test on the Web. They chose to use Gangestad and Snyder's (1985) revision of the Self-Monitoring Scale. First a

Table 1

Correlational Studies Using the Web That Allow the Determination of Validity

Study	Variables measured	Method of validity determination
Buchanan (1998)	Self-monitoring, attractiveness	Comparison with previously found relationships using a traditional version of the material
Buchanan and Smith (1999)	Self-monitoring, criterion groups	Comparison with previous publication of psychometric properties of the text and simultaneous collection of a laboratory sample and criterion validity
Pasveer and Ellard (1998)	Self-trust	Comparison with a simultaneous collection of a laboratory sample, measures of internal consistency, and traditional psychometric analysis
Smith and Leigh (1997)	Gender, elements of sexual fantasy	Comparison with previously published research and simultaneous collection of a laboratory sample

Web version of the test was developed and then a sample was collected. Then the authors collected a Web sample and a traditional laboratory sample to obtain a data set that would allow the determination of the psychometric properties of the test. They compared their findings to two previously published attempts in order to determine the psychometric properties of this test. The internal consistency of the Web sample was found to compare very favorably to that of both the lab sample and previous reports using this scale. Moreover, going beyond this simple examination of the null hypothesis (a dangerous exercise logically), Buchanan and Smith (1999) ran a confirmatory factor analysis based upon one published factor structure. The two goodness-of-fit measures were greater than 0.9, and the root mean square (RMS) was near zero and comparable to the fit from their own lab sample. In addition to this basic determination of the validity of a personality scale, the authors collected samples from discussion groups that were based upon the earlier published relationships found with the Self-Monitoring scale. They identified two groups—discussion groups presumably containing predominantly high self-monitors and discussion groups presumably containing predominantly low self-monitors. As predicted, these groups differed in their scores on the Web-based Self-Monitoring Scale (Buchanan and Smith, 1999). Buchanan (1998) followed up these findings by determining the relationship between self-monitoring and judgments of attractiveness. As with the criterion groups, the relationship found with the Web survey agrees with earlier published research though the relationship is not as strong.

Pasveer and Ellard's (1998) experience is very similar. Instead of translating an existing scale, they developed a new scale. They developed their scale on Self-Trust by using traditional approaches for scale development. Then they placed a version of the survey on the Web and gave a paper-and-pencil version to a laboratory sample. The measures of internal consistency, interitem correlation, and item mean and standard deviations were all very similar across two sets of Web and laboratory data. Although much work is required to determine the actual validity of the Self-Trust questionnaire for both Web and laboratory versions, it is clear that both versions of the form measure very much the same thing.

Smith and Leigh (1997) employ a slightly different type of correlational design. The authors basically replicated Ellis and Symons' (1990) research on gender differences in sexual fantasies. Smith and Leigh asked both a laboratory and a Web sample the same questions as Ellis and Symons did. The first three items used a rating scale and allowed direct comparisons of the means of the responses between the Web and the laboratory samples. In no cases were the responses different between these two groups. In addition, all the trends were the same and significant; this is congruent with Ellis and Symons. The second three items were categorical so a χ^2 analysis was performed to determine differences in response across the four categories in both Ellis and Symons and Smith and Leigh. Again, both the earlier laboratory study and the Web study found the same trends.

Thus, in all cases, Web data in correlational studies match very well with traditional laboratory methods. In addition, the Web versions of the scales seem to show the same psychometric properties as their laboratory cousins. The biggest limitation of these results seems to be the limited range of studies that have been conducted to date where comparisons of laboratory and Web data are possible.

EXPERIMENTAL DESIGNS

Table 2 shows the experimental studies that allow for some determination of the validity of the findings. The variables that have been manipulated, and the measures used, are quite diverse considering the paucity of studies. In all cases, the comparisons have indicated that the Web findings are quite valid or at least are comparable to those of laboratory studies of the same phenomena. The first published and the most extensive experimental study of the set to date is Krantz et al. (1997). These studies are replications with extensions of both Fallon and Rozin (1985) and Wiggins, Wiggins, and Conger (1968), both

Table 2

Experimental Studies Using the Web That Allow the Determination of Validity

Study	Independent variable	Dependent variable	Method of validity determination
Allen (1999)	Principally, presence and absence of shadows	Relative distance of objects	Simultaneous comparison of Web and laboratory samples
Birnbaum (1999)	Probabilities associated with gambles	Choices of which set of probabilities the subjects would prefer	Simultaneous collection of Web and laboratory samples; examination of consistency (see text)
Duker (1997)	Managed vs. fee-for-service physician	Ratings of reasonableness, agency, competence, confidence, trust, and responsibility of the physician	Simultaneous collection of Web and laboratory samples
Klauer et al. (1999)	Within subject: logical validity and believability of a syllogism Between subject: suggested base rate of valid conclusions	Solution frequency of the syllogisms	Simultaneous collection of Web and laboratory samples; χ^2 comparison of solution frequency of different groups
Krantz (1998a)	Monocular depth cues	Magnitude estimations of depth	Comparison of Web results with theoretical expectations
Krantz et al. (1997)	Weight, hip-to-waist proportion, bust size, and buttock size of female figures	Magnitude estimations of attractiveness	Simultaneous collection of Web and laboratory samples; correlation and regression of Web on laboratory sample as test of goodness of fit
Senior et al. (1999)	Eyebrow height and smiling or not on schematic faces	Forced choice selection of the more dominant face	Simultaneous collection of Web and laboratory samples with use of χ^2 as a goodness of fit measure
Stern and Faber (1997)	Social appropriateness and controversial nature of e-mail messages	Frequency of returned vs. forwarded e-mail	Comparison with previously published laboratory study of same phenomenon
Welch and Krantz (1996)	Parameters of auditory stimuli	Various	Comparison with previously published laboratory study of same phenomena

of which examined factors that influence the perceived attractiveness of female figures. Specifically, in the replication of Fallon and Rozin (1985), which manipulated the weight of front-facing female figures, the independent variable of hip-to-bust proportion was added. For the study that replicated Wiggins et al. (1968), the female figures were viewed from the side, and the independent variables were weight, breast size, and buttock size.

To best tackle the issue of the validity of the Web-based studies, the researchers needed to find a way to measure the match between the laboratory and Web results. One solution used was to correlate means from the two experiments. For both front-view and side-view studies the highest order interaction that was significant was used in the correlation. The higher the order of the interaction, the greater the number of means that can be entered into the analysis. If the interaction is not significant, it does not make sense to use it as the pattern in the data is not considered reliable. For the front-view study, the interaction between weight, body proportion, and the gender of the participants was the highest order significant interaction. The interaction is seen in that, although both genders found moderate weights most attractive, at this weight females clearly preferred figures where the hips were either wider than the bust or equal to the bust. Males did not make as clear a distinction but tended to prefer the figures where the hips equaled the bust. For thinner figures, males preferred figures where the bust was larger than the hips while females did not show any preferences among the different types of figures. For the side-view study, the interaction of weight, breast size, and the gender of the subject was the highest order interaction. Again a moderate weight was seen as most attractive by both genders. Females preferred the moderate breast size except for the thinnest figures, where they preferred the larger breast size, while males preferred the large breast size across all weights where they showed a preference. These trends were clearly seen in both the Web and laboratory samples of both studies.

For the front-view study there were 54 pairs of means and in the side-view study there were 36 pairs of means in these interactions, respectively. These mean pairs were entered into a Pearson's correlation to assess whether the patterns of the means in the laboratory studies were comparable to the Web versions of the same study. For the front-view study $r = .96$, and for the side-view study $r = .95$. In both cases, a high degree of correspondence between the laboratory and Web versions of the study is indicated. However, correlations are not sensitive to differences in the magnitudes of the values of the two data sets; for example, it is quite possible to correlate SAT scores, which vary from 400 to 1600, with GPAs, which vary from about 0 to 4 on most scales. Thus a linear regression analysis was applied which is sensitive to the magnitude of the two data sets. The slope will differ from 1 if the range of values of the two variables being compared is of different scales and the intercept will differ from 0 if the values of one variable are offset from the values of the other variable. For both studies, the regression analyses yielded slopes both nearly 1 and not significantly different from 1 and intercepts near 0 (Krantz et al., 1997). These results indicate that the means from the Web and laboratory versions of each study are essentially interchangeable.

Stern and Faber (1997) used e-mail as opposed to the Web, but their findings reveal some important issues regarding using any new media for research. They replicated Milgram's (1977) lost-letter paradigm, but used e-mail as opposed to dropping letters. In the Milgram study letters were dropped in a public location. Both the return address and the destination address would go to Milgram so he could measure how many letters were sent on or returned. Milgram found that few letters ever reappeared and all that did were sent on to the addressee. Thus, instead of collecting both an Internet and a laboratory sample, Stern and Faber compared the results of an Internet study to an already published traditionally collected data set. In contrast to the letters in the original study, the e-mail appeared to have been misdelivered to the subject. The "To:" address and the "From:" address involved a code such that either forwarding the e-mail to the supposedly intended person or using the "Reply" option would send the e-mail back to the experimenters. This study becomes an experiment, because the authors manipulated the message content to see whether that might affect how subjects handled this apparently missent e-mail. The manipulation did not yield significant results, but there was an important difference in the results of this Internet study from that of Milgram's original study. Whereas in the Milgram (1977) study, the letters were sent on to the intended recipient of the letters, in Stern and Faber's (1997) study, the e-mail was sent back to the sender. This difference in results, rather than showing how one method is inadequate, indicates how the two methods taken together reveal a clearer view of behavior in these circumstances. Either study, taken alone, might suggest that who the mail was sent to might be important. However, together, it is clear that people who sent or returned the mail did so in the easiest manner. In regular mail, it is easier to just drop the letter into a mailbox (to continue on its way) than to return it to the sender (because this would involve writing on the envelope). In contrast, it is easier to return a misdirected e-mail than to forward it on (because the forwarded address must be typed in, which is not the case when returning a message). Those who helped, therefore, did so in the easiest way possible.

Duker (1997) also simultaneously collected laboratory and Web samples. Duker was interested in the issue of whether the way a physician was paid (HMO or fee-for-service) affected how people evaluated treatment given. The study used a scenario and then manipulated whether the doctor in the scenario was either an HMO doctor or a fee-for-service doctor to investigate attitudes toward these types of physicians. Instead of a correlation or regression analysis to determine if the results were comparable, Duker examined the data to see if the same effects were significant and used the type of data collection as a factor in an analysis of variance design. A nonsignificant result on the type of sample factor was taken to imply that the results were comparable. At first glance, this method seems adequate; however, it relies on the logically flawed acceptance of the null hypothesis to make a conclusion.

Senior, Phillips, Barnes, and David (1999) actually combined the techniques of both Stern and Faber (1997) and Duker (1997) by not only replicating a published study but also collecting both Web and laboratory data. In this sense, Senior et al. took the same approach as Smith and Leigh (1997). In most ways, Senior et al. (1999) replicated the earlier published study on the perception of dominance by Keating, Mazur, and Segall (1977). These studies used simple drawings of faces with the face drawn as an outline, eyebrows drawn as single lines, and eyes, nose, and mouth simply drawn in. The independent variables were the positions of the eyebrows and the mouth. The dependent variable was subjects' judgments of which of a pair of these faces appeared more dominant (a forced-choice method). The two studies have very similar findings except that Senior et al. found that smiling faces were perceived as dominant, which was not true in Keating et al. The interesting feature of this difference was that Senior et al. found that smiling was seen as dominant on both their Web and laboratory studies (though the results in the lab were not as strong as those on the Web). Thus, the difference should not be attributed to the use of the Web but perhaps to changes in perception over time given the interval of two decades between the two studies.

Allen (1999) combined a series of laboratory studies with a parallel set of studies on the Web. Allen was interested in examining the role that shadows can play in disambiguating depth perception. Laboratory studies used a shadow chamber with two bars. One rod was 0.5 m from the subject, the other was 0.507 m from the subject. The rods could be lit in a way—either to have shadow or not—that accurately indicated their distance. To confuse the situation, the nearer stimulus was thinner and higher, in opposition to the normal situation of depth cues. The subjects were asked which bar was farther away. In the first study the lighting came from the left in the shadow condition. When the shadows were present, subjects were correct most of the time (12/13) and without shadows they were correct only rarely (3/13). Binomial probabilities show that subjects were correct more than chance with shadows and incorrect more often than chance without shadows. The second laboratory study changed the angle of light so that it came from in front of the objects. In the third study, there were four bars instead of two. The results were essentially the same; the subjects were almost always correct in the shadow condition and almost always incorrect when no shadows were present. Allen was interested in replicating the studies on the Web for two reasons. The first reason was that he wished to see if the results would continue to hold true when photographs were used. In this way the depth cue of accommodation was eliminated. In addition, in the lab, the researcher could not keep the subjects from changing their viewpoints, thereby adding another depth cue due to motion parallax. All three studies yielded exactly the same results as the laboratory studies. In addition, the Web study added a new experiment, with the lighting from the right. The results, too, agreed with those of the other studies.

Birnbaum's (1999) results from his study of decision making are very similar to what has been reported here. He studied decision making in probabilistic situations. In particular he used subjects' choices of which gambling situation they would prefer, to examine how people weigh probabilities and possible outcomes to make a decision. A lab and a Web version of the study were run simultaneously. Both used the same Web pages but the lab study was run in a lab with experimenters present to help with information on how to use the equipment. The choices of the lab and Internet samples correlated at .94. One other test of the data was to check a very basic criterion for consistent responding by subjects. Here, the criterion is called monotonicity. In monotonicity, the two choices of gambles are identical except that one outcome has a higher value. For example, one gamble would be $5 at a probability of .25 and $10 at a probability of .75. The other possible gamble would be $5 with a probability of .25 and $50 with a probability of .75. Now, in this case, it seems obvious that the person ought to pick the second gamble (and most subjects do). There were several trials in Birnbaum's study that directly and indirectly tested monotonicity and the Web study proved to be slightly but significantly more consistent with this basic principle. Thus in this case, if anything, the Web sample was found to give better data than the laboratory sample.

Klauer, Musch, and Naumer (1999) also investigated cognitive functioning as did Birnbaum (1999) but they investigated reasoning using syllogisms. They manipulated the validity of the syllogism as well as its believability (it could be believable or not). They were trying to replicate the traditional finding that we are more likely to accept a conclusion if it is believable than if it is not. This phenomenon has been called the belief bias. In addition they manipulated across groups the suggested base rate of valid conclusions. In a series of three experiments, using different types of syllogisms but the same independent variables, they ran both traditional laboratory and Web-based versions of the experiments. The Web-based and laboratory data very successfully replicated the earlier findings about the belief bias. In addition, both the Web and laboratory studies showed the same effects of suggested base rate on the results. One interesting analysis possible with the Web-based studies that was not possible with the laboratory studies is the examination of the effect of experience with logic on the findings. None of the laboratory subjects reported any formal training with logic while 60% of the participants in the Web-based studies reported some level of logic training. Using a χ^2 analysis of the solution frequencies, there were no significant differences in the pattern of the results for the different groups of subjects (laboratory, logic-naïve Web subjects, and logic-experienced Web subjects). Although this conclusion rests on the null hypothesis, the number of subjects is greater than 2000 for each experiment, suggesting that loss of power due to small n's is less likely to be a problem here.

Krantz (1998a) used a different technique to establish the validity of experimental results from the Web. This study examined the well-studied and understood phenomenon of depth perception with monocular cues. Different monocular cues were presented either alone or in combination. The participants' task was to judge how far apart two objects were. Instead of comparing the results to those of a previously existing study, of which there is not one that is similar enough, the results were compared to general expectation that the presence of more depth cues tends to lead to greater depth being presented in the image. In this case, the results matched well with the predictions made from a general basic understanding of depth perception.

TRENDS IN SUBJECT POPULATIONS

The overwhelming majority of traditional psychology studies make no effort whatsoever to ensure that the samples used are randomly selected (and, therefore, representative of the larger population being studied). Therefore, as alluded to earlier, the external validity of traditional laboratory studies is fairly low. In fact, it has been said that psychology has become the study of the behavior of the suburban White American college sophomore. The World Wide Web is seen as a tool to redress the problem and to dramatically increase the external validity of psychological findings. The potential for extremely large sample sizes (thereby resulting in a decrease in the Type II error rate and a corresponding increase in power) has been touted as another benefit of the Web. Other oft-quoted benefits are the low cost of conducting studies on the Web and the ease of data collection. On the other hand, along with the benefits come some definite threats to the internal validity of the studies. These threats stem from variation in equipment at the participants' end (Welch and Krantz, 1996), variation in download time, variation in the environment, and potential for participant fraud (Schmidt, 1997). These issues are discussed more fully by Reips (1996), Schmidt (1997), and Smith and Leigh (1997).

But does the Web really provide representative samples? This section traces potential trends in the demographic characteristics of participants in Web studies. A summary of the data from previous Web studies is provided in Table 3.

Table 3

Demographic Characteristics of WWW Participants

Study	Gender (% female)	Ethnicity	Country of origin	Age (years)
Kiesler and Sproull (1986)	16			
Brenner (1997)	≤ 27			Average = 34
Reips (1996)				
English version	42.9			
German version	17.5			
Duker (1997)	56.3	81.3% White; 3.1% each Asian/PI, Hispanic, and Latino/a	68.8% U.S.A	
Krantz et al. (1997)				
Front view	44	89% White	86% N. Am.; 7% Eur.; 3% Aust.; 2% Asia; 1% S. Am.; 1% Afr.	24% 18–22; 33% 23–30; 37% 31–50; 6% > 50
Side view	44	84% White	82% N. Am.; 8% Eur.; 2% Aust.; 3% Asia; 1% S. Am.; 0% Afr.	27% 18–22; 37% 23–30; 30% 31–50; 6% > 50
Schiano (1997)	26	45–50% White Am.; 20–25% White Other		
Smith and Leigh (1997)	26	86% White		65% ≤ 30
Swoboda et al. (1997)	8		64% N. Am.; 23% Eur.; 4% Aus./N.Z.; 3% Asia; 1% Africa	$M = 30$ $SD = 10$
Pasveer and Ellard (1998)				
Study 1— WWW section	62		78% Can.+ U.S.; 11% Eur.; 11% Other	4% unknown & < 16; 24% 16–20; 27% 21–25; 45% > 25 range = 13–62 $M = 27.5$ $SD = 9.7$
Study 3	71		83% Can.+ U.S.; 9% Eur.; 8% Other	7% unknown & < 16; 29% 16–20; 25% 21–25; 39% > 25 range = 11–78 $M = 25.9$ $SD = 9.4$

(*continues*)

Table 3 (*continued*)

Study	Gender (% female)	Ethnicity	Country of origin	Age (years)
Senior et al. (1999)		10–15% White British; 5–10% Chinese; < 5% (each) Other		
Buchanan and Smith (1999)	49			$M = 32$ $SD = 10.79$
Birnbaum (1999)	56		44 countries, but 73% from U.S.	23% 18–22; 27% 23–28; 30% 29–39; 20% ≥ 40
GVU 1st survey (1994a)	5.1			6.32% < 20; 28.27% 21–25; 26.93% 26–30; 16.22% 31–35; 10.71% 36–40; 7.66% 41–50; 1.93% > 50
GVU 2nd survey (1994b)	9.68		71.52% N. Am.; 23.27% Eur; 3.41% Aus.; 1.7% Other	Mean = 31.37 median = 29 range = 12–73
GVU 3rd survey (1995a)	15.5 (17.1% U.S.)		80.6% U.S.; 9.8% Eur.; 5.8% Can. + Mex.	Mean = 35.01 median = 35.00
Granered (1995a) (based on non-U.S. data from GVU 3rd survey, 1995a)	< 10 (7% Eur.)	84% White		
GVU 4th survey (1995b)	29.3		76.2% U.S.; 8.4% Eur.; 10.2% Can. + Mex.	Mean = 32.7
Granered (1995b) (based on European data from GVU 4th survey, 1995b)	15 (U.K. /Ire); 8–9 (rest)			Mean = 29.7
Recker and Greenwood (1995) (based on Oceania data from GVU 4th survey, 1995b)	28			Mean = 31.2
GVU 5th survey (1996a)	31.5 (34.4% U.S.)		73.4% U.S.; 10.8% Eur.; 8.4% Can. + Mex.	Mean = 33.0

(*continues*)

Table 3 (*continued*)

Study	Gender (% female)	Ethnicity	Country of origin	Age (years)
Granered (1996) (based on European data from GVU 5th survey, 1996a)	15.2			Mean = 28.8
Recker and Greenwood (1996) (based on New Zealand data from GVU 5th survey, 1996a)	25			Mean = 30.3
GVU 6th survey (1996b)	31.4 (19.8% Eur.)			Mean = 34.9
GVU 7th survey (1997a)	31.3 (33.41% U.S.)			Mean = 35.2
GVU 8th survey (1997b)	38.5 (22% Eur.; 40% U.S.)	88% White; 2.6% Asian		
GVU 9th survey (1998a)	38.7 (16.3% Eur.)	87.4% White; 3.1% Asian		17.2% 11−20; 23% 21−25; 36.6% 26−50; 58.11% > 50; $M = 35.1$
GVU 10th survey (1998b)	33.6	87.2% White	84.7% U.S.; 7.3% Eur.; 3.8% Can.	6% ≤ 20; 12.5% 21−25; 16.1% 26−30; 13.6% 31−35; 11.4% 36−40; 12.2% 41−45; 26.8% ≥ 46

GENDER

The overall picture that emerges with respect to gender is fairly ambiguous, due to large variability in the percentage of women subjects reported in the various studies.

On the one hand, the surveys conducted by the Georgia Institute of Technology—the Graphics, Visualization, and Usability (hereafter referred to as GVU) Center's semiannual general survey of Web users—show a clear and comforting trend toward gender equality in Internet study participants. The percentage of women participating in the GVU surveys grew consistently, from a modest 5.1% in the 1st survey (GVU, 1994a) to a promising 38.7% in the 9th survey (GVU, 1998a), before dropping to 33.6% in the 10th survey (GVU, 1998b).

In the non-GVU studies, on the other hand, the percentage of women Web participants ranged from 8% (Swoboda, Mühlberger, Weitkunat, & Schneeweiß, 1997) to 71% (Pasveer & Ellard, 1998 [Study 3]). Intervening percentages in other non-GVU studies were as follows (in ascending order): 16% (Kiesler & Sproull, 1986), 26% (Schiano, 1997; Smith & Leigh, 1997), ≤ 27% (Brenner, 1997), 42.9% (Reips, 1996), 44% (Krantz et al., 1997), 49% (Buchanan & Smith, 1999), 56% (Birnbaum, 1999), 56.3% (Duker, 1997), and 62% (Study 1—Web section; Pasveer & Ellard, 1998). It appears that the gender proportion found in a study may, in part, be determined by the topic and/or method used to recruit participants. Pasveer and Ellard (1998) acknowledge this as a possible explanation for their high percentage of female participants. The issue of participant recruitment is considered at further length in the next section of this chapter.

In an analysis of European participants in the GVU surveys, Granered (1995a, 1996) reported an increase in women from 7% in the third survey (GVU, 1995a) to 15.2% in the fifth survey (GVU, 1996a). In Granered's (1995b) analysis of the GVU fourth survey European data (GVU, 1995b), females composed 15% of all participants for the United Kingdom and the Republic of Ireland, but only between 8 and 9% for the rest of Europe. Recker and Greenwood's (1995) analysis of Oceania data from the GVU fourth survey (GVU, 1995b) indicated 28% female participants, while their analysis (Recker & Greenwood, 1996) of New Zealand data from the GVU fifth survey (GVU, 1996a) indicated 25% female participants.

Interestingly, Reips (1996) reported 17.5% females in the German language version of the same study for which there were 42.9% females in the English language version. This appears to suggest either that women form a larger percentage of Web users in English-speaking areas than in German-speaking areas or—rather less interestingly—that the result is an artifact, because Reips' (1996) study was of greater appeal to English-speaking women than to their German-speaking counterparts.

ETHNICITY

The findings with respect to ethnicity are fairly straightforward: the overwhelming majority of participants in Web studies are White. No changing trends appear to be taking place. However, it should be noted that, of all the studies considered in this review that revealed information about the ethnicity of participants, none were published before 1995; 3 years may represent too short a time for obvious trends in subject ethnicity to manifest themselves.

Whites generally constitute between 80 and 90% of all participants in Web studies (Duker, 1997; Krantz et al., 1997; Smith & Leigh, 1997; GVU 8th survey, 1997b; GVU 9th survey, 1998a; GVU 10th survey, 1998b). Schiano (1997) is the lone exception: this study reported between 65 and 75% White respondents. No other ethnic group constituted more than 5% of subjects in any of the Web studies reviewed with the one exception being the Senior et al. (1999) study. In this study, people of Chinese ethnicity constituted between 5 and 10%.

Among European subjects in the GVU third survey (GVU, 1995a), Granered (1995a) reports that approximately 84% were White.

COUNTRY OF ORIGIN

As with ethnicity, there is little ambiguity about participant demographics with respect to country of origin. North Americans, especially people from the United States, form by far the largest single grouping of participants in English-language studies conducted on the Web.

Several studies have shown the percentage of participants of North American origin to be between 80 and 90% of the total number of participants (GVU 3rd survey, 1995a; GVU 4th survey, 1995b; GVU 5th survey, 1996a; Krantz, et al, 1997; Pasveer & Ellard, 1998 [Study 3]; GVU 10th survey, 1998b). The GVU 2nd survey (1994b) reports a comparatively low 71.52%, and the Swoboda et al. (1997) study reports an even lower 64%. In Pasveer and Ellard's (1998) Study 1 (Web section), the percentage of participants whose country of current residence was either the United States or Canada was 78%.

Some studies have reported the specific percentages of total respondents who were from the United States. The percentages of U.S. participants in the GVU 3rd survey (1995a), GVU 4th survey (1995b), GVU 5th survey (1996a), Duker (1997), and the GVU 10th survey (1998b) were 80.6, 76.2, 73.4, 68.8, and 84.7%, respectively. The paucity of studies does not facilitate the making of educated guesses regarding trends.

The percentage of respondents from Europe appears to fluctuate mostly between 7 and 11% (GVU 3rd survey, 1995a; GVU 4th survey, 1995b; GVU 5th survey, 1996a; Krantz et al., 1997; Pasveer & Ellard, 1998; GVU 10th survey, 1998b). In stark contrast, the GVU 2nd survey (1994b) reported 23.27% European participants, and the Swoboda et al. (1997) study reported 23% Europeans (21% citizens of the European Community, plus 2% citizens of the former Eastern Europe).

No other area of the world has contributed more than 5% of the total number of subjects to any of the studies reviewed. As alluded to before, the language employed (English) may influence these data, as may the fact that the studies quoted were overwhelmingly authored by authors in North America.

AGE

Both mean and median measures of central tendency for age have identified that the average age of respondents to Web studies lies between 26 and 35.2 years (Brenner, 1997; Buchanan & Smith, 1999; GVU's WWW User Surveys (1999); Klauer et al., 1999; Pasveer & Ellard, 1998; Swoboda et al., 1997). In the GVU 10th survey (1998b), the median age fell between 36 and 40 years. The median age in the Krantz et al, (1997) study fell between 23 and 30 years, while the median age in the Smith and Leigh (1997) study also fell below 30 years. From Granered's (1995b, 1996) and Recker and Greenwood's (1995, 1996) analysis of the data from the fourth (GVU, 1995b) and fifth (GVU, 1996a) GVU surveys, it appears that the mean age of participants from Europe and Oceania is similar to that of American participants.

A few studies also mention measures of dispersion for age. Pasveer and Ellard (1998) report a standard deviation, for participant age, of 9.7 (Study 1—Web section) and 9.4 (Study 3). Swoboda et al. (1997) report a standard deviation of 10, while Buchanan and Smith (1999) report a standard deviation of 10.79. Klauer et al. (1999) report standard deviations also about 10 with ranges in their studies from 10 to 90 years of age. The distribution of age is wider for Web participants than for laboratory studies (Reips, 1996).

LANGUAGE EXPERIENCE

Klauer et al. (1999) report some interesting data on the language skills of the subjects in the two versions of their studies. They ran both a German and an English version of their studies. In the German version of the study, 92% said they were native German speakers and an additional 5% said they were fluent in German. In English only 72% said they were native English speakers and 12% said they were fluent in English. Thus, many more nonnative speakers will take an English version of a study. In addition, many more people using the English version of the study had relatively weak English. It seems that many more subjects are more willing to struggle through an English version of the study than a German version of the study. It seems advisable to assess the knowledge of the language in which the study is written in future Web-based studies.

SUMMARY OF SUBJECT CHARACTERISTICS

We now return to the question posed earlier in this section: Does the World Wide Web provide an appropriate medium for gathering globally representative samples? The demographic data presented above suggest that, for the moment at least, the question must be answered largely in the negative. A major reason for this, of course, is the problem of nonprobabilistic sampling and self-selection. Today's Web participants appear to be mostly White, mostly male (especially in non-U.S. samples), and overwhelmingly from the United States, Europe, Canada, and Oceania. Reips (Chap. 4, this volume) discusses how the Web can be used to collect samples from subsets of this global population.

However, the wider distribution of age of Web samples than of laboratory samples may be interpreted as a step in the right direction as far as an increase in external validity is concerned. Furthermore, as a medium, the Web must be said to be in its infancy and still growing at a prodigious rate. It is not inconceivable that, within the next decade or two, Web samples will become fairly representative of the global population.

SUBJECT RECRUITMENT

One topic that will affect the validity of all studies is the manner in which subjects are obtained. There are several basic techniques that have been used across these studies:

- Soliciting on newsgroups or lists related to the research topic (Birnbaum, 1999, Buchanan & Smith, 1999; Mehta & Sivadas, 1995; Reips, 1995)
- Posting to search engines (Birnbaum, 1999; 2000, Chapter 1, this volume; Duker, 1997)
- Waiting for search engines to find the study (sometimes using the metatags to assist the search engines) (this really will affect all posted Web studies unless protected from general access)
- Posting on the APS list of experiments online or similar pages (Allen, 1999; Buchanan & Smith, 1999; Duker, 1997; Krantz, et al., 1997; Reips, 1995)

There are some studies that used more unique methods, but the methods just detailed seem to be the most common means of obtaining subjects. These methods are both general (e.g., using the search engines) and more focused (e.g., using the newsgroups).

One study found one method to be very unsuccessful. Klauer et al. (1999) received very little response from a radio interview about the study based upon examination of the log files of the study shortly after the interview (Musch, personal communication). This experience contrasts strongly with the effect of being mentioned on a Web page related by the NBC news magazine *Dateline* of the studies reported in Krantz, et al., (1997). In the next few days after the show, the server recorded at least a fourfold level of activity on the studies. The activity was easily noticed from the regular examinations of the log files, but only responding to e-mails from some of the subjects allowed the author to discover the source of the activity as the NBC show had not asked permission for the link. Part of the difference is that the participants of the radio show had to remember the esoteric address off the air. In the television example, the link was embedded in a Web page related to the TV story. However, the media may increase the tendency to make links to studies if they are relevant to their stories and how that link is made may greatly increase the activity on the site.

We wish to reiterate that the participant population accessed may well depend on which of the preceding (or unique, for that matter) methods are used. Furthermore, the participant population tapped may also vary according to the topic of the study. These problems are a consequence of participant self-selection on the Web.

A related issue for Web research involves the methods employed to induce subjects to complete the study. Most researchers merely try to keep the study short to keep participation rates up. Some have offered incentives such as a chance at money or a small piece of code or other prize for completion of the study. Reips (1995) has been one of the more active users of this method of getting subject compliance. The use of incentives should be in accordance with APA guidelines, but, given the topics of the studies thus far, this does not seem to be a problem (yet).

CONCLUSIONS

In all cases, there seems to be a surprising match between laboratory and Web versions of surveys, scales, and experimental variables. At least this seems to be true for the surveys and variables researched to date. These results seem to be obtained despite often great differences between the subject characteristics, even on some personality variables that would be expected to affect the findings. For example, in Krantz, et al. (1997), the subject groups were highly different but the results indicated that the Web and laboratory data could essentially replace each other. The same result was found by Buchanan and Smith (1999), who validated the online version of the Self-Monitoring Scale.

Although it would be premature (and in fact ridiculous) to conclude that individual difference variables that might distinguish one sample from another and one population from another are irrelevant to psychological research, it is possible that they are not as relevant as once thought. Whatever the case, the ability to collect large sample sizes should allow for the determination of when and which person variables are important for which independent and dependent variables. This feature of the Web may be one of the most useful as the use of the Web as a research tool develops over time.

It appears as though a similar conclusion can be made for many environmental variables. Although there is no way to quantify the range of environments that subjects encounter in a Web version of the experiment, the environments we use to work on computers are varied—as we know from our own experiences. It is very likely, therefore, that these environments are varied for our Web users as well. Again, in many cases these environmental variables will be important to the psychological variables studied, but for many variables of psychological interest, environmental variables seem to play a small role. In other words, the findings may be relatively robust to variations in the environment (this may also hold true for participant demographics). One obvious caveat exists with respect to attempts to deliver stimuli for sensory and perceptual research. Here the environment will be paramount. This issue is probably part of the difficulty experienced in the study of auditory perception by Welch and Krantz (1996).

As we have observed, it would be incorrect to suggest that all findings from the Web match the corresponding findings from the laboratory. Stern and Faber (1997) found very different results from Milgram's (1977) original lost-letter technique. However, this difference, in itself, was illustrative, demonstrating that helping behavior in this situation was driven partly by ease and not just by a desire to send the letter to where it belonged. Buchanan (1998) found that the relationship between attractiveness and self-monitoring was not as strong on the Web as in a previously published laboratory study of the relationship. Senior et al. (1999) found a similar weakening of a relationship over the Web in their study of facial expression and dominance. A tentative explanation is that, in the latter case, the disparate findings may reflect a change in social attitudes, because the simultaneous laboratory sample showed the same weakening in the trends. Thus, not only similarities but also differences between Web and laboratory samples may be informative whether the difference turns out to be dependent on the Internet itself (Stern and Faber, 1997) or on the change in social attitudes (Buchanan, 1998; Senior et al., 1999). The Web itself, being such a drastically different environment from that of the laboratory, may itself constitute an important psychological variable, helping researchers to obtain a clearer view of psychological processes.

In conclusion, the Web appears to be a powerful tool for research. Across a wide range of designs and variables the Web seems to access the same psychological variables as does the laboratory. Obviously many more variables will need to be studied, but this is a very encouraging start.

REFERENCES

Ainsworth, M. D., & Bell, S. M. (1970). Attachment, exploration, and separation: Illustrated by the behavior of one-year-olds in a strange situation. *Child Development, 41,* 49–67.

Allen, B. P. (1999). *Shadows as sources of cues for distance of shadow casting objects*. Manuscript in preparation.

Bachmann, D., Elfrink, J., & Vazzana, G. (1996). Tracking the progress of e mail vs. snail mail. *Marketing Research, 8,* 31–35.

Birnbaum, M. H. (1999). Testing critical properties of decision making on the Internet. *Psychological Science, 10,* 399–407.

Birnbaum, M. H. (2000). Decision making in the lab and on the Web. In M. H. Birnbaum (Ed.), *Psychological Experiments on the Internet,* (pp. 3–34). San Diego: Academic Press.

Bonnenburg, A. V., & Gosling, S. D. (1998). *Geeks not freaks: Personality of Internet users compared to college students*. Presented at the 10th Annual Convention of the American Psychological Society, Washington, DC.

Brenner, V. (1997). Psychology of computer use: XLVII. Parameters of Internet use, abuse and addiction: The first 90 days of the Internet usage survey. *Psychological Reports, 80,* 879–882.

Buchanan, T. (1998). *Internet research: Self-monitoring and judgements of attractiveness*. Presented at the 28th annual convention of the Society for Computers in Psychology, Dallas, TX.

Buchanan, T., & Smith, J. L. (1999). Using the Internet for psychological research: Personality testing on the World-Wide Web. *British Journal of Psychology, 90,* 125–144.

Chen, B., Wang, H., Proctor, R. W., & Salvendy, G. (1997). A human-centered approach for designing World-Wide Web browsers. *Behavior Research Methods, Instruments & Computers, 29,* 172–179.

Duker, A. P. (1997). *The equivalency of Internet research to conventional testing: An experiment on the effects of managed care on trust in the physician–patient relationship*. Unpublished senior thesis, College of Wooster.

Ellis, B. J., & Symons, D. (1990). Sex differences in sexual fantasies: An evolutionary psychological approach. *Journal of Sex Research, 27,* 527–555.

Fallon, A., & Rozin, P. (1985). Sex differences in perceptions of desirable body shape. *Journal of Abnormal Psychology, 94,* 102–105.

Gangestad, S. W., & Snyder, M. (1985). "To carve nature at its joints": On the existence of discrete classes in personality. *Psychological Review, 92,* 317–340.

Georgia Institute of Technology: Georgia Tech's Graphics, Visualization, and Usability Center. (1994a). *GVU's first WWW user survey* [Online]. Available URL: http://www.cc.gatech.edu/gvu/user_surveys/survey-01-1994/

Georgia Institute of Technology: Georgia Tech's Graphics, Visualization, and Usability Center. (1994b). *GVU's second WWW user survey* [Online]. Available URL: http://www.cc.gatech.edu/gvu/user_surveys/survey-09-1994/

Georgia Institute of Technology: Georgia Tech's Graphics, Visualization, and Usability Center. (1995a). *GVU's third WWW user survey* [Online]. Available URL: http://www.cc.gatech.edu/gvu/user_surveys/survey-04-1995/

Georgia Institute of Technology: Georgia Tech's Graphics, Visualization, and Usability Center. (1995b). *GVU's fourth WWW user survey* [Online]. Available URL: http://www.cc.gatech.edu/gvu/user_surveys/survey-10-1995/

Georgia Institute of Technology: Georgia Tech's Graphics, Visualization, and Usability Center. (1996a). *GVU's fifth WWW user survey* [Online]. Available URL: http://www.cc.gatech.edu/gvu/user_surveys/survey-04-1996/

Georgia Institute of Technology: Georgia Tech's Graphics, Visualization, and Usability Center. (1996b). *GVU's sixth WWW user survey* [Online]. Available URL: http://www.cc.gatech.edu/gvu/user_surveys/survey-10-1996/

Georgia Institute of Technology: Georgia Tech's Graphics, Visualization, and Usability Center. (1997a). *GVU's seventh WWW user survey* [Online]. Available URL: http://www.cc.gatech.edu/gvu/user_surveys/survey-1997-04/

Georgia Institute of Technology: Georgia Tech's Graphics, Visualization, and Usability Center. (1997b). *GVU's eighth WWW user survey* [Online]. Available URL: `http:// www.cc.gatech.edu/ gvu / user_surveys / survey-1997-10 /`

Georgia Institute of Technology: Georgia Tech's Graphics, Visualization, and Usability Center. (1998a). *GVU's ninth WWW user survey* [Online]. Available URL: `http:// www.cc.gatech.edu/ gvu / user_surveys / survey-1998-04 /`

Georgia Institute of Technology: Georgia Tech's Graphics, Visualization, and Usability Center. (1998b). *GVU's tenth WWW user survey* [Online]. Available URL: `http:// www.cc.gatech.edu/ gvu / user_surveys / survey-1998-10 /`

Georgia Institute of Technology. (1999). *GVU's WWW user surveys* [Online]. Available URL: `http:// www.gvu.gatech.edu/ user_surveys /`

Granered, E. (1995a). *Analysis of non-US data from GVU 3rd survey* [Online]. Available URL: `http:// www.cc.gatech.edu/ gvu / user_surveys / europe / egworld.html`

Granered, E. (1995b). *Analysis of European data from GVU 4th survey* [Online]. Available URL: `http:// www.cc.gatech.edu/ gvu / user_surveys / europe /`

Granered, E. (1996). *Analysis of European data from GVU 5th survey* [Online]. Available URL: `http:// www.vuw.ac.nz / ~ mimi / survey / survey4th / general.html`

Keating, C., Mazur, A., & Segall, M. (1977). Facial gestures which influence the perception of status. *Sociometry, 40,* 374–378.

Kiesler, S., & Sproull, L. S. (1986). Response effects in the electronic survey. *Public Opinion Quarterly, 50,* 402–413.

Kittleson, M. J. (1995). An assessment of the response rate via the postal service and e-mail. *Health Values, 18,* 27–29.

Klauer, K. C., Musch, J., & Naumer, B. (1999). *On belief bias in syllogistic reasoning.* Manuscript submitted for publication.

Krantz, J. H. (1998a). *Depth perception* [Online]. Needham, MA: Peregrine. Available URL: `http:// www.psychplace.com/ learning / depth / intro.html`

Krantz, J. H. (1998b). *Psychological research on the net* [Online]. Available URL: `http:// psych.hanover.edu/ APS / exponnet.html`

Krantz, J. H., Ballard, J., & Scher, J. (1997). Comparing the results of laboratory and World-Wide Web samples on the determinants of female attractiveness. *Behavior Research Methods, Instruments & Computers, 29,* 264–269.

Kuffler, S. W. (1953). Discharge patterns and functional organization of mammalian retina. *Journal of Neurophysiology, 16,* 37–68.

Levy, C. M. (1995). Mosaic and the information superhighway: A virtual tiger in your tank. *Behavior Research Methods, Instruments & Computers, 27,* 187–192.

Marlowe, D., & Crowne, D. (1964). *The approval motive.* New York: Wiley.

Mehta, R., & Sivadas, E. (1995). Comparing response rates and response content in mail versus electronic mail surveys. *Journal of the Market Research Society, 37,* 429–439.

Milgram, S. (1977). *The individual in a social world.* New York: McGraw-Hill.

Pasveer, K. A., & Ellard, J. H. (1998). The making of a personality inventory: Help from the WWW. *Behavior Research Methods, Instruments, & Computers, 30,* 309–313.

Recker, M., & Greenwood, J. (1995). *Analysis of Oceania data from GVU 4th survey* [Online]. Available URL: `http:// www.vuw.ac.nz / ~ mimi / survey / survey4th / general.html`

Recker, M., & Greenwood, J. (1996). *Analysis of New Zealand data from GVU 5th survey* [Online]. Available URL: `http:// www.vuw.ac.nz / ~ mimi / survey / survey 5th / general.html`

Reips, U.-D. (1995). *The Web's experimental psychology lab* [Online]. Available URL: `http:// www.psych.unizh.ch/ genpsy / Ulf / Lab / WebExpPsyLab.html`

Reips, U.-D. (1996). *Experimenting in the World-Wide Web.* Presented at the 26th Annual Meeting of the Society for Computers in Psychology, Chicago, IL.

Schiano, D. J. (1997). Convergent methodologies in cyber-psychology: A case study. *Behavior Research Methods, Instruments & Computers, 29,* 270–273.

Schmidt, W. (1997). World-Wide Web survey research: Benefits, potential problems, and solutions. *Behavior Research Methods, Instruments & Computers, 29,* 274–279.

Schuldt, B., & Totten, J. (1994). Electronic mail vs. mail survey response rates. *Marketing Research, 6,* 36–39.

Senior, C., Phillips, M. L., Barnes, J., & David, A. S. (1999). An investigation in the perception of dominance from schematic faces: A study using the World-Wide Web. *Behavior Research Methods, Instruments, & Computers, 31,* 341–346.

Smith, M. A., & Leigh, B. (1997). Virtual subjects: Using the Internet as an alternative source of subjects and research environment. *Behavior Research Methods, Instruments, & Computers, 29,* 496–505.

Stern, S. E., & Faber, J. E. (1997). The lost e-mail method: Milgram's lost-letter technique in the age of the Internet. *Behavior Research Methods & Computers, 29,* 260–263.

Swoboda, Mühlberger, Weitkunat, & Schneeweiß. (1997). Internet surveys by direct mailing: An innovative way of collecting data. *Social Science Computer Review, 15,* 242–255.

Weible, R., & Wallace, J. (1998). Cyber research: The impact of the Internet on data collection. *Marketing Research, 10,* 19–24.

Welch, N., & Krantz, J. H. (1996). The World-Wide Web as a medium for psychoacoustical demonstrations and experiments: Experience and results. *Behavior Research Methods, Instruments, & Computers, 28,* 192–196.

Wiggins, J., Wiggins, N., & Conger, J. (1968). Correlates of heterosexual preference. *Journal of Personality & Social Psychology, 10,* 82–90.

CHAPTER 3

A Brief History of Web Experimenting

Jochen Musch
Psychological Institute
University of Bonn
D-53117 Bonn
Germany

Ulf-Dietrich Reips
Experimental and Developmental
 Psychology
University of Zürich
CH-8032 Zürich
Switzerland

A small, but growing number of researchers have begun to use the World Wide Web as a medium for experimental research. To learn more about the circumstances and results of the first Web experiments, we conducted a WWW-based online survey directed to researchers currently engaged in Web experimenting. We hoped to get an impression of the experiences of the pioneering generation of Web researchers. We summarize the results of this survey, which showed that an increasing number of Web experiments with promising results is now being conducted, and give a brief overview on the short history of Web experiments.

THE HISTORY OF WEB EXPERIMENTS

The introduction of computerized experimenting in the 1970s (e.g., Connes, 1972; Hoggatt, 1977) revolutionized traditional laboratory research. Among the attractive new features were a standardized and controlled presentation of stimuli, item-branching capabilities, immediacy of data entry, elimination of missing responses, elimination of transcription costs and errors, and accurate measurements of response times. Adaptivity, interactivity, and ease of data storage and analysis were additional advantages of the new technology. It has also been argued that the use of computers reduces the tendency to respond in a socially desirable way (Booth-Kewley, Edwards, & Rosenfeld, 1992;

Psychological Experiments on the Internet

Martin & Nagao, 1989) and helps to avoid experimenter biases and demand characteristics (Hewson, Laurent, & Vogel, 1996; Reips, chap. 4, this volume; Smith & Leigh, 1997). Clearly, the computerized administration of experiments and questionnaires offered possibilities unavailable in traditional paper-and-pencil research. With hindsight, it is hardly surprising therefore that the computer revolution in experimental psychology in the 1970s was an overwhelming success.

Twenty years later, most human experimental research in psychology is aided by computer automation. Extending computerized experimenting beyond single PCs, local computer networks have been used for the collection of data (Hoffman & MacDonald, 1993). Programs are written in high-level languages such as C + +, Pascal, or Delphi, or with program packages such as SuperLab, PsyScope, MEL (Micro Experiment Laboratory), and ERTS (Experimental Run Time System). Although computerized experiments have become the method of choice in conducting psychological research, there are many signs that another revolution is now beginning. It is associated with the recent exponential growth of the Internet.

The Internet's early purpose in the 1960s was to link a U.S. Defense Department network called the Advanced Research Projects Agency Network (ARPAnet) with a variety of other radio and satellite networks (Abbate, 1994; Hardy, 1995). In the 1980s, Ethernet local area networks were developed to allow computers at a single site to connect to a time-sharing computer site (Salus, 1995). These capabilities were extended to include access to the ARPAnet. The latest and most influential part of the Internet, a global hypertext system called the World Wide Web, was born in the early 1990s at the European Laboratory for Particle Physics (CERN). Within a few years it became clear that it might become the basis of the next generation of computerized experiments in psychology.

Although the term "hypertext" was coined by Theodor Nelson in 1960, the concept of hypertext dates back to the work of Vanevar Bush (1945). Around 1980, Tim Berners-Lee wrote a notebook program based on the hypertext concept and called it "Enquire-Within-Upon-Everything." The program created links between arbitrary nodes which were given a title and a list of bidirectional typed links. While working at CERN, Berners-Lee proposed a hypertext project in 1989 that extended his program to a more global level. It was created under the pretense that many people would be able to work collaboratively by putting information on a web of hypertext documents. The documents would be put on servers and client software, called a browser, would allow one to access the information stored on the server. The software calls up the information by searching for a link's uniform resource locator (URL). It then uses the hypertext transfer protocol (HTTP) to get the document, which is coded in hypertext markup language (HTML). The world's first Web browser ran on a NeXt computer at CERN in 1990. In 1991, Marc Andreesen and a group of students at the National Center for Supercomputing Applications (NCSA), located on the campus of the University of Illinois at Urbana Champaign began work on what would be the first publicly available browser, called Mosaic. Mosaic, released in 1993, was the first point-and-click graphical user interface for the World Wide Web. The ability to combine words, pictures, and sounds on Web pages excited many computer programmers who saw the potential for publishing information on the Internet in a way that can be as easy as using a word processor.

When the people that previously constructed Mosaic started developing the Netscape Navigator in 1994, they decided to implement several new HTML features, and the Navigator soon became the dominant tool for browsing the Web. A little later, Microsoft came along and created another browser also based on HTML, the Internet Explorer. HTML—the hypertext markup language—became the lingua franca for publishing on the World Wide Web.

The World Wide Web Consortium (W3C), the most prominent members of which are Netscape and Microsoft, works on and publishes proposed recommendations of new HTML specifications. To date, the W3C has released three versions of HTML. The first one, in 1995, was HTML 2.0, which was a simple language that attempted to gather the various previous implementations and concatenate them into a concrete specification. (Whatever existed earlier is collectively called HTML 1.0, although there never was such a specification). Then came HTML 3.2, which aimed to gather all the most popular features Netscape had introduced into a concrete specification. HTML 3.2 still is the most reliable specification to refer to for simple applications and allows for the creation of simple Web pages. W3C's latest HTML specification is version 4.0, which was released in December 1997. It is supported by the latest version of both Netscape (version 4.0) and Internet Explorer (version 4.0). Today, starting a browser and going online gives the user access to millions of Web servers and hundreds of millions of HTML pages. Having gone through several stages of evolution, HTML 4.0 has a wide range of features reflecting the needs of a very diverse and international community wishing to make information available on the Web. Among the most important of these features are forms.

Forms (or "fill-out forms") were first introduced in HTML 2.0. They are interactive, unlike the typical static Web page, and their introduction changed things in an important way. For the first time, the reader of a Web document could communicate back to the server. Forms in HTML are the computer equivalent of paper forms, such as an application form. There is a button or link at the end of every WWW form, often labeled "Submit." When this button is pushed, two things are sent to the server: the data that were typed into the form, and an ACTION, which basically tells the server the name of the program that knows how to process that form's data. The server simply invokes that program and passes the form's data to it (using CGI, the common gateway interface), and arranges for the output of that program to be sent back to the browser (ordinarily another document that contains some form of feedback).

Common uses of forms are surveys, online order forms, or really any Web page in which input is required from the user to accomplish a given task or provide a service to the user. Of course, for a psychologist, sending a participant's experimental or questionnaire data back to the experimenter is the most interesting application of forms. Drawing on forms, the WWW first offered the possibility of conducting psychological surveys and experiments independent of any geographical constraints.

HTML was soon supplemented by JavaScript, a compact, cross-platform, object-based scripting language that was first supported in version 2.0 of the Netscape Navigator and was also adopted by Microsoft in version 3.0 of its Internet Explorer (Flanagan, 1998). JavaScript code is embedded directly into the HTML page and can be used to create interactive Web pages. The browser interprets the JavaScript statements embedded in an HTML page and executes them. JavaScript statements can respond to user events such as mouse-clicks, form input, and page navigation. For example, JavaScript functions can be used to verify that users enter valid information into a form requesting a fixed number format. Without any network transmission, the HTML page with embedded JavaScript can check the entered data and alert the user with a dialog box if the input is invalid.

Another important technology became available in 1995, when James Gosling and a team of programmers at Sun Microsystems released an Internet programming language called Java. It again radically altered the way applications and information could be retrieved, displayed, and used over the Internet. Client-side Java applets are small programs that are transmitted over the Web and run on the user's machine, offering a large variety of possibilities for sophisticated experiments. Java was first built into version 3.0 of the Navigator and version 3.0 of the Explorer. Owing to these technological developments and its exponential growth during the past few years, the World Wide Web presents researchers with an unprecedented opportunity to conduct experiments with participants from all over the world rather than with the usual student sample from their local universities. It thus has the potential to serve as an alternative or supplemental source of subjects and research environment for traditional psychological investigations (Buchanan & Smith, 1999; Reips, 1996a, 1996b, 1997b; Smith & Leigh, 1997). Using the Internet to conduct research offers several advantages over traditional research practices (see Hewson et al., 1996, and Reips, 1995b, 1996a, 1996b, 1997b, this volume, for a summary).

In a sense, using worldwide networks such as the Internet for experimental research therefore is the logical next step in what began with the first experiments on stand-alone computers (cf. Buchanan & Smith, 1999).

However, the use of the WWW as a medium for experimental research also poses a unique set of challenges (Reips, 1999a). To learn more about the circumstances and results of the recently growing number of Web experiments, we conducted two online surveys directed to researchers currently engaged in Web experimenting. We thus hoped to get an impression of the experiences of the pioneering generation of Web researchers. In the present chapter we summarize the results of this survey and make an attempt to write the early history of Web experiments.

As in writing a general history of the Internet (e.g., Musch, 1997), the frequency and ease with which WWW documents are changed, combined with the lack of an effort to comprehensively collect those documents during the first years of the WWW, make it a difficult task to determine what really happened when. This difficulty is even reflected in recommendations for references to online documents (e.g., Ott, Krüger, & Funke, 1997), which advise adding the lookup date to the reference. On the other hand, the WWW is still very young, the number of Web experiments is rather small, and so people's memory (including our own) should be still fresh.

In the fall of 1994, when one of us began planning what later became the *Web's Experimental Psychology Lab* (Reips, 1995a), an Internet scan for Web experiments produced no results. However, before the Web's Experimental Psychology Lab went online with its first two experiments in September 1995 there were already a few experiments online, as we later discovered. Obviously, the time for Web experimenting had come.

As it seems, the very first Web experiments were Norma Welch's (1995) experiments on auditory perception, which were simultaneously run at McGill University, Montreal, Canada, and Technical University, Darmstadt, Germany (Welch & Krantz, 1996). However, as Krantz and Dalal (chap. 2, this volume) put it, these experiments "could not be really called studies carried out over the Web" as they were attached to tutorials in auditory perception. In May 1995, Andreas Weigend and a class he taught at Colorado University put up three Web experiments on music recognition (Weigend, 1995). Unfortunately, the code of these Web experiments was lost when Weigend left Colorado University (A. Weigend, personal communication, November 6, 1998), and we were not able to determine whether these studies were really experiments in the sense that some variable was manipulated (as contrasted with an online questionnaire). A little later John Krantz and colleagues started their Web experiment on the determinants of female attractiveness (Krantz, Ballard, & Scher, 1997). This might well have been the first true Web experiment that went online. It appears to be the first psychology Web experiment that was published in a scientific journal.

Krantz et al. used a within-subjects design, the first Web experiment with a between-subjects design appears to be the Web experiment on cognitive consistency of causal mechanisms (Reips, 1996a, 1996b, 1997b), with which the first virtual experimental psychology laboratory (Reips, 1995a) opened its doors. Between-subject designs require random assignment of participants to experimental conditions, which can be realized in Web experiments through the use of CGIs (Kieley, 1996; Reips, 1996b, 1997b, 1999a), JavaScript, or Java. Today, the Web's Experimental Psychology Lab at Tübingen (Reips, 1995a), which is now at Zurich, is still a place for methodological discussions on Web experimenting and actively invites participation of experiments from other researchers which can be hosted by the lab.

Since 1995, the following sites (with their opening dates) have gone online:

- Interactive CyberLab for Decision-Making Research (http://www.etl.go.jp/~e6930, April 1996)
- Laboratory of Social Psychology Jena (http://www.uni-jena.de/~ssw/labor.htm, June 1996)
- Experimental Server Trier (http://cogpsy.uni-trier.de:8000/TEServ-e.html, June 1997)
- Max-Planck Institute for Biological Cybernetics Tübingen (http://exp.kyb.tuebingen.mpg.de/web-experiment/ndex.html, November 1997)
- Online Psychology Lab Padua (http://www.psy.unipd.it/personal/laboratorio/surprise/htmltesi/index.html, May 1997)
- Decision Research Center (http://psych.fullerton.edu/mbirnbaum/dec.html) (started online experiments in March 1998)
- Psycholinguist Laboratory Scotland (http://surf.to/experiments, September 1998)
- PsychExps (http://www.olemiss.edu/PsychExps/, fall 1998; invites participation of Web experiments from other researchers)
- Systems Analysis Lab at Helsinki University (http://www.hut.fi/Units/SAL)
- Jonathan Baron's questionnaires (http://www.psych.upenn.edu/~baron/qs.html)

Some additional WWW laboratories engage in teaching or demonstration of experiments, for example, the excellently designed Internet Psychology Lab (http://kahuna.psych.uiuc.edu/ipl/), which went online in April 1998. However, all of the laboratories in this list are mainly used for experimental data collection. In addition to the preceding list of Web laboratories and sites where Web experiments are being conducted, a growing number of other sites have gone online to offer participation in psychological experiments.

The most comprehensive list of Web experiments on the WWW can be found on the Psychological Research on the Net page (American Psychological Society, 1995), which was created and is maintained by John Krantz. John Krantz and many (probably more than half) of the other currently active Web experimenters generously agreed to participate in our survey on the experiences of the first generation of Web researchers.

METHOD

All respondents were recruited via the Internet. To promote its existence, we announced the Web experimenter survey to the following mailing lists:

- PSYCGRAD (Psychology Graduate Student Internet Project)
- RESEARCH (Psychology of the Internet: Research and Theory)
- GIR-L (German Internet Research List)
- SCiP (Society for Computers in Psychology)

Additional invitations to participate were posted to the following Usenet newsgroups:

- sci.psychology.research
- sci.psychology.announce
- sci.psychology.misc
- alt.usenet.surveys
- bit.listserv.psycgrad
- de.alt.umfragen
- de.sci.psychologie
- de.sci.misc
- z-netz.wissenschaft.psychologie

Personal invitations were sent via e-mail to all researchers who announced a Web experiment at one of the following places:

- The Psychological Research on the Net page of the American Psychological Society, maintained by John Krantz

http:// psych.hanover.edu / APS / exponnet .html

- The list of Online Social Psychology Studies by Scott Plous

  `http://www.wesleyan.edu/spn/expts.htm`

- Ulf-Dietrich Reips' Web Experimental Psychology Lab in Zürich and Tübingen

  `http://www.psych.unizh.ch/genpsy/Ulf/Lab/`

  `WebExpPsyLab.html`

- The Psychology/Tests-and-Experiments pages at Yahoo International

  `http://www.yahoo.com/Social_Science/Psychology/`

  `Disciplines/Personality/Online_Tests/`

- The Psychology/Tests-and-Experiments pages at Yahoo Germany

  `http://www.yahoo.de/Geisteswissenschaften/`

  `Psychologie/Online_Tests_und_Versuche/`

Finally, we sent a call for participation to a number of researchers that we knew had conducted or planned to conduct a Web experiment.

In a first wave of the survey, we received 21 submissions from Web experimenters between October 17 and October 30, 1998. Additional submissions came from researchers who had conducted surveys. Conducting surveys on the Web is a promising new way of online research (cf. Batinic, 1997; Batinic, Gräf, Werner, & Bandilla, 1999). However, because we were interested in Web experiments rather than surveys, we did not include them in the analysis. The criterion used for classifying submissions as describing experiments was that at least one independent variable was manipulated.

In this first wave of the survey, we told the respondents that if they conducted more than one Web experiment, they should answer all questions with regard to their first Web experiment. A second wave was online from April 16 to April 28, 1999. In this second wave, we asked participants who had already participated in the first wave to answer some questions with respect to the last Web experiment they had conducted. First-time participants were asked to describe the first experiment they had conducted. The number of questions was reduced for the second wave of the survey, which was announced to the same mailing lists and to the same newsgroups to which the first wave had been announced. In addition, it was announced to SJDM, the mailing list of the Society for Judgment and Decision Making. There were 14 submissions from researchers who conducted a Web experiment in the second wave of the survey. Additional submissions from researchers who conducted a survey rather than an experiment were not included in the analysis. Thus, the final sample consisted of 35 submissions from 29 different researchers currently engaged in Web experimenting. The regional distribution of the 29 researchers was as follows: Germany (8), United States (7), United Kingdom (6), Canada (1), Austria (1), Switzerland (1), Australia (1), Soviet Union (1), Finland (1), New Zealand (1), Unknown (1). After the data were collected and analyzed, all respondents were provided with a summary of the results. An additional WWW scan and notes from the Web Experimental Psychology Lab's archives (Reips, 1995a) showed that at least eight more people have conducted Web experiments, but did not respond to either wave of our survey.

PROCEDURE

The survey consisted of three WWW pages and was written in HTML, the computer programming language most often used to display pages on the WWW. On the first page survey participants were greeted and informed about the rationale for conducting the survey. Also, participants were told that only online data collection was considered a *Web experiment* that met the definition of "any undertaking in which some variable is manipulated; thus, in contrast with a survey, at least two conditions must be involved in an experiment." Then, participants were asked to indicate the number of Web experiments they had conducted and to provide us with their e-mail address for feedback and possibly additional questions. Most researchers had conducted one ($N = 15$) or two ($N = 6$) Web experiments at the time of the survey. Eight experimenters already had conducted a higher number of studies (ranging from 3 to 20 experiments).

Submission of the first page of the survey sent the form data (i.e., the data that were filled in by the respondent) to a server-side plug-in (Mailagent 1.1, Netdrams Software, 1998), which wrote the data to a tab-delimited file. Also, it triggered the display of the second survey page in the respondent's Web browser window. This second page contained almost all of the questions asked. A variety of WWW specific answering formats was used. For example, to answer the question on announcement media respondents had to use their mouse arrow to click on *checkboxes*. Checkboxes allow for multiple nonexclusive selections. To limit responses to one out of several possible answers both possibilities offered by HTML were used: a question about the area of research, for example, was presented as a *pop-up menu*, while a question about the use of counterbalancing had to be answered by clicking on *radio buttons*. Such electronic answering formats, which allow for only one answer, have been shown to reduce the frequency of response errors (Kiesler & Sproull, 1986). Certain answers, especially to open-ended questions such as the question on the experimental factors used, required *text fields*. Text fields can be limited to a maximum number of characters. When a survey respondent sent off the second page by clicking on its submit button, again the data were sent to the Web server (WebSTAR by StarNine Technologies) and processed by the Mailagent plug-in. In addition to writing the data to a file the plug-in sent an e-mail to the respondent and the experimenters to report the processing of the data.

RESULTS

When did you start the experiment? When did you end the experiment?

John Krantz and colleagues from Hanover College started their first Web experiment in April 1995. We are not aware of any psychology Web experiment with at least two conditions (i.e., two levels of an independent variable) that appeared on the WWW before this date. The number of Web experiments has been constantly rising since, with the majority of Web studies starting during 1997 and 1998.

In the first wave of our survey, we told the respondents that if they conducted more than one Web experiment, they should answer the following questions for their first Web experiment for which they had reported the starting date.

How important were the following factors for your decision to conduct the Web experiment (1, not important at all; 7, very important)?

	Mean	SD	N
large number of participants	5.5	1.9	20
high statistical power	4.5	2.2	20
high speed	3.6	2.4	20
ability to reach participants from other countries	3.6	2.2	20
high external or ecological validity	3.4	2.1	20
low cost	3.2	2.2	21
ability to replicate a lab experiment with more power	2.9	2.5	20
chance to better reach a special subpopulation on the Web (e.g., handicapped, rape victims, chess players)	2.6	2.5	20

The factor that experimenters rated as most important was reaching a large number of participants. The high statistical power associated with a large sample size, the high speed with which Web experimenting is possible, and the chance to reach participants from other countries were also considered important by most of the respondents.

How problematic do you think were the following potential problems in your Web experiment (1, not problematic at all; 7, very problematic)?

	Mean	SD	N
no control of a participant's behavior during participation	3.6	2.0	21
no control of participant's motivation	3.4	1.7	21
inability of participants to ask questions	3.3	1.7	21
no control of participant's hardware and equipment	2.9	2.1	21
nonrepresentative samples	2.8	1.8	21
manipulation and fraud	2.4	1.4	21
ethical problems	1.5	1.0	21

The biggest concern of the Web experimenters participating in the first wave of our survey was the lack of control of a participant's behavior during participation. However, a numeric value of 3.6 translates to not more than an assessment of this lack of control as "somewhat problematic." Ethical problems were not considered a problem by most Web experimenters. Obviously, it is important to note that all these ratings came from researchers who themselves are conducting Web experiments, and the results may well have been different if another sample of researchers had been asked.

In which media did you announce your experiment?

Naturally, the WWW was used most often to promote Web experiments (22 out of 35 experiments were promoted on the Web). Many researchers also relied on newsgroups (18), e-mails (15), and search engines (14) to advertise their experiment. Few experiments were also announced in print media (2) and radio programs (1).

How many design factors did you include in your experiment? For each of these factors, please specify the number of levels on which it was varied.

The mean number of factors participants of the first wave of the survey indicated they had manipulated was 2.1 (with a median and a mode of 2.0). There were six experiments in which as many as three or more factors were varied. The following designs were reported in the first wave of the survey:

Levels per factor	N
$5 \times 5 \times 2 \times n$	1
$5 \times 5 \times 4$	1
$5 \times 3 \times 2$	1
$3 \times 3 \times n$	2
$3 \times 2 \times 2$	1
5×2	2
3×3	1
3×2	1
2×2	5
$n \times 2$	1
3	1
2	4
not specified	1

60% of the designs involved between-subjects factor manipulations, another 20% of the designs involved within-subjects factor manipulations, and 20% of the designs involved both kinds of experimental manipulation.

In what area of research did you conduct the experiment?

To aid the respondents' decision, we offered a list of 54 subject areas used for classifying poster contributions to the 10th Annual Convention of the American Psychological Society (1998). Just as one would expect from a theoretical perspective (Reips, 1997b), the Web experimental method obviously seems best suited for cognitively oriented areas of research (see, e.g., Klauer, Musch, & Naumer, 1999). The areas in which most experiments were conducted are Cognition (4), Thinking and Reasoning (3), Psycholinguistics (2), Sensation/Perception (1), Memory (1), Judgment/Decision Making (1), Attention/Performance (1), Personality (1), Social/Groups (1), Social/Cognition (1), Social/Attitudes (1), and Computers in Psychology (1).

What was the main hypothesis? What were other hypotheses?
Please name the factors you varied and their levels.

The following selective list gives an impression of the theories and hypotheses that were tested in Web experiments and the independent variables that were manipulated. Hypotheses that are difficult to understand without sufficient knowledge of the subject domain or that were not explained by the survey respondents are not included in the list.

- Judges violate stochastic dominance in coalesced gambles, but satisfy stochastic dominance when gambles are presented in split form (high versus low variance of gambles; .01, .50, .99 probability of winning higher prize; value of prizes; combined versus split consequences of gamble; stochastic dominance between gambles). There is a lower degree of violation among people with more training and education in judgment and decision-making.
- Comparison of Bayes Theorem, Subjective Bayesian Model, and Averaging Model of Inference—participants use the base rate in the taxicab problem contrary to the idea of base rate fallacy (base rate, witness credibility, witness report).
- Persons relying on schema-based interpretation of incoming text information are less likely to have accurate recall than aschematic readers (schematic versus aschematic text, temporal delay between reading and recall).
- Pronominal case-ambiguous objects elicit a preference toward accusative case assignment, whereas nonpronominal, case-ambiguous objects elicit no preference (object noun phrase type is ambiguous nonpronominal, ambiguous pronominal, or unambiguous pronominal; object case is accusative or dative).
- Answers to questions in online surveys are potentially subject to biases, depending on the number of questions per page (one, two), scale type (pop-up, radio buttons), reading directionality (from left–top, from right–bottom), cursor entry position (top, bottom), question order (donation question first, expense question first), and numerical labeling (-5 to $+5$, 0 to 10).
- Experts use their specific and their general knowledge for data evaluation (expertise, high versus low; data are in accordance with versus in contradiction to expert knowledge).
- Subjects perceive feminine male and female faces as more attractive (masculinity of male face, more feminine to more masculine).
- Background color influences response to emotionally laden statements (different shades of background color, print color white versus red).
- Web questionnaires produce response effects that are similar to paper-and-pencil questionnaire response effects (questionnaire length is short or long).
- People with low context constraint encode individual words deeper (context constraint is low or high).
- Syllogisms with believable conclusions are accepted more often than unbelievable ones, irrespective of their validity ("belief bias"). The suggested base rate of valid conclusions influences the willingness to accept a given conclusion if the participant cannot determine its

validity (suggested base rate of valid conclusions is low, medium, or high; validity of conclusion is valid or invalid; believability of conclusion is believable or unbelievable).

- What kind of errors are being made when reconstructing 2D information from a 3D model (object colors, object shape, map orientation)?
- Is syntactic priming (in German verb-final constructions) sensitive to subcategorization information or linear precedence, or both? What is the baseline proportion of ditransitive versus simple transitive responses, given different target types (prime type is accusative < dative, dative < accusative, accusative, dative, or control; target type is accusative object or dative object)?
- Previously acquired knowledge about causal mechanisms influences later acquisition and use of causal knowledge involving those mechanisms (acquired type of causal mechanism is consistent, inconsistent, or none).
- Syntactic primes affect completions of targets; there is a possible interaction with case, especially dative (prime type is neutral, ditransitive–accusative–dative, ditransitive–dative–accusative, transitive–accusative, or transitive–dative; target type is accusative or dative).
- Participants recruited from newsgroups likely to be read by people who are high self-monitors score higher on a WWW-mediated version of the Self-Monitoring scale than participants recruited through newsgroups likely to be read by people who are low self-monitors (likely self-monitoring is low or high).
- Does bimodal presentation (hearing, seeing) of objects increase memory performance? Does contradictory bimodal presentation decrease memory performance (acoustic naming of pictures shown is no acoustic naming, true naming, or wrong naming).
- Content of sites visited before answering a survey systematically influences answer behavior; time of watching instructions influences strength of context effects (content of simulated WWW site is pictured or not; social desirability via instruction is high or low).
- Important computer-specific concepts are explained in more detail if addressee is a beginner (concept importance is important or less important; addressee's knowledge level is beginner or advanced).

Did you assign participants to the experimental conditions randomly? If yes, what did you use to obtain random assignment?

Of the 34 experimenters who answered this question, 29 assigned participants to the experimental conditions in a random order. (Four of the remaining experiments varied conditions within subjects, and one study was a quasi experiment). The techniques that were used most often to obtain random assignment were CGI, Java, and JavaScript. Few respondents indicated they used yet another (unspecified) technique to obtain random assignment. (Birth month, birthday, social security number, etc. are alternative criteria that can be used to obtain random assignment, for example, by offering different hyperlinks to participants born in odd vs. even months of the year; cf. Birnbaum, 1999a, in press).

Did you apply counterbalancing of any sort?

Although the use of counterbalance is certainly an important aspect of internal control in many experimental designs, only a little more than half of the experiments (20 out of 35) applied counterbalancing of some kind. This may in part be attributable to the technical and programming difficulties associated with the use of counterbalancing. Five of the 14 experiments that did not make use of counterbalancing measures were one-factor experiments, however, which may have been simple enough not to require this technique.

What did you do to guard against multiple submissions?

Entry errors, the intent to foil the experiment, and curiosity are just some of the possible reasons respondents may have for submitting their answers more than once. Because all WWW browsers have a "back button" built in, it is not easy to prevent users from reexamining their Web form page and submitting it again, possibly after altering their data (Schmidt, 1997; cf. Schmidt, chap. 12, this volume). However, several techniques exist that can be used to deal with the problem (Buchanan & Smith, 1999; Reips, 1996b, 1997b, 1999a; Schmidt, 1997; Smith & Leigh, 1997). Most of them try to uniquely identify each participant and to filter out all suspicious submissions. This can be done by examining a variety of aspects of the data provided by the participants. We wanted to know what data Web experimenters used to tackle the problem of multiple submissions. In many of the 35 experiments, researchers relied on checking the e-mail (24) and IP addresses (18). Both variables help to uniquely identify the participants. However, e-mail addresses can be faked, repeated participation may take place from a different computer address, and proxy servers can make the submissions of different users falsely appear to have been sent from one and the same person. Perhaps because of these problems, passwords were used in addition to control of e-mail and IP addresses in three experiments. In two experiments, no special precautionary measures against multiple submissions were taken.

Several researchers also used the following procedures to secure data integrity:

- Cookies (3)
- Date or time (2)
- Bank account (2)
- Asking not to participate more than once (2)
- Asking for seriousness of the submission (1)
- Checking for identical records arriving in close temporal interval (1)

One researcher told us that he felt any attempts to cheat by multiple submissions would have been very unattractive regarding the low reward participants received in his experiment.

On what technical HTML level was your Web experiment programmed?

Advanced HTML levels offer a number of sophisticated layout features such as tables, frames, and style sheets. However, the lower the HTML level used, the wider the population of potential respondents will be. This is because not all users have installed the latest version of their Web browser, and older versions do not support the latest HTML features.

Only three researchers made use of features of the latest HTML 4 version. The vast majority of researchers preferred a conservative approach and restricted themselves to the more established HTML versions 2 and 3.

Which of the following techniques, programming languages, and tools did you use?

A large variety of techniques and programming languages is being used to implement Web experiments. CGI was used by 19 respondents; other popular tools that were named are Perl (13), JavaScript (11), Java client-side (10), Java server-side (7), and Cookies (4). A few experiments were also conducted using VRML (2), C/C++ (2), DHTML (1), XML (1), and ActiveX (1).

What operating system was your Web server running on?

To conduct a Web experiment, one requires access to a WWW server (Kieley, 1996). This can be practically any machine connected to the Internet: an account on a multiuser UNIX system or a networked PC or Macintosh is all the hardware that is required (Reips, 1996b, 1997b; Schmidt, Hoffmann, & MacDonald, 1997). Because the software available for implementing Web experiments largely depends on the type of operating system that is installed on the WWW server, we asked participants of the first wave of the survey which operating systems they used. Answers indicated a clear preference for Unix and Unix derivatives such as Solaris, Linux, and so on, followed in this order by MacOS and Windows 95/98/NT.

In which language(s) did you offer your experiment?

There were 17 experiments that were offered in English and 10 experiments that were offered in German. Offering experiments in parallel versions for different languages reliably increases the number of participants and allows for cross-cultural comparisons. This possibility was used by seven researchers.

What was the total number of participants included for final data analysis (after deletion of multiple submissions etc.)?

Respondents indicated the final sample size for 26 of the 27 experiments that were already finished at the time of the survey. The mean number of participants in these experiments was 427, with a standard deviation of 650. The median number of participants was 158. The smallest number of participants was 13 and the largest was 2649.

Can you tell (in percent) how many of those who looked at the very first access page to your experiment decided to start the experiment?

Several experiments recorded how many of the visitors of the first access page proceeded to start the experiment. However, it is important to note that the definitions of "the first access page" to a web experiment may vary quite extensively, as indicated by the responses. This first access page could be the main page of an online laboratory, an informed consent page, the first instructions page, or the last page of a "warm-up phase" (a technique used to reduce dropout during Web experiments; see Reips, 1996b, 1997b, 1999a). On average, 68% (median, 80%) of all visitors of the very first access page proceeded to start the experiment ($N = 10$). The minimum click-through rate was 7%, the maximum was 100%. The chance to obtain this information is a unique advantage of Web experiments if one considers the number of visitors to the first access page of a Web experiment as equivalent to the number of people who consider or are asked to take part in a standard laboratory experiment. In the case of a laboratory experiment, the researcher usually does not know how many students decide *not* to sign up for an experiment (or would have decided to do so if given the right to choose among studies).

Can you tell (in percent) how many of those who started the experiment by looking at the first page after the instructions page did complete it?

On average, 66% (median, 65%) of the participants who started an experiment also completed it ($N = 20$). The respective figures ranged from 13 to 99%. In 15 experiments, the dropout rate was not (yet) determined; four of these experiments were still running at the time of the survey.

> Did your participants have to download a plug-in or an applet first to be able to participate?

The only plug-ins used were VRML (virtual reality modeling language), offering the opportunity to display three-dimensional objects, and Macromedia Flash. With these two exceptions, all participating researchers indicated that their experiments did not require the (somewhat time-consuming and troublesome) download of a plug-in. (Note, however, that the PsychExps group [McGraw, Tew, & Williams, this volume] at the University of Mississippi uses the Shockwave plug-in to deliver its experiments; /http://www.olemiss.edu/PsychExps/). Eight experiments required the download of an applet prior to participation.

> Did you ever have a problem with a hacker trying to intrude your experiment? If yes, please give a description of what happened.

On the WWW, nothing prevents anybody from downloading and examining the HTML source code of Web experiments. Hackers can attempt to foil the experimental results, and they may even try to gain control over the Web server (Schmidt, 1997). One possibility to do so is to send manipulative data to the CGI program for processing.[1] We wanted to know whether Web experimenters had faced such problems.

No respondent indicated having observed a hacker attack. Of course, this does not mean that there were no such attacks. Although one may assume that successful attempts to damage the experiment would have been noticed, the possibility that a hidden hacker went undetected cannot be excluded.

> Which demographic questions did you ask your participants?

To know which denizens of the Web chose to participate in their online experiments, investigators have asked a variety of demographic questions. The variables Web experimenters gathered most often from their participants were age (32 out of 35), sex (32), occupation (16), language (11), nationality (9), insider knowledge concerning the field of research (7), and education (6).

---

[1] To prevent this, experimenters can set up their CGI program to restrict acceptance to data from only certain referers.

Several researchers asked respondents to provide additional data regarding

- Their handedness (3)
- Their marital status (2)
- Their dialect (2)
- Their circumstances of housing or job
- Their religion
- Their socioeconomic status
- Their status as student or nonstudent
- Their college major
- Their class (for credit assignment)
- Their name
- The Web browser they used
- The size and color (yes or no) of their monitor display
- The speed of their Internet connection

> Did you provide the participants with the possibility
> to contact you via e-mail?

The vast majority of researchers (94%) offered an e-mail link, thus allowing participants to ask questions, to make comments, and to point out errors. The chance to obtain this kind of feedback is a notable advantage of Web experiments (Welch & Krantz, 1996).

> Did your experimental material contain any graphics or sounds?

Advanced facilities for viewing graphics are available in the HTML language and 16 out of 35 experiments contained graphics in some form.

A modality less frequently used than graphics in a typical experiment is sound. Only two experiments were based on acoustical stimuli. This might well be the result of the technical difficulties associated with the large differences in the hardware and software used to interpret and play sound files, and in the audio formats they can handle (cf. Welch & Krantz, 1996).

> Did you measure any reaction times (below 1 second)?

In spite of the technical difficulties associated with reaction time measurement on the World Wide Web, eight experiments made use of such measurements. This surprisingly high number might be due to the fact that many Web servers automatically log access time in fractions of a second.

> Did you measure any time intervals (above 1 second)?

The measurement of time intervals provides valuable information about the participant's behavior during the experiment, and 14 out of the 34 experiments recorded time intervals.

Monetary rewards can be expected to increase both the motivation and the number of participants.

Did you offer a monetary reward to each participant?

Three out of 34 experiments offered a monetary reward to each participant. In these experiments, the amount every respondent received was $15 (on average), $13, and DM 10.– (approximately $6).

Did you offer monetary or other prizes in a lottery? If yes, what was the total amount of money (the value of your prizes) in dollars?

Ten experiments offered a lottery. The total value of the prizes was $1224, $750, $500, $192, $150, $100, $100, $100, $85, and $11, respectively. One experiment offered a 1% chance to actually play (with real money) one of the attractive gambles that were part of the experiment. To investigate whether financial incentives have a beneficial effect, we conducted some additional analyses. We found that if some kind of monetary compensation (individual payments or lottery prizes) was offered, the percentage of participants who completed the experiment was significantly higher (86%, $N = 13$) than if no rewards were at stake (55%, $N = 7$; $t = 2.61$, $df = 18$, $p < .05$). Although the sample sizes are very small, this observation might indicate that financial incentives can help to reduce the number of dropouts. There was a similar (though nonsignificant) trend for a higher number of participants per week when a financial incentive was offered (49 versus 37 participants per week).

On average, how much time did it take to participate in your experiment (in minutes)?

The average duration of the experiments was 22 minutes ($N = 33$), with a median of 15 minutes. The minimum duration that was reported was 5 minutes, the maximum was 90 minutes.

Did you inform your participants in advance about the duration of the experiment?

The 29 experiments which informed potential participants in advance about how much time they would need to complete it attracted a higher number of participants (mean $N = 496$) than the 5 experiments that did not provide this information (mean $N = 230$). However, because of the small sample sizes and the large variance in participation rates, this difference was not significant.

Did you offer an individual feedback to each participant?

Web experiments, as other computer-based forms of experimenting, offer the opportunity to provide dynamic and interactive forms of feedback to the participants (Schmidt, 1997). This feedback can be specifically tailored to the responses given, and it can provide summary statistics about the results of other respondents. It is thus possible to give respondents interesting pieces of information in return for their efforts, probably a powerful motivation to participate in an experiment. Schmidt (1997) conjectured that if respondents know that the feedback they receive is about themselves and based on the data they provide, they are likely to supply accurate and thoughtful responses. However, apparently because much effort is needed to implement an individualized feedback, only 9 out of 34 experiments included this feature. Of these 9 experiments, 6 provided feedback immediately after participation, and 3 provided feedback with some temporal delay.

Did you offer feedback concerning the goals and hypotheses of the experiment to the participants?

Most experiments offered feedback about what was being investigated, either immediately after participation (10) or with some temporal delay (16). In eight experiments, participants were not offered feedback about the goals of the study.

Did you offer feedback concerning the design of the experiment?

About half of the experiments conveyed the experimental design to the participants, either immediately after participation (4) or with some temporal delay (12). Participants in 18 experiments were not informed about the design of the study in which they participated.

Did you also run the experiment with non-Internet participants (for comparison)? If yes, how would you rate the convergence of Web and lab data? If there was less than complete agreement, please describe the differences.

To assess the validity of their findings, 18 experimenters conducted a replication study in a traditional setting. (The results of another 5 replication studies were not yet available at the time of the survey).

Almost all experimenters observed complete or good agreement between their Web and lab data. There were no experiments for which a lack of agreement between lab and Web data was observed. Low agreement between data collected in a traditional versus an Internet-based setting was found in one case where an effect of stimulus material was found in the lab but not in the Web data. The author of this experiment conjectures that the stimulus images were too small to be seen properly in the Web version of his experiment. Higher variances in the Web were observed in one experiment for which the experimenter otherwise observed good agreement between lab and Web data. Another experimenter also described the agreement between lab and Web data as good but observed slightly more outliers (in the form of extreme or illogical judgements) in the Web version of his experiment. The author of an experiment that showed only partial agreement between the Web and the lab data assumed that this difference might be due to the small sample size in his lab experiment. Another researcher observed that Internet participants were more highly educated than the participants in his lab sample and showed lower rates of violation of stochastic dominance in their choices.

> Overall, how much time (person hours) did you put into the Web experiment, compared to a similar laboratory experiment?
> If you plan to conduct another Web experiment, how much time do you expect to need, compared to your first Web experiment?
> And how much money did you put into the Web experiment, compared to a similar laboratory experiment?

There was no clear pattern with regard to the question whether first-time Web experiments need less working time than more traditional approaches; about one third of participants indicated they needed more time for the Web experiment than they would have needed for a similar laboratory experiment, another third needed about the same amount of time, and another third indicated that they needed less time for the Web experiment. A majority of researchers stated that in their opinion, much time can be saved when more than one Web experiment is conducted. This seems consequential regarding the effort one has to put into learning and implementing a whole new research method. Naturally, the difficulties of getting the first Web experiment running will be reduced in subsequent Web experiments, and the computer setup as well as other materials can be recycled (although rapid changes in technology may create obsolescence quickly). Experimenters also indicated that Web experimenting is a quite inexpensive undertaking. The vast majority of respondents estimated the costs of Web experiments to be smaller or much smaller than the costs of a traditional laboratory experiment.

> Overall, how much space or how many rooms did you need for the Web experiment, compared to a similar laboratory experiment?

Another benefit of using the Web for experiments stems from savings of space and rooms needed for laboratory experiments (Reips, 1995b, 1996a, 1996b, 1997b; chap. 4, this volume). All researchers indicated that they needed less or much less space for their Web experiment than they would have needed for a laboratory experiment.

Are you planning to conduct another Web experiment?

The experiences Web experimenters reported seem overwhelmingly positive. With only one exception, all researchers said they would certainly, or at least perhaps, conduct another Web experiment.

Did you present your experiment to a scientific conference or is your presentation accepted for an upcoming conference? If yes, which conference?

More than two thirds of the data of already finished Web experiments have been presented to a scientific conference or have been accepted for presentation at an upcoming conference. On the following occasions Web experiments were (or will be) reported:

- Virtual Reality Modeling Language Conference, 1998
- European Conference on Visual Perception, 1998
- Annual Workshop on Object Perception and Memory, 1998
- Society for Computers in Psychology, 1996, 1998
- British Psychological Society, 1998
- German Online Research, 1998
- Economic Science Association, 1998
- Conference of the Society for Research in Experimental Economics (Tagung der Gesellschaft für Experimentelle Wirtschaftsforschung), 1998
- Annual Convention of the Canadian Psychological Association
- Congress of the German Psychological Society, 1998
- Experimental Psychologists' Conference (Tagung Experimentell Arbeitender Psychologen), 1998, 1999
- Annual Conference of the Text and Discourse Society
- Annual Conference of the Cognitive Science Society, 1999
- Annual Conference of the German Linguistic Society (Jahrestagung der Deutschen Gesellschaft für Sprachwissenschaft), 1999
- International Society for Research in Emotion Conference, 1998

Did you already write a paper on your experiment? If yes, did you report comparison data from non-Web participants? Which journal did you submit it to? What is the current status of the first submission of your paper? If the paper was not accepted when you first submitted it, what were the stated reasons? If the paper was not accepted, did you submit it to another journal afterward?

The respondents had written 12 papers on their Web experiments by the time of the survey, 5 of which reported comparison data from a traditional lab sample. Several manuscripts were not yet completed. The journals to which the completed manuscripts were submitted to are:

- *Behavior Research Methods, Instruments, and Computers* (three submissions—two manuscripts were accepted; one was rejected but not because Web data were reported; the manuscript has not yet been resubmitted)
- *Journal of Economic Behavior and Organization* (under review)
- *Journal of Behavioral Decision Making* (not accepted for reasons other than the Web data)
- *British Journal of Psychology* (accepted but wanted it as a short report; the authors elected to resubmit elsewhere rather than rewrite)
- *Psychological Review* (under review)
- *Psychology and Marketing* (not accepted for reasons other than the Web data)

Four articles and a book by survey participants are already in press or published (Birnbaum, 1999a, 1999b, in press; Morrow & McKee, 1998; Schmalhofer, Elst, Aschoff, Bärenfänger, & Bourne, in press). However, the number of Web experiments that already found their way into scientific journals is still very low (but see Hänze, Hildebrandt, & Meyer, 1998; Krantz et al., 1997; Welch & Krantz, 1996). Of course, one reason for this is that the first Web experiments were started only a few years before our survey. It remains to be seen whether the editors and reviewers of traditional journals will accept the growing number of papers reporting data from Web experiments.

Web experiments offer a number of advantages compared to traditional laboratory experiments. This has mostly been explored theoretically or concluded from experience with very few Web experiments (Krantz & Dalal, chap. 2, this volume; Reips, 1995b, 1996a, 1996b, 1997b; chap. 4, this volume) and, of course, a number of traditional experiments. Our survey shows for the first time on an empirical basis that many of those advantages hold true in the impressions of those who have used Web experiments as a method for doing research.

Although online data collection efforts are undertaken in many areas of research (American Psychological Society, 1995), it seems that the core areas for Web experiments are those that deal with cognition. Combined with the practical advantages and the ease with which Web experiments can be conducted this might lead to an increase in cognitive research, especially in light of the integration of online research and online publication (Reips, 1997a, 1998).

Taken together, we feel that the results of this survey give a number of interesting insights into the experiences of the first generation of Web experimenters. At the moment, the number of Web experiments is still small, but a rapid growth can be predicted on the basis of the present results. We would not be surprised if within the next few years, a fair proportion of psychological experiments will be conducted on the Web. It will be interesting to see how the experiences of the early researchers shape this new direction in psychological research.

REFERENCES

Abbate, J. E. (1994). *From Arpanet to Internet: A history of ARPA-sponsored computer networks, 1966–1988.* Unpublished doctoral dissertation, University of Pennsylvania.

American Psychological Society. (1995). *Psychology experiments on the Net* [WWW document]. Available URL: http:// psych.hanover.edu/ APS / exponnet.html

American Psychological Society. (1998). [WWW document]. Available URL: http:// www.psychologicalscience.org

Batinic, B. (1997). How to make an Internet based survey? In W. Bandilla & F. Faulbaum (Eds.), *SoftStat '97—Advances in statistical software 6* (pp. 125–132). Stuttgart: Lucius & Lucius.

Batinic, B., Gräf, L., Werner, A., & Bandilla, W. (1999). *Online research.* Göttingen: Hogrefe.

Birnbaum, M. H. (1999a). How to show that 9 > 221: Collect judgments in a between-subjects design. *Psychological Methods, 4,* 243–249.

Birnbaum, M. H. (1999b). Testing critical properties of decision making on the Internet. *Psychological Science, 10,* 399–407.

Birnbaum, M. H. (in press). *Introduction to behavioral research on the Internet.* Upper Saddle River, NJ: Prentice-Hall.

Booth-Kewley, S., Edwards, J., & Rosenfeld, P. (1992). Impression management, social desirability, and computer administration of attitude questionnaires: Does the computer make a difference? *Journal of Applied Psychology, 77,* 562–566.

Buchanan, T., & Smith, J. L. (1999). Using the Internet for psychological research: Personality testing on the World Wide Web. *British Journal of Psychology, 90,* 125–144.

Bush, V. (1945). As we may think. *Atlantic Monthly, 1,* 101–103.

Connes, B. (1972). The use of electronic desk computers in psychological experiments. *Journal of Structural Learning, 3,* 51–72.

Flanagan, D. (1998). *Javascript: The definitive guide* (3rd ed.). Cambridge: O'Reilly.

Hänze, M., Hildebrandt, M., & Meyer, H. A. (1998). Feldexperimente im World Wide Web: Zur Verhaltenswirksamkeit des "mere-exposure"-Effekts bei der Informationssuche [Field experiments in the World Wide Web: Effectiveness of the "mere exposure" effect on information seeking]. *Psychologische Beiträge, 40,* 363–372.

Hardy, H. E. (1995). *A short history of the Net* [WWW document]. Available URL: http://www.ocean.ic.net/ftp/doc/snethistnew.html

Hewson, C. M., Laurent, D., & Vogel, C. M. (1996). Proper methodologies for psychological and sociological studies conducted via the Internet. *Behavioral Research Methods, Instruments, & Computers, 28,* 186–191.

Hoffman, R., & MacDonald, J. (1993). Using HyperCard and Apple events in a network environment: Collecting data from simultaneous experimental sessions. *Behavior Research Methods, Instruments, & Computers, 25,* 114–126.

Hoggatt, A. C. (1977). On the uses of computers for experimental control and data acquisition. *American Behavioral Scientist, 20,* 347–365.

Kieley, J. M. (1996). CGI scripts: Gateways to World-Wide Web power. *Behavior Research Methods, Instruments, & Computers, 28,* 165–169.

Kiesler, S., & Sproull, L. S. (1986). Response effects in the electronic survey. *Public Opinion Quarterly, 50,* 402–413.

Klauer, K. C., Musch, J., & Naumer, B. (1999). *On belief bias in syllogistic reasoning.* Manuscript submitted for publication.

Krantz, J. H., Ballard, J., & Scher, J. (1997). Comparing the results of laboratory and World-Wide Web samples on the determinants of female attractiveness. *Behavioral Research Methods, Instruments, & Computers, 29,* 264–269.

Martin, C. L., & Nagao, D. H. (1989). Some effects of computerized interviewing on job applicant responses. *Journal of Applied Psychology, 74,* 72–80.

Morrow, R., & McKee, J. (1998). CGI scripts: A strategy for between-subjects Web designs. *Behavior Research Methods, Instruments, & Computers, 30,* 306–308.

Musch, J. (1997). Die Geschichte des Netzes: Ein historischer Abriß [The Net's history: A synopsis]. In B. Batinic (Ed.), *Internet für Psychologen* [Internet for psychologists] (pp. 27–48). Göttingen: Hogrefe.

Mailagent 1.1 [Computer software]. (1998). Rohnert Park, CA: Netdrams Software.

Ott, R., Krüger, T., & Funke, J. (1997). Wissenschaftliches Publizieren im Internet [Scientific publishing on the Internet]. In B. Batinic (Ed.), *Internet für Psychologen* [Internet for psychologists] (pp. 199–220). Göttingen: Hogrefe.

Reips, U.-D. (1995a). *The Web's Experimental Psychology Lab* [WWW document]. Available URL: http://www.psych.unizh.ch/genpsy/Ulf/Lab/WebExpPsyLab.html

Reips, U.-D. (1995b). *The Web experiment method* [WWW document]. Available URL: http://www.psych.unizh.ch/genpsy/Ulf/Lab/WWWExpMethod.html

Reips, U.-D. (1996a, April). Experimentieren im World Wide Web [Experimenting in the World Wide Web] [Abstract]. *Experimentelle Psychologie: Tagung experimentell arbeitender Psychologen* [Proceedings of the experimental psychologist's conference], *Germany, 38,* 256–257.

Reips, U.-D. (1996b, October). *Experimenting in the World Wide Web.* Paper presented at the 1996 Society for Computers in Psychology conference, Chicago.

Reips, U.-D. (1997a). Forschen im Jahr 2007: Integration von Web-Experimentieren, Online-Publizieren und Multimedia-Kommunikation [Science in the year 2007: Integration of Web experimenting, online publishing, and multimedia communication]. In D. Janetzko, B. Batinic, D. Schoder, M. Mattingley-Scott, & G. Strube (Eds.), *CAW-97. Beiträge zum Workshop "Cognition & Web"* [Articles presented at the workshop "Cognition & Web"]. Freiburg: IIG-Berichte 1/97.

Reips, U.-D. (1997b). Das psychologische Experimentieren im Internet [Psychological experimenting on the Internet]. In B. Batinic (Ed.), *Internet für Psychologen* [Internet for psychologists] (pp. 245–265). Göttingen: Hogrefe.

Reips, U.-D. (1998). Forschung in der Zukunft [Future science]. In T. Krüger & J. Funke (Eds.), *Psychologie im Internet: Ein Wegweiser für psychologisch interessierte User* [Psychology in the Internet: a pathfinder for psychologically interested users] (pp. 115–123). Weinheim: Beltz.

Reips, U.-D. (1999a). Theorie und Techniken des Web-Experimentierens [Theory and techniques of Web experimenting]. In B. Batinic, L. Gräf, A. Werner, & W. Bandilla (Eds.), *Online research*. Göttingen: Hogrefe.

Reips, U.-D. (1999b). *Online answering biases.* Manuscript submitted for publication.

Salus, P. H. (1995). *Casting the net: from ARPANET to Internet and beyond.* Reading, MA: Addison-Wesley.

Schmalhofer, F., Elst, L., Aschoff, R., Bärenfänger, O., & Bourne, L. (in press). Mentale Modelle sozialer Interaktionen: Wie Texte über Sozialbetrügereien verstanden werden [Mental models of social interactions: How readers comprehend texts about cheating behaviors]. *Zeitschrift für Experimentelle Psychologie.*

Schmidt, W. (1997). World-Wide Web survey research: Benefits, potential problems, and solutions. *Behavior Research Methods, Instruments, & Computers, 29,* 274–279.

Schmidt, W. Hoffman, R., & MacDonald, J. (1997). Operate your own World-Wide Web server. *Behavior Research Methods, Instruments, & Computers, 29,* 189–193.

Smith, M., & Leigh, B. (1997). Virtual subjects: Using the Internet as an alternative source of subjects and research environment. *Behavior Research Methods, Instruments, and Computers, 29,* 496–505.

Weigend, A. (1995). *Music recognition experiments.* [WWW document]. Available URL: `http://www.cs.colorado.edu/~andreas/Teaching/Music/Experiments.html`

Welch, N. (1995). *Demonstrations in auditory perception.* [WWW document]. Available URLs: `http://www.music.mcgill.ca/auditory/Auditory.html` and `http://gl15.bio.tu-darmstadt.de/auditory/auditory.html`

Welch, N., & Krantz, J. (1996). The World-Wide Web as a medium for psychoacoustical demonstrations and experiments: Experience and results. *Behavior Research Methods, Instruments, & Computers, 28,* 192–196.

CHAPTER 4

The Web Experiment Method:
Advantages, Disadvantages, and Solutions

Ulf-Dietrich Reips
Experimental and Developmental Psychology
University of Zürich
CH-8032 Zürich
Switzerland

The World Wide Web (WWW) provides a new tool for experimental research. The Web experiment method differs in fundamental aspects from traditional laboratory and field experiments; therefore it can be used to validate previous findings. Web experiments offer (1) easy access to a demographically and culturally diverse participant population, including participants from unique and previously inaccessible target populations; (2) bringing the experiment to the participant instead of the opposite; (3) high statistical power by enabling access to large samples; (4) the direct assessment of motivational confounding; and (5) cost savings of lab space, person-hours, equipment, and administration. These and 13 other advantages of Web experiments are reviewed and contrasted with 7 disadvantages, such as (1) multiple submissions, (2) lack of experimental control, (3) self-selection, and (4) dropout. Several techniques and other detailed solutions are described that avoid potential problems or even turn them into useful features of Web experimentation.

INTRODUCTION

Web experimenting has only just begun, and the method is thriving. Since Norma Welch, John Krantz, and others conducted the first Web experiments in 1995 (Krantz, Ballard, & Scher, 1997; Reips, 1996a, 1996b;

Psychological Experiments on the Internet

Welch, 1995; Welch & Krantz, 1996), this method has been used with increasing frequency, and in more and more areas (see American Psychological Society 1995; Musch & Reips, chap. 3, this volume; Reips & Musch, 1999). There has been a steady increase in the number of Web experiments as well as in the number of researchers using this method. Musch and Reips (chap. 3, this volume) conducted a survey among Web experimenters which confirmed that factors considered important by most of the respondents were, in order of importance, large numbers of participants, high statistical power, time saving, and the chance to reach participants from other countries. Although they were not considered most important, all predictions of cost-savings postulated by theoretical analyses of Web experimental methodology (e.g., Reips, 1995c, 1997b) were supported by the survey. Consequently, most survey respondents stated that they would certainly conduct another Web experiment. This shows that advantages outweigh the disadvantages in Web experimenting.

The term "Web experiment" was coined to underline this method's categorical distinctiveness from laboratory and field experiments (Reips, 1995a, 1995c, 1998b). However, the underlying logical criteria are the same as those in the other experimental methods. Hence, the definition of "experiment" used here requires manipulation of the independent variable(s) and repeatability. If an independent variable is manipulated between-subjects, then participants must be randomly assigned to conditions. Likewise, a quasi Web experiment would involve nonrandom assignment of subjects to conditions (see Bredenkamp, 1996; Campbell & Stanley, 1963; Kirk, 1995). Many of the issues discussed in this chapter are also relevant to other forms of Web research, such as surveys and tests.

Traditionally, in the behavioral sciences, there are two forms of experiments: the laboratory experiment and the field experiment. Both forms are distinct from simple observation in being active ways of manipulating variables to gain knowledge. They come with certain theoretical and practical disadvantages, which often limit their power of explanation in principle. Throughout the chapter I will discuss in more detail how and why Web experiments might provide solutions to these issues. The problems are listed next:

- Number of participants or measures is too small in many studies, because researchers set the Type I error probability α to a conventional level (and therefore the power of these studies is low; Erdfelder, Faul, & Buchner, 1996)
- Very limited sample populations, which raises the question whether psychological theories and body of research are too narrow in scope (For decades subjects have been mostly young students of local nationality [Reips & Bächtiger, 1999; Schultz, 1972; Smart, 1966]; therefore

many results may be specific for young students and/or the culture in which a study was conducted)

- Limited external validity (in laboratory experiments) or limited control (in field studies)
- Less than optimal voluntariness of participation (a twofold issue: (1) although nobody is forced to participate in psychological experiments, many students feel they need to do it to fulfill course requirements, given low attractiveness of possible alternatives; (2) for situational, social, and procedural reasons participants may develop a sense of obligation to stay in the experiment once they have agreed to participate)
- Motivational confounding, in part following from the previous point
- Institutional and organizational limitations (e.g., lab hours are typically limited to daytimes during weekdays; equipment may limit the number of participants that can be tested in a given interval of time)
- Experimenter bias
- Nontransparency of much of the research process
- Frequently, under the traditional methods, limitation of what *can* be done experimentally (partly to avoid the preceding issues becoming too relevant) and what *is* done (due to the ease of conducting some experiments and the hardship of conducting others; Devereux, 1967; for an example of an experiment that was only feasible to be conducted as a Web experiment see Klauer, Musch, & Naumer, 1999).

Consequently, findings from laboratory experiments should be validated using other methods. This is one general application of Web experiments; another one is to allow for experimental research in previously unexplored areas. The new Web experiment category offers the chance of extending the validity and acceptance of experimental research. This chapter is intended to be a comprehensive overview of methodological issues of online experiments.

To understand why conducting Web experiments is an opportunity for our science, we have to look at some of the problems with traditional experiments. For a certain time, in the late 1960s and 1970s, there was a heightened interest in flaws of these methods. Researchers like Rosenthal (e.g., 1965, 1966) and Cohen (e.g., 1977) relentlessly directed their enlightening spotlights to some of the dark corners in psychology's methodological basement. They discovered experimenter effects such as the Pygmalion effect (Brophy & Good, 1974; Rosenthal & Jacobsen, 1968), volunteer bias (Rosenthal, 1965; Rosenthal & Rosnow, 1969; Rosnow & Rosenthal, 1966), low power and other problems in experimental design (Cohen, 1977; Gigerenzer et al., 1989), demand characteristics (Orne, 1962; Rosenthal & Fode, 1973), and predominance of undergraduate psychology students as experiment participants (Jung,

1969; Schultz, 1972; Smart, 1966). Some issues were addressed, for example, the Hawthorne effect[1] (Roethlisberger, 1977) through use of nonexperimental control groups (Adair, 1973). All other problems listed here remain, however, and because they could not be resolved with the methods at hand or were too complicated to deal with, they have more or less been treated with a certain slippery indifference. Of course, these problems do not affect all areas of psychological research to the same degree. Also, in many studies, many researchers work very hard to minimize many of these effects in their studies. However, there are reasons many researchers have to work so hard to minimize these effects, and some issues are so fundamentally linked to the method that no measures can be taken to reduce their influence. Here Web experiments add some support to the basement.

MOIST BEAMS AND MILDEW STAINS ROTTING IN INDIFFERENCE (AND HOW WEB EXPERIMENTS MIGHT BE USED FOR STRUCTURAL SUPPORT)

GENERALIZABILITY (DEMOGRAPHIC)

One of the most obvious reasons for criticism is that most psychological research is done with undergraduate psychology students. As McNemar put it in 1942: "The existing science of human behavior is largely the science of the behavior of sophomores" (p. 333). Although in hypothetico-deductive research it might not really matter who the participants are (Bredenkamp, 1996; Reips, 1999a), it would matter if results from psychological research are to be generalized to the general population and if the results of experiments differ in different populations (Reips, 1999a). Smart (1966) and Schultz (1972) noted that more than 80% of all psychological studies are conducted with students as participants, while only about 3% of the general population are students. Basically, this picture has not changed (Reips & Bächtiger, 1999).

Birnbaum (1999, p. 399) has written: "Some say that psychological science is based on research with rats, the mentally disturbed, and college students. We study rats because they can be controlled, the disturbed because they need help, and college students because they are available." If in research using traditional methods the main reason for the restriction in participant

---

[1]Although the original "Hawthorne effect" at the Hawthorne plant may well not have been what is meant by the term (Parsons, 1974) "it is certainly possible for an experimental manipulation to cause a change in behavior independent of what the manipulation was" (Martin, 1996).

demography is the limited availability of participants, then Web experiments should be looked at as a serious alternative. Demographic characteristics of self-selected participants in Web experiments include a much greater diversity than is found in laboratory studies (e.g., Reips, 1996b). Demographics of Internet users is expected to rapidly approach similarity with demographics of the general population (Graphics, Visualization, & Usability Center, 2000). Therefore, a promising application of Web experiments would be the replication of results found in laboratory experiments, aiming at increasing the external validity of the body of research. For instance, in a recent Web experiment (Reips, 1999b) I was able to replicate findings from a study that looked at question context effects in answering behavior depending on whether a survey was administered by mail or by telephone (Schwarz & Hippler, 1994a). Apparently these context effects produced similar differences. It mattered whether survey questions were presented on one Web page (the "mail survey" situation) or on consecutive Web pages (the "telephone survey" situation). However, I could not replicate a numerical labeling effect (Schwarz & Hippler, 1994b) in that Web experiment (this is probably due to a different question used as the material, though).

Supporting the practice of using a demographically narrow sample within a study, one can argue that the processes studied in much of psychological research are independent of person type, and studying a uniform population to reduce error variance increases power holding N constant. This applies to Web experiments also, and the Web offers a nice feature for aiming at specific person types. One can direct Web participants to different Web studies using *characteristics-dependent redirecting*, which displays different Web pages depending on what was answered on earlier Web pages.

How can we be sure that the results of our studies are not specific to one culture? We need more replications with people from different cultures. The Web experimental method offers paths right onto the desktops of people from all over the world.

Web experiments provide the researcher with easy access to a much wider and geographically diverse participant population. As the term implies, the World Wide Web spans the whole globe and even extends into outer space (there have been live WWW conferences with space shuttle crews). The powerful implication of this development for psychological research comes from particular characteristics of the Internet, namely the nearly complete freedom of space and time. Communication is almost instantaneous between any two points on earth. Basically, this means that in Web experiments many persons from the general population are as accessible to the researcher as students in the local campus cafeteria have always been.

Nevertheless, local accessibility and density of the Web remain unbalanced. The numbers both of Web servers and of Web clients are the highest in industrialized countries. It is estimated that "Internetization" of U.S. house-holds will approach 58% by 2003 (Internet.com LCC, 1999). Because average income and education of Internet users are higher than the average of the general population (Graphics, Visualization, & Usability Center, 2000), certain strata of the population might be overrepresented in Web research.

On the other hand, the vast size of the Web offers room for tens of thousands of small "virtual communities" with a wide variety of user profiles (Rheingold, 1993). This allows for targeted recruitment, including participants from very unusual or previously inaccessible populations such as drug dealers (Coomber, 1997), people with particular head injuries (Browndyke, Santa Maria, Pinkston, & Gouvier, 1999), or people suffering from panic attacks (Stones & Perry, 1997).

The advantage of eased access is twofold, as Web experiments allow people to experience psychological research who would never have had the chance to do so due to geographical, cultural, or social barriers. Scientific psychology becomes more accessible. Web sites with Web experiments, especially online laboratories (e.g., Birnbaum, 1998; Bülthoff, van Veen, Givaty, Braun, & Georg, 1997; Pagani & Lombardi, 1997; PsychExps, 1998; Reips, 1995a; Schubert & Waldzus, 1996), mostly include a rationale of the research at hand and give an explanation of what experimental psychologists are doing. This might well heighten the visibility of psychological research.

GENERALIZABILITY (SITUATION) AND EXTERNAL VALIDITY

It has long been seen as one of the major disadvantages of laboratory experiments that in this highly controlled situation people might produce results that cannot be transferred to their behavior in the "real world" (Martin, 1996). Chapanis (1970) argues that the external validity of laboratory experiments is generally low (however, for a different view see Anderson & Bushman, 1997). If one wants to generalize findings that have originated in laboratory research one runs into the difficulty that the laboratory situation is mostly very different from what is a natural setting for the participants. This gap might create an "artificial" or "sterile" atmosphere in many laboratories, as participants find themselves being in an often unfamiliar place they cannot personally relate to. It seems quite obvious that it is possible that many people will behave unusually under these circumstances. In Web experiments a large percentage of participants remain in the familiar situation at the computer at home or at work. According to the 10th GVU WWW user survey 79% of respondents *daily* browse the WWW from home, and 57% from work, while

77% *never* browse from school, 72% *never* browse from public terminals, and 60% say they *never* access the WWW from places other than the previous choices (Graphics, Visualization, & Usability Center, 1998).

Besides familiarity with the physical situation and its associated comfort there is another important aspect to Web experimenting: bringing the experiment to the subject instead of the opposite. Web experiments spare participants from scheduling, from transportation, from hassles finding campuses, buildings, rooms within buildings, and the right person to talk to. No walks through long hallways, only a few mouse clicks. Extrapolating current technical development, it will soon be common to connect to the WWW with wireless laptop and palmtop computers. While the dependence on a technical interface may limit external validity in Web experiments, the wide variety of situations that allow for access will increase external validity in Web experiments, compared to laboratory experiments. To make another point for this claim: Participants in Web experiments can freely choose at which time of day (or night) and on which day they wish to participate.

GENERALIZABILITY (TIME)

Laboratories usually are subject to all kinds of institutional regulations, including limited access times. It is probably no overstatement that (with certain exceptions, such as sleep research laboratories) psychology's body of research says a lot about people's behavior during weekday daytime working hours. Web experiments can be accessed all the time, all around the clock. Data from Web experiments lend themselves very easily to making post-hoc comparisons depending on time of day. Furthermore, these data might be less influenced by interactions between participants' biological rhythms and levels of the independent variable(s) used, as it is likely that in Web experiments with self-selected access personally comfortable participation times will be chosen. Because thousands of Web pages can be served at the same time, there is practically no limit to simultaneous use of the materials. Consequently, no scheduling difficulties arise, and overlapping sessions do not produce organizational nightmares as well.

This sounds like complete freedom for participants. But what if an experimenter wants to control for time of day or weekday? Web experiments offer a previously unattainable technical capability of interactively controlling display of experimental materials dependent on preset variables. For example, it is possible to only serve an experiment's materials during a certain hour while during all other times logging in leads to a different experiment. That way one might do a study limited to people surfing the Internet during their local nighttime between 2 and 3 a.m. Additionally, one could cross this *time-dependent redirecting* with a second factor, such as one that is based on the participant's domain. That way one could determine whether persons connecting from U.S. American educational institutions (.edu) differ from those connecting from commercial institutions (.com). In turn, this way one can test whether it makes a difference when and from where someone participates. Other variables readily available for redirecting are the Web page a surfer comes from, the operating system he or she is using, the screen resolution the monitor is set to, left- versus right-handedness (determined by type of mouse arrow movement), or any input the participant might give in a form built into the first page.

VOLUNTEER BIAS

It has been shown that complete voluntariness of participation in laboratory experiments may lead to results different from those obtained with less voluntary participation (Rosenthal & Rosnow, 1969; Rosnow & Rosenthal, 1966; Spiel, 1988). Also, there is evidence that motivation for participation may be a moderating variable. Oakes (1972) compared behavior in group discussions of persons recruited through advertisements in two newspapers with such behavior by "coerced" students and found dramatic differences. In most studies with psychology students, the students participate to fulfill an assignment for a class. As has been noted before, the psychological body of research is mainly based on studies conducted with students (Buchanan & Smith, 1999; Reips & Bächtiger, 1999). Having to fulfill a research assignment in a college course often leaves students with the choice between serving as a subject for extra credit and a not particularly desirable alternative (such as writing a paper). These students are likely to be less-than-eager participants. Consequently, much of our current psychological knowledge has been derived from the behavior of students in "not perfectly voluntary" situations. These people are probably less motivated than people who seek out and choose to participate in Web experiments. Perhaps these Internet participants are more likely to exercise their freedom to quit the experiment than those who serve in the lab. Participants in Web experiments can "leave" with the touch of a button.

Of course, something has to be said about the downside of the lower commitment to participation in Web experiments. Resulting dropouts could adversely affect the conclusion. Techniques for reducing the dropout rate and limiting its impact will be discussed later in this chapter.

STATISTICAL POWER

It has been noted that the statistical power of studies in psychological research is notoriously low (Erdfelder et al., 1996). As Erdfelder et al. remind us: "There are only two ways to raise the power if the null hypothesis (H0), the alternative hypothesis (H1), and the test statistics have already been specified: One must increase either the sample size N or the Type I error probability α" (p. 2). In laboratory experiments one often is forced to take the unusual step of increasing α, if one wants to draw meaningful conclusions from experiments, as there are theoretical limits to increased precision of the error measurement and more control of unwanted variability, and pragmatic barriers to an increase of N. Time, lab space, and finances limit the number of participants one can afford. In Web experiments, however, it is no problem to reach the "ideal" calculated sample size (not too small and not too large) while remaining at a conventional α-level. On the WWW the participant pool is of almost unlimited size.

To support the claim that in Web experiments it is no problem to achieve the optimal calculated sample size, Figure 1 shows monthly visits to

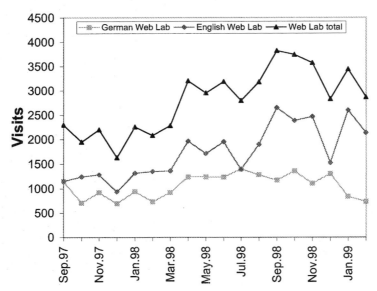

Figure 1   Number of monthly visits to the Web's Experimental Psychology Lab, September 1997 to February 1999.

the *Web's Experimental Psychology Lab* (Reips, 1995a). Currently, the number of visits is about 4000 a month. The issue of "hits" and "visits" is a complicated one. In Figure 1 visits are single downloads of the plain (not the animated) entry pages to the Web's Experimental Psychology Lab. This gives a rough estimate of true visits by people, as I could determine by four other methods: WebTracker (FxWeb Web Technologies, 1999); JavaScript; figures for certain images; figures for visits from certain IP addresses. The estimate has to be corrected by subtracting robot visits and cases when users switch between language versions, when they reload the pages, when their cache is turned off and they go back, and when they return to the page at the end of an experiment (unless they went to the experiment directly). On the other hand, one has to add those cases when people get the pages from proxies (this number has been increasing in recent years), when several persons connect using the same IP addresses, and all cases for the Zurich version of the lab, as these are not included. On both the positive and the negative side a few other cases are possible. Of course, visits are not "people who have been in the Web lab exactly one time." However, with the help of persistent Cookies I am able to estimate quite accurately how many people return (about 75% do not), and how often.

Figures similar to the number of visitors to the Web's Experimental Psychology Lab can be reached for single Web experiments through extensive advertising in newsgroups and on highly frequented Web sites (Jochen Musch, personal communication, April 6, 1998). Being able to potentially reach large numbers of participants is the single most important factor for Web experimenters to conduct Web experiments (Musch & Reips, chap. 3, this volume).

DETECTABILITY OF MOTIVATIONAL CONFOUNDING

An issue strongly related to the voluntariness of (respectively eagerness for) participation is possible confounding of experimental manipulation with motivation and/or task difficulty. In traditional laboratory experiments, levels of a participant's motivation to engage in the experimental task might be confounded with levels of the independent variable. However, those participants who are in the less motivating condition usually will not indicate so by leaving the situation. They will stay and finish the experiment, thereby possibly contaminating the data. In Web experiments with a between-subjects design a differential dropout rate in experimental conditions would indicate such a motivational confounding. This information can then be used to address issues such as task difficulty or task attractiveness, for example by introducing control conditions.

With participants being able to terminate the experiment at any time during a Web experiment, *condition-independent* dropout due to motivational issues can become much more problematic than in laboratory experiments. It can be assumed that many participants in Web experiments will not stay in the experimental situation, as their commitment might be lower. On the other hand, their commitment is not based on reasons such as course credit consider-ations or "peer pressure" by the experimenter, thereby creating less error variance (Reips, 1996b, 1997b, 1999a, 1999b).

How can dropout behavior be used to detect motivational confounding? Spotting motivational confounding requires a between-subjects design for the Web experiment, that is, random distribution of participants to at least two conditions. Generally, selective dropout in one condition might make an experiment worthless (unless dropout is the dependent variable, of course). Participants in a less motivating or boring experimental condition, who in a laboratory experiment would have stayed due to, for example, course credit considerations, might very likely drop out of a Web experiment. In this case the laboratory experiment data would be contaminated by motivational con-founding; the Web experiment data would allow for detection of this effect. Put as a general rule: The less free participants are to leave the experimental situation the less likely it is that motivation-related confounding variables will become salient. Consequently, the heightened degree of voluntariness in Web experiments allows for detecting confounds with variables that potentially decrease motivation, such as task difficulty. Between-subjects Web experi-ments with voluntary participation have a built-in detection device for this type of confounding, which will be discussed in the section on "Solutions."

EXPERIMENTER EFFECTS AND
DEMAND CHARACTERISTICS

Basic problems that trouble experimental research and tie in with the issue of external validity are demand characteristics (Orne, 1962) and experi-menter effects (e.g., Barber & Silver, 1968; Rosenthal & Fode, 1973). Demand characteristics are—often subtle—clues that influence participants in the experimental situation by "demanding" certain reactions. They include such clues given by the experimenters. Experimenter effects are "mildew stains" in psychological science, as they might have biased a large portion of experimen-tal results. As long as experimenters are present in experiments, there is the potential that they might give subtle clues or make errors that might systemat-ically bias their data. However, the notion of experimenter effects also includes biases introduced by the experimenters during execution of the experiment, data transformation, data analysis, and interpretation of the results. "Every attempt should be made to minimize those demand characteristics that might become confounding variables. ... Demand characteristics can be controlled by automating as much of the experiment as possible" (Martin, 1996, p. 72). Although automation might reduce external validity in some cases due to the artificiality of the situation, it will increase it as long as some laboratory-specific demand characteristics are avoided. Web experiments are automated by definition, and experimenter influence is minimized to preparation and data analysis.

Which advantages does the Web experiment method offer regarding experimenter effects? In most Web experiments there is no interaction between experimenters and participants. This avoids a large source of potential experimenter effects. However, experimenters also bias experiments by making errors in the preparation of the experiment, data transformation, data analysis, and interpretation of the results. The more a Web experiment is automated, the less opportunity there is for undetectable experimenter effects (however, because there is no one to ask questions of, instructions for Web experiments must be particularly clear—this problem is addressed later in this chapter). Also, there might be a higher chance for detection of experimenter errors in these tasks, because the material and the records are available on the Internet and are open to review. On this issue another Web experimenter commented:

> I do not believe that detecting subtle errors in experimental design or data analysis is going to be easier for Web experiments than traditional lab-based ones. We have a reaction time study using visual and sound stimuli. Unbeknownst to us, the sound files included about 25 msec of silence at the start of each sound. This was being added to reaction times. This type of error can occur in the lab as easily as on the Web, of course, but in either case it may go undetected for some time (Kenneth McGraw, personal communication, January 15, 1999).

Incidentally, I had heard about a problem with this particular experiment from one participant, before reading the comment. The participant wrote:

> Try the reaction time experiments. Some of the experiments on reaction time, in my browser, give me an unintended advance warning of the coming of the sound cue (on my Netscape screen, I see the system's hourglass just before the sound is presented—clearly, that is a problem in the software—if the sound is delivered before the trial starts, I won't have that cue ....If all the sounds are delivered well before the start of the experiment, then I may have too long a wait and give up on doing the experiment. Instead, the sound is being delivered as part of each trial's pretrial waiting period, so it gives a cue of the timing of the sound onset.

Although this participant erroneously attributed the faulty material issue to the Web experiment software and concluded to critically look at these issues with Web experiments, he noticed that something must be wrong and nicely showed how the open nature of Web research indeed allows for detection and quick correction of errors through feedback by participants and the research community.

Taken together, the mildew stains in psychological laboratory research might well cover some established findings, identifying them as tainted beams, as Web experiments now allow for the validation of traditional research methods. The point is that some of the problems that have plagued the methodology of psychology experiments can be eliminated or at least addressed through the use of Web experiments in lieu of or alongside traditional field or lab research.

OTHER ADVANTAGES OF WEB EXPERIMENTING

COSTS

Web experimenting reduces costs, because of savings of lab space, experimenters, equipment, and administration. Web experiments run around the clock and allow for simultaneous access by a large number of participants. Several participants might use the experimental material at the same time without knowing of each other. Consequently, there are no scheduling problems. Institutional regulations (e.g., limited lab hours) lose their confining impact on research. Most Web server programs allow for thousands of simultaneous connections. To deal with large numbers of simultaneous participants in Web experiments is only feasible because no experimenter needs to be present during the experiment. Once a Web experiment is programmed and on the WWW no salaries have to be paid for experimenters.

To conduct Web experiments is financially attractive in even more ways: no rooms for laboratories are needed, and no bureaucracy regarding scheduling, insurance, and so forth. In their simplest form, Web experiments can be run from a desktop computer, which can still function as a personal computer. Although some money for the transmission of the data has to be paid, comparable Web experiments are much more cost-effective than traditional experiments.

The cost argument should be seen within the proper scope. Although one could argue that costs of data coding and data entry from paper to computer are also saved by most Web studies that use scripts to code and store the data, this is no additional advantage in comparison to other computer-driven experiments. Furthermore, one has to bear in mind that some very expensive areas within psychology are not likely to profit from the advantages of Web experimentation, as they rely on specialized equipment (PET scans, MRIs, EEGs, etc.).

GENERAL ADVANTAGES FOR THE RESEARCH PROCESS

Openness, one of the fundamental principles of science (Merton, 1942/1973), can be achieved much better in Web experiments than in laboratory experiments. Traditional experiments may contain features that are not described in the method section that may turn out to be important. Public Web experiments (there are also hidden Web experiments resembling the field experiment type, e.g., Hänze & Meyer, 1997) are openly accessible and can remain indefinitely on the WWW for documentation purposes. Institutions such as publishing houses or online libraries can house these materials and guarantee their accuracy. Also, there might be development of online agencies (e.g., by funding institutions) that will do searches and collect experimental materials. This allows other researchers to look at the materials and to know in detail the procedure used. Direct hypertext links to articles in online journals such as *Psycoloquy* (1999) may be established and will provide readers with the possibility of experiencing the described experiment from a participant's perspective. Interactive editing of the materials will allow fast setup and modification of Web experiments. The data can also be made accessible online and open for reanalysis. All stages of psychological research will become more public. (For a more elaborate vision of the future research process see Reips, 1997a, 1998a).

The Web experimental method opens the door to research areas that were almost inaccessible for established methods. Examples include studies with children (Reips, 1999c) or with participants from very unusual, specific target populations such as Melungeons (Melungeon Heritage Association, 1999), people with diabetes (newsgroups `alt.support.diabetes`, `alt.support.diabetes.kids`, `de.sci.medizin.diabetes`, `misc.health.diabetes`), disabled artists (newsgroup `alt.support.disabled.artists`), mothers of triplets (newsgroup `alt.parenting.twins-triplets`), people living in long-distance relationships (`alt.support.relationships.long-distance`), drug dealers (Coomber, 1997), or people with panic attacks (Stones & Perry, 1997). In the past, finding and contacting people who had the desired characteristics would have required an enormous effort, not to mention transportation to the laboratory. By using newsgroups and Web experiments, studies with specific, unusual samples can be conducted almost as easily as those with standard sample populations.

OTHER PROCEDURAL ADVANTAGES

Literal Web experiments (i.e., those conducted on the WWW) technically permit one to check for the number of nonparticipants. Because all visits to a Web page are written to a log file the number of visitors to the Web page with a hyperlink to the first page of a Web experiment that do not follow the link approximately equals the number of nonparticipants in that Web experiment (for Web experiments using no-cache tags in the HTML headers, and corrected for robot visits). Of course, such a comparison is only an assessment of participation rate among those people who visit the Web page or Web pages that offer a hyperlink to the Web experiment, if there are no other ways the experiment is announced (finding Web experiments through search engines can be prohibited by using so-called *robot exclusion tags* in the header of the Web pages containing the experimental material). In laboratory experiments usually one does not know how many people walked past the sign advertising an experiment. Another way participants' traces on the Web (by analyzing "referer" information) can be used is mentioned later as the *multiple site entry technique*.

With Web experiments it is always possible to validate results by administering the same materials to a local sample in the laboratory. This allows specifically for assessment of volunteer bias, demand characteristics, experimenter effects, and external validity. Another advantage of Web experiments is the technical variance. This issue will be discussed in the "Disadvantages" section, as it might appear to be a disadvantage on first view.

ETHICAL ISSUES

In Web experiments, participation is completely voluntary throughout the whole experiment. Participants may drop out of the experiment at any time, and therefore a Web experiment might have much less of a restricting influence on participants than laboratory experiments.

Public display of Web experiments allows for better control of ethical standards. Participants, peers or other members of the scientific community might look at an experiment and communicate any objections by e-mail. As in other research, if an experimenter were to violate ethical guidelines, that person would face the disapprobation of peers and possible sanctions from organizations (e.g., American Psychological Association) that also restrict membership and publication to people who are ethical in their research. Also, the Internet allows for sanctions by individual participants, an issue that needs further discussion among Web experimenters, as the implications can be grave.

Although current ethical standards in psychological research, such as those published by national psychological associations (e.g., American Psychological Association, 1992; Föderation der Schweizer Psychologinnen und Psychologen, 1997), cover most of the ethical issues related to conduct of Web experiments, the international character of the WWW might create some conflicts. Standards are not the same everywhere, and feelings about ethical issues in conducting research might vary internationally just as those about uncovering faces in public, the death penalty, or the limitation of free speech for certain controversial issues in some countries but not others (e.g., Nazi propaganda is legal in the United States, but not in Germany). For example, ethical aspects of research conducted at British or American institutions is mostly controlled by local review boards. These boards often require a "participant consent form," which is rather unusual at continental European institutions.

DISADVANTAGES AND SOLUTIONS

The list of advantages of Web experiments is long. Nevertheless, Web experimenters should not overlook the beams in their own eyes. In this section, potential problems will be discussed and some solutions offered.

CONTROL ISSUES ("CHEATING")

It seems that for most researchers questions about control of possible "cheating" are the first ones that come to mind when they think about conducting Web experiments, and indeed almost all Web experimenters take some precautionary measures to ensure a minimal degree of control (Musch & Reips, chap. 3, this volume). To guard against multiple submissions, one may simply ask participants not to participate more than once or ask them about their seriousness regarding their answers. Another solution is to provide repeaters with a checkbox to indicate their status. Also, it is common to check the participants' e-mail addresses or computer addresses (IPs). Both pieces of information help to uniquely identify the participants. However, this information is not completely accurate. One cannot easily draw the conclusion that independence of observations is guaranteed. People could also log in twice from different computers (a rare case) or—increasingly more likely—be assigned different IPs through dynamic addressing (Reips, 1999a). Hence, checking for multiple participation by using a more conservative combination of IP address and e-mail address might be a reliable alternative. Although e-mail addresses can be checked for validity, it is difficult to determine whether the same person participates repeatedly using more than one valid e-mail address. Most such cases can be sorted out by only including the first data set from a given IP address. Unfortunately, this conservative procedure will also abandon some valid data, as the same IP may be used by different people working on the same computer. Another case of shared IPs are proxy servers that can be used by a large number of people. Nevertheless, relying only on the first data sets from IPs also decreases the likelihood of biasing effects produced by participants talking to each other. The chance that a whole group of participants enters an experiment with the same hypothesis in mind seems less likely on the Web than in labs on campuses where students may exchange information on experiments and speculate on what the experiments are about (a phenomenon that can also be observed if Web experiments are announced in newsgroups; in this case the experimenter knows about what is being speculated, however).

At a time when occurrence of dynamic addressing was still very rare, I conducted an experiment on learning of consistency of causal mechanisms (Reips, 1995b, 1996a, 1996b, 1997b), which turned out to be the earliest between-subject experiment conducted on the Web (Musch & Reips, chap. 3, this volume). I had to exclude only 4 cases out of 880 in that Web experiment using a strong criterion of IP plus e-mail address plus "similar IP (all but digits after last period) within a 2 day period." Although there may be more cases of multiple participation in Web experiments of shorter duration (the one mentioned took about 45 minutes to complete), we may be safe to assume that "cheating behavior" is rare. However, if one wants to be cautious or wishes to determine true percentage of "individual identities" one might use measures such as the techniques described next.

Proxy servers can make the submissions of different users appear to have been sent from a single person. To counter this as well as other problems, one may use a *password technique* (Reips, 1997b, 1999; see Figure 2, top). Although handing out passwords reduces the number of participants prior to start of the Web experiment and may be used as a way of countering the problem of self-selection, it requires considerable effort. Individual user IDs and passwords have to be created and set in the Web server, and both need to be mailed to preselected participants. A technique that can be applied after conducting a Web experiment is the *subsampling technique* (Reips, 1997b, 1999; see Figure 2, bottom). This procedure consists of randomly drawing a number of participants' e-mail addresses and mailing them a follow-up questionnaire, in which one might repeat some of the questions from the Web experiment to control for the proportion of false answers. Also, one might ask for faxing of a personal ID.

Another procedure that may be used to secure data integrity is to ask for various personal identification items that can be checked independently or are

◇ **Password technique**

◇ **Subsampling technique**

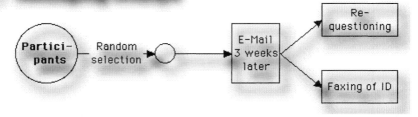

Figure 2 The password technique (top) and the subsampling technique (bottom).

difficult to counterfeit:

- Ask for fax of a personal ID
- Ask for bank account number, if a small monetary reward is to be transferred for participation
- Ask for e-mail addresses of two people who will confirm identity
- Ask for URL of personal home page
- Any combination of items above

Additionally, data quality can be controlled for by checking internal consistency and date and time consistency of answers. A feature that is built into newer versions of HTML are so-called Cookies, which allow for checking of repeated visits to a Web page. A Cookie is

> a unique string of letters and numbers that the Web server stores in a file on your hard drive. This method is used by Web designers to track visitors to a Web site so the visitors do not have to enter the same information every time they go to a new page or revisit a site. For example, Web designers use Cookies to keep track of purchases a visitor wants to make while shopping through a Web catalog. Cookies may work through a single visit to a Web site, such as when tracking a shopping trip, or may be set to work through multiple sessions when a visitor returns to the site (Netscape, 1999).

However, using Cookies is frowned upon in the Internet community, as they can be misused to create user profiles for commercial purposes. Using Cookies in Web experiments will not capture those participants who have this feature turned off in their Web browser. Generally, multiple participation by the same persons is not very likely, as most Web experiments are not that thrilling. It seems unlikely that people would repeat long or boring experiments. As mentioned above, dynamic addressing makes it increasingly difficult to detect individual computers, but looking at data collected at a time of almost no dynamic addressing supports the presumption that multiple participation is rare.

CONTROL ISSUES (EXPERIMENTAL CONTROL)

Another issue is the desire to have as much control of the experimental situation as possible. Earlier in the chapter it was discussed how this desire contradicts external validity of experiments. Much of the situation cannot be controlled in Web experiments. Consequently, conducting Web experiments requires careful experimental design, including criteria such as factorial between-subjects design with randomized distribution of participants to the experimental conditions (Reips, 1996b, 1997b). Randomization can be realized in Web experiments through the use of so-called CGIs, small computer programs that cooperate with the Web server (Kieley, 1996; Reips, 1996b). Consequent use of these techniques, in combination with a large sample, will almost always detect an effect, which will be highly generalizable, as most variables (apart from the independent variables, of course) are allowed to vary freely. As Martin (1996) states: "As a rule of thumb, the more highly controlled the experiment, the less generally applicable the results. ... if you want to generalize the results of your experiment, do not control all the variables." Some experimenters might disagree with this rule, and I am in accord with them for certain quasi-experimental and correlational designs. However, as a rule of thumb the rule is quite logical for between-subjects experiments with random distribution of participants to conditions, as this also means random distribution of all uncontrolled influences to the experimental conditions.

Finally, one technique that might be attractive for researchers who want to know who their participants are is the *participant pool technique* (see Figure 3). Persons who sign up for this pool provide the Web experimenter with their demographic data and can be paid for participation. Additionally, the experimenter keeps a record of who participated in which Web experiments. This technique also allows for drawing stratified samples.

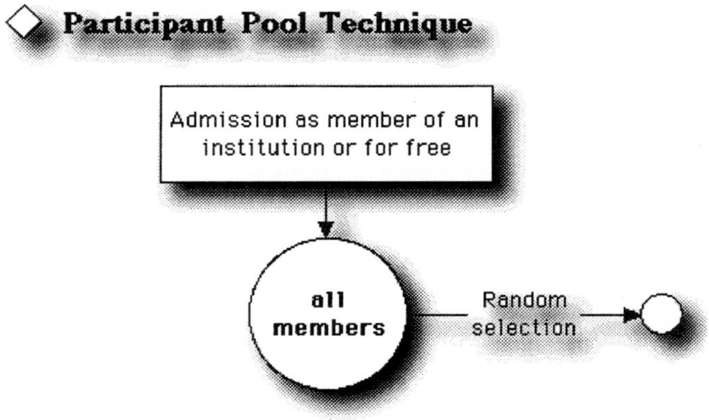

Figure 3 The participant pool technique.

SELF - SELECTION

Self-selection can be considered the most serious problem in online research, as there is no perfect solution as long as participation is voluntary. Just as one might expect selective participation of politically interested persons in a survey on a Web page titled "To participate in a survey on political ignorance, click here" there seem to be pockets of self-selected areas in the WWW between which there is not much surfing traffic. Although we cannot do much about the possibly detrimental nature of self-selection, we can make an attempt to estimate its influence on our results. The technique used here is the *multiple site entry technique* (see Figure 4). Several entry pages or entry hyperlinks on different Web sites lead to the first page of the Web experiment. Later the data of participants coming from the different sources are compared. If they are similar for entry pages with very different content, then one is safe to conclude that self-selection did not play much of a role in determining the results.

DROP - OUT

Comparatively high dropout rates are the downside of the voluntary nature of participation in Web experiments. Birnbaum and Mellers (1989) showed that even with equal dropout rates in all conditions, if there are dropouts, even a between-subjects experiment can lead to wrong conclusions about the direction of an experimental causal effect. This happens if partici-

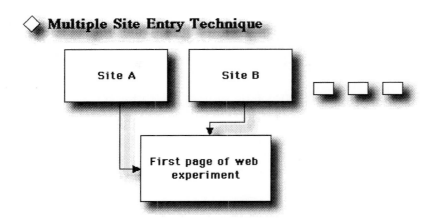

Figure 4   The multiple site entry technique.

pants drop out of different conditions for different reasons. Therefore, Birnbaum and Mellers recommend checking dropouts for any correlations of
demographic or other background variables with the experimental conditions.
This requires assessment of these variables before introduction of conditions. A
way of countering dropout in Web experiments is a *warm-up phase* before the
point of random distribution of participants to experimental conditions. I used
this technique in one of my first Web experiments, where the experimental
manipulation was not introduced until about 20 minutes into the Web experiment, resulting in a dropout rate of only 9.7% (dropout was defined as not
filling out any of the questionnaires at the end of the Web experiment; Reips,
1996a, 1996b, 1997b). Musch and Reips (chap. 3, this volume) found that the
average drop-out rate in Web experiments is 34% (median, 35%), with a
range from 1 to 87%. The large range suggests that there are other motivational factors that influence dropout, two of which could be verified empiri-
cally: monetary rewards for participation and placement of assessment of
personal information (PI). Frick, Bächtiger, and Reips (1999) manipulated these
two factors in a Web experiment and found the following drop out rates:
5.7% in the condition with PI and financial incentive information (FI) at the
beginning of the experiment, 13.2% with PI at end and FI present, 14.9% with
PI at start and no FI, and 21.9% in the PI at end/no FI condition. Musch and
Reips showed that completion of Web experiments was 86% if some form of
monetary reward (individual payments or lottery prizes) was offered, up from
55% without such rewards.

Other factors might also be at work determining continued participation. Some might be technical in nature: In a Web experiment on the reversed hindsight bias, we found that a Javascript version of the Web experiment resulted in a 13.4% larger drop out than an otherwise identical CGI version (Schwarz & Reips, 1999). Several factors have been theoretically explored (Reips, 1996b, 1997b, 1999a) and can be turned into a list of recommendations for Web experimenters:

- Create an attractive Web site by
  - Using a nice looking Web design
  - Having people create links to your site
  - Putting up signs that this could be an interesting site (awards, comments)
  - Not using commercial banners
  - Having multilingual pages
  - Offering various versions (frames, no frames, text).
- Emphasize your site's high trustworthiness by
  - Providing the name of your institution
  - Emphasizing the scientific purpose
  - Ensuring (and keeping) confidentiality
  - Providing contact information.
- Offer a gratification (e.g., the chance of winning a prize).
- Offer feedback (individual or general; for a procedure that can be used to offer individual feedback see Schmidt, chap. 12, this volume).
- Use a Web design that results in systematic shortening of loading times.
- Provide participants with information about their current position in the time structure of the experiment.
- Use the "high entrance barrier" technique.

The *high entrance barrier technique* (Reips, 1999a) is a package of procedures that can be applied to provoke early dropout and ensure continued participation after someone makes the decision to stay. This means bundling of demotivating factors at the very beginning of a Web experiment (i.e., on the general instructions page). Motivating factors should come to work increasingly thereafter, enticing participants to continue with the experiment. Several high entrance barrier techniques are listed here:

- Tell participants participation is serious, and that science needs good data.
- Personalize—ask for e-mail address and/or phone number.
- Tell them you can trace them (via their computer's IP address).
- Be credible: tell them who you are, and what is your institutional affiliation.

- Tell them how long the Web experiment will take.
- Prepare them for any sensitive aspects of your experiment (e.g. "you will be asked about your financial situation").
- Introduce your experimental manipulation after a warm-up phase.
- Tell them what software they will need (and provide them with hyperlinks to get it)
- Perform Java, JavaScript, and plug-in tests (but avoid Active-X).
- Make compliance a prerequisite for winning the reward.

Despite all precautions, dropout in self-selected within-subjects designs poses a serious threat to the validity of this type of research. In between-subjects designs, dropout can be turned into a tool for detecting confoundings, as has been described in the "Advantages" section.

TECHNICAL VARIANCE

Usually, in a highly controlled experiment, a researcher tries to minimize all error variance, such as that which comes from the technical instruments used. Conducting experiments over the Internet involves a worldwide network of cables, routers (computers at cross points of Internet traffic), satellites, plugs, and so on, so that naturally there is a fluctuation in "net lag." This is a very fundamental property of the Internet, as information never goes the same way, but is split up into thousands of "packets" which try to find their own way to later be reassembled. A second source of technical variance lies in the wide range of computers, monitors, speakers or ear phones, Web browsers, and net connections used by Web surfers.

In between-subjects Web experiments these types of technical variables can be seen as advantageous, because possible undetected sources of systematic error are replaced by random error (Reips, 1996b, 1997b). For example, if a technical problem with a monitor used in a laboratory experiment interferes with whatever is studied, then it will systematically change the results. This will not happen in a Web experiment, because every participant sits at a different monitor. Control is replaced by randomness, and therefore generalizability is increased. Of course, generalizability might be limited by *systematic* changes in the environment, such as uniform changes of Web browser features.

INTERACTION WITH PARTICIPANTS

Often in experiments it happens that participants have questions regarding the understanding of the instructions. Then they ask the experimenters. Because this is not feasible in Web experiments, comprehension of material and task cannot be supported by the experimenters. Although this lack of interaction in Web experiments may reduce experimenter effects, lack of comprehension may become a serious threat to the experiment's validity. A solution to this problem is to use pretests for comprehension difficulties with the materials. Also, providing participants with the opportunity of giving feedback by writing e-mail or using comment text boxes on Web pages might allow for quick detection of misunderstandings and for appropriate revision of instructions.

COMPARATIVE BASIS

One might argue that the comparative basis (i.e., other similarly conducted studies of the same questions) for research done using the Web experimental method is too small to draw any valid conclusions from Web experiments. However, the number of Web experiments is increasing rapidly (Musch & Reips, chap. 3, this volume). So far, the evidence for high validity of Web experiments, if compared with laboratory experiments (or, for that matter, validity of laboratory experiments, if one reverses the argument as a consequence of the discussed problems with local laboratory experiments) is overwhelmingly positive (Krantz & Dalal, chap. 2, this volume; Musch & Reips, chap. 3, this volume).

LIMITS (EPILOGUE ON EXTERNAL VALIDITY)

Not all experiments can be done on the Web as there are some things that cannot be done on the Web. It has not been implemented in Web experiments yet to attach sensors to people, take PET or MRI scans, take EEGs, inject drugs, feed foods to taste, touch others over the Web, or do any of a number of other things. Has it? It might just be a matter of a few weeks....

A disadvantage of Web experiments that cannot be changed, as it is built-in, is that participants will always be at computers. Consequently, computer-independent behaviors cannot yet be measured in Web experiments. However, good psychological theories should be able to predict behavior of people sitting at computers as well!

SUMMARY

In this chapter I discussed methodological advantages and disadvantages of Web experiments, in part comparing the Web experimental method with the traditional laboratory experimental method. Advantages I presented were

(1) ease of access to a large number of demographically and culturally diverse participants as well as (2) ease of access to very rare, specific participant populations; (3) a certain justification for generalization of findings in Web experiments to the general population; (4) generalizability of findings to more settings and situations, as there are reasons to believe that external validity in Web experiments is high; (5) avoidance of time constraints; (6) avoidance of organizational problems, such as scheduling difficulties, as thousands of participants may participate simultaneously; (7) completely voluntary participation; (8) ease of acquisition of just the optimal number of participants for achieving high statistical power while being able to draw meaningful conclusions from the experiment; (9) detectability of motivational confounding; (10) reduction of experimenter effects; (11) reduction of demand characteristics; (12) cost savings of lab space, person hours, equipment, administration; (13) greater openness of the research process; (14) ability to assess the number of nonparticipants; (15) ease of comparing results with results from a locally tested sample; (16) greater external validity through greater technical variance; (17) ease of access for participants (bringing the experiment to the participant instead of the opposite); (18) public control of ethical standards.

The presentation of disadvantages was accompanied by suggestions of possible solutions. (1) Possible multiple submissions can be avoided or controlled by collecting personal identification items, by checking internal consistency as well as date and time consistency of answers, and by using techniques such as subsampling, participant pools, or handing out passwords. Evidence was presented that multiple submissions are rare in Web experiments. (2) Generally, experimental control may be an issue in some experimental designs, but is less of an issue when using a between-subjects design with random distribution of participants to experimental conditions. (3) Self-selection can be controlled by using the multiple site entry technique. (4) Dropout is high in Web experiments, especially, if no financial incentives are given for participation. However, dropout can be turned into a detection device for motivational confounding. Also, dropout can be reduced by implementing a number of measures, which are listed in this chapter. (5) The reduced or absent interaction with participants during a Web experiment creates problems, if instructions are misunderstood. Possible solutions are pretests of the materials and providing the participants with the opportunity for giving feedback. (6) The comparative basis for the Web experiment method is low. This will change. (7) External validity of Web experiments may be limited by their dependence on computers and networks. Also, many studies cannot be done on the Web.

For many areas of experimental psychology, advantages of the Web method outweigh the disadvantages. As more data are collected by this method, new problems will no doubt be discovered and new solutions proposed. Nevertheless, it seems safe to venture that the Web method will soon stand as a new structure side by side with older methods in psychology's research basement, supporting our house and driving out the moisture that threatens laboratory research.

REFERENCES

Adair, J. G. (1973). *The human subject.* Boston: Little, Brown.

Anderson, C., & Bushman, B. (1997). External validity of "trivial" experiments: The case of laboratory aggression. *Review of General Psychology, 1,* 19–41.

American Psychological Association. (1992). *Ethical principles of psychologists and code of conduct* [WWW document]. Available URL: http:// www.apa.org/ ethics / code.html

American Psychological Society. (1995). *Psychology experiments on the Net* [WWW document]. Available URL: http:// psych.hanover.edu/ APS / exponnet.html

Barber, T. X., & Silver, J. J. (1968). Fact, fiction, and the experimenter bias effect. *Psychological Bulletin Monograph Supplement, 70,* 1–29.

Birnbaum, M. H. (1998). *Decision research center* [WWW document]. Available URL: http:// psych.fullerton.edu/ mbirnbaum / dec.htm

Birnbaum, M. H. (1999). Testing critical properties of decision making on the Internet. *Psychological Science, 10,* 399–407.

Birnbaum, M. H., & Mellers, B. A. (1989). Mediated models for the analysis of confounded variables and self-selected samples. *Journal of Educational Statistics, 14,* 146–158.

Bredenkamp, J. (1996). Grundlagen experimenteller Methoden [Foundations of experimental methods]. In E. Erdfelder, R. Mausfeld, T. Meiser, & G. Rudinger (Eds.), *Handbuch Quantitative Methoden* (pp. 37–46). Weinheim, Germany: Psychologie Verlags Union.

Brophy, J. E., & Good, T. L. (1974). *Teacher–student relationships: Causes and consequences.* New York: Holt, Rinehart & Winston.

Browndyke, J. N., Santa Maria, M., Pinkston, J., & Gouvier, W. D. (1999). *Online neuropsychology project: Head injury and prevention knowledge among professionals and laypersons.* Manuscript submitted for publication.

Buchanan, T., & Smith, J. L. (1999). Using the Internet for psychological research: Personality testing on the World Wide Web. *British Journal of Psychology, 90,* 125–144.

Bülthoff, H., van Veen, H.-J., Givaty, G., Braun, S., & Georg, P. (1997). *Web-experiments: Psychophysics on the Internet* [WWW document]. Available URL: http:// exp.kyb.tuebingen.mpg.de/ web- experiment / index.html

Campbell, D. T., & Stanley, J. C. (1963). Experimental and quasi-experimental designs for research on teaching. In N. L. Gage (Ed.), *Handbook of research on teaching* (pp. 171–246). Chicago: Rand McNally.

Chapanis, A. (1970). The relevance of laboratory studies to practical situations. In D. P. Schultz (Ed.), *The science of psychology: Critical reflections.* New York: Appleton Century Crofts.

Cohen, J. (1977). *Statistical power analysis for the behavioral sciences* (2nd ed.). New York: Academic Press.

Coomber, R. (1997). Using the Internet for survey research. *Sociological Research Online, 2* [WWW document]. Available URL: http:// www.socresonline.org.uk/ socresonline/ 2 / 2 / 2.html

Devereux, G. (1967). *From anxiety to method in the behavioral sciences.* The Hague: Mouton.

Erdfelder, E., Faul, F., & Buchner, A. (1996). GPOWER: A general power analysis program. *Behavior Research Methods, Instruments, & Computers, 28,* 1–11.

Föderation der Schweizer Psychologinnen und Psychologen. (1997). *Berufsordnung der Föderation der Schweizer Psychologinnen und Psychologen FSP* [Occupation principles of the Confederation of

Swiss Psychologists [WWW document]. Available URL: http://www.fsp.psy.ch/BerufsordnungD.html

Frick, A., Bächtiger, M. T., Reips, U.-D. (1999). Financial incentives, personal information and drop-out rate in online studies. In U.-D. Reips, B. Batinic, W. Bandilla, M. Bosnjak, L. Gräf, K. Moser, & A. Werner (Eds./Hrsg.), *Current Internet science — trends, techniques, results. Aktuelle Online-Forschung — Trends, Techniken, Ergebnisse.* Zürich: Online Press. [WWW document]. Available: URL http://dgof.de/tband99/

FxWeb Web Technologies. (1999). *WebTracker version 2* [WWW document]. Available URL: http://www.fxweb.com/tracker/

Gigerenzer, G., Swijtink, Z., Porter, T., Daston, L., Beatty, J., & Krüger, L. (1989). *The empire of chance: How probability changed science and everyday life.* Cambridge, UK: Cambridge University Press.

Graphics, Visualization, & Usability Center. (1998). *GVU's tenth WWW user survey graphs* [WWW document]. Available URL: http://www.cc.gatech.edu/gvu/user_surveys/survey-1998-10/graphs/graphs.html#general

Graphics, Visualization, & Usability Center. (2000). *GVU's WWW user surveys* [WWW document]. Available URL: http://www.cc.gatech.edu/gvu/user_surveys

Hänze, M., & Meyer, H. A. (1997). Feldexperimente und nicht-reaktive Messung im World Wide Web [Field experiments and nonreactive measurement on the World Wide Web]. In D. Janetzko, B. Batinic, D. Schoder, M. Mattingley-Scott, & G. Strube (Eds.), *CAW-97. Beiträge zum Workshop "Cognition & Web"* (pp. 141–148). Freiburg, Germany: IIG-Berichte 1/97.

Internet.com LCC. (1999). *One-quarter of US households online* [WWW document]. Available URL: http://www.cyberatlas.com/big_picture/demographics/household.html

Jung, J. (1969). Current practices and problems in the use of college students for psychological research. *Canadian Psychologist, 10*(3), 280–290.

Kieley, J. M. (1996). CGI scripts: Gateways to World-Wide Web power. *Behavior Research Methods, Instruments, & Computers, 28,* 165–169.

Kirk, R. E. (1995). *Experimental Design: Procedures for the behavioral sciences* (3rd ed.). Pacific Grove, CA: Brooks/Cole.

Klauer, K. C., Musch, J., & Naumer, B. (1999). *On belief bias in syllogistic reasoning.* Manuscript submitted for publication.

Krantz, J. H., Ballard, J., & Scher, J. (1997). Comparing the results of laboratory and World-Wide Web samples on the determinants of female attractiveness. *Behavioral Research Methods, Instruments, & Computers, 29,* 264–269.

Martin, D. W. (1996). *Doing psychology experiments* (4th ed.). Pacific Grove, CA: Brooks/Cole.

McNemar, Q. (1942). Opinion–attitude methodology. *Psychological Bulletin, 43,* 289–374.

Melungeon Heritage Association. (1999). *Melungeon Heritage Association* [WWW document]. Available URL: http://pluto.clinch.edu/appalachia/melungeon/index.html

Merton, R. K. (1973). The normative structure of science. In N. W. Storer (Ed.), *The sociology of science: Theoretical and empirical investigations* (pp. 267–278). Chicago: University of Chicago Press. (Original work published 1942)

Netscape. (1999). *Netscape communicator glossary* [WWW document]. Available URL: http://home.netscape.com/communicator/glossary.html

Oakes, W. (1972). External validity and the use of real people as subjects. *American Psychologist, 27,* 959–962.

Orne, M. T. (1962). On the social psychology of the psychological experiment: With particular reference to demand characteristics and their implications. *American Psychologist, 17,* 776–783.

Pagani, D., & Lombardi, L. (1997). *Online Psychology Lab Padua* [WWW document]. Available URL: http://www.psy.unipd.it/personal/laboratorio/surprise/htmltesi/index.html

Parsons, H. M. (1974). What happened at Hawthorne? *Science, 183,* 922–932.

PsychExps. (1998). [WWW document]. Available URL: http://www.olemiss.edu/PsychExps/

Psycoloquy. (1999). [WWW document]. Available URL: http://www.princeton.edu/~harnad/psyc.html

Reips, U.-D. (1995a). *The Web's Experimental Psychology Lab* [WWW document]. Available URL: http://www.psych.unizh.ch/genpsy/Ulf/Lab/WebExpPsyLab.html

Reips, U.-D. (1995b). *AAAbacus, the first cognitive learning experiment on the WWW* [WWW document]. Available URL: http://www.psych.unizh.ch/genpsy/Ulf/Lab/archiv/aaabacus.html

Reips, U.-D. (1995c). *The Web experiment method* [WWW document]. Available URL: http://www.psych.unizh.ch/genpsy/Ulf/Lab/WWWExpMethod.html

Reips, U.-D. (1996a, April). Experimentieren im World Wide Web [Experimenting in the World Wide Web] [Abstract]. *Experimentelle Psychologie: Tagung experimentell arbeitender Psychologen* [Proceedings of the Experimental Psychologist's Conference], *Germany, 38,* 256–257.

Reips, U.-D. (1996b, October). *Experimenting in the World Wide Web.* Paper presented at the 1996 Society for Computers in Psychology conference, Chicago. [Also as WWW document]. Available URL: http://www.psych.unizh.ch/genpsy/reips/slides/scipchicago96.html

Reips, U.-D. (1997a). Forschen im Jahr 2007: Integration von Web-Experimentieren, Online-Publizieren und Multimedia-Kommunikation [Science in the year 2007: Integration of Web experimenting, online publishing, and multimedia communication]. In D. Janetzko, B. Batinic, D. Schoder, M. Mattingley-Scott, & G. Strube (Eds.), *CAW-97. Beiträge zum Workshop "Cognition & Web"* (pp. 141–148). Freiburg, Germany: IIG-Berichte 1/97.

Reips, U.-D. (1997b). Das psychologische Experimentieren im Internet [Psychological experimenting on the Internet]. In B. Batinic (Ed.), *Internet für Psychologen* (pp. 245–265). Göttingen: Hogrefe.

Reips, U.-D. (1998a). Forschung in der Zukunft [Future science]. In T. Krüger & J. Funke (Eds.), *Psychologie im Internet: Ein Wegweiser für psychologisch interessierte User* (pp. 115–123). Weinheim: Beltz.

Reips, U.-D. (1998b). Web-Experiment [Web experiment]. In F. Dorsch, H. Häcker, & K.-H. Stapf (Eds.), *Psychologisches Wörterbuch* (Vol. 13, pp. 943–944). Bern: Huber.

Reips, U.-D. (1999a). Theorie und Techniken des Web-Experimentierens [Theory and techniques of Web experimenting]. In B. Batinic, A. Werner, L. Gräf, & W. Bandilla (Eds.), *Online Research: Methoden, Anwendungen und Ergebnisse.* Göttingen: Hogrefe.

Reips, U.-D. (1999b). *Online answering biases.* Manuscript submitted for publication.

Reips, U.-D. (1999c). Online-Forschung mit Kindern [Online research with children]. In U.-D. Reips, B. Batinic, W. Bandilla, M. Bosnjak, L. Gräf, K. Moser, & A. Werner (Eds./Hrsg.), *Current Internet science—trends, techniques, results. Aktuelle Online-Forschung—Trends, Techniken, Ergebnisse.* Zürich: Online Press. [WWW document]. Available: URL http://dgof.de/tband99/

Reips, U.-D., & Bächtiger, M.-T. (1999). *Are all flies drosophilae? Participant selection bias in psychological research.* Manuscript in preparation.

Reips, U.-D., & Musch, J. (1999). *Web experiment list* [WWW document]. Available URL: http://www.psych.unizh.ch/genpsy/Ulf/Lab/webexplist.html

Rheingold, H. (1993). *The virtual community: Homesteading at the electronic frontier* [Also as WWW document, available URL: http://www.rheingold.com/vc/book/]. Reading, MA: Addison-Wesley.

Rice, B. (1983). The Hawthorne defect: Persistence of a flawed theory. *Psychology Today, 16,* 70–74.

Roethlisberger, F. J. (1977). *The elusive phenomena: An autobiographical account of my work in the field of organized behavior at the Harvard Business School.* Cambridge, MA: Division of Research, Graduate School of Business Administration. (Distributed by Harvard University Press)

Rosenthal, R. (1965). The volunteer subject. *Human relations, 18,* 389–406.

Rosenthal, R. (1966). *Experimenter effects in behavioral research.* New York: Appleton-Century-Crofts.

Rosenthal, R., & Fode, K. L. (1973). The effect of experimenter bias on the performance of the albino rat. *Behavioral Science, 8,* 183–189.

Rosenthal, R., & Jacobson, L. (1968). *Pygmalion in the classroom: Teacher expectation and pupils' intellectual development.* San Francisco, CA: Holt, Rinehart & Winston.

Rosenthal, R., & Rosnow, R. L. (1969). The volunteer subject. In R. Rosenthal & R. L. Rosnow (Eds.), *Artifact in behavioral research.* New York: Academic Press.

Rosnow, R. L., & Rosenthal, R. (1966). Volunteer subjects and the results of opinion change studies. *Psychological Reports, 19,* 1183–1187.

Schubert, T., & Waldzus, S. (1996). *Laboratory of Social Psychology Jena* [WWW document]. Available URL: http: // www.uni-jena.de / ~ ssw / labor.htm

Schultz, D. P. (1972). The human subject in psychological research. In C. L. Sheridan (Ed.), *Readings for experimental psychology* (pp. 263–282). New York: Holt.

Schwarz, N., & Hippler, H. (1994a). Subsequent questions may influence answers to preceding questions in mail surveys. *ZUMA-Arbeitsberichte,* 94/07.

Schwarz, N., & Hippler, H. (1994b). The numeric values of rating scales: A comparison of their impact in mail surveys and telephone interviews. *ZUMA-Arbeitsberichte, 94/08.*

Schwarz, S., & Reips, U.-D. (1999). Drop-out wegen JavaScript: "Das habe ich unmöglich wissen können"—Ein Web-Experiment zum Reversed Hindsight Bias [Drop out caused by JavaScript: "I could not have expected this to happen"—A Web experiment on the reversed hindsight bias]. In U.-D. Reips, B. Batinic, W. Bandilla, M. Bosnjak, L. Gräf, K. Moser, & A. Werner (Eds./Hrsg.), *Current Internet science—trends, techniques, results. Aktuelle Online-Forschung—Trends, Techniken, Ergebnisse.* Zürich: Online Press. [WWW document]. Available: URL http: // dgof.de / tband99 /

Smart, R. (1966). Subject selection bias in psychological research. *Canadian Psychologist, 7a,* 115–121.

Spiel, C. (1988). Experiment versus Quasiexperiment: Eine Untersuchung zur Freiwilligkeit der Teilnahme an wissenschaftlichen Studien [Experiment versus quasi-experiment: An investigation of voluntariness of participation in scientific studies]. *Zeitschrift für experimentelle und angewandte Psychologie, 25,* 303–316.

Stones, A., & Perry, D. (1997). Survey questionnaire data on panic attacks gathered using the World Wide Web. *Depression and Anxiety, 6,* 86–87.

Welch, N. (1995). *Demonstrations in auditory perception* [WWW document]. Available URLs: http: // www.music.mcgill.ca / auditory / Auditory.html and http: // gl15.bio.tu-darmstadt.de / auditory / auditory.html

Welch, N., & Krantz, J. (1996). The World-Wide Web as a medium for psychoacoustical demonstrations and experiments: Experience and results. *Behavior Research Methods, Instruments, & Computers, 28,* 192–196.

SECTION II

Individual Differences and Cross-Cultural Studies

CHAPTER 5

Potential of the Internet for Personality Research

Tom Buchanan
Department of Psychology
University of Westminster
London Wir 8AL
United Kingdom

POTENTIAL OF THE INTERNET FOR PERSONALITY RESEARCH

With every passing day, the Internet plays a larger role in the western world: a source of information and entertainment, a medium for communication and commerce, and an important resource for educators, scholars, and scientists. The potential it offers for teaching and research has been brought to the attention of the academic psychological community (e.g., Allie, 1995; Batinic, 1997; Hewson, Laurent, & Vogel, 1996; Krantz, 1995; Reips, 1995; Szabo & Frenkl, 1996), and that community has been swift to embrace it. This chapter addresses the opportunities the Internet offers for the psychometric approach to personality research. It aims to explore some of the problems facing online personality research, to describe a series of studies exploring the feasibility of such an endeavor, and to offer some methodological recommendations on the basis of findings to date.

WHY DO PERSONALITY RESEARCH ON THE INTERNET?

Much personality research, especially in the psychometric and factor analytic traditions, relies on participants completing questionnaires, checklists,

Psychological Experiments on the Internet

or inventories. Although relatively simple to implement, such studies often require large numbers of participants. For researchers without easy access to large "captive" participant populations—such as undergraduate students who may participate in return for course credit—recruiting the numbers needed may prove difficult (Smith & Leigh, 1997).

The Internet offers access to very large numbers of participants with little cost or effort (e.g., Buchanan & Smith, 1999; Reips, 1995; Smith & Leigh, 1997). It is easy to convert traditional pencil-and-paper tests to online versions which can automatically acquire data. HTML (the code in which WWW pages are written) forms which reproduce the items of traditional tests are easily created—the test is effectively transferred from the printed page to the screen. Various response formats (e.g., drop-down menus, radio buttons, or free text entry boxes) are possible, and there is evidence (Reips, 1998) that these may be used interchangeably. Participants' responses may then be e-mailed to the researcher or automatically scored and feedback presented if desired. Software which will facilitate the process is becoming available.

Although the tests and assessment instruments used in online studies are usually presented as forms on Web pages, other Internet resources and technologies will also typically be employed. For instance, communication between experimenter and participant may occur by e-mail, or participants may be recruited by means of advertisements placed in Usenet newsgroups (online discussion groups which function rather like bulletin boards, with people posting messages relating to the topic of the group). Online data acquisition is not unique to the WWW: studies have in the past been performed using bulletin board systems (BBSs), e-mail, and procedures where participants access experimental materials through FTP or Telnet protocols (e.g., Hewson et al., 1996; Kiesler & Sproull, 1986; Smith & Leigh, 1997). Such methods differ in some ways from the type of work being discussed in this chapter: that in which a participant—recruited by whatever means—accesses a Web page and fills out an interactive form. Other types of study, where for instance a questionnaire is posted to a Usenet newsgroup or is completed interactively in a virtual environment (e.g., Schiano, 1997), obviously share many features but also differ in ways which place them beyond the scope of this discussion.

Increasing numbers of psychological studies are being conducted using such methods, and the number of reports of serious empirical work is growing. In the commercial sector, alongside market research and other applications, there is also considerable potential for using the Internet in automated (where narrative reports are automatically generated) or semiautomated (where data are collected online but reports are generated and communicated to clients by traditional means) personality and ability assessment. A number of professional psychologists and test publishers are already beginning to offer such services:

Bartram (1998) considers the testing industry is "on the threshold of a revolution."

POTENTIAL STRENGTHS OF
INTERNET - MEDIATED RESEARCH

As well as the ease with which large amounts of data may be obtained at very low cost, there are scientifically underpinned reasons for doing such work. These mainly involve the nature of the sample(s) one may recruit. Psychological research is often criticized for overuse of undergraduate student samples (e.g., Smart, 1966). Overreliance on student samples (which are relatively homogeneous) may diminish the possibility of finding true relations between individual differences and behavior, and limits generalizability. Homogeneity also presents a problem for researchers using factor analysis: if variance on a characteristic is restricted, an incomplete picture may be obtained of the latent variables underlying responses to the test (Kline, 1993).

Internet samples are likely to include a broader range of participants than a traditional undergraduate sample and by virtue of their size are expected to include a larger number of people with extreme scores. They are thus likely to have increased heterogeneity with regard to whatever constructs are of interest to the researcher (demonstrated by the greater variance in WWW samples relative to student samples reported by Pasveer & Ellard, 1998), suggesting that, in factor analytic studies, a better picture of the latent variables underlying responses to the test instrument may be obtained.

Along with the relative ease of participant recruitment and data collection, the greater diversity of WWW samples suggests that the Internet may have much to offer as a tool for test development. Pasveer and Ellard (1998), who used WWW samples in developing a psychometric measure of self-trust, suggest that in this regard the benefits of large samples outweigh the generalizability problems (which also exist with traditional captive—e.g., student—samples). Commercial test users and developers are similarly using Internet samples for creating tests and gathering validation and normative data (L. Healy, personal communication, 1998).

Another suggested advantage of Internet-mediated research is anonymity —both of participant and of researcher. Anonymity of participants may increase levels of self-disclosure (as observed by Locke and Gilbert, 1995, with stand-alone computerized tests), while anonymity of experimenters (or minimal information about and interaction with them) may serve to reduce demand characteristics and other experimental biases (Hewson et al., 1996). However, this lack of contact may also cause problems if participants misunderstand experimenters' instructions, and anonymity might interact with motivation to finish the experiment (see Reips, chap. 4, this volume).

POTENTIAL PROBLEMS FOR INTERNET - MEDIATED RESEARCH

Despite the possibilities just outlined, there are significant queries about Internet-mediated research. Most crucially, are Web-mediated tests psychometrically and psychologically equivalent to traditional instruments?

Psychometric Properties and Challenges to Reliability and Validity

When stand-alone personal computers began to become widely available, their usefulness as instruments for psychometric test administration and scoring was quickly exploited. This led to concerns about the adequacy of computer-based instruments—were they equivalent to the traditional tests on which they were based? (Skinner & Pakula, 1986). Research has suggested that in most cases computerized versions of tests do measure the same variables as their traditional counterparts (Bartram and Bayliss, 1984; Cohen, Swerdlik, & Smith, 1992) although they sometimes do differ (particularly when tests are timed). It is generally considered that equivalence of computerized and traditional tests must be demonstrated and not simply assumed (Cohen et al., 1992; Meier, 1994). This is probably even more important for Internet-mediated tests, which face extra challenges to reliability and validity (Buchanan & Smith, 1999).

Sample heterogeneity has just been suggested as one of the strengths of Internet research. Although Internet samples are indeed likely to be relatively heterogeneous with regard to some factors (e.g., age, ethnicity, language), they may also be homogeneous with regard to others (e.g., interest or skill in using computers, and computer anxiety). Such homogeneity could restrict variance on the construct(s) of interest and furthermore leave one with a biased sample—both of which are undesirable in individual differences research (the same argument as is leveled against the overuse of undergraduate samples).

The status of participants as self-selected volunteers may also have an effect (Hewson et al., 1996). It has been shown that participant motivation may affect research outcomes (Oakes, 1972)—and the motivation of participants in Internet mediated studies is likely to differ from that of traditional samples (Buchanan & Smith, 1999). Findings may also be influenced by environmental factors such as the situation in which the test is completed (Reips, 1996) and temporary attributes of the individual such as fatigue or intoxication (Buchanan & Smith, 1999). Also of great import is the possibility of multiple or mischievous responses (Schmidt, 1997; Pasveer & Ellard, 1998) which if not detected and corrected for (e.g., by deletion of duplicate submissions) may compromise studies.

It is obviously essential to establish the reliability and validity of a test designed from scratch as a Web-mediated instrument (e.g., Pasveer & Ellard, 1998). This is equally true of tests converted from pencil-and-paper formats: the validity of the original will not necessarily transfer to the Web version, as there are likely to be numerous factors which may influence participants' responses. Any study using Web-mediated tests must either control for these factors or demonstrate that they will not affect the testing of hypotheses. The first strategy is unlikely to be possible, due to the likely number of such factors and the fact that many of them have probably not yet been discovered. One must therefore establish that any Web-mediated test has satisfactory psychometric properties prior to its use in research.

Generalizability of Findings

Caution has in the past been expressed about the generalizability of Internet research findings to other populations (e.g., Buchanan & Smith, 1999). Hewson et al. (1996) suggested strategies for increasing generalizability, including recruiting from randomly selected newsgroups to achieve a sample representative of the larger population of Internet users. The extent to which findings from a particular sample are true of Internet samples in general may be increased (and assessed) using the "multiple site entry" technique described by Reips (chap. 4, this volume). Both these strategies would probably produce a sample more representative than one recruited through psychology-related newsgroups—but would it be representative of the general population?

Schmidt (1997) recommends gathering demographic data so that one can make judgments about the populations to which results may be generalized. Studies which have done this to date suggest that generalizability may not be such a problem as many fear. For example, Pasveer and Ellard (1998) compared the demographic characteristics of their WWW sample with the findings of a Georgia Tech (1997) survey of WWW user characteristics and their own student sample. They suggest that although their WWW sample was not representative of the general population, there was evidence that the WWW and student samples were comparable—so findings obtained with WWW samples may be just as generalizable as those obtained using traditional captive samples. There are also increasing numbers of accounts (e.g., Mueller, Jacobsen, & Schwarzer, chap. 8, this volume) indicating that Internet samples probably are more representative of "the real world" than stereotypes would suggest.

Sampling Strategies

However, sample characteristics are still likely to affect research outcomes. For instance, Smith & Leigh (1997) might have found very different answers to their questionnaire on sexual fantasies had they advertised in one of the numerous sex-related newsgroups (which cater to many varied sexual preferences) rather than sci.psychology.research. This suggests that instead of seeking representativeness, one might deliberately target specific types of sample—a strategy which allows questions of psychological interest to be addressed through use of criterion groups.

Criterion Group Approaches

Criterion group oriented methods (where by "criterion group" we mean a section of the population which fits some set of criteria or has some special characteristics) play an important role in personality research, often being used in test development to establish construct validity. For example, Maiuro, Vitaliano, & Cahn (1987) compared men with violent and nonviolent histories when developing an aggression test. Clinical samples are often used in developing or validating measures of psychopathology, and Binet and Simon (1916), postulating that ability developed with age, constructed an intelligence test which differentiated between children of different ages. Such methods also play a role in theory development and testing (although in that situation groups are usually selected on the basis of extreme test scores).

It has been suggested that the Internet presents the opportunity for recruiting large numbers of people from such special populations (e.g., Schmidt, 1997; Smith & Leigh, 1997; Szabo & Frenkl, 1996). This may be done through links from appropriate Web pages (Stones & Perry, 1997) or advertising in newsgroups likely to be read by people with the characteristics of interest (e.g., Buchanan & Smith, in press; Smith & Leigh, 1997).

GOALS OF RESEARCH PROGRAM

Three main themes were addressed in the research program described in this chapter. The first priority was to establish that an Internet-mediated assessment instrument could meet the criteria used to assess any psychometric test. We considered it essential that the instrument chosen be robust to the challenges to reliability and validity outlined previously. The second theme relates to the targeting of specific sample populations or criterion groups through the Internet. The intention here was to ascertain whether or not such samples could be effectively recruited and whether they would then respond in ways consistent with experimental hypotheses. A third major priority was to demonstrate the relations between Internet and traditional methods, in terms of the findings obtained using the two techniques—do both methods lead to the same conclusions?

Implementation Strategy

Experiment 1 (Buchanan & Smith, 1999) examined equivalence of the Internet-mediated and pencil-and-paper tests in terms of reliability and factor structure. If two instruments purport to measure the same characteristic(s), the same factor structure should underlie responses to both. It is hard to see how test–retest reliability could be assessed with an Internet sample, but coefficient α is an easily calculated index of reliability. The next requirement was to demonstrate construct validity. Achieving this via a criterion-group approach would also demonstrate the feasibility of criterion-group methods in Internet research. The objectives of Experiments 2 and 3 (Buchanan & Smith, in press) were therefore to demonstrate that criterion groups could be located and that the instrument would differentiate between them. Finally, the goal of Experiment 4 (Buchanan, 1998) was to investigate whether it could serve as a useful research tool, putting hypotheses about self-monitoring to empirical test.

Choice of Instrument

Practical and ethical factors determined the choice of personality scale for use in these studies (Buchanan & Smith, 1999). These included possession of satisfactory psychometric properties (and for the purposes of this research having a well-known factor structure), the length and format of the test, the status of the instrument in terms of previous publication (for test security and copyright reasons), and the subject matter of the test—for ethical reasons this should be relatively innocuous, especially if feedback is provided to respondents.

The instrument chosen was the SMS-R (Gangestad & Snyder, 1985), the 18-item revision of Snyder's Self-Monitoring Scale, a widely used measure of personality which measures the tendency to observe and regulate expressive behaviors and manipulate the way one presents oneself to others. Individuals high in self-monitoring are sensitive to social and situational cues and adjust their behavior accordingly. Individuals low in self-monitoring, on the other hand, lack either the ability or motivation to adjust to the situation and tend to behave in ways consistent with their stable personality attributes or internal states (Snyder & Gangestad, 1986). The SMS-R has adequate internal reliability (α of 0.70—Briggs & Cheek, 1988; Gangestad & Snyder, 1985) and test–retest reliability (test–retest correlation of .55 after two years; Anderson, 1991). Its construct validity is generally considered to be well established (e.g., Snyder, 1987). The SMS-R therefore appeared to fit all the desired criteria.

EMPIRICAL WORK

EXPERIMENT 1 (BUCHANAN & SMITH, 1999)

Factor analytic studies of the traditional version of the SMS-R (Miller & Thayer, 1989; Hoyle & Lennox, 1991) have established that three factors[1] seem to underlie variance in responses (Gangestad and Snyder, 1991). The purpose here was to ascertain, through confirmatory factor analysis, whether the same structure underlies the Internet version. Participants were solicited through postings to several Usenet newsgroups. These requested people to go to a URL which, after some information and a consent form, allowed access to an HTML form bearing the instructions and questions of the SMS-R and demographic questions on age, sex, and student status. Responses were automatically scored by a CGI script which saved data to a file and fed back scores along with sufficient information for respondents to be able to interpret them. Participants were also given the opportunity to give feedback via another online form.[2] Over a period of 14 weeks, 1181 sets of responses were obtained. After deletion of multiple submissions (defined as repeat accesses from the same Internet address) 963 valid records remained. For comparison, a second sample (224 undergraduate psychology students) was recruited and tested using traditional means: volunteers were asked to participate in the study after classes.

Reliability (coefficient α) of the Web test was calculated, and at 0.75 compared favorably with those reported in SMS-R literature and with the pencil-and-paper sample (0.73). The fit of the three-factor model to the pencil-and-paper version SMS-R has been tested in two main confirmatory factor analyses (Hoyle and Lennox, 1991; Miller and Thayer, 1989). The same analysis, performed upon the Internet data, produced fit indices that were better than the corresponding indices reported in those studies. The level of fit for the Internet data was also better than that of the student sample on four out of the six indices employed. Other analyses (for instance, comparison of

[1]Although three factors, labeled "Other-Directedness," "Extraversion," and "Acting Ability" by Lennox (1998), appear to underlie the SMS-R, its authors argue that the total score on the scale represents the self-monitoring construct. Gangestad and Snyder (e.g., 1991) argue that the three factors do tap certain behavioral tendencies, but that self-monitoring *per se* is tapped by the first unrotated factor which accounts for most of the variance on the SMS-R. Hence the total score was used as an index of self-monitoring in the studies reported in this chapter.

[2]A demonstration of the experimental materials can be seen at URL http://www.mailbase.ac.uk/lists/psy-net-research/files/tbdemo1.htm

the pattern and strength of item loadings upon the first unrotated factor) also indicated factorial similarity.

EXPERIMENT 2 (BUCHANAN & SMITH, IN PRESS)

It has been suggested that one may recruit specific samples by selective advertising in Usenet newsgroups. This study attempted to identify suitable newsgroups by examining the incidence of a behavior associated with self-monitoring. A defining characteristic of high self-monitors is that they are likely to engage in expressive self-presentation—that is, they will try to portray themselves in a way consistent with an image they wish to adopt, to manipulate others' perceptions of them. This activity is an important aspect of online life. In multiuser environments such as MUDs (multiuser domains) and MOOs (MUDs, object-oriented), the focus is usually on adopting and playing out a fictional persona. This occurs to a lesser extent in "Internet relay chat" (IRC) and "chat rooms," where a nickname is chosen by the user as the front seen by others: there the focus is less on creating and role-playing another character than on choosing how other users see you (Bechar-Israeli, 1995, discusses the use of nicknames in IRC). The use of nicknames has a long history[3] on the Internet in the form of "handles" or "screen names," seen in every participatory medium from BBSs to Usenet newsgroups. Many, but not all, contributors to Usenet newsgroups use such screen names. If use of a handle is an example of expressive self-presentation, a person who is a high self-monitor would be more likely to use a handle instead of their real name than would one who is a low self-monitor.[4]

Classes of people likely to be high (e.g., overweight people and actors) or low (e.g., shy people and people with a commitment to single-issue politics such as environmental activists) self-monitors were identified on the basis of the self-monitoring literature. Usenet newsgroups likely to be read by people belonging to these groups were identified: alt.support.big-folks, soc.support.fat-acceptance, rec.arts.theatre.misc, and rec.arts.theatre.plays for the high self-monitors; alt.support.shyness, uk.environment, and talk.environment for the low self-monitors. The names under which people posted messages to these newsgroups were then examined and classified as either real names or handles by two independent raters (see Buchanan & Smith, in press, for more details). A χ^2

---

[3]And it has an even longer one in other communications media such as citizens band (CB) and amateur (ham) radio.

[4]Use of handles is also likely to reflect Internet expertise (U. Reips, personal communication, 1999) with "old hands" more likely to use them. However, there is no reason to believe the distribution of Internet expertise to be anything other than random in the newsgroups selected (which might not have been the case for other groups).

test for independence indicated that handles were used more frequently in the newsgroups thought to be used by high self-monitors than in those likely to be frequented by low self-monitors.

EXPERIMENT 3 (BUCHANAN & SMITH, IN PRESS)

The validity of this Internet-mediated test remains to be established—does it actually measure self-monitoring? To test this, we recruited groups of participants who should differ in self-monitoring tendency (i.e., the readers of the newsgroups identified in Experiment 2), had them complete the instrument, then compared scores to establish whether or not it differentiated between them. Recruitment notices were posted to newsgroups in the "high" and "low" self-monitoring categories. Participants completed the electronic version of the SMS-R and answered additional questions about why they had taken part and whether they could provide any examples of self-monitoring behavior. A different URL was used for each participant group, enabling the CGI script which scored the responses to automatically include participants' self-monitoring classification in the data file. The sample eventually comprised 218 participants.

Mean self-monitoring scores in the two conditions were compared, and participants recruited from "high self-monitoring" newsgroups were found to score significantly higher than those from "low self-monitoring" groups. Participants' responses to the request for examples of self-monitoring behavior were also examined. Of the 114 who responded, 99 provided an example. However, 7 denied ever engaging in such behavior. These 7 had self-monitoring scores significantly lower than those providing examples.

This study suggests the test has some degree of construct validity, and it reinforces the suggestion that targeted recruitment through newsgroups is a viable procedure. The final study addressed the question of whether meaningful WWW research can be done and whether similar findings can be obtained using WWW-mediated and traditional methods.

EXPERIMENT 4 (BUCHANAN, 1998)

Traditional research on self-monitoring suggests that when choosing romantic partners high self-monitors seem to attend mainly to external characteristics (physical attractiveness) of potential partners. Low self-monitors, on the other hand, place more value on the potential partner's personality (Snyder, Berscheid, & Glick, 1985; Snyder, 1987). Experiment 4 examined whether the same held true in an Internet sample. It seemed likely that it would: Krantz, Ballard, & Scher (1997) found that the same variables seemed to influence judgments of female attractiveness in samples tested via both the WWW and traditional means. The study was also intended to extend Snyder et al.'s findings to a more diverse sample. The findings reported in the literature were obtained using relatively small samples of heterosexual male college students. It has yet to be established whether self-monitoring tendencies have the same effect upon determinants of attraction in women (there is evidence, for instance, that in general men pay more attention than women to physical characteristics of romantic partners, Pines, 1998) or people who are attracted to members of their own sex.

Photographs of two male and two female faces differing significantly in raters' judgments of physical attractiveness were selected for use in the study and two short personality profiles including either desirable or undesirable trait descriptions (drawn from Snyder et al., 1985, and Glick, 1985) were generated. Participants were recruited through newsgroups thought likely to be read by people of varying sexual orientations. The procedure and materials were similar to those in Experiments 1 and 3, except that participants were also asked to indicate whether they were primarily attracted to men or to women. Based on their response, participants then saw a page bearing the faces of their preferred gender. The images were paired with the personality descriptions such that the more physically attractive face was presented as having a less attractive personality, while the less physically attractive face was paired with the more desirable personality description. Participants were then asked to indicate which of the two people they would find most attractive and, after debriefing, why they had chosen to take part in the study.

After deletion of duplicates and incomplete data, 320 valid records (from 380) were obtained. High and low self-monitors were identified by reference to norms (cf. Snyder, 1987). Their choices of target were compared using the same analysis as employed by Snyder et al. (1985). The conclusions were the same: high self-monitors most often chose the more physically attractive target (57%), while low self-monitors most often chose the target with the more desirable personality (61%).

This study seems to confirm that recruitment of criterion groups by advertising in appropriate newsgroups then asking screening questions is viable. Like Krantz et al. (1997), it also seems to demonstrate that empirical findings obtained using traditional methods are replicable in Internet-mediated research.

GENERAL FINDINGS ACROSS ALL STUDIES

These studies find encouraging answers to all three questions addressed. Although these results are limited to the SMS-R, for that instrument at least it seems to make little difference whether the instrument is administered on paper to a group of students or via the WWW to anyone who sees a recruitment notice and has the opportunity and motivation to take part: the psychometric properties of the instrument are similar, and the psychological meaning of the construct it taps seems unaffected by the research method. The viability of criterion group methods also seems to be supported. A number of other observations were made over the course of the program. These are outlined next.

Multiple Completions

One problem with online research is the fact that the same participants may, for various reasons, complete the test more than once (Buchanan & Smith, 1999; Schmidt, 1997). In these studies, multiple submissions were controlled for by examining the data file for multiple hits from the same Internet address and, if any were found, deleting all but the (chronologically) first occurrence. This method assumes that the first occurrence is a genuine submission and that others may be due to the participant's clicking on the "Submit" button twice or investigating what happened if they made different choices. Although a conservative method likely to result in the loss of some genuine data (e.g., when multiple individuals use the same machine), this technique seemed the best way of achieving independence of observations (although it is not a guarantee; see Reips, chap. 4, this volume).

The number of multiple completions differed across studies. In Experiment 1, 18.5% of submissions were deleted. In Experiment 3, only 0.9% were deleted, and in Experiment 4, 8.7% required deletion. It is not clear why rates differed, but the nature of the study and the targeted sample are likely to play a part. In Experiment 1, people with an interest in psychology, personality, or testing were the main targets of recruitment. As the instrument gave feedback on test scores, it is likely these people went back and experimented to see how varying their answers would affect their scores. Another possible reason for multiple submissions from the same Internet address might be when two or more people sharing a home PC (or machine in a computer classroom) completed the test, perhaps to compare their scores. In Experiment 4, participants saw different versions of the experimental materials depending on how they answered the question about their sexuality. Examination of the data file suggested that in many cases when people participated more than once, the only difference in their data was the answer to this question: perhaps people who had completed the experiment went back to see what faces they would have seen had they answered the opposite way. In Experiment 3, however, the occurrence of multiple completions was very low, perhaps because the populations targeted in that study were not particularly interested in psychology or personality testing.

Table 1

Reasons for Participation

Reason	Frequency	
	Experiment 3	Experiment 4
Said "no reason"	10 (9%)	10 (9%)
Curious or interested	31 (29%)	46 (40%)
Enjoys tests or surveys	17 (16%)	2 (2%)
Helping research	9 (8%)	9 (8%)
Bored	4 (4%)	5 (4%)
Reference to posted request	14 (13%)	8 (7%)
Combination of above categories	10 (9%)	7 (6%)
Other	13 (12%)	28 (24%)

Reasons for Participation

In Studies 3 and 4, people were asked why they had chosen to participate. The numbers who answered were 108 (49%) and 115 (34%), respectively. Reasons given, coded by two independent raters using the categories described by Buchanan & Smith (in press), are presented in Table 1. In both studies the main motivation of participants was curiosity or interest in the study.

Composition of Sample

Part of the debate about Internet samples concerns demographic variables such as age, sex, or occupational status (e.g., Hewson, 1998). Respondents in Studies 1 and 3 were asked about their age, gender, and whether or not they were students. Results are summarized in Table 2. Although respondents in Study 4 also gave their age and gender, their data are excluded due to the

Table 2

Demographic Characteristics of Internet Samples

	Experiment 1	Experiment 3
Total N	963	218
Males	491 (51%)	126 (58%)
Females	472 (49%)	92 (42%)
Students	405 (43%)	75 (34%)
Mean age	32.02	32.42
SD	10.79	10.77

different sampling strategy (which involved targeting of specific gender-related newsgroups) used in that study.

Given the stereotypical profile of the "typical Internet user" (e.g., Georgia Tech., 1998), should there actually be such a person, some authors have suggested that women will be underrepresented in Internet samples. It is therefore worth noting the near equivalent numbers of men and women (especially in Experiment 1). Buchanan & Smith (1999) suggested that even though comparatively low numbers of women used the Internet, more women than men had an interest in psychology and thus read the newsgroups where recruitment notices were posted. Similarly, among the Internet-recruited panic attack sufferers of Stones & Perry (1997), there were around twice as many women as men—unsurprising, as the disorder is more prevalent among women. As Pasveer & Ellard (1998) note, "...specific WWW samples need not fit the profile of the prototypical Internet user" (p. 132). With respect to gender (or any attribute), the only realistic conclusion is that there are bound to be differences depending on the topic and recruitment strategy. An important finding is the low number of students in each sample. In a sense, WWW samples may therefore be more representative of the general population than are student samples.

DISCUSSION

COMMENTS ON CRITERION GROUP APPROACH

Studies 3 and 4 seemed to demonstrate that groups of people with special characteristics can be successfully located and recruited via Usenet newsgroups. However, some groups seemed easier to recruit than others. This may be because some newsgroups have larger readerships than others. People with the characteristic of interest may be rare even in the targeted population, and people in some criterion groups may be less inclined to participate.

A problem with criterion group methods is the purity of the groups. With the method used in Experiment 3, there is no guarantee that participants are who we think they are. It is perfectly possible for an underweight person to read `alt.support.big-folks` or for a buoyant extravert to be casually browsing through `alt.support.shyness`—as indeed happened, according to an account given by one of our participants. Aside from such browsers, other readers might include people who have an interest in the topic of the newsgroup but do not necessarily possess whatever characteristics discussion revolves around—might, for example, a dietitian (or a psychologist) read `alt.support.big-folks`?

It seems fairly common for participants to pass a study's URL on to friends—either because their friends might be interested or to help the research. Participants sometimes also suggest places to post the URLs of studies or offer to actually do it. Other researchers have also found this (M. Birnbaum, personal communication, 1998). Such offers of help are heartwarming, but may also wreck a study that intends to recruit special populations (such as Experiment 3).

The method we adopted for addressing this problem was to ask people why they participated. Those who indicated that they were recruited via a friend could thus be excluded. The problem with this technique is that not all participants may answer such a question (as shown in Table 1). A second technique might be to ask supplementary questions to help ascertain group membership (as was done in Experiment 4, where people answered questions about their sexuality and were assigned to experimental conditions on that basis) or to use a "filter page" where people would classify themselves as members of particular groups, this classification being either recorded or used to assign them to different experimental conditions (M. Birnbaum, personal communication, 1999). A third would be to assign people to groups based on test scores. Classifications would be made on the basis of actual measured possession of an attribute, not just postulated likelihood of possession.

Although of little use in studies such as Experiment 3, this last method would be appropriate in research where one wishes to compare the performance of people high or low in some personality trait on another test or task. For example, there is evidence that high self-monitors are more accurate eyewitnesses than low self-monitors (Hosch & Platz, 1984). If one wished to test this hypothesis, it is easy to imagine an experiment in which recruitment notices would be placed in selected newsgroups likely to recruit persons high or low in self-monitoring. Participants would complete the SMS-R, and those with sufficiently high or low scores would proceed to the next stage of the experiment, in which they would be tested for accuracy in an eyewitness task. Such combinations of questionnaire-based and experimental paradigms, in which participants are automatically categorized or assigned to experimental conditions, will likely become an important research use of online personality tests.

SAMPLE "CONTAMINATION"

A problem with recruiting through a newsgroup is the strong chance that a study will be discussed in that newsgroup. In the course of this research, newsgroups in which recruitment postings had been made were monitored. It was found that occasional expressions of interest or "flames" (hostile replies) were typical. In only one instance was there more extensive discussion than this: the readers of `alt.support.shyness` posted a total of 15 articles discussing the study, comparing scores, and speculating about what the study was all about (nobody guessed the purpose of the study or the fact that other groups were being compared, and most of the discourse centered around a misconception that shyness or extraversion was being measured). It is believed that naiveté of potential participants was maintained, and that the study was not compromised—any information about the research which could be gleaned from this discussion could also be found on the informed consent page at the start of the experiment. If the discussion had any effect at all it was probably to stimulate curiosity and thereby increase the participation rate. Anecdotal information and personal experience of acting as a "subject pool" member suggests that members of captive student populations do discuss their experiences—often with people who have yet to participate. The discussion in `alt.support.shyness` simply revealed a problem usually hidden from the experimenter.

It seems advisable for researchers recruiting through newsgroups to monitor those groups during their studies. Any threats to the integrity of the experiment can be assessed (of course, should group members exchange private e-mails discussing the study, some of the discussion would still be hidden), and one might also gain insights into the psychology of participation.

PARTICIPANTS, NOT SUBJECTS

One apparent difference between participants in traditional and Internet-mediated research is the increased empowerment and ownership of the research by people participating via the Internet. Respondents gave feedback, offered help and advice, used the experiments for their own ends, and demanded more information about the studies. Perhaps because taking part in such a study requires the respondent to actively seek it out, or because respondents are more in control of the experience or engage with the research more fully, there is a very real shift from being a subject of experimentation to being a participant. Others (e.g., Gibbs & Robinson, 1998, in the case of qualitative research conducted through e-mail) have reported similar observations: a phenomenon worthy of future examination?

PEOPLE'S REACTIONS TO RECRUITMENT STRATEGIES AND POSSIBLE ALTERNATIVES

Hewson et al. (1996) noted that the recruitment strategy used here (postings to newsgroups) may result in hostile responses from some newsgroup readers. On the whole, this was not a major problem. Although a couple of flames were received—both in newsgroups and via e-mail—these were outweighed by expressions of interest and good wishes. However, in the interests of "netiquette" (standards of behavior Internet users expect of each other), a policy was adopted whereby if a single complaint was received, no further advertisements were posted to that group.[5]

Alternative recruitment techniques, which might in many ways be preferable to newsgroup advertising, have also been used successfully. These include placing links or banner ads (Batinic, 1997) in appropriate Web pages such as psychology sites (e.g., Krantz et al., 1997) or pages relevant to the sample one wishes to recruit (e.g., Stones & Perry, 1997). In the longer term, to avoid saturation of newsgroups with participation requests, these may be more appropriate. One technique which seems unlikely to succeed, and which cannot be recommended on netiquette and ethical grounds, is e-mail "spamming" (indiscriminately e-mailing recruitment messages to large numbers of people).

CONCLUSIONS

It has been demonstrated that one specific personality test administered via the Internet can have satisfactory psychometric properties and be functionally equivalent to its pencil-and-paper antecedent. This does not, of course, mean that all tests will behave in this way. Until more is known about this medium of research, each research problem will need to be tested for the effects of Internet presentation.

It is likely to be difficult to obtain a "representative" sample for survey-type research. The composition of any Internet-recruited sample not only will incorporate known (but changing) biases, but also will depend on the nature of the research question and recruiting strategy. It may therefore be better to focus on specific groups with whom interesting and important psychological questions may be answered. However, should one seek to maximize representativeness, a possible strategy is to recruit a very large sample, gathering demographic data, and use that information to select a subsample with a composition similar to the population of interest.

Studies should somehow control for multiple submissions. As well as using information from Internet addresses, asking supplementary questions (Pasveer & Ellard, 1998) may be advisable. A very useful supplementary question to ask is why participants took part in the study; another is to offer the opportunity for people to make any other comments they might wish: many people do seem to have things they wish to say.

[5]Reips (personal communication, 1999) suggests that one method of avoiding flames would be to approach regular posters and ask them to introduce you to the group—this would probably make requests for participation appear more legitimate, reducing hostile reactions.

Finally, it should be noted that the focus of this research has been very narrow: only one part of one approach to the study of personality has been addressed. The Internet offers the potential for research in other areas of the discipline. It will be exciting to see how this potential is realized.

REFERENCES

Allie, D. A. (1995). The Internet and research: Explanation and resources. *The Journal of Mind and Behavior, 16,* 339–368.

Anderson, L. R. (1991). Test-retest reliability of the Revised Self-monitoring scale over a two-year period. *Psychological Reports, 68,* 1057–1058.

Bartram, D. (1998). *Distance assessment: Psychological assessment through the Internet.* Paper presented at the 1998 British Psychological Society Division of Occupational Psychology Conference.

Bartram, D., & Bayliss, R. (1984). Automated testing: Past, present and future. *Journal of Occupational Psychology, 57,* 221–237.

Batinic, B. (1997). How to make an Internet based survey? In W. Bandilla and F. Faulbaum (Eds.), *SoftStat '97 Advances in statistical software 6* (pp. 125–132). Stuttgart: Lucius & Lucius.

Bechar-Israeli, H. (1995). From (Bonehead) to (cLoNehEAd): Nicknames, play and identity on Internet relay chat. *Journal of Computer-Mediated Communication* [Online serial] *1*(2). Available URL: http://jcmc.huji.ac.il/vol1/issue2/bechar.html

Binet, A., & Simon, T. (1916). *The development of intelligence in children.* Baltimore: Williams & Wilkins.

Briggs, S. R., & Cheek, J. M. (1988). On the nature of self monitoring: Problems with assessment, problems with validity. *Journal of Personality and Social Psychology, 54,* 663–678.

Buchanan, T. (1998). *Internet research: Self-monitoring and judgments of attractiveness.* Paper presented at the 1998 Society for Computers in Psychology Conference, Dallas, TX.

Buchanan, T., & Smith, J. L. (1999). Using the Internet for psychological research: Personality testing on the World-Wide Web. *British Journal of Psychology, 90,* 125–144.

Buchanan, T., & Smith, J. L. (in press). Research on the Internet: Validation of a World-Wide Web mediated personality scale. *Behavior Research Methods, Instruments, & Computers.*

Cohen, R. J., Swerdlik, M. E., & Smith, D. K. (1992). *Psychological testing and assessment* (2nd ed.). Mountain View, CA: Mayfield.

Gangestad, S. W., & Snyder, M. (1985). "To carve nature at its joints": On the existence of discrete classes in personality. *Psychological Review, 92,* 317–340.

Gangestad, S. W., & Snyder, M. (1991). Taxonomic analysis redux: Some statistical considerations for testing a latent class model. *Journal of Personality and Social Psychology, 61,* 141–146.

Georgia Tech's Graphics, Visualization and Usability Center. (1997). *GVU's WWW Users Surveys* [Online]. Available URL: http://www.cc.gatech.edu/gvu/user_surveys/

Georgia Tech's Graphics, Visualization and Usability Center. (1998). *GVU's 9th WWW User Survey* [Online]. Available URL: http://www.cc.gatech.edu/gvu/user_surveys/survey-1998-04/

Gibbs, G., & Robinson, D. (1998). Using the Internet for qualitative research—methodological issues. In A. Trapp, N. Hammond, & C. Manning (Eds.), *CiP98 Conference Proceedings* (p. 33). York: CTI Centre for Psychology.

Glick, P. (1985). Orientations toward relationships: Choosing a situation in which to begin a relationship. *Journal of Experimental Social Psychology, 21,* 544–562.

Hewson, C. M. (1998). The scope of the Internet for conducting psychological studies. In A. Trapp, N. Hammond, & C. Manning (Eds.), *CiP98 Conference Proceedings* (p. 40). York: CTI Centre for Psychology.

Hewson, C. M., Laurent, D., & Vogel, C. M. (1996). Proper methodologies for psychological and sociological studies conducted via the Internet. *Behavior Research Methods, Instruments, & Computers, 28,* 186–191.

Hosch, H. M., & Platz, S. J. (1984). Self-monitoring and eyewitness accuracy. *Personality and Social Psychology Bulletin, 10,* 189–292.

Hoyle, R. H., & Lennox, R. D. (1991). Latent structure of self-monitoring. *Multivariate Behavior Research, 26,* 511–540.

Kiesler, S., & Sproull, L. S. (1986). Response effects in the electronic survey. *Public Opinion Quarterly, 50,* 402–413.

Kline, P. (1993). *Personality: The psychometric view.* London: Routledge.

Krantz, J. H. (1995). Linked Gopher and World-Wide Web services for the American Psychological Society and Hanover College Psychology Department. *Behavior Research Methods, Instruments, & Computers, 27,* 193–197.

Krantz, J. H., Ballard, J., & Scher, J. (1997). Comparing the results of laboratory and World-Wide Web samples of the determinants of female attractiveness. *Behavior Research Methods, Instruments, & Computers, 29,* 264–269.

Lennox, R. D. (1988). The problem with self-monitoring: A two-sided scale and a one-sided theory. *Journal of Personality Assessment, 52,* 58–73.

Locke, S. D., & Gilbert, B. O. (1995). Method of psychological assessment, self disclosure, and experiential differences: A study of computer, questionnaire and interview assessment formats. *Journal of Social Behavior and Personality, 10,* 255–263.

Maiuro, R. D., Vitaliano, P. P., & Cahn, T. S. (1987). A brief measure for the assessment of anger and aggression. *Journal of Interpersonal Violence, 2,* 166–178.

Meier, S. (1994). *The chronic crisis in psychological measurement and assessment: A historical survey.* San Diego: Academic Press.

Miller, M. L., & Thayer, J. F. (1989). On the existence of discrete classes in personality: Is self-monitoring the correct joint to carve? *Journal of Personality and Social Psychology, 57,* 143–155.

Oakes, W. (1972). External validity and the use of real people as subjects. *American Psychologist, 27,* 959–962.

Pasveer, K. A., & Ellard, J. H. (1998). The making of a personality inventory: Help from the WWW. *Behavior Research Methods, Instruments, & Computers, 30,* 309–313.

Pines, A. M. (1998). A prospective study of personality and gender differences in romantic attraction. *Personality and Individual Differences, 25,* 147–157.

Reips, U.-D. (1995). *The Web's Experimental Psychology Lab* [Online]. Available URL: `http://www.psych.unizh.ch/genpsy/Ulf/Lab/WebExpPsyLab.html`

Reips, U.-D. (1996). *Experimenting in the World-Wide Web.* Paper presented at the 1996 Society for Computers in Psychology Conference, Chicago, IL.

Reips, U.-D. (1998). *Online answering biases.* Paper presented at the 1998 Society for Computers in Psychology Conference, Dallas, TX.

Schiano, D. J. (1997). Convergent methodologies in cyber-psychology: A case study. *Behavior Research Methods, Instruments, & Computers, 29,* 270–273.

Schmidt, W. C. (1997). World-Wide Web survey research: Benefits, potential problems, and solutions. *Behavior Research Methods, Instruments, & Computers, 29,* 274–279.

Skinner, H. A., & Pakula, A. (1986). Challenge of computers in psychological assessment. *Professional Psychology: Research and Practice, 17,* 44–50.

Smart, R. (1966). Subject selection bias in psychological research. *Canadian Psychologist, 7,* 115–121.

Smith, M. A., & Leigh, B. (1997). Virtual subjects: Using the Internet as an alternative source of subjects and research environment. *Behavior Research Methods, Instruments, & Computers, 29,* 496–505.

Snyder, M. (1987). *Public appearances / private realities.* New York: Freeman.

Snyder, M., Berscheid, E., & Glick, P. (1985). Focusing on the exterior and the interior: Two investigations of the initiation of personal relationships. *Journal of Personality and Social Psychology, 48,* 1427–1439.

Snyder, M., & Gangestad, S. W. (1986). On the nature of self-monitoring: Matters of assessment, matters of validity. *Journal of Personality and Social Psychology, 51,* 125–139.

Stones, A., & Perry, D. (1997). Survey questionnaire data on panic attacks gathered using the World Wide Web. *Depression and Anxiety, 6,* 86–87.

Szabo, A., & Frenkl, R. (1996). Consideration of research on Internet: Guidelines and implications for human movement studies. *Clinical Kinesiology, 50,* 58–65.

CHAPTER 6

Human Sexual Behavior:
A Comparison of College and
Internet Surveys

Robert D. Bailey
Department of Psychology
California State University, Fullerton
Fullerton, California 92834

Winona E. Foote
Department of Psychology
California State University, Fullerton
Fullerton, California 92834

Barbara Throckmorton
Department of Psychology
California State University, Fullerton
Fullerton, California 92834

How can one investigate sexual histories and opinions without introducing demand characteristics imposed by the presence of interviewers, experimenters, or concerns for privacy? What are the differences between those who participate as part of a college class and those who actively volunteer? These issues of response bias and self-selection have long troubled researches of human sexuality.

PREVIOUS STUDIES OF HUMAN SEXUALITY

Many of the largest and most well known studies of human sexuality have come under criticism for not adequately addressing such biases. One large study, the *Psychology Today* survey, comprised 100 items, to which 20,000 readers of the magazine responded (Athanasiou, Shaver, & Tavris, 1970). Another large magazine mail-in survey was the *Redbook* magazine study of over 100,000 married women (Tavris & Sadd, 1976). These two magazine surveys have been criticized on two grounds: First, readers of the magazine are a biased sample; second, those who choose to mail in the survey may differ in some systematic way from those who do not (a self-selection bias).

Psychological Experiments on the Internet

The Hunt (1974) study, another well-known, large-scale study of human sexuality, was commissioned by the Playboy Foundation. The purpose was to replicate Kinsey's original work using procedures intended to produce a representative sample. Although the Hunt study went to greater lengths to secure a representative sample than did the *Psychology Today* and *Redbook* studies, Klassen, Williams, and Levitt (1989) have noted that the Hunt sample was underrepresentative of rural and less educated people.

A more serious attempt to secure a representative sample was made by Kinsey, Pomeroy, and Martin, in their well-known 1948 and 1953 surveys of American sexuality (Kinsey, Pomeroy, & Martin, 1948; Kinsey, Pomeroy, Martin, & Gebhard, 1953). Kinsey et al. went to great lengths to secure a diverse sample of American citizens, while assuring and protecting their anonymity. They recruited from a wide variety of social groups, from housewives and clergymen to pimps and prostitutes. Using face-to-face interviewing techniques and "one hundred percent" sampling (the gathering of comprehensive responses from *all* members of intact social groups) they secured sexual histories from many different social strata in American society. Nevertheless, even the Kinsey et al. studies were unable to convince the skeptics.

As these examples illustrate, true representative samples are difficult, if not impossible, to secure. This chapter will explore an alternative respondent pool, namely, that of Internet users. Although Internet data collection is certainly not the answer to obtaining a representative sample, it does provide an interesting new way to reach a large and diverse sample of individuals.

THE INTERNET ENVIRONMENT

Internet studies are capable of reaching large numbers of individuals at a low cost. In the United States about 36% of households currently own a computer, and 17.3% of these are connected to the Internet, representing nearly 50 million individuals (McConnaughey, Lader, Chin, & Everette, 1998). This figure certainly underestimates the number of Internet users in the United States because it does not take into account those having access from colleges, libraries, other public institutions, and the international community.

The Internet is also an environment where some individuals appear willing to divulge personal information to complete strangers (e.g., in "chat rooms"), and freely post their artistic or intellectual labors for the benefit of others in forms from poetry to computer programs. Those who may not otherwise spend time writing or advertising their experiences and opinions may spend hours meticulously placing facts, advice, art, and other personal information on "home pages." The congregation of like-minded individuals sharing common interests in discussion groups has created what can be described as "virtual communities."

It has been suggested that individuals who feel separated from mainstream culture are increasingly using the Internet to share information and common experiences they may not otherwise disclose in public (McKenna & Bargh, 1998). This suggestion raises an interesting question for researchers of human sexuality. That is, might individuals share private information concerning their sexual behaviors via a computer when they might not reveal this information directly to a researcher under more common survey conditions? Can sexual histories and attitudes be collected reliably via the Internet? The present study suggests that many individuals may indeed be willing to share this information. We will now turn to the issue of how to go about collecting these data and some advantages and disadvantages of doing so via the Internet.

INTERNET DATA COLLECTION

Collection of Internet data shares many advantages with the more traditional method of participant recruitment using the convenient college student "subject pools," where data collection can proceed rapidly and at low cost. On the other hand, Internet data collection possesses some advantages the traditional college subject pools do not, such as geographic diversity, an increased potential for very large samples, and a saving of human resources involved in laboratory testing. Finally, some have suggested the Internet may also create new opportunities for cross-cultural research (Hewson, Laurent, & Vogel, 1996; Smith & Leigh, 1997).

Despite its advantages, effective implementation of Internet research poses a number of new challenges which concern, among other things, response solicitation and data collection techniques (Hewson et al., 1996). Two response solicitation methods seem to predominate, namely, active versus passive advertisement. Active advertisement (or *call for participation*) often uses e-mail solicitations aimed at intact newsgroups whose subscribers share a common interest. Smith and Leigh (1997) provide an extensive discussion of how users of such groups can be solicited via e-mail, and the proper course to take when doing so. Some of these issues include proper etiquette for contacting newsgroups via the moderator, because mass e-mailing is considered rude and is prohibited by many such groups.

Alternatives to active recruitment or advertisement can include indexing a questionnaire under search engines. This method recruits in a "passive" manner. In this case the recruit "finds" the protocol after engaging in a search for a related subject or term. The researcher using this method is taking the passive role in recruitment by throwing out a "broad net" and should remain mindful of self-selection biases.

Once the questionnaire is indexed under a category- or directory-based search engine, search terms can affect the sample the researcher is able to recruit. For instance, a survey (or experiment) indexed under a relatively unfamiliar search term, such as "Bayesian probability," will not generate as many "hits" as would a survey indexed under terms combined with the key word "sex." Using passive recruitment effectively therefore requires very general and widely appealing search term(s) and/or topic.

After solicitation issues are considered, data collection techniques must also be addressed. Two data collection methods predominate: those that rely on server-based HTML forms to automate the data collection process and those that rely on respondent e-mail submissions of data.

Most passively and actively recruited questionnaires or experiments use server-based HTML forms.[1] Often HTML forms are used in conjunction with server-based software packages capable of handling the details of data submission and collection, which frees the respondent from the responsibility of directly returning the data. This method provides an advantage to both the researcher and the respondent in that data are written anonymously and immediately upon submittal to the local file server.

Alternatively, the respondents can manually return data via e-mail, or the respondent's e-mail system can be stimulated to respond through special HTML form tags.[2] E-mail is the least expensive and technically uncomplicated of the two methods, but it provides the least degree of anonymity for the participant's responses and presents additional data analysis challenges for the researcher. For example, data submitted via e-mail can be difficult to format for analysis, while server-based HTML form software automates the data formatting process for easier importation into a variety of spreadsheets and statistical programs. Finally, if sensitive information is collected a respondent may be unwilling to submit data via e-mail or even to finish the protocol in the absence of some extra incentive.

Given the sensitive nature of our questionnaire and the relatively nonspecific and popular search terms needed to find it, we chose a passive server-based method of data collection. Using HTML *forms* on a local server allowed the participant's responses to remain anonymous and allowed for data collection and consolidation to remain under our control.

---

[1] Experiments could be contained in a downloadable program indexed as an ftp address, but this is not common with questionnaires.

[2] This technique is useful in cases when a server under direct control of the researcher is not available; however, it requires the respondent's browser to be configured as the respondents primary e-mail device.

THE CURRENT STUDY

The present research began in 1995 at California State University, Fullerton (CSUF), under the leadership of Barbara Throckmorton. The original purpose of the study was to assess the sexual knowledge, attitudes, and behaviors of undergraduates. A battery of questionnaires was combined into a printed survey of over 400 variables assessing aspects of human sexuality. After several hundred students had been tested in college classrooms using paper-and-pencil methods, it was decided to post the survey on the Internet. The questionnaire was converted to HTML and posted to the CSUF Web server in mid-1995 (URL `http:// psych. fullerton.edu/ throck`).

At the time, Internet data collection on this scale had not yet been attempted in our department, so we were uncertain of what to expect. Following an initial 3-month period of server-based data collection, we were excited to discover that nearly 1000 individuals had submitted responses, though some were incomplete. Over time, the momentum and popularity of the Web site rose and, by early 1999, we had collected more than 10,000 sets of data. After screening the data (described in the Method section) we were left with 7217 analyzable sets.

This chapter will review some of our results. The responses of college students and Internet participants will be compared. We will also compare our results (where possible) to those of other large-scale studies of human sexuality, such as the Kinsey Institute's original studies (Kinsey et al., 1948, 1953; Klassen et al., 1989; Reinisch & Beasley, 1990), the *Redbook* study (Tavris & Sadd, 1976), and the *Psychology Today* study (Athanasiou, et al., 1970). Finally, issues and challenges we encountered in our data will be discussed as they may apply to other researchers considering Internet research, including a discussion of the demographic characteristics of our Internet respondents.

METHOD

PARTICIPANTS

College Participants

A total of 597 college students were tested in college classrooms. Of these, 195 records were excluded because of incomplete or invalid data, leaving 402 participants. Twenty percent of this group was recruited from an upper-division human sexuality class at CSUF and the remaining portion was recruited from lower-division critical thinking classes at a local community college. Of this sample, 156 were male and 246 were female. The mean age was 23 and 9% were married. Ninety-five percent described themselves as heterosexual, 2% bisexual, and 2% homosexual. Thirty percent were Hispanic, 28% Caucasian, 24% Asian, 7% African American, 4% Middle Eastern, and 3% Pacific Islanders.

Internet Participants

The majority of Internet respondents discovered the survey by means of a search engine link or by engaging in a search using the search terms "sex," "survey," or some combination of the two. In at least one case a respondent found the survey through a link placed at a Web site dealing with domestic abuse. To help clarify how Internet respondents were finding the survey, a question was appended to the original survey which asked respondents to indicate if they found the survey through the University home page (1.7%), a search engine (84.4%), a friend (3.1%), a human sexuality class (0.7%), non-search-engine-related link (4.7%), or "other" (5.3%). In the small number of cases where respondents did specify "other," they indicated they learned of the survey from an individual's home page or e-mail address.

After excluding cases in which gender and age were not given, a total of 7217 respondents (mean age = 26) were included for analysis from the Internet. There were 3860 men and 3357 women. Out of this group, 2998 subjects submitted at least partial information on all five sections of the questionnaire. Thirteen percent of the participants were married, 82% described themselves as heterosexual, 12% as bisexual, and 5% as homosexual. Eighty-four percent were Caucasian, 4% African American, 4% Asian, 0.8% Middle Eastern, 0.3% Pacific Islanders, 4% Hispanic, and 4% "other."

Based on a comparison between counter "hits" to the Web site and the actual data submitted, it was estimated that approximately 10–12% of those who encountered the survey actually participated by giving responses (using a counter which did not increment on reloads). A question about geographic location was added later to the survey. Responses (1148) to this question indicated that about 12% of participants were located outside the United States.

MATERIALS

Questionnaire

Only paper-and-pencil materials were used for the college student sample. The questionnaire consisted of 416 items.

Prior to responding, participants first read a consent page informing them of the nature of the questionnaire, assuring them that their responses

were confidential and anonymous, and that they could terminate their participation at any time. Participants were informed they needed to be at least 18
years of age to participate. To assure anonymity in the college sample, the
consent form was separated from the survey and placed in a separate box for
collection in accordance with our university's Institutional Review Board's
(IRB) standards. Because Internet respondents could not sign the consent, they
clicked a link indicating their acknowledgment of it. If Internet respondents
were under 18 years of age or did not agree to the conditions of the informed
consent, they were provided with an alternative link which delivered them
back to the Psychology department's Web page.

The survey began with several demographic items, followed by more
sensitive questions regarding sexual behaviors and opinions. Demographic
items queried participants about their age, gender, residence, birthplace,
religious and political affiliations, income, and marital status. These items were
followed by a series of questions regarding behaviors, attitudes, sexual orientation, frequency of sexual intercourse, HIV/AIDS, and questions regarding
attitudes toward the behaviors of others. Within this body of questions were
scales that assessed attitudes toward homosexuals, sexual self-esteem, sexual
knowledge, loneliness, and a social desirability indicator. These scales are
briefly described here:

1. *Index of Homophobia (IHP) scale (Hudson & Ricketts, 1980).* This 25-item
scale consists of hypothetical questions assaying an individual's level of comfort
in the social and physical proximity of homosexuals. Items are responded to on
a 5-point scale from "strongly agree" to "strongly disagree." An example
question would be

I would be upset if I learned that my brother or sister was a homosexual.

Higher scores on this inventory indicate greater degrees of discomfort around
homosexuals. Reported scores are grouped according to Hudson and Ricketts
(1980) along the 25th, 50th, and 75th percentiles into "highly homophobic."
"moderately homophobic," "moderately nonhomophobic," and "highly nonhomophobic" categories.

2. *Sexual Self-Esteem (Beck, 1988).* This scale is a 19-item checklist of
statements requesting that the respondent indicate whether they have experienced the following thoughts while engaged in or thinking about sex. A
typical item would be

I know I'm not pleasing you.

This scale is supposed to differentiate between those who have feelings of
sexual inadequacy and those who do not. Scores were divided at the 33rd and

66th percentiles into the groups "low," "average," and "high" sexual self-esteem.

3. *Kinsey Institute / Roper Organization National Sex Knowledge Test (Reinisch & Beasley, 1990).* This 18-item scale of sexual knowledge consists of an array of multiple choice questions assessing accurate knowledge of extramarital intercourse, HIV, birth control, and other aspects of sexual behavior, as well as popular myths surrounding such issues. Reinisch & Beasley (1990) categorized the scores along the break points of 1–9, 10–11, 12–13, 14–15, and 16–18 points into the letter grades "F" to "A," respectively. A 1989 survey by the Kinsey Institute found that 55% of American adults failed the test. Moreover, approximately 27% received D's, 14% received C's, 4% B's, and less than 1% received A's (Reinisch & Beasley, 1990). An example item would be

A woman or teenage girl can get pregnant during her menstrual flow

(her period).

4. *UCLA Loneliness Scale (Rathus & Nevid, 1992).* This scale consisted of a 10-item version of a test assessing degrees of loneliness. Responses were given on a 4-point scale from "never" (1) to "often" (4). For example,

How often do you feel you have nobody to talk to?

Scores are grouped into three categories: "very lonely," "average loneliness," and "low loneliness." Rathus and Nevid (1992) suggest that individuals scoring in the very lonely category may be at risk of socioemotional adjustment difficulties.

5. *Social-Desirability Scale (Crowne & Marlowe, 1960).* A 26-item (reduced) version of this questionnaire was included to assess the tendency of an individual to color responses in a socially desirable direction. According to Crowne and Marlowe (1960), higher scores indicate a greater degree of concern over the social appropriateness of responses, while lower scores indicate more candor and forthrightness. A typical item would be:

I am sometimes irritated by people who ask favors of me.

Scores on this test were broken at the 16th and 84th percentiles into 'high social desirability', 'average social desirability', and 'low social desirability'.

Internet

A Microsoft NT server with the Internet forms software package PolyForm (see www.oreilly.de/catalog/polyform) was used to deliver the Internet protocol. Five consecutive HTML pages (forms) containing up to 99 questions each were posted to http://psych.fullerton.edu/throck. PolyForm combined with JavaScript embedded in the HTML pages handled the details of writing a single data file to the university server. The data file was written in ASCII (∗.csv) format and contained five records for each subject. After reaching the end of a section, respondents continued to the next by clicking a "Submit" button at the bottom of the form. The "Submit" button created a timestamp for each record in the data. An estimate of the time spent per section was computed from differences between consecutive timestamps. The questionnaire's URL was submitted and indexed in the Yahoo search engine's directory (http://dir.yahoo.com/Society_and_Culture/Sexuality/Surveys/). This link could be reached indirectly by typing "survey" as a general search term, or more directly by entering any combination of the words "sex" and "survey" as search terms.

   Some challenges were encountered upon our initial attempts to analyze the data. For example, PolyForm was set to write a comma-delimited file to our server. Each record of this file contained the entire response set of the individual participant. When data were imported into statistical software it was discovered that some open-ended responses (stored as strings) contained commas, which created extra variable columns. Needless to say, this was very disruptive of initial attempts to analyze the data, so several public domain JavaScript form-validation functions were modified from the archive at Netscape (http://www.netscape.com) in an attempt to deal with this problem. These functions removed unwanted characters (e.g., commas) and were triggered by the "OnChange" event of their associated input boxes.

   Another challenge was that of multiple submissions on the part of respondents. As a precaution against multiple submissions we used PolyForm to append the IP of each respondent to each record in the data file. A simple sort by this number revealed a very small number of multiple submissions, which were filtered from the data. As mentioned by Smith and Leigh (1997), it is possible for multiple submissions to come from a single institutional entity (e.g., two students in a computer laboratory). Among our Internet responses, however, these instances appeared to be rare. Additionally, many online service providers use dynamic IP assignment whereby an individual might disconnect from the service and subsequently return to the survey with a new IP number. Given the large sample size and the rarity of these cases, it is unlikely that this factor significantly influenced or changed results. We hope the simple measures described next helped reduce the likelihood of bookmarking a spot within the survey, and thus made it more difficult to return at a later time.

   In an effort to prevent blatant misbehavior by respondents (i.e., automated and repeated multiple submissions), the script was restricted to process data only from our form on the server. In addition, a JavaScript function instantiated a new browser window devoid of viewing and navigation windows. The instantiated browser helped hide potential distractions normally present within the default browser window (e.g., titlebars and navigation buttons) and hid the actual URL of the survey, which would make difficult any tendency to navigate backward through the protocol.

PROCEDURE

College Respondents

Participants were told that a professor was conducting a survey on human sexual behaviors and attitudes. They were asked as a group to voluntarily participate in the survey as part of a class activity. Respondents were seated next to one another within the classroom and given the survey at the beginning of the class period. Participants took between 35 and 50 minutes to complete the survey, during which time talking was prohibited.

After participants read and signed the consent form cover page, they proceeded to complete the questionnaire. Following completion, participants were thanked for their time and provided with telephone numbers for AIDS/STD clinics and domestic abuse hotlines. Respondents were instructed to tear off the cover page with their signature and place it and their survey responses in *separate* boxes. No information linked the signed consent with the survey responses. Responses were submitted simultaneously at the end of the session and participants were assured of their anonymity.

Internet

After indicating their acceptance of the informed consent (by clicking a button on the form), participants were allowed to proceed to the survey. Following completion, participants were thanked for their time and provided with some preliminary demographic results, in addition to links to AIDS/STD clinics and domestic abuse hotline numbers.

RESULTS

Sample N's of both college and Internet respondents may vary from the total given previously due to missing values. For example, if an item was missing from a computed scale the scale value was not calculated for that participant. Items tagged with the symbol "†" differed significantly between college and Internet respondents at the $p < .05$ level using χ^2 tests. Because of the large sample sizes, small differences can be significant.

DEMOGRAPHIC CHARACTERISTICS

Table 1a shows the gender breakdown for the Internet, college, and other large sex surveys. The Internet sample, Klassen et al. (1989), Athanasiou et al. (1970), and Reinisch & Beasley (1990) had nearly equal proportions of males and females. The college sample has relatively more females; Tavris and Sadd (1976) only sampled married females.

Table 1b presents the age breakdown for all participants. The median ages of male and female Internet respondents were 28 and 24, respectively. The median and mean age for both sexes in the college sample was 23.

The majority of both Internet and college student respondents reported having at least "some college education" (Table 1c). A higher percentage of college graduates was found among Internet participants than among college students.

Nearly 85% of the Internet respondents were Caucasian, showing greater homogeneity of ethnicity compared to the college participants (Table 1d). Conversely, the ethnic breakdown of the college student sample was much more heterogeneous than the U.S. population, but was representative of the colleges in which the samples were recruited.

The median household income distributions (Table 1e) for male and female college students were approximately equal, while the income distributions for male and female Internet respondents differed in the lowest and highest income categories. χ^2 tests[†] (disregarding sex) revealed significant income differences between the college and Internet samples.

According to 1997 U.S. Census (Data) the median household income (for all households) was $37,005. Approximately 41% of male and 54% of female Internet respondents fell below the median household income. For the college students, approximately 57% of males and 62% of females fell below the median U.S. household income. After considering age, however, it was found that the Internet and college participants were actually a bit wealthier, given

Table 1a

Sex by Participant Group

	Internet	College	Klassen et al. (1989)	Tavris & Sadd (1976)	Athanasiou et al. (1970)	Reinisch & Beasley (1990)
Male	53.5%	38.8%	48.5%	0.0%	47%	48%
Female	46.5%	61.1%	51.5%	100%	53%	52%
Sample N	7217	402	3018	2278	20,000	1974

Table 1b

Age Breakdown for Participant Group

Age	Internet	College	Klassen et al. (1989)[a]	Athanasiou et al. (1970)	Tavris & Sadd (1976)[b]	Reinisch & Beasley (1990)[c]
Under 20	24.0%	29.4%	~1.3%	11%	2.6%	—
20–24	33.0%	48.5%	11.0%	32%	23.4%	58%
25–34	27.6%	15.7%	23.1%	34%	> 19.8%	—
35–44	9.9%	4.5%	19.4%	14%	< 9.1%	—
45–54	4.0%	1.7%	17.9%	6%	< 13.0%	—
55 and over	1.5%	0.2%	27.3%	3%	< 13.0%	42%
Sample N	7217	402	3015	20,000	2278	1974

[a] Percentage categories are collapsed from original studies for visual comparison in this table.
[b] Percentage categories are collapsed from original studies for visual comparison in this table.
[c] Percentage categories are collapsed from original studies for visual comparison in this table. Age breakdown is approximated with 23% < 29 years old, and remaining 42% 55 years and older.

that the 1997 household income (for all households) was $22,583 for those under the age of 24, and $38,174 for those between the ages of 25 and 34.

Table 1f presents the geographic breakdown of current residence for Internet respondents across four geographic areas of the United States along with percentages found in other studies. All values have been rounded and coded into our classification scheme of four regions. "East" applies to all Atlantic and mid-Atlantic states, "South" is all southern states east of Texas, "Midwest" extends from mid-Atlantic states west to the Rocky Mountains, and "West" includes the Rocky Mountain states and Texas to the Pacific.

Table 1c

Education by Participant Group

Education	Internet	College	Tavris & Sadd (1976)	Athanasiou et al. (1970)	Klassen et al. (1989)	Reinisch & Beasley (1990)
1–8 years	0.2%	—	1.2%	2%	21.8%	—
Some high school	3.4%	—	—	—	19.9%	21%
High school grad	16.6%	17.3%	37.4%	9%	30.9%	34%
Some college	48.8%	77.9%	37.7%	37%	16.6%	—
College grad	22.4%	3.8%	6.9%	18%	6.5%	45%
Graduate work +	8.5%	0.3%	3.6%	34%	4.1%	—
Total N	7053	399	2278	20,000	3013	1974

Table 1d

Ethnicity by Participant Group

Ethnic Group	Internet	College	Reinisch & Beasley (1990)
Asian	3.7%	24.2%	N/A
African	3.9%	6.6%	11%
Caucasian	83.5%	27.6%	80%
Middle Eastern	0.8%	4.1%	N/A
Pacific Islander	0.3%	2.8%	N/A
Hispanic	3.5%	29.8%	6%
Other	4.4%	4.8%	1%
Sample N	7147	392	1974

Table 1g indicates that the majority of college student and Internet respondents fell into the "single" category. A greater proportion of Internet respondents reported being married, separated, divorced, or widowed.

Percentages in Table 1h show a greater proportion of self-described homosexual and bisexual respondents among Internet participants.

Percentages of self-described liberal versus conservative respondents were similar for the Internet and college participants (Table 1i). The *Redbook* sample (Tavris & Sadd, 1976) of married women showed a similar pattern of responses. By far, the Athanasiou et al. (1970) survey had the greatest degree of liberal views.

Tables 2a and 2b show the breakdown between samples for each sex on the loneliness, social desirability, and sexual self-esteem scales. χ^2 tests

Table 1e

Overall Household Income by Sex and Participant Group

Income	Internet		College	
	Males	Females	Males	Females
$0–10,999	9.8%	17.9%	20.4%	24.5%
$11,000–15,999	6.2%	8.3%	11.2%	13.9%
$16,000–20,999	6.6%	8.1%	3.9%	8.9%
$21,000–35,999	19.2%	19.3%	21.7%	14.3%
$36,000–50,999	20.0%	16.7%	13.8%	11.0%
$51,000–70,999	16.7%	14.2%	11.8%	10.5%
$71,000–99,999	10.9%	7.5%	7.2%	7.2%
$100,000 >	10.6%	7.9%	9.9%	9.7%
Sample N	3748	3247	152	237

Table 1f

U.S. Geographic Region (Internet Participants) by Other Large Studies

U.S. Region	Internet	Tavris & Sadd (1976)[a]	Athanasiou et al. (1970)	Klassen et al. (1989)[b]	Reinisch & Beasley (1990)
West	30%	19%	34%	26%	19%
East	19%	28%	32%	38%	22%
South	18%	24%	8%	19%	33%
Midwest	33%	25%	26%	19%	26%
Sample N	4946	2278	20,000	2940	1974

[a] Tavris & Sadd (1976) Redbook 1974 study results were randomly sampled from within their 100,000 mail-in responses.
[b] Klassen et al. (1989) is the only study closely approximating the 1970 Census.

Table 1g

Relationship Status by Participant Group

	Internet	College	Klassen et al. (1989)	Athanasiou et al. (1970)	Tavris & Sadd (1976)	Reinisch & Beasley (1990)
Single	63.6%	89.3%	6.5%	45.0%	0.0%	20%
Married	13.1%	9.0%	77.6%	42.0%	100.0%	60%
Widowed, separated, or divorced	23.2%	1.6%	4.1%	13.0%	0.0%	20%
Sample N	3287	365	3018	20,000	2278	1974

Table 1h

Reported Sexual Orientation by Sex and Participant Group

	Internet		College	
	Male	Female	Male	Female
Heterosexual	83.2%	83.1%	96.1%	95.9%
Bisexual	10.5%	13.3%	0.6%	2.9%
Homosexual	6.4%	3.5%	3.2%	1.2%
Sample N	3784	3297	154	245

Table 1i

Liberal versus Conservative Views

	Internet	College	Athanasiou et al. (1970)	Tavris & Sadd (1976)	Reinisch & Beasley (1990)[a]
Very liberal	11.1%	6.9%	28%	4%	N/A
Liberal	27.7%	26.4%	39%	23%	23%
Moderate	42.9%	50.0%	21%	57%	32%
Conservative	15.6%	14.4%	10%	15%	42%
Very conservative	2.7%	2.3%	2%	2%	N/A
Sample N	6832	390	20,000	2278	1974

[a] "Very liberal" and "very conservative" categories were not used.

Table 2a

Computable Scales by Participant Group for Males

	Internet				College			
	Score range				Score range			
	Low	Avg.	High	Count	Low	Avg.	High	Count
UCLA Loneliness	35.5%	34.3%	30.2%	1659	32.6%	43.9%	23.5%	132
Social Desirability	12.7%	75.2%	12.1%	621	32.8%	41.6%	25.6%	125
Sexual Self-Esteem	38.5%	32.5%	29.0%	1592	22.0%	23.5%	54.5%	132

Table 2b

Computable Scales by Participant Group for Females

	Internet				College			
	Score range				Score range			
	Low	Avg.	High	Count	Low	Avg.	High	Count
UCLA Loneliness	32.9%	36.3%	30.8%	1490	40.3%	36.8%	22.9%	231
Social Desirability	18.0%	70.0%	12.0%	520	39.0%	36.0%	25.0%	217
Sexual Self-Esteem	51.6%	29.2%	19.2%	1434	28.7%	26.5%	44.8%	223

Table 2c

Index of Homophobia Scale (IHP)

	Internet		College	
	Male	Female	Male	Female
Highly nonhomophobic	28.9%	46.5%	8.6%	19.3%
Moderately nonhomophobic	36.4%	33.9%	25.7%	42.4%
Moderately homophobic	25.6%	15.7%	46.4%	30.3%
Highly homophobic	9.1%	3.9%	19.3%	8.3%
Sample N	3325	3002	140	218

showed Internet respondents tended to be lonelier than college students,[†] while college females tended to be slightly less lonely than college males.

The distribution of social desirability scores was similar for males and females, but differences emerged between college and Internet participants. In regard to proportions, twice as many college students fell into both high and low categories for this scale, as compared to Internet respondents. The mean raw score of Internet participants was 13.81 with a 95% confidence interval range of 0.26; the mean for college students was 13.09 with a 95% confidence interval range of 0.96.[3]

Disregarding sex, Internet participants had a greater proportion of individuals in the lowest self-esteem category as compared to college students.[†] A greater proportion of males were classified as having high sexual self-esteem scores.

The breakdown of IHP score differences between the two groups and between males and females is shown in Table 2c. Females were less homophobic than males in both samples, while overall the Internet participants were significantly less homophobic than the college students.[†]

Table 2d lists the "grade breakdowns" of sexual knowledge scores for Internet and college samples. The Internet participants showed greater sexual knowledge than the college students[†] and far more than the Kinsey–Roper findings (Reinisch & Beasley, 1990). Recall that 90% or better is required for an "A."

BEHAVIORS

As shown in Table 3a, responses of Internet males to the first question were consistent with the findings of Kinsey et al. (1948), who found that nearly 46% of males report engaging in same-sex homosexual play by adolescence.

---

[3] Means are based upon a 26-item version of the social desirability scale.

Table 2d
Kinsey Knowledge Scale (Reinisch & Beasley, 1990); Grade by Respondent Group

Grade	Internet	College	Reinisch & Beasley (1990)
A	11.2%	5.6%	< 1%
B	22.0%	15.1%	4%
C	33.4%	28.9%	14%
D	22.7%	24.9%	27%
F	10.7%	25.6%	55%
Sample N	3010	305	1711

Strikingly, rates for female respondents were more than 15% higher for the Internet sample and about 8% lower in the college sample in comparison to the Kinsey et al. (1953) findings.

Internet and colleges samples responded similarly to the second question; the majority of these sexual encounters were premarital. Response frequencies for the Internet participants on the third question were higher than those found by Kinsey et al (1948, 1953). The fourth question shows that high proportions of both samples reported having had an HIV test, yet none of the college students and only 0.2% of Internet participants reported being HIV positive. It may be reasonable to assume that many do not know their HIV status and simply left the question blank.

Results for the average age of one's first sexual experience (Table 3b, Item 1) corresponded with the findings reported by Reinisch and Beasley

Table 3a
Percentages of Those Responding "Yes"

Question[a]	Internet			College		
	Male	Female	Count	Male	Female	Count
(1)	37.7%	67.9%	3688	11.0%	12.1%	385
(2)	79.3%	84.5%	3795	77.8%	83.6%	382
(3)	93.4%	96.1%	3794	77.1%	56.4%	380
(4)	45.0%	49.0%	1557	37.0%	37.9%	140
(5)	0.2%	0.1%	2644	0.0%	0.0%	0

[a] (1) Have you ever experienced *same* sex genital stimulation? (2) Have you ever experienced genital stimulation with someone of the *opposite* sex? (3) Have you ever engaged in self-stimulation (masturbation)? (4) Have you ever been tested for HIV? (5) Are you HIV positive? (If you don't know, leave blank)

Table 3b

Mean Age of First Sexual Experience and Monthly Frequency of Masturbation

Item[a]	Internet				College			
	Male	Female	Count	SD	Male	Female	Count	SD
(1)	17.5	16.7	7217	2.9	17.0	16.8	402	2.4
(2)	17.0	10.0	7217	22.0	11.0	4.0	402	8.0

[a] (1) Average age for first sexual experience. (2) Mean reported frequency of masturbation per month.

(1990), which indicate that the typical individual has the first sexual contact around the age of 17. Males reported masturbating nearly twice as often as females (Item 2), and Internet participants reported masturbating at twice the frequency of college students. Internet males fell within the range reported by Kinsey et al. (1948) for their age group on this item, and females had slightly lower frequencies than those reported by Kinsey et al. (1953).

ATTITUDES

Table 4a shows that Internet respondents reported being less likely than college students to share their personal sexual experiences with others.[†]

PREMARITAL INTERCOURSE

From Table 4b a double standard is clearly evident in that females and males within the college and Klassen et al. (1989) groups were less accepting of

Table 4a

Response to "I Am Open with Others Regarding My Personal Sexual Experiences"

	Internet		College	
	Male	Female	Male	Female
Almost always	9.6%	5.7%	13.4%	15.4%
Often	13.4%	9.9%	23.9%	19.3%
Sometimes	27.2%	26.2%	36.6%	36.0%
Seldom	32.8%	37.4%	14.9%	14.9%
Almost never	17.1%	20.7%	11.2%	14.5%
Sample N	1569	1346	134	228

Table 4b

Percentage Responding with Acceptance to Each Premarital Sex Situation

	Internet		College		Klassen et al. (1989)[a]	
	Male	Female	Male	Female	Male	Female
Always acceptable w/o love or affection for male	58.8%	52.9%	43.3%	37.1%	22.9%	10.8%
Always acceptable w/o love or affection for female	58.1%	49.6%	30.9%	23.0%	20.7%	7.1%
Sample N	850	684	81	99	~1450	~1546

[a] Totals for male and female categories under Klassen et al. (1989) vary by less ±5 due to these questions being collapsed from larger categories.

females engaging in premarital sex without love than for males engaging in this same behavior. A more equal distribution between the sexes was observed among the Internet participants, who exhibited less of a double standard. The Internet sample was also more accepting than college students, who were more accepting than those in Klassen et al. (1989).

EXTRAMARITAL INTERCOURSE

Table 4c shows that both Internet and college participants had more liberal attitudes toward extramarital sex than the mostly married subjects of Klassen et al. (1989). Overall, males tended to have more tolerant attitudes toward extramarital sex than did females. In comparison to Klassen et al.

Table 4c

Attitudes toward Extramarital Intercourse

	Internet		College		Klassen et al. (1989)[a]	
	Male	Female	Male	Female	Male	Female
Unacceptable	53.7%	64.3%	68.6%	76.4%	83.1%	90.1%
Neutral	24.0%	18.5%	16.8%	11.4%	N/A	N/A
Acceptable	17.8%	15.1%	14.5%	12.3%	16.5%	9.6%
Sample N	1596	1375	137	237	1463	1553

[a] Klassen et al. (1989) used "don't know" instead of a "neutral" category (frequencies were 0.5% and 0.3% for males and females, respectively). This study worded the question in terms of "unacceptable/acceptable" whereas Klassen et al. used "wrong/not wrong" in their actual wording.

(1989), college and Internet respondents of both sexes were far more accepting of this behavior.

DISCUSSION

The purpose of our investigation has been to compare a traditional sample of convenience (college students) with the Internet sample and with previous studies. Although the Internet and college participants differed in some respects, they also shared some similarities. The following sections review the results of these comparisons under three primary categories: demographics, behaviors, and attitudes. We feel the best measures for comparison between the two respondent groups are from the classic Kinsey reports. Although these data were collected more than 40 years ago, they remain today the best available.

DEMOGRAPHIC DIFFERENCES

Internet participants tended to be older, more liberal, and ethnically less diverse than the college group. When compared to the U.S. population (based on 1997 Census Bureau estimates), Internet participants were younger, had higher incomes for their age group, and were less ethnically diverse. In comparison to the Klassen et al. (1989) sample, both the Internet and college respondents were younger. We, like Smith and Leigh (1997), as well as Sell (1997), found a slightly greater proportion of males among our Internet respondents, although males and females were more equally represented than they were among our group of college students.

Although the original survey did ask participants about their country of origin, it did not query them about the location they were logging in from. When we added the item about location, we estimated that about 12% of the responses originated outside the United States. Out of the 37 different countries represented in this group, the highest proportion came from Canada and other Western countries. No particular effort was made to recruit foreign respondents, but a link to the AltaVista language translation engine was given at the beginning of the survey.

Because approximately 85% of the Internet respondents were within the United States, a further comparison of demographic characteristics from the latest U.S. census data seemed relevant. According to the U.S. Census (1997) and the National Telecommunications and Information Administration (NTIA; Report 1998), American households with incomes between $5,000 and $10,000 account for the lowest percentage of computer owners (7.9%), and the online access rate within this group is only 2.3%. In contrast, people earning more than $75,000 in urban areas have the highest computer ownership (76%) with 50.3% of this group having Internet access (McConnaughey et al., 1998). In comparison to census population estimates, the Internet respondents had a greater representation in the lower income categories. However, when the age of these respondents was taken into account it became clear that they actually had higher incomes than other U.S. residents of their age. For example, approximately 64% of Internet respondents between 18 and 23 years of age were above the median household income for their age group. Overall, Internet participants had higher incomes than college students (holding age constant).

In terms of ethnicity, the college sample was overrepresentative of Hispanics, Asians, and women in comparison to U.S. Census projections for the year 2000. According to the Census Bureau, by July 2000 the U.S. population will be approximately 12% African American, 11% Hispanic, 4% Asian or Pacific Islander, and 72% Caucasian. African Americans were underrepresented among both college and Internet respondents. Among the Internet participants the proportion of Asians was close to population estimates, but Hispanics were underrepresented. Caucasians were slightly overrepresented on the Internet, and under-represented in our college sample. Finally, the underrepresentation of African Americans and Hispanics within the Internet responses is consistent with estimates that show Whites are twice as likely as Blacks or Hispanics to own a computer (McConnaughey et al., 1998). In conclusion, individuals from both the college and Internet groups appear to be similar in many ways to the large-scale popular magazine surveys of the past, in that they are underrepresentative of certain demographic groups (see Klassen et al., 1989; Smith 1991).

Despite the lack of ethnic diversity among our Internet respondents, we did have good representation from each major geographic region in the United States. Interestingly, our sample had a large number of Midwestern respondents during a particularly harsh winter season. It may be that a relationship exists between seasonal variations of weather and recreational computer use. This is an intriguing proposition that future research should investigate.

Both of our samples had large numbers of unmarried people. Ninety percent of college students and 63% of Internet participants were not married. In comparison to other samples, the Athanasiou et al. (1970) survey had the most equal representation of married and single individuals, while Klassen et al. (1989) overrepresented married individuals, and the Tavris and Sadd (1976) sample contained only married women.

One of the most striking differences between our two sets of respondents was the larger proportion of self-reported homosexual and bisexual participants from the Internet. As speculated earlier, it may be that opinions and behavioral histories, especially those that are sensitive in nature, can be shared more freely on the Internet, where there is relative privacy, anonymity, and acceptance. Similarly, and as McKenna and Bargh (1998) have suggested, socially marginalized people experience fewer negative consequences within the Internet environment, where they can remain anonymous or seek out others with similar experiences. We found that older homosexual and bisexual participants spent on average more time per survey section than did heterosexuals. In this case the amount of time spent on each section was unrelated to social desirability scores, ethnicity, or income level and perhaps suggests a greater interest or comfort with the subject matter. The lack of relationship between the time spent on each section and other variables within this group is interesting, and future research should investigate what factors, if any, are related to time.

Finally, we suspect that the lower frequency of self-described homosexual and bisexual activity among college students may represent an unwillingness to divulge sexual orientation in a classroom test environment (again, underscoring the role of demand characteristics). This lower frequency may also have reflected a general lack of stable sexual attitudes and preferences among the comparatively younger college students.

The frequency distributions of liberal and conservative views were similar for the two groups of respondents, both of which had larger representations in the "liberal" to "moderate" categories. On the other hand, magazine surveys, such as that of *Psychology Today* (Athanasiou et al., 1970), showed an even stronger liberal bias, with 67% falling into the "liberal" to "very liberal" categories. The liberal and conservative views of our two respondent groups were more similar to the results of the *Redbook* magazine's survey of married women (Tavris & Sadd, 1976). Finally, in Klassen et al.'s (1989) stratified sample of U.S. citizens, although not queried directly with a specific question, these respondents were conservative if judged by other indicators. In general, however, meaningful comparisons on this item are difficult because the meaning of "liberal" or "conservative" varies over time and over generations.

In conclusion, although our results do not refute U.S. Census statistics suggesting certain groups of people are still limited in their ability to access the World Wide Web, we do not believe this prevents the Internet from serving as a valuable medium for research (see also Hewson, et al., 1996). Rather, the Internet presents new possibilities for cross-cultural research, opening the door to convenient recruitment of participants from around the world, and in ways not possible before. Nevertheless, the observed demographic characteristics of our Internet respondents underscore the importance of global and regional differences in Socio Economic Status, race, and education, which of course must be taken into account when conducting research potentially affected by these factors. Moreover, some have suggested that demographic information collected from the Web can be very unstable regardless of sampling techniques (see Schillewaert, Langerak, & Duhamel, 1998), underscoring that census comparisons may be of limited use for understanding demographic characteristics more detailed than basic computer and online penetration rates.

COMPUTED SCALE DIFFERENCES

A general pattern emerges from the results based on the five computed scales. Although the Reinisch and Beasley (1990) Sexual Knowledge Test has been questioned (Sell, 1997), it is nonetheless useful in serving as an indicator of one's basic understanding of human sexuality. Results from this scale indicated that Internet participants tended to be more knowledgeable about sexuality than the college students and Reinisch & Beasley's (1989) sample. The differences between these groups is not surprising given the greater education, increased age for males, marital status, and overall greater sexual experience among Internet participants compared to college students. Moreover, many Internet respondents undoubtedly came upon the survey while actively seeking out sex-related content. This also underscores a self-selection bias inherent in passive Internet recruitment in that many respondents had a prior interest in the subject of sex in order to find our survey. In fact, some may consider this a case of Internet respondents *recruiting us*, rather then the reverse.

Contrary to our expectations, Internet participants were only slightly lonelier than the college students, yet not lonely enough to affect emotional adjustment according to the Rathus and Nevid Loneliness Scale (Rathus and Nevid, 1992).

Although the mean social desirability scores were slightly higher for Internet participants, the distribution of scores had lower variance than that of college students. Since 86% of Internet responses to these items were missing, meaningful comparisons with college students are difficult, if not impossible. It may be that the greater mean scores for Internet respondents were likely due to a self-selection bias among those higher in this dimension already. In other words, they may have been "socially" concerned or interested enough to answer all the questions.

Despite this source of bias, the distribution (proportion of those within each category) of social desirability scores for Internet participants resembled the expected distribution of scores based upon the findings of Crowne and Marlowe (1960). Finally, differences in recruitment, as well as differences in perceived anonymity under the two survey conditions, surely contributed to differences in the proportional distribution of scores between the two groups of respondents.

One of the most notable differences between Internet and college participants emerged on the Hudson and Ricketts (1980) Index of Homophobia (IHP) scale. Regardless of sex, the average college student in our sample was classified as moderately *homophobic*, while the Internet respondents were classified as moderately *nonhomophobic*. Additionally, we found an increase in IHP scores with age that was dependent upon relationship status. In other words, older married individuals, but not singles, had significantly greater homophobia scores. These findings concur with those of Hudson and Ricketts (1980).

Finally, sexual self-esteem scores (Beck, 1988) were lower among women than men, and among Internet respondents than college students. This is consistent with the large body of research which has shown that females often score lower than males on measures of self-esteem.

Lower self-esteem among Internet respondents provides further support for the proposition that the Internet may serve as a social "sanctuary" for individuals who feel marginalized because of physical appearance, sexual orientation, or sexual inadequacy and dysfunction. These individuals may also be more likely to search for sex-related terms on the Internet. Interestingly, the sexual self-esteem of male and female homosexual Internet respondents did not differ. However, homosexuals had the lowest average sexual self-esteem in comparison to bisexuals, who scored slightly higher, and heterosexuals, who scored the highest.

BEHAVIORS

Overall, behavioral items such as genital stimulation with members of the opposite sex, masturbation experiences, monthly frequency of sexual intercourse, and age of first intercourse did not substantially differ between Internet and college students.[†] Hence, with the exception of *same-sex* genital stimulation and monthly frequency of masturbation, the two groups were similar to each other and to the respondents of past research. For example, Internet and college student self-reported behaviors were similar to the findings of Kinsey et al. (1948, 1953), including the mean age of first intercourse, frequency and incidence of masturbation by gender, and the frequency or incidence of premarital sex. Additionally, more than 79% of respondents in both samples reported having experienced genital stimulation with the members of the opposite sex. Given the age and low incidence of marriage among each set of respondents, most of these sexual and "petting" contacts must be premarital.

Results for monthly frequency of masturbation indicate that college and Internet male participants reported masturbating almost twice as often as females. College respondents of both sexes reported masturbating at about half the frequency of Internet respondents. Kinsey's original work, based on averages from his data, suggests that preadolescent boys masturbate about 2.4 times a week, a number slightly lower than that reported by the older male college students. Kinsey et al. (1948) found that these frequencies decline for males as they age and suggested that they may vary by as much as 300%.

In an effort to further investigate this finding, an examination of social desirability scores showed that social desirability was not correlated with the reported frequency of masturbation in either the college or Internet sample. The high frequencies of masturbation by Internet participants then may have been the result of greater honesty on the part of Internet participants. It may also be that subject–experimenter biases (which can impose demand character-istics and perhaps increase socially desirable responses) are absent on the Internet, or at least less prevalent in comparison to more traditional testing environments.

Finally, findings regarding same-sex genital stimulation indicated that over 36% of males on the Internet reported having had same sex genital stimulation, while over 67% of females reported engaging in this behavior. The percentage for Internet males matches that of Kinsey et al. (1948) for men, yet the incidence for females in this group was strikingly higher than the 20% reported by Kinsey et al. (1953). This response pattern appears independent of sexual orientation, and several exploratory descriptive discriminant analyses with a wide range of predictor variables were unable to give us insight into this unusual result.

ATTITUDES

Beyond behavioral inquiries, participants were asked to respond to several questions regarding attitudes and beliefs about human sexuality. Of particular interest were the responses to the statement: "I am open with others regarding my personal sexual experiences." College participants were twice as likely as Internet participants to report being open, and their response patterns more often resembled those found in previous research. This result is not particularly surprising, given that many participants were surveyed at the beginning of a human sexuality course. Somewhat surprisingly, however, there were no strong correlations between answers to this question and the social desirability scores for either the Internet or college samples.

Attitudes toward premarital intercourse among both the college and Internet respondents were far more liberal than those found by Klassen et al.

(1989), whose sample contained primarily older, married individuals, of a different generation. Overall, comparisons with other large studies are difficult if not impossible because the exact wording of questions differed. However, over 53% of those surveyed by *Psychology Today* (Athanasiou et al., 1970) agreed that premarital sex is "ok" either under any circumstances or for consenting adults and young adults alike. An additional 36% approved of this behavior in the presence of affection, and only 9% responded that it is *not* ok under any circumstances. Participants from the Internet exhibited less evidence of the double standard than did college students. Additionally, sex differences within the Internet group were smaller than those observed among college students.

CONCLUSIONS

In conclusion, although some demographic differences emerged, our college student and Internet respondents did not differ on the majority of the behavior characteristics assessed, and differed only moderately on some of the attitudinal variables. Of course, one should bear in mind that large sample sizes likely influenced significance tests. This suggests that the Internet is at least as good a source for some forms of data collection as the "subject pool" in colleges. Where differences between the groups were observed, they were related to items such as attitudes toward homosexuals, sexual knowledge, and sexual self-esteem (where college students emerged as more homophobic, possessed less knowledge, and had slightly higher sexual self-esteem scores than Internet respondents). Collectively, the differences between college and Internet respondents suggest that those from the Internet represent a more diverse set of individuals in terms of age, sex, attitudes, and the tendency to share behavioral information. With socially "sensitive" topics such as sex, Internet participants may be willing to disclose information that might not otherwise be readily secured from a college student tested in a classroom.

As stated previously, it is important to bear in mind that the Internet respondents may represent individuals who were seeking sex-related material. One should recognize the great individual variability in the purposes and motivations for being online and should take caution in treating the Internet as a single population. This fact underscores the need for future research exploring the wide variety of participants available through this new medium. Specifically, various methods of recruitment (see Buchanan, chap. 5, this volume; Birnbaum, chap. 1, this volume), from passive recruitment via search engines to active recruitment from newsgroups and other member-oriented areas, should be further examined. More must also be known about how calls for participation, the subject matter, the testing environment, and other factors combine to influence a respondent's willingness to participate.

Internet data collection is inexpensive and progresses quickly and efficiently, and the environment is international, which can open new doors in social research. It allows researchers to survey individuals from social groups that are both geographically remote and previously difficult to contact. The Internet's growing potential demands that it be studied to determine the characteristics of its users and the viability of this new approach to social science research.

ACKNOWLEDGMENTS

The authors thank Jennifer Blum, John DeLosReyes, Patrick Irwin, and all undergraduates involved on this project for their assistance.

REFERENCES

Athanasiou, R., Shaver, P., & Tavris, C. (1970). Sex: Once again a function of religion. *Psychology Today, 4,* 39–52.

Beck, A. (1988). *Love is never enough.* New York: Harper & Row.

Crowne, D. P., & Marlowe, D. A. (1960). A new scale of social desirability independent of pathology. *Journal of Consulting Psychology, 24,* 351.

Hewson, C. M., Laurent, D., & Vogel, C. M. (1996). Proper methodologies for psychological and sociological studies conducted via the Internet. *Behavior Research Methods, Instruments, & Computers, 28*(2), 186–191.

Hudson, W. W., & Ricketts, W. A. (1980). A strategy for the measurement of homophobia. *Journal of Homosexuality, 5*(4), 357–372.

Hunt, M. (1974). *Sexual behavior in the 1970's.* New York: Dell.

Kinsey, A. C., Pomeroy, W. B., Martin, C. E. (1948). *Sexual behavior in the human male.* Philadelphia: Saunders.

Kinsey, A. C., Pomeroy, W. B., Martin, C. E., & Gebhard, P. H. (1953). *Sexual behavior in the human female.* Philadelphia: Saunders.

Klassen, D. A., Williams, C. J., & Levitt, E. E. (1989). *Sex and morality in the U.S.: An empirical inquiry under the auspices of the Kinsey Institute.* Middletown, CT: Wesleyan University Press.

Lamison-White, Leatha, (1997) U.S. Bureau of the Census, *Current Population Reports,* Series p60-198, Poverty in the United States: 1996, U.S. Government Printing Office, Washington, D.C., 1997.

McConnaughey, J. W., Lader, W., Chin, R., & Everette, D. (1998). *Falling through the Net II: New data on the digital divide.* National Telecommunications and Information Administration. Available URL: http://www.ntia.doc.gov/ntiahome/

McKenna, Y. K., & Bargh, A. J. (1998). Coming out in the age of the Internet: Internet "demarginalization" through virtual group participation. *Journal of Personality and Social Psychology, 75*(3), 681–694.

Rathus, S. A., & Nevid, J. S. (1992). *Adjustment and growth: The challenges of life.* (5th ed., pp. 420–597). Fort Worth, TX: Harcourt Brace Jovanovich.

Reinisch, J. M., & Beasley, R. (1990). *The Kinsey Institute new report on sex: What you must know to be sexually literate.* New York: St. Martin's Press.

Schillewaert, N., Langerak, F., & Duhamel, T. (1998). Non-probability sampling for WWW surveys: A comparison of methods. *Journal of the Market Research Society, 40*(1), 307–322.

Sell, R. L. (1997). Research and the Internet: An e-mail survey of sexual orientation. *American Journal of Public Health, 87,* 297.

Smith, M. A., & Leigh, B. (1997). Virtual subjects: Using the Internet as an alternative source of subjects and research environment. *Behavior Research Methods, Instruments, & Computers, 29*(4), 496–505.

Smith, T. M. (1991). A critique of the Kinsey Institute/Roper organization national sex knowledge survey. *Public Opinion Quarterly, 55,* 449–457. American Association for Public Opinion Research.

Tavris, C., & Sadd, S. (1976). The Redbook report on female sexuality: 100,000 married women disclose the good news about sex. New York: Delacorete Press.

CHAPTER 7

An Intercultural Examination of Facial Features Communicating Surprise

Donatella Pagani*
University of Padua
Department of Social and
  Developmental Psychology
35131 Padova
Italy

Luigi Lombardi
University of Padua
Department of Social and
  Developmental Psychology
35131 Padova
Italy

INTRODUCTION

The Internet has features of great interest for all scientific disciplines. For psychology in particular, cyberspace is not only a useful research tool (Krantz, Ballard, & Scher, 1997; Reips, 1996a; Welch & Krantz, 1996), but also a new object to investigate (Bordia, 1996; Smith and Leigh, 1997). Because the Internet now supports multimedia, it offers an ideal ecological context in which topics related to *pictorial communication* may be scrutinized by the models and methods of experimental psychology. Pictorial communication is a research area that studies the processes of communicating information through particular iconographic codes. Several fields of research such as (visual communication, visual sociology, the psychology of art, and the psychology of perception) as well as those of virtual reality (VR) and human–computer interaction (HCI) share a common interest in this framework (Ellis, Kaiser, & Grunwald, 1993).

In this chapter we present an exploratory intercultural study, conducted via the Internet, on the iconographic communication of the emotion of surprise in various groups of participants classifiable according to distinct cultural and

*Equal authorship implied.

Psychological Experiments on the Internet

geographical areas. For this aim, we conducted an online experiment to investigate the role of upper facial features in evaluating the emotion of surprise in a set of synthetic pictograms generated by a graphical interface called the model of structural analysis (MSA) (Lombardi, 1997; Lombardi & Burigana, 1999).

THE FACIAL EXPRESSIONS OF THE EMOTION OF SURPRISE

Research on facial expressions is currently exploring new concepts, findings, and methods (Russell & Fernàndez-Dols, 1997).

An interesting debate involves the principal theorists of the relations between faces and emotions. There are different positions concerning the issue of the innateness and universality of facial expressions that express human emotions (Ekman, 1994; Izard, 1994; Russell, 1994). Darwin's treatise on emotions (1872/1965) inspired those who postulate the existence of at least six facial expressions of emotions that are recognized cross-culturally (e.g., Ekman, 1994; Izard, 1994). These are happiness, surprise, fear, disgust, anger, and sadness. Ekman and Friesen (1978) elaborated a procedure called the facial action coding system (FACS) to measure and describe each visible facial expression.

Cross-cultural studies have investigated the recognition of emotions from facial expressions (Boucher & Carlson, 1980; Ducci, Arcuri, W/Georgis, & Sineshaw, 1982; Kilbride & Yarczower, 1980; Matsumoto, 1990, 1992; McAndrew, 1986). These studies consider similarities and differences between subjects from at least two cultures. In general, there is consensus that there are universals of facial expressions of emotions. Even so, there is also consensus that there are differences between cultures and that cultural influence may be compatible with the universality thesis (Matsumoto, 1992).

Results of various studies of facial expression show that the emotion of surprise often occupies a unique position among other emotions considered "universal." For example, Frijda & Tcherkassof (1997) noted that expressions of surprise have been considered as ones of fear by a certain percentage of subjects in various studies (Ekman & Friesen, 1975). This may be because, as Ekman (1973) suggests, fearful events can also be surprising, and because the facial features of fear and surprise are similar. In a cross-cultural study, McAndrew (1986) compared Malaysian and American subjects: he found that females were significantly better than males at recognizing surprise and that Malaysian females were more accurate than American females. Matsumoto (1992) carried out a study on American–Japanese cultural differences in the recognition of universal facial expressions and found that Americans were better than Japanese at identifying anger, disgust, fear, and sadness, but that there were no differences in scores for happiness or surprise.

There are also other differences among authors in relation to the facial expression of surprise. For example, Russel (1997) identifies a "space of psychological judgment" defined by two dimensions: pleasantness and arousal. In this space, he sets the action unit of surprise very near the peak of arousal, but in a neutral position with regard to the dimension pleasantness—unpleasantness. Katsikitis (1997) used a multidimensional-scaling procedure to obtain a spatial representation of emotion categories in a two-dimensional space: horizontal, labeled as pleasant—unpleasant, and vertical, labeled as dimension of upper-face—lower-face dominance. The emotion of surprise is placed in the upper right-hand quadrant: thus surprise is labeled as pleasant and is characterized by upper-face dominance. The eyebrows and eye region predominate in the facial configuration of surprise.

If we consider only the upper facial features (eyes and eyebrows), the expression of surprise is caused by the combined action of two distinct muscular units, respectively the *medial* and *lateral* portions of the *frontalis*. Contraction of the former raises the inner part of the eyebrows, producing corrugation of the central portion of the forehead. Contraction of the latter raises the outer part of the eyebrows, corrugating the external portions of the forehead. As a consequence, the visual field "opens" and the structural configuration of the facial features appears to be "expanded." In one sense, we may interpret the expression of surprise as the need to "see better" or "know better" (Eibl-Eibesfeldt, 1984).

In their review of the "componential" approach to the study of facial expressions, Smith and Scott (1997) report that raising eyebrows and upper eyelids is associated with attention (Darwin, 1872/1965; Frijda, 1969; Smith, 1989), the perception of newness in the environment (Scherer, 1984), and low levels of control of the situation (Darwin, 1872/1965; Scherer, 1984; Smith, 1989). Smith (1989) also noted that raising eyebrows in particular is associated with a state of uncertainty.

From the structural point of view, the expression of surprise has a definite configuration. Lombardi and Burigana (1999) have shown how level of surprise is associated with a particular structural organization in artificial pictograms. The prototype used for the construction of simplified models of facial expressions was a graphical interface created by Lombardi (1997). Called MSA, it is characterized by variation of a small set of facial features (eyes, eyebrows, mouth, etc.). This parametrization is *ad hoc*, based on observation and common knowledge of the underlying structure of the face. Two separate components, structural and procedural, define the MSA. The structural component is defined by a complex structural organization called the *symbolic knowledge model*, which organizes all necessary information (phenomenological, geometrical, etc.) to describe the expressions and morphological aspects of the face. The procedural component consists of the computational and graphical procedures for producing the pictograms. Variations in the values of appropriate parameters produce a large set of pictograms that can be used as models of specific facial expressions. For example, we can modify mouth opening or the degree of inclination of the eyebrows, simply by assigning particular values to their associated parameters.

An example of a structural unit of the MSA is the *extension coefficient* (*EC*), by which it is possible to represent the various levels of surprise in a pictogram. The *EC* (Figure 1) indicates the degree of topological expansion of the chief components (eyes and eyebrows; see the Appendix for the analytical description of *EC*).

The literature contains several other works on the structural configuration of the face. Several computational models inspired by the FACS have been proposed (Katsikitis, Pilowsky, & Innes, 1990; Thornton & Pilowsky, 1982; Yamada, 1993). Computer graphics have been implemented by programs that simulate the anatomical behavior of facial expressions (Cohen & Massaro, 1990; Magnenat Thalmann, Primeau, & Thalmann, 1988; Massaro & Ellison, 1996; Parke, 1982; Platt & Badler, 1981; Terzopoulos & Waters, 1990; Waters, 1987; Williams, 1990).

All these studies describe human facial expressions through physical models of the face, based on anatomy of facial muscle structures, histology of facial tissues, physics of deformations, geometry of shape, and realism of graphical visualization. The task of human face modeling and animation has become more complex to accommodate psychological and behavioral dynamics (Kalra, 1996). Problems associated with the use of pictorial codes in the communication of emotions have received less attention from researchers. This

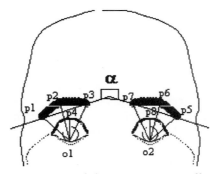

Figure 1   Pict *x* structural elements; extension coefficient (*EC*).

may be considered a serious omission, because artificial facial communication definitely offers a new dimension for human–machine interactions and interfaces (Kalra, 1996). The latest computer technologies support hypertext and multimedia, creating complex graphical interfaces. As a consequence, we think that the communication of emotions via pictorial codes, defined by a highly structured set of pictograms, represents a real and interesting object of study.

ONLINE EXPERIMENT: "HOW SURPRISED IS HE?"

We designed an online experiment to investigate the role of the upper facial features in evaluating the emotion of surprise in a small set of pictograms generated by the MSA. In this study, subjects viewed stimuli represented by MSA pictograms and rated the appropriate degree of surprise expressed. The studies of Katsikitis (1997), Ekman & Friesen (1978), and Izard (1971) highlighted the role of upper-face components in the emotion of surprise. Therefore, our research focused on the most salient features of this expression.

(a) Unlike other studies in this field (Matsumoto, 1992; Katsikitis, 1997) we chose not to use facial stimuli previously classified by raters: the peculiarity of the set of our stimuli is the structural organization of their components. It is the empirical evaluation of subjects to reveal which configurations from the set of pictograms are candidates for prototypical expressions of surprise.

(b) We decided to adopt the expression *intercultural research* to indicate a comparative study conducted via the Internet regarding evaluation of the emotion of surprise in different groups of participants classifiable according to distinct cultural and geographical areas.

The issues of universality of emotions and methodological problems in cross-cultural studies on facial expressions are raised by Russel (1993), Russell (1994), Russell & Fernàndez-Dols (1997), and Wagner (1997).

In our case, experimental subjects are Internet users who may be classified (accepting the assumption of honesty), according to their *declared* geographical provenance and their *declared* mother tongue, into distinct "virtual" cultural groups.

(c) The choice to operate on artificial pictograms, as opposed to simple photographic stimuli, affords an advantage: we have a precise analytical description of the structural elements of the face, and thus a more accurate description of the experimental stimuli.

This was very much an exploratory study. However, some general aspects were examined:

Structural aspect

- To value the reliability of the extension coefficient (*EC*) of the MSA as regards the effects of structural components of stimuli, "eye opening," "position of eyebrows," and "inclination of eyebrows"

Demographic and intercultural aspects—in the evaluation of degree of surprise in pictograms of the online experiment, to check:

- The presence of any differences between males and females, and possible accordances with or variances from results of researches conducted in the laboratory or in the field (McAndrew, 1986; Matsumoto, 1992)
- The presence of intercultural or intergeographic differences

Validity aspects

- The lack of influence of different hardware and software components and configurations used by the subjects who took part in the experiment via the Internet
- The strength of the experimental design (type of stimuli chosen) as regards possible influences from particular skills in iconographic decoding acquired by assiduous reading of comics or a passion for video games
- Comparison of the results of the same experiment conducted both over the Internet and in the laboratory under well-controlled conditions

METHOD

SUBJECTS

Self-reported subject characteristics of the online sample are listed in Table 1.

One unexpected demographic result was gender distribution: 69% of our participants were females. This fact is particularly interesting, because it clearly contradicts the results of all major demographic studies of the Internet population (Georgia Institute of Technology, 1998; hereafter, Georgia Tech).[1] Pasveer and Ellard (1998) also found results similar to ours in one of their

---

[1] The Georgia Tech research reports the following percentages: 33.6% female; 66.4% male.

Table 1

Self-Reported Subject Characteristics

	No.	%
Total N	742	
Sex		
Female	511	68.9
Male	223	30.1
Missing	8	1.1
Age		
< 18	80	10.8
18–22	244	32.9
23–30	235	31.7
31–50	154	20.8
> 50	22	3.0
Missing	7	0.9
Geographical area		
N. America (NA)	478	64.4
S. America (SA)	15	2.0
N. Europe (NE)	99	13.3
S. Europe (SE)	87	11.7
E. Europe (EE)	6	0.8
Africa (AF)	2	0.3
Asia (A)	33	4.4
M. Orient (MO)	4	0.5
Missing	18	2.4
Play video games		
Never	214	28.2
Rarely	302	40.7
Monthly	96	12.9
Weekly	71	9.6
More	41	5.5
Missing	18	2.4
Read comics		
Never	191	25.7
Rarely	332	44.7
Monthly	85	11.5
Weekly	71	9.6
More	48	6.5
Missing	15	2.0

studies conducted on the WWW. They interpreted their results as a consequence of the fact that their research aroused mainly female interest; we think the same explanation applies to our study as well.

The size of the sample and the heterogeneous provenance of the participants allowed us to subdivide them into eight geographical groups (Table 1).

Four of these groups (Northern Americans (NA), Northern Europeans (NE), Southern Europeans (SE), and Asians (A)) were sufficiently large to permit statistical comparisons.

STIMULI

The pictograms varied in degree of eye opening (3 levels: medium; medium wide; wide), position of eyebrows (3 levels: medium; medium high; high) and inclination of eyebrows (3 levels: no inclination; converging upward; converging downward) (Figure 2). The 3 levels of each variable were selected from a larger set of pictograms that had been used in a pilot study (Pagani, 1997; Pagani & Lombardi, 1999). In particular, we selected 9 pictograms from the 27 possible combinations of features, using a Latin square randomly chosen from the 12 Latin squares that could be generated given the 3 variables (with 3 levels per variable). Three different orders of presentation were devised, to avoid effects related to stimulus order and sequence.

PROCEDURES

Within the Web site of the Department of Psychology of the University of Padua, we implemented the first Italian online lab. Participants had access to the experiment through four possible Internet links.[2]

Guests were welcomed by the first page of the experiment, which gave information regarding the experiment title, the aim of the research, and the experimenters' names. Further on was a brief description of the experiment, information about the time required to execute it, and a short list of instructions. A link called "Start the Experiment" allowed the trials to begin.

If guests decided to click the link and participate, they were granted access to the main page of the online experiment. Here, they found a series of nine pictograms and, for each one, were asked to rate the degree of *surprise* that seemed to be expressed using a 7-point scale (from 0 = *total absence of surprise* to 6 = *maximum surprise*). After this task, subjects answered a list of questions: demographic (e.g., sex, language, age, country, etc.), technical (type

[2](1) "Online Lab" link on our Psychology Department home page (Pagani & Lombardi, 1997); (2) a link in the online research page of the American Psychological Society (Krantz, 1996); (3) a link in the page devoted to sites relevant to data collection on the Internet of The Web Experimental Psychology Lab, University of Tuebingen (Reips, 1996b); (4) a link in the page concerning methodologies for experimentation on the Internet of the Department of Psychology, University of Plymouth (Kenyon, 1996).

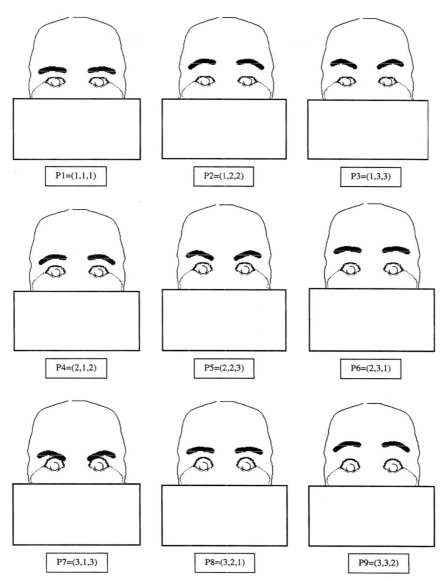

Figure 2   Experimental stimuli: labels (x_1, x_2, x_3), where $x_1 \in$ EYE_OP. = {1 = medium, 2 = medium-wide, 3 = wide}; $x_2 \in$ EYEBR_POS. = {1 = medium, 2 = medium-high, 3 = high}; $x_3 \in$ EYEBR_INCL. = {1 = no_inclination, 2 = converging_upwards, 3 = converging_downwards}.

of computer, monitor, and browser used), and behavioral (degree of reading of comics and degree of video-game playing). There was also a text area for any comments or suggestions. A "Submit" button sent their data to our server. Participation was voluntary, and only those subjects who completed an entire experiment were included in data analyses.

MAIN ANALYSES AND PLANNED COMPARISONS (STRUCTURAL, DEMOGRAPHIC, AND INTERCULTURAL ASPECTS)

We carried out three four-way ANOVAs ((a), (b), and (c)) on the three possible pairs of structural factors studied:

(a) 3 (Position of Eyebrows) $\times$ 3 (Eye opening) $\times$ 2 (Gender) $\times$ 4 (Geographical Area)

(b) 3 (Position of Eyebrows) $\times$ 3 (Inclination of Eyebrows) $\times$ 2 (Gender) $\times$ 4 (Geographical Area)

(c) 3 (Inclination of Eyebrows) $\times$ 3 (Eye Opening) $\times$ 2 (Gender) $\times$ 4 (Geographical Area)

Results of ANOVAs with repeated measures on position of eyebrows, eye opening, and inclination of eyebrows are given in Table 2.

Data analysis provided some interesting information regarding the effects of the structural components of the pictograms on the evaluation of the degree of surprise, as shown in the joint analysis of Figures 3–5 and Table 2. In particular, qualitatively, we can observe the relation between the "configurations" of the within-subject factor interactions (Eye Opening (C) $\times$ Position of Eyebrows (D); Eye Opening (C) $\times$ Inclination of Eyebrows (E); Position of Eyebrows (D) $\times$ Inclination of Eyebrows (E)) and the EC equation (see the Appendix). Moreover, the predictive power of the extension coefficient (EC) is assessed through the high correlation between the *simulated* stimuli means (EC-data) and the *empirical* stimuli means over the total sample ($r = 0.984$; $p < .001$) (Figure 6).

Other significant interactions (Sex (A) $\times$ Eye Opening (C); Sex (A) $\times$ inclination of eyebrows (E)) allowed examination of *gender* differences, separately, for combinations of levels of eye opening (inclination of eyebrows, respectively) by appropriate interaction contrasts (Table 3, Figures 7 and 8). As regards the female group (vs. the male group), results show a relatively more accentuated trend in attributing higher degrees of surprise with increase in eye opening ($\epsilon_{male} - \epsilon_{female} = -.354$).

Table 2

Results of Four-Factor Analyses of Variance [(a), (b), and (c)]

Effect	df	F	p [a]
Sex (A)	(1, 623)	1.33	(n.s.) .249
Geographical area (B)	(3, 623)	1.33	(n.s.) .265
Eye opening (C)	(2, 1246)	205.58	< .001
Position of eyebrows (D)	(2, 1246)	204.09	< .001
Inclination of eyebrows (E)	(2, 1246)	87.14	< .001
A × B	(3, 623)	0.67	(n.s.) .569
A × C	(2, 1246)	6.07	< .005
A × D	(2, 1246)	0.91	(n.s.) .404
A × E	(2, 1246)	13.37	< .001
B × C	(6, 1246)	4.30	< .001
B × D	(6, 1246)	2.40	.026
B × E	(6, 1246)	1.87	.083
C × D	(4, 2492)	59.91	< .001
C × E	(4, 2492)	128.46	< .001
D × E	(4, 2492)	116.15	< .001
A × B × C	(6, 1246)	2.02	.060
A × B × D	(6, 1246)	0.57	(n.s.) .753
A × B × E	(6, 1246)	3.04	< .010
A × C × D	(4, 2492)	9.06	< .001
A × C × E	(4, 2492)	0.63	(n.s.) .645
A × D × E	(4, 2492)	3.46	< .010
B × C × D	(12, 2492)	1.92	.028
B × C × E	(12, 2492)	2.26	< .010
B × D × E	(12, 2492)	3.30	< .001
A × B × C × D	(12, 2492)	2.19	.010
A × B × C × E	(12, 2492)	0.52	(n.s.) .902
A × B × D × E	(12, 2492)	1.32	(n.s.) .198

[a] n.s. = not significant.

Instead, the male group (vs. the female group) evaluates as a higher degree of surprise the change from pictograms with no eyebrow inclination to those with eyebrows converging downward ($\epsilon_{male} - \epsilon_{female} = .5$).

Differences between ratings for distinct geographical groups were also tested separately for eye opening (position and inclination of eyebrows, respectively) (Table 4, Figures 9 and 10). Results show the trend of Northern Americans (NA) versus Asians (A) to evaluates a relatively higher degree of surprise in *relation to* an increase in eye opening ($\epsilon_{NA} - \epsilon_{A} = .969$). An analogous trend emerges between Southern Europeans (SE) and Asians (A) ($\epsilon_{SE} - \epsilon_{A} = .621$). In relation to Factor D (position of eyebrows), we observe the inverse trend between Group NA and Group A with respect to eye

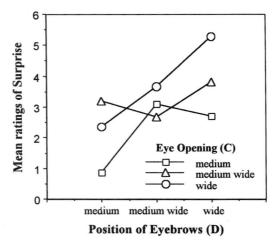

Figure 3 Mean ratings of surprise plotted as a function of the positions of the eyebrows (Factor D), with a separate type of marker and curve for each eye opening (Factor C).

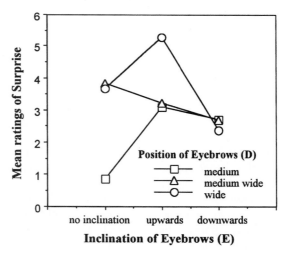

Figure 4 Mean ratings of surprise plotted as a function of the inclinations of the eyebrows (Factor E), with a separate type of marker and curve for each position of the eyebrows (Factor D).

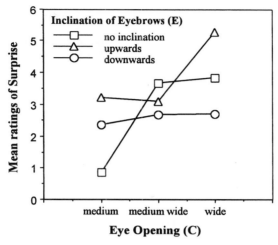

Figure 5 Mean ratings of surprise plotted as a function of eye opening (Factor C), with a separate type of marker and curve for each inclination of the eyebrows (Factor E).

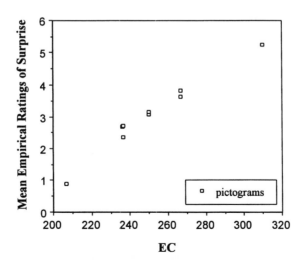

Figure 6 The empirical values associated with the pictograms plotted as a function of the EC values produced with the $\oplus = +$ linear operator, $b = 10.0$; μd_eyebr_sx and μd_eyebr_sx in [70.0, 100.0]; eye opening $d \in [30.0, 50.0]$ (see the Appendix).

Table 3

Contrasts

Contrast[a]	$\varepsilon_1 - \varepsilon_2$	Std. err.	t-Value	Sig. t[b]
I (C)	−.354	.1242	−2.857	.004
II (C)	.066	.095	.693	n.s. .488
I (E)	.500	.142	3.519	.001
II (E)	−.177	.142	−1.247	n.s. .212

[a] Contrast I (type polynomial) is defined by comparing difference ε_1 between the marginal means on the third and first levels of the within-subjects factor for the male group with the corresponding difference ε_2 for the female group. Contrast II (type polynomial) is defined by comparing difference ε_1 between the sum of the marginal means of the first and third levels and two times the value of the marginal means of the second level of the within-subjects factor for the male group with the corresponding difference ε_2 for the female group. C = eye opening; E = inclination of eyebrows.
[b] n.s. = not significant.

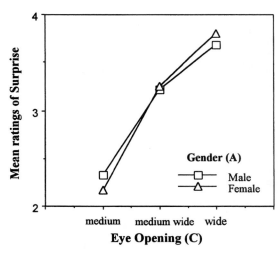

Figure 7 Mean ratings of surprise plotted as a function of eye opening (Factor C), with a separate type of marker and curve for male group and female group (Factor A).

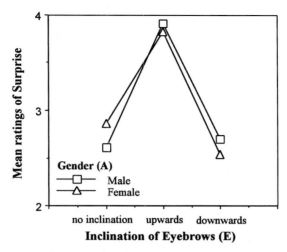

Figure 8 Mean ratings of surprise plotted as a function of the inclinations of the eyebrows (Factor E), with a separate type of marker and curve for male group and female group (Factor A).

opening evaluation ($\epsilon_{NA} - \epsilon_A = -.699$). The trend of group SE versus group NE to evaluate a *relatively* higher degree of surprise in *relation to* an increase in eyebrow raising ($\epsilon_{NE} - \epsilon_{SE} = -.631$) is interesting. In relation to Factor E (inclination of eyebrows), Group NA with respect to Group A evaluates as a higher degree of surprise the change from pictograms with no eyebrow inclination to those with eyebrows converging upward ($\epsilon_{NA} - \epsilon_A = -.929$).

However, we also found a strong relation between the modalities of evaluation of surprise in the four geographical groups as clearly shown by the cross-cultural measures of correlations ($r_{NA-NE} = .994$, $r_{NA-SE} = .973$, $r_{NE-SE} = .958$, $r_{SE-A} = .902$, $r_{NA-A} = .812 = r_{NE-A}$).[3] In conclusion, Table 5 reports the rank order of the stimuli between the geographical groups.

MAIN ANALYSIS OF HARDWARE AND SOFTWARE EFFECTS (VALIDITY ASPECT A)

Three six-way ANOVAs were designed, with the same within-subject factor component and with type of *hardware* and *software* as new between-factors.

[3]Correlations are significant at the 0.1 level.

Table 4

Contrasts

Contrast[a]	Comparisons G_1–G_2[b]	$\varepsilon_1 - \varepsilon_2$	Std. err.	t-Value	Sig. t[c]
I (C)	NA–A	.969	.271	3.575	.001
	NE–SE	.217	.219	0.991	n.s. .321
	SE–A	.621	.306	2.024	.043
II (C)	NA–A	.043	.209	0.205	n.s. .837
	NE–SE	−.252	.169	−1.490	n.s. .136
	SE–A	.276	.237	1.164	n.s. .244
I (D)	NA–A	−.699	.319	−2.188	.029
	NE–SE	−.631	.258	−2.444	.014
	SE–A	−.381	.361	−1.054	n.s. .292
II (D)	NA–A	−.277	.224	−1.237	n.s. .216
	NE–SE	.013	.181	0.076	n.s. .938
	SE–A	−.248	.254	−0.977	n.s. .328
I (E)	NA–A	.129	.314	0.412	n.s. .679
	NE–SE	.367	.253	1.445	n.s. .148
	SE–A	−.093	.355	−0.263	n.s. .791
II (E)	NA–A	−.929	.309	−3.004	.002
	NE–SE	−.378	.250	−1.512	n.s. .131
	SE–A	−.474	.350	−1.354	n.s. .175

[a] Contrast I (type polynomial) is defined by comparing difference ε_1 between the marginal means on the third and first levels of the within-subjects factor for Geographical group G_1 with the corresponding difference ε_2 for Geographical group G_2. Contrast II (type polynomial) is defined by comparing difference ε_1 between the sum of the marginal means of the first and third level and two times the value of the marginal means of the second level of the within-subjects factor for Geographical group G_1 with the corresponding difference ε_2 for Geographical group G_2. C = eye opening; D = position of eyebrows; E = inclination of eyebrows.
[b] Geographical groups **G** = (NA, NE, SE, A); Between-factor matrix of contrasts **M** = $[(1, 1, 1, 1), (1, 0, 0, -1), (0, 1, -1, 0), (0, 0, 1, -1)]$.
[c] n.s. = not significant.

No important significant effect emerged for different types of software and hardware configurations used by participants. In fact, the local settings of the experiment, which varied in relation to the types of monitor, PC, and browser used (Table 6), did not produce any substantial difference in evaluation except for some particular cases (see Table 7).

MAIN ANALYSES OF VIDEO GAMES AND COMICS EFFECTS (VALIDITY ASPECT B)

Three four-way ANOVAs were considered, with *reading of comics* and *passion for video games* as between-factors. We did not find any significant effect

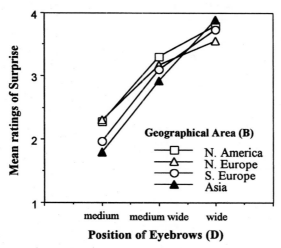

Figure 9 Mean ratings of surprise plotted as a function of the eye position of eyebrows (Factor D) with a separate type of marker and curve for each geographical group (Factor B).

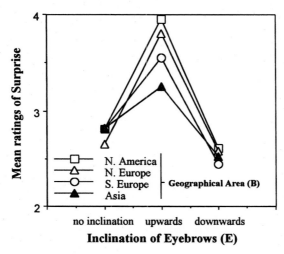

Figure 10 Mean ratings of surprise plotted as a function of the inclinations of the eyebrows (Factor E), with a separate type of marker and curve for each geographical group (Factor B).

Table 5

Rank Order of the Stimuli Pi (Mean Values in Parentheses) for Different Geographical Groups

Rank	N. America	N. Europe	S. Europe	Asia
1	P1 (0.83)	P1 (0.93)	P1 (0.88)	P1 (1.35)
2	P7 (2.32)	P7 (2.10)	P7 (2.43)	P3 (1.88)
3	P5 (2.72)	P5 (2.79)	P2 (2.44)	P4 (2.52)
4	P3 (2.76)	P3 (2.82)	P3 (2.49)	P2 (2.53)
5	P4 (3.23)	P4 (3.08)	P5 (2.56)	P5 (2.82)
6	P2 (3.24)	P2 (3.10)	P4 (3.17)	P7 (3.36)
7	P8 (3.66)	P8 (3.40)	P6 (3.76)	P6 (3.62)
8	P6 (3.92)	P6 (3.56)	P8 (3.80)	P8 (3.81)
9	P9 (5.37)	P9 (5.11)	P9 (5.06)	P9 (4.76)

Note. Differences between groups exceeding 0.5 of a category is significant by a t-test, with $p < .05$.

Table 6

Hardware and Software Variables

	No.	%
Total N	742	
Browser		
I.E.	241	32.5
Netscape	409	55.1
Others	26	3.5
Missing	66	8.9
Computer		
PC	634	85.4
MAC	69	9.3
Missing	39	5.3
Monitor dimension		
Don't know	203	27.4
14 in.	157	21.2
15 in.	188	25.3
17 in.	151	20.4
More	27	3.6
Missing	16	2.2
Monitor resolution		
Don't know	392	52.8
600 × 400	44	5.9
800 × 600	176	23.7
1024 × 800	108	14.6
Missing	22	3.0

Table 7

Main Results of Six-Factor Analyses of Variance

Effect[a]	df	F	p[b]
Browser (F)	(2, 509)	0.119	(n.s.) .888
Computer (G)	(1, 509)	0.003	(n.s.) .960
Monitor dimension (H)	(4, 509)	2.39	.050
Monitor resolution (I)	(3, 509)	0.667	(n.s.) .573
C × D × I	(12, 2036)	2.01	.020
C × D × F × G	(8, 2036)	2.03	.039

[a] C = eye opening, D = position of eyebrows.
[b] n.s. = not significant.

related to the learning of previous visual and semantic codes in pictogram evaluation. No differences emerged between groups who had contrasting levels of interest in video games and comics.

COMPARISONS BETWEEN THE RESULTS OF WWW SAMPLE AND LABORATORY SAMPLE (VALIDITY ASPECT c)

A traditional laboratory is usually a room with essential and functional furnishings: the environment in which the experimental setting is immersed appears as an aseptic, strongly controlled context, planned by the experimenter.

The context associated with an online lab has two distinct environmental components, one characterized by specific planning of the online lab in terms of aspects related to human–computer interaction, and the other by the real, or physical, context in which the participant is situated (e.g., office, house). Although the former component does allow us some kind of control, the latter cannot be controlled. It is therefore necessary to use special statistical or empirical procedures that allow us to bypass this problem and establish the validity of the Internet procedures used.

Krantz et al. (1997) proposed a comparative method to evaluate results obtained via the two modalities (classical vs. online). The procedure consists of conducting the same experiment both in the laboratory and over the WWW. According to Krantz et al., if the same psychological variables are driving the results of both data sets, their trends should turn out to be very similar, leading to a high correlation between the results of the two studies.

Like Krantz et al. (1997), we replicated our online experiment in a laboratory version. Participants were 53 undergraduate and graduate psychology students at the University of Padua, and the stimuli were the same pictograms used in the WWW experiment. Participants were read the Italian version of the same instructions of the online experiment, and a randomized sequence of stimuli was then presented to them on a PC monitor (resolution, 800 × 600; size, 15 in.). The task was identical to that of the online experiment.

The laboratory data were analyzed by three two-way ANOVAs on the three possible pairs of within-structural factors. As can be seen from Table 8 and Figure 11, both studies yielded similar data trends.

Moreover, comparing data from a subsample of online, Southern Europeans with laboratory data (of Italians, also in Southern Europe), we found a high correlation between means of the two experimental designs ($r = .948$, $p < .001$). Regressing these data, we found:

$$\text{online mean} = 0.958(\text{laboratory mean}) + 0.02,$$

which shows a slope of 0.958 (with standard error of .122) and an intercept value of 0.02 (with standard error of .397), which shows the similarity of lab to comparable online data.[4]

---

[4] The slope (0.958) was significantly different from 1 ($t = 7.856$, $p < .001$); the intercept (0.02) was not significantly different from 0 ($t = 0.124$, $p = .905$).

Table 8

Results of Two-Factor Analyses of Variance—Laboratory Sample

Effect	df	F	p
Eye opening (C)	(2, 104)	77.03	< .001
Position of eyebrows (D)	(2, 104)	31.43	< .001
Inclination of eyebrows (E)	(2, 104)	40.0	< .001
C × D	(4, 208)	28.05	< .001
C × E	(4, 208)	22.39	< .001
D × E	(4, 208)	48.51	< .001

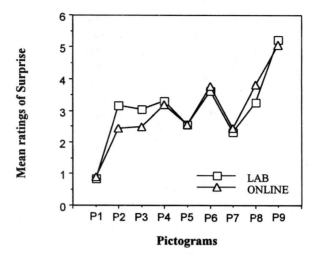

Pictograms

Figure 11   Mean ratings of surprise plotted as a function of the pictograms with a separate type of marker and curve for the laboratory group and the online group (Southern European group (SE)).

DISCUSSION

DEMOGRAPHIC AND INTERCULTURAL ASPECTS

We found a small (but statistically significant) difference between males and females in the evaluation of surprise.

Previous studies showed the presence of some differences in the recognition of emotions between males and females (Hall, 1978, 1984). McAndrew (1986) found that the emotions on which females were consistently more accurate than males were fear and surprise, which are traditionally the two most often confused. Brody and Hall (1993) summarize research and theory concerning gender differences in emotional experience, emotional expression, and nonverbal communication behaviors relating to emotion. The evidence indicates that females are superior to males both at recognizing feelings in others and at verbally and facially expressing a wide variety of feelings themselves. Brody and Hall also summarize evidence for socialization and developmental processes, including the development of verbal language and gender roles that may underlie gender differences in these domains.

Moreover, the fact that our study was accessed by a greater number of females than males is perhaps not coincidental: if the topic of emotions mostly attracts female interest, it should not surprise us more females chose to participate in a task of judging emotions.

Some significant differences between geographical groups also emerged from our study (see Table 4). They may be discussed from several points of view.

Cultural variations in the judgment of the intensity of emotion are relevant because facial expressions may be modulated by culture-specific display norms, such as intensification, deintensification, masking, and neutralization (Ekman, 1994).

It would be interesting to speculate how the results obtained might be related to plausible geographical, historical, and social–cultural differences. However, considering the small number of stimuli used in our study, we think it would be premature to make too much of these interesting relations.

It is also important to note that some cross-cultural studies on the recognition of facial expressions raised the issue of race depicted in the photos (Kilbride & Yarczower, 1980; Matsumoto, 1990). For example, Matsumoto (1992) stated that expressions must be portrayed by faces of people whose culture matches that of the judges, to separate judgments of emotions from judgments concerning race. However, Massaro & Ellison (1996) tested Japanese and U.S. students on computer-generated faces from these two countries and found that "the perceptual processing of facial affect follows well-established principles of pattern recognition, independent of the ethnicity and culture of the perceiver and of the perceived face." Moreover, Katsikitis (1997) found that the mode of stimulus presentation (i.e., photographs or line drawings) produces similar judgments of emotion. In consideration of these findings, we believe that the results of cross-cultural differences that emerged in our experiment may also be facilitated by the rating procedure, which probably allowed finer measures.

VALIDITY ASPECTS

(a) From the methodological point of view, it is important that the different types of software and hardware configurations used by participants did not produce substantial influences in pictogram evaluation. This result is very interesting, because it shows how a proper, robust experimental design allows the potential noise induced by different settings to be tolerated or minimized.

(b) The fact that no differences emerged between groups with distinct levels of interest in video games and comics shows a homogeneity that we believe is related to the high structural organization of the stimuli. We also think that our pictograms permit a more general level of decoding, which is independent of specific experiences in iconographic decoding.

(c) Our Internet data were comparable to those of the laboratory experiment: both correlational and regression analyses showed that our Internet data are valid. According to Krantz et al. (1997), this kind of comparison is needed to determine what types of research will yield similar results on the WWW and to establish the validity of the Internet as an experimental medium.

In conclusion, we verified that, with the Internet, very large, geographically diverse samples could be obtained (Reips, 1996a): people from 45 different countries completed our online experiment. A large sample permits division into subgroups of sufficient size for statistical analysis.

One limitation of our method of recruitment is the large disparity in number of participants that volunteered from different countries. An alternative way of recruiting subjects would have been a "call for participation" (Hewson, Laurent, & Vogel, 1996) by targeted invitation to specific newsgroups and listservers from specific countries. However, with the immediate adoption of such a strategy we would not have been able to acquire any idea of a "hypothetical baseline" of the number of completely voluntary participants and from how many and which countries they were able to connect. We are currently giving serious consideration to this alternative strategy, which may allow us a more specific focus on cultural differences in the evaluation of facial expressions.

In sum, we have studied cross-cultural differences and similarities in the judgment of emotions from pictorial stimuli. Our experience in this project leads us to the conclusion that the Internet is the most cost-effective and practical method for such cross-cultural research.

APPENDIX

Schematically, given the pictogram Pict x (Figure 1), the extension coefficient (EC) is defined by

$$EC = \left[\mu d\_eyebr\_sx \oplus d(O1, P4) \right] \oplus \left[\mu d\_eyebr\_dx \oplus d(O2, P8) \right] \oplus \omega,$$

$$(1)$$

where $\mu d\_eyebr\_sx = \mu(d(O1, P1), d(O1, P2), d(O1, P3))$ is the mean of the distances between origin O1 and points P1, P2, and P3; $\mu d\_eyebr\_dx = \mu(d(O2, P5), d(O2, P6), d(O2, P7))$ is the mean of the distances between origin O2 and points P5, P6, and P7; $d(O1, P4)$ and $d(O2, P8)$ indicate respectively the degree of expansion of the left and right eyes; and ω identifies a parameter that is dependent on angular measurement α,

$$\omega = \begin{cases} +b & \text{if } \alpha \geq 180° \\ 0 & \text{if } \alpha \cong 180°\,, \\ -b & \text{if } \alpha \leq 180° \end{cases} \qquad (2)$$

where b is a whole number. Lastly, $\oplus$ represents a generic function operator, if $\oplus = +$, EC specifies a simple linear equation.

REFERENCES

Bordia, P. (1996). Studying verbal interaction on the Internet: The case of rumor transmission research. *Behavior Research Methods, Instruments, & Computers, 28,* 149–151.

Boucher, J. D., & Carlson, G. E. (1980). Recognition of facial expression in three cultures. *Journal of Cross-Cultural Psychology, 11,* 263–280.

Brody, L. R., & Hall, J. A. (1993). *Gender and emotion.* In M. Lewis & J. M. Haviland (Eds.), *Handbook of emotions.* New York: Guilford Press.

Cohen, M. M., & Massaro, D. W. (1990). Synthesis of visible speech. *Behavior Research Methods, Instruments, & Computers, 28,* 260–263.

Darwin, C. (1965). *The expression of emotions in man and animals.* London: John Murray. (Original work published 1872)

Ducci, L., Arcuri, L., W/Georgis, T., & Sineshaw, T. (1982). Emotion recognition in Ethiopia. *Journal of Cross-Cultural Psychology, 13,* 340–351.

Eibl-Eibesfeldt, I. (1984). *Die Biologie des menschlichen Verhaltens. Grundriss der Humanethologie.* Munich: Piper.

Ekman, P. (1973). *Darwin and facial expression: A century of research in review.* New York: Academic Press.

Ekman, P. (1994). Strong evidence for universals in facial expressions: A reply to Russell's mistaken critique. *Psychological Bulletin, 115,* 268–287.

Ekman, P., & Friesen, W. V. (1975). *Unmasking the face: A guide to recognizing emotions from facial clues.* Englewood Cliffs, NJ: Prentice-Hall.

Ekman, P., & Friesen, W. V. (1978). *Facial action coding system.* Palo Alto: Consulting Psychologists Press.

Ellis, S. R., Kaiser, M. K., & Grunwald, A. J. (1993). *Pictorial communication in virtual and real environments* (2nd ed.). Bristol: Taylor & Francis.

Frijda, N. H. (1969). *Recognition of emotion.* In L. Berkowitz (Ed.), *Advances in experimental social psychology.* New York: Academic Press.

Frijda, N. H., & Tcherkassof, A. (1997). *Facial expressions as modes of action readiness.* In J. A. Russell & J. M. Fernàndez Dols (Eds.), *The psychology of expression.* New York: Cambridge University Press.

Georgia Institute of Technology: Georgia Tech's Graphics, Visualization, and Usability Center. (1998). *GVU's WWW Users Surveys* [Online]. Available URL: http://www.cc.gatech.edu/gv/user_survey/

Hall, J. A. (1978). Gender effects in decoding non verbal cues. *Psychological Bulletin, 85,* 845–857.

Hall, J. A. (1984). *Nonverbal sex differences: Communication accuracy and expressive style.* Baltimore: Johns Hopkins University Press.

Hewson, C., Laurent, D., & Vogel, C. M. (1996). Proper methodologies for psychological and sociological studies conducted via the Internet. *Behavior Research Methods, Instruments, & Computers, 28,* 186–191.

Izard, C. E. (1971). *The face of emotion.* New York: Appleton Century Crofts.

Izard, C. E. (1994). Innate and universal facial expressions: Evidence from developmental and cross-cultural research. *Psychological Bulletin, 115,* 288–299.

Kalra, P. (1996). Human facial animation. In N. Magnenat Thalmann & D. Thalmann (Eds.), *Interactive computer animation.* London: Prentice Hall.

Katsikitis, M. (1997). The classification of facial expressions of emotion: A multidimensional-scaling approach. *Perception, 26,* 613–626.

Katsikitis, M., Pilowsky, I., & Innes, J. M. (1990). The quantification of smiling using a microcomputer-based approach. *Journal of Nonverbal Behavior, 14,* 3–18.

Kenyon, P. (1996). *What other experiments are there on the Internet?* [Online]. Available URL: http://salmon.psy.plym.ac.uk/mscprm/forms2.htm#Supplementary

Kilbride, J. E., & Yarczower, M. (1980). Recognition and imitation of facial expressions: A cross cultural comparison between Zambia and the United States. *Journal of Cross-Cultural Psychology, 11,* 281–296.

Krantz, J. H. (1996). *Psychological Research on the Net* [Online]. Available URL: http://psych.hanover.edu/APS/exponnet.html

Krantz, J. H., Ballard, J., & Scher J. (1997). Comparing the results of laboratory and World-Wide Web samples on the determinants of female attractiveness. *Behavior Research Methods, Instruments, & Computers, 29,* 264–269.

Lombardi, L. (1997, September). *Rappresentazione delle espressioni del volto: Proposta di un modello insiemistico orientato ad oggetti.* Paper presented at the 1997 Congresso Nazionale della Sezione di Psicologia Sperimentale, Capri.

Lombardi, L., & Burigana, L. (1999). MSA (Model of Structural Analysis): An example of formal analysis on the emotion of surprise. In M. Zanforlin & M. Tommasi (Eds.), *Research in perception: Proceedings of the Meeting in Memory of Fabio Metelli.* Padua: Logos Press.

Magnenat Thalmann, N., Primeau, E., & Thalmann, D. (1988). Abstract muscle action procedures for human face animation. *The Visual Computer, 5,* 290–297.

Massaro, D. L., & Ellison, J. W. (1996). Perceptual recognition of facial affect: Cross-cultural comparisons. *Memory & Cognition, 24,* 812–822.

Matsumoto, D. (1990). Cultural similarities and differences in display rules. *Motivation and Emotion, 14,* 195–214.

Matsumoto, D. (1992). American–Japanese cultural differences in the recognition of universal facial expressions. *Journal of Cross-Cultural Psychology, 23,* 72–84.

McAndrew, F. (1986). A cross-cultural study of recognition thresholds for facial expression of emotion. *Journal of Cross-Cultural Psychology, 17,* 211–224.

Pagani, D. (1997). *Potenzialità applicative nell'uso di Internet per la ricerca in psicologia: Proposta di un laboratorio online.* Unpublished thesis. Università di Padova.

Pagani, D., & Lombardi, L. (1997). *Online psychology lab* [Online]. Available URL: http://www.psy.unipd.it/personal/laboratorio/surprise/htmltesi/first3.html

Pagani, D., & Lombardi, L. (1999). An experiment conducted on the Internet: The evaluation of the emotion of surprise. In M. Zanforlin & L. Tommasi (Eds.), *Research in perception: Proceedings of the Meeting in Memory of Fabio Metelli.* Padua: Logos Press.

Parke, F. I. (1982). Parametrized models for facial animation. *IEEE Computer Graphics and Applications, 9,* 61–68.

Pasveer, K. A., & Ellard, J. H. (1998). The making of personality inventory: Help from the WWW. *Behavior Research Methods, Instruments, & Computers, 30,* 309–313.

Platt, S. M., & Badler, N. I. (1981). Animating facial expressions. *Computer Graphics, 15,* 245–251.

Reips, U. (1996a, October). *Experimenting in the World-Wide Web.* Paper presented at the 1996 Society for Computers in Psychology Conference, Chicago.

Reips, U. (1996b). *Other sites relevant to data collection on the internet* [Online]. Available URL: http://www.psych.unizh.ch/genpsy/UIF/Lab/WebLabLinksE.html

Russel, J. A. (1993). Forced-choice response format in the study of facial expression. *Motivation and Emotion, 17,* 41–51.

Russel, J. A. (1997). *Reading emotions from and into faces: Resurrecting a dimensional–contextual perspective.* In J. A. Russell & J. M. Fernàndez Dols (Eds.), *The psychology of expression.* New York: Cambridge University Press.

Russell, J. (1994). Is there universal recognition of emotion from facial expression? A review of the cross-cultural studies. *Psychological Bulletin, 115,* 102–141.

Russell, J., & Fernandèz-Dols, J. M. (1997). *The psychology of facial expression.* Cambridge: Cambridge University Press.

Scherer, K. R. (1984). *On the nature and function of emotion: A component process approach.* In K. R. Scherer & P. Ekman (Eds.), *Approaches to emotion.* Hillsdale, NJ: Erlbaum.

Smith, C. A. (1989). Dimensions of appraisal and physiological response in emotion. *Journal of Personality and Social Psychology, 57,* 329–353.

Smith, C. A., & Scott, H. (1997). *A componential approach to the meaning of facial expressions.* In J. A. Russell, J. M. Fernàndez Dols (Eds.), *The psychology of expression.* New York: Cambridge University Press.

Smith, M. A., & Leigh, B. (1997). Virtual subjects: Using the Internet as an alternative source of subjects and research environment. *Behavior Research Methods, Instruments, & Computers, 29,* 496–505.

Terzopoulos, D., & Waters, K. (1990). Physically-based facial modeling, analysis and animation. *Journal of Visualization and Computer Animation, 1,* 73–80.

CHAPTER 8

What Are Computing Experiences Good For?: A Case Study in Online Research

John H. Mueller
EDPS Department
University of Calgary,
Calgary, Alberta T2N 1N4
Canada

D. Michele Jacobsen
EDPS Department
University of Calgary
Calgary, Alberta T2N 1N4
Canada

Ralf Schwarzer
Institute of Psychology
Freie University of Berlin
Habelschwerdter Allee 45
Berlin 14195
Germany

The argument has been made that discovery-based experiences in learning to program in LOGO on computers reduce mathematics anxiety. Broadening this perspective, we speculated that the result should be a decrease in test anxiety and an increase in self-confidence, with enhanced general academic performance, not just mathematics performance. Further, we hypothesized that this benefit would not be limited to the LOGO language, rather it should be a general by-product of self-instruction (discovery) experiences with computers in general. We developed an on-line survey to explore this possibility. This chapter will summarize some of the results of this survey and our experiences with on-line data collection.

What good comes from all this time and money spent on computers? Among others, Internet widows and widowers alike seem to ask this question daily. This chapter chronicles our efforts to achieve an answer to this question from data collected via an online survey. We view this survey as a case study, an exploration of the question, and a test of online technology as a data collection format, rather than a theory-testing venture. Thus any answers will necessarily be tentative. We report here some preliminary results from about 2000 respondents. In addition to summarizing our findings, we will also address

Psychological Experiments on the Internet

how our own experiences may provide some "lessons learned" for others contemplating such data collection.

We note in passing that in the "real world," out there beyond our ivory tower, the "payoff" for using computers is often thought of simply in terms of "productivity increases." In other words, the "good" is reflected in annual profit reports, stock values, and such. In spite of substantial investment, it has been difficult to document regular, direct gains from computer expenditures in the workplace (e.g., Gibbs, 1997; Landauer, 1995; Norman, 1988, 1993). The disappointing results on the "return on investment" issue are beyond the scope of the present discussion, though one may reasonably suspect that there is some connection with the issues that we will discuss here, compounded by missteps in the manner of technological implementation (cf. Adams, 1996).

PERSONAL GROWTH AS VALUE

In the educational domain, computing experiences have long been justified in other terms, in terms of benefits to the individual, warm and fuzzy things compared to the bottom line. In academe, computing experience is viewed as a possible contributor to an individual's skill set, in terms of either some specific task mastery (e.g., graphics software), as in learning a trade, or some broader personal improvement related to general intellectual stimulation.

This personal growth perspective was emphasized in *Mindstorms*, a popular book by Seymour Papert (1980). Papert was concerned with declining mathematics competence, as well as increased mathematics avoidance in course selection and related problems. He argued that declining mathematics competence might be traceable to the conventional classroom assessment environment, whereby performance is usually dichotomized as "right" or "wrong." In the traditional classroom context, failing to solve mathematics problems is an unpleasant experience. Being "wrong" connotes personal failure, and eventually fear of being wrong generates anxiety and avoidant strategies designed to preserve self-esteem. It was argued that declining mathematics scores might be traced to this characterization of "error" as "bad me."

As an antidote for this fear-of-failure approach, Papert seized upon the LOGO programming language as a way to reduce mathematics anxiety in young children. Children learn to make the "turtle" cursor move about the computer screen using LOGO commands, in an unstructured, playlike environment. In the process, they learn that programs do not always work as planned, even for the teacher and other adults. Papert argued that this experience of an error as a mere step in problem solving changes the experience of making a "mistake" to something less personal. Errors become less threatening to self-esteem, and thus merely a challenge to further constructive (i.e., on-task) action. In this discovery framework, a mistake has at least some benefits, rather than becoming a stimulus for avoidant or escape behavior with concomitant negative emotional reactions.

Thus Papert expected to find improved mathematics performance following LOGO experiences, at least if LOGO was experienced in a "discovery" manner rather than being "taught," and a substantial literature developed to examine LOGO (e.g., Littlefield et al., 1988). At the risk of overgeneralizing, students do routinely report more positive attitudes about school following LOGO training, but the evidence for improvement in mathematics or problem solving is less consistently obtained. Still, the anecdotal reports of teachers that students seem to have fun during LOGO sessions is consistent with the notion that a changed perception of the significance of mistakes has taken place. This recharacterization of the meaning of an error should be beneficial for the child's self-image and other academic endeavors if that more relaxed perception of errors can be generalized beyond the LOGO setting. (In passing, it is worth noting that the association of the computer with play extends beyond LOGO and computer games. I have long found that if my office door is open and I am at my computer keyboard, passersby do not hesitate to pop in and see what I am doing—I am seen as "playing" with my computer, so interruption is socially acceptable. However, if I were sitting there at a typewriter, a potential visitor would quietly pass by; I would be perceived as "working"—and there is less often interest in sharing work.)

Although the LOGO research does provide some context for our project, we do not believe that it is broad enough to provide a complete framework, and so we note LOGO only in passing. For present purposes, "structured" instruction will refer to the conventional format, that is, syllabus-driven, going from A to Z on each topic in sequence, with the prospect of formal evaluation. "Discovery" learning here will refer to alternative approaches such as the undirected playlike format described by Papert, but we will also include other learner-driven formats, such as self-directed problem solving. Obviously there is no inviolate definition of these, and unfortunately some uses of the term "discovery" have a legacy of connotations that may mislead. And surely there are any number of formats that would be problematic of classification. However, the extremes of such a continuum seem identifiable, and our concern is that the extremes provide environments potentially different in terms of the perceived meaning of making a mistake.

Observing children at the computer, one may see that structured approaches to learning about computers may not be optimal. Specifically, the child will confront a specific, limited problem or issue of immediate interest, such as, "how do I change the font for this material." This specific problem is pursued to satisfaction, and then the next specific issue is dealt with. In other words, that is not the time to intrude with a comprehensive discourse about the differences between bitmap, TrueType, and PostScript fonts, screen versus printer appearance differences, kerning, ad nauseam. Unfortunately the comprehensive format is all too characteristic of formal course presentation, covering all aspects of a topic whether needed at the moment or not, in contrast to the "just-in-time" nature of learning that seems to occur naturalistically. More broadly, this just-in-time perspective is championed by other observers of the way in which computers can promote children's learning (e.g., Tapscott, 1998).

On closer reflection, we decided Papert's analysis stopped short of a complete realization. In particular, it was too conservative in viewing the benefits as limited to mathematics performance. We think that there is appeal to the idea that computer learning experiences may alter one's perception of errors during learning, but we extend Papert's analysis in two ways. First, there seems no reason to think that this benefit would be restricted to just LOGO experiences to the exclusion of other programming languages *provided* that the computer experience occurs in a "discovery" mode. That is, the benefit should accrue whenever the learning experience occurs for immediate problem-solving benefit rather than under the structured instruction format. For this reason we will not pursue an extended review of the literature on LOGO per se. Although LOGO is an intellectual ancestor for our survey, the original concerns are just too specific. Likewise, to appreciate this potential benefit from an altered view of errors, one need not be a constructivist theorist, because even the classic Thorndikian tradition will suffice. That is, *any* viewpoint whereby errors tell us something and lead us partway toward a solution will do—error elimination as information gain, not errors as "bad me." Therefore, the main question for us became "do self-instruction and/or discovery experiences involving computers in general yield a changed attitude about how errors fit into problem solving, compared to more traditional structured experiences?"

Second, we see no reason to think that the benefits of such a change in attribution about the meaning of an error would be restricted to just mathematics performance, nor, for that matter, to just computer use. That is, reduced test anxiety and enhanced self-confidence should show broad, general performance gains, as reflected in measures such as cumulative GPA rather than scores in a single course or even a single subject area. If so, then assessing the benefits of such a changed attitude about errors requires looking beyond changes in grades in mathematics courses. Further, because these more general effects involve changes in self-confidence and related dimensions, the effects may not be fully manifest in improved general performance until a few years later, another reason to look beyond effects in a single, immediate course.

Therefore, what are computer experiences good for? We decided to look at the way computer experiences might be associated with learner features such as test anxiety and self-efficacy, and whether they were a benefit to academic performance. Do they just affect mathematics performance or are the results broader? Do the results derive equally for structured courses and self-instruction? More specifically, does an open-ended computer experience reduce evaluative anxiety? Does it increase self-efficacy? Do these self-enhancements improve overall academic performance, but perhaps only in a long-term or delayed timeframe, years after the elementary school experience with the LOGO turtle?

APPROACHING THE QUESTION

How to address these questions? One traditional strategy would be to follow a group of kindergarten children through their elementary and high-school years. However, longitudinal research at best provides exasperatingly delayed reinforcement to the investigator, and further a longitudinal sample like this would be quite restricted in terms of size, locale, curriculum, and so forth. Another traditional source of respondents would be to survey first-year students at university. However, the campus sample misses out on those who do not continue on to college, restricts the experiences to a specific geographic locale and educational regimen, and has other generalization problems as well.

We decided it was appropriate to throw this question open to the world by setting it up so that the survey could be accessed by anyone via the Internet, using a Web browser such as Netscape. This procedure raises some potential issues of sample representativeness, but it does assure a wider variety of background experiences in computing, it taps ages beyond high school and university, and it allows the assessment of long-term benefits. Further, it potentially taps a wider range of test anxiety and efficacy than would be the case by restricting the sample to university students. That is, students who really have test anxiety may be less likely to continue on to university, so a university subject pool would tend to be lower in test anxiety than the population at large. (Of course, it might be asked whether really high-anxiety people would seek out a WWW survey, but presumably an online survey is not construed as a personal evaluation and thus would not elicit such evaluative concerns.) Likewise, a college-only sample would presumably reflect a group with self-efficacy scores biased to the high end, warranted or not.

The most obvious "bias" to a sample gathered online is that the respondents will all be computer users, but that after all is what *this* particular study is about—what benefits derive from computer experiences. No matter how we might have alternatively approached the question, it would have involved computer users. Having said that, though, there may be general issues of representativeness for other survey topics, but some of our results may be heartening in that regard, even, and there may be some general strategies which will help allay some concerns about generalizability. On the plus side for any topic, there are trade-offs to be gained in terms of breaking down regional educational practices and other localized sampling constraints. That is, if we avoid the homogeneity of the introductory psychology class, we will get heterogeneity and thus perhaps results closer to the population at large. However, it is not necessary to always throw your survey open to the world; one can restrict it to a recruited local subject pool, even use password access, basically just using the Web browser software in lieu of paper and pencil. Likewise, in some cases it may be useful to simultaneously conduct a traditional paper-and-pencil survey for comparison (e.g., Pasveer & Ellard, 1998).

These and related sampling issues have been discussed by Smith and Leigh (1997) and others (including this volume), and though we might have wished for such counsel when we started this project (December 1995), the best resolution of these concerns remains to collect the online data to see whether the potential concerns materialize or not. Interestingly, as will be discussed later, some of the concerns we have often heard expressed (e.g., gender bias) simply have not shown up in our sample, even with minimal control on access.

Ultimately we must be realistic: a survey is a very limited way to test a hypothesis, it is a far better way to set up a hypothesis. Thus the more reasonable expectation in most cases should be to gather some evidence in an exploratory fashion, then pursue a controlled laboratory experiment if indicated.

GETTING STARTED

With this idea in late 1995, we were stimulated by the appearance of commercially oriented surveys implemented as Web pages, something which by now has become ubiquitous. These marketing surveys made it clear that this online methodology was mechanically possible. It would have helped to have had models and turnkey software to set up our survey Web page (e.g., Baron, 1998; Schmidt, 1997), but that part actually turned out to be fairly straightforward, just using local help files and online guides to programming in hypertext markup language (HTML), a little discovery learning of our own. Your institution likely provides some common shared (CGI, or common gateway interface) scripts for processing forms and likely allows you to host your survey on the institution's server; if not, almost any commercial Internet service provider will do so for a very nominal fee. Looking back, the HTML part of the project was not much of a problem at all, and by now undergraduates can do it over lunch. But we have enhanced our own self-efficacy as a result.

ETHICAL CONSIDERATIONS

We noted in our initial deliberations that there did appear to be some notable omissions in the commercial or nonacademic surveys. For example, in contrast to our often tedious campus procedures for informed consent, nonacademic surveys generally launched right into the questions without any component such as our obligatory consent form. Specifically, these nonacademic surveys involved no or minimal assurance about the anonymity and/or confidentiality of the answers that a respondent provides. Even when such "assurance" was offered, the credibility of the offer seemed suspect as soon as follow-up e-mail contacts began to arrive. Although this is not the place to pursue it, there does seem to be an issue here having to do with differential standards in the academic and private sector with regard to data collection online.

Nonetheless, as academics we thought we needed to model the paper-and-pencil informed consent format. We included a preliminary consent form as a Web page with the usual basic information about the purposes of the survey. It also assured the potential respondent that they could quit at any time with no penalty. The consent form also included the usual assurance about anonymity and confidentiality. Most routines save the data with the numerical IP address as part of the subject's data, and this is usually sufficiently anonymous (e.g., 136.159.200.9 or 24.64.69.5). In general, to further reinforce the assurance of anonymity, it is a good idea to not ask for an e-mail address. Alternatively, one can ask for an e-mail address (e.g., to provide follow-up results) after storing the data, on a separate Web page, so that the e-mail address goes into a separate file from the survey answers.

Another variation from a paper survey is the impossibility of getting the Web-page consent form "signed" to acknowledge consent. With the Web page, the participant can only click on the "Agree" button. One can imagine the campus lawyers worrying profusely at this point. However, from a broader, real-world perspective, this practice has been commonplace with computers for sometime now. For example, when installing software one invariably has to only click on a series of "Accept" buttons for the license agreement. Thus we decided that if clicking an "Agree" button is good enough to be binding for Microsoft's lawyers, it should suffice for online research. Guidelines incorporating these and other points for the consent page can be found at Mueller (1997) and also in Smith and Leigh (1997).

In reality, it is hard to imagine a more "voluntary participation" format than Web surfing. For this reason if no other, it seems wise to keep the consent form as *brief* as possible, within the constraint of informed consent. If participants elect to stop, there are no face-to-face social cues to stop them going elsewhere, no chance to answer questions for clarification, and so on. And, for similar reasons, it is hard to imagine that there could be any sense in which a penalty could be imposed for a decision to withdraw. In pragmatic terms, one can hardly imagine a more superfluous clause to be issued to someone halfway around the world than the assurance they could stop at any point without penalty. There may be circumstances that dictate a "high entrance barrier" to minimize dropout (cf. Reips, chap. 4, this volume), but we think that one should avoid implementing that strategy except by deliberate design.

It will be detached in time from the consent form, but it also seems desirable to provide a debriefing document after the survey answers are submitted. This is done as a matter of courtesy and as a matter of completing the informed consent agenda, but it also should avoid a flood of e-mail asking repetitious questions.

Thus the usual academic constraints for informed consent can be honored. Further, the Web-based survey is cheap compared to a hard-copy mailed survey, the survey is there 24 hours a day without the need to pay a research assistant, there is no need to barter with a department head for lab space, and the data so collected routinely accumulate in a data file without even the need for data entry for statistical analysis. Clearly there are merits to the online approach, whether the sample is controlled or open-ended, and whether the survey topic concerns computer-related issues or not. But in any event a question about the effect of computer experiences certainly seemed appropriately examined online.

METHOD

Thus, in January of 1996, we launched a virtual survey, exploring the issue of how computer experiences might be related to self-efficacy and similar traits, and whether there would be any concomitant benefits to academic performance or other measures of achievement. First we located some measures of test anxiety and self-efficacy to convert to the online format. This online use requires honoring the usual conventions around copyrights, so we obtained such permissions and noted this fact on the Web page as a caution for others.

We adopted the *Test Anxiety Inventory* (TAI; Spielberger, 1980) to assess test anxiety. The TAI provides two subscale test-anxiety scores: *worry* (task-irrelevant cognitions), which reliably has a negative association with performance, and *emotionality* or arousal per se, which may or may not hinder performance. We elected to stay with these traditional two subscales for analysis, though there is recent evidence to suggest that other factors may be identified (e.g., Hodapp & Benson, 1997).

To assess self-efficacy, we adopted the *Generalized Self-Efficacy Inventory*, developed by Schwarzer and Jerusalem (1995). In other words, we did not just look at "computer anxiety" (the negative perspective traditionally taken in educational technology research), nor even its positive counterpart, "computer efficacy." We could have looked at specific efficacy as well as general, but as noted previously re the consent form, there is a need to keep the online experience digestibly short. In fact, finding an effect for generalized self-efficacy seems more problematic, and thus our procedure constitutes a more conservative or demanding test than a more focused measure such as "computer efficacy."

We then developed several demographic items having to do with the usual suspects, *age, gender, education, grade point average*, but also *income, geographic region, handedness*, and *extraversion*. Handedness was assessed by a 9-point self-report rating, having to do with writing, sighting, swinging a hammer or racquet (1 = left, 9 = right). Extraversion was also a 9-point self-report rating, with 1 being "extraverted and liking to work in groups" and 9 being "introverted and liking to work alone." Although there are other reasons for looking at interactions between anxiety measures and extraversion, in this case the purpose was more modest: presumably extraversion could have some connection with preferences for self-instruction (solitary) versus structured (group) classes, for example. Single-item assessments such as this may not usually have high reliability, but a longer assessment would have extended the online experience. Therefore, given the exploratory nature of the project and because handedness and extraversion were secondary concerns, single-item coverage seemed sufficient at this stage.

Finally we developed some items having to do with specific computer experiences, especially *programming languages*, including LOGO, BASIC, HTML. We also asked how that expertise was obtained, that is, self-instruction versus courses, with no detailed explanation of these formats. To some extent, self-instruction may be somewhat age-linked, in that some years ago there were few courses in computer programming, and thus most older respondents may be self-taught without choice have been a factor.

The complete survey is at http://www.acs.ucalgary.ca/~ mueller/tai-consent.html. To start soliciting participants, we seeded this site's address (URL) into several Web search engine databases (e.g., WebCrawler, YAHOO, Alta Vista, and so forth). Thus Web users searching for "anxiety," "efficacy," "computer programming," and such at these search engines would find our Web site. Entering the URL into several search engines seemed desirable as a way to overcome any selection bias that might be present for visitors to a specific database.

Respondents finding it by those search engine databases would be somewhat delayed because updates to the database may take several days or even weeks. Therefore, to get more immediate response, we also directly announced the survey URL to several educational technology discussion groups (both Listservs and Usenet newsgroups), psychology discussion groups, computer magazine Web pages, educational technology sites (e.g., International Society for Technology in Education), psychology sites (e.g., American Psychological Society), and otherwise promoted its existence more directly than the Web search engine route.

At this point, over two years later, any differences in respondent origin have presumably changed and averaged out. That is, the early respondents likely came primarily from the discussion groups, whereas later respondents came largely if not entirely from the search engines. Because of the anonymous nature of the identification in the date file, we are not able to classify respondents in terms of how they found the survey. In hindsight, one could duplicate the survey with multiple URLs, and then seed one URL to psychology discussion groups and the other URL to technology discussion groups, for example. Then one could record the probable origins of the respondents by simply creating separate data files from each URL, but we did not incorporate this scheme here. By using a variety of search engine seedings and a variety of discussion group postings, we presumably obtained broader representation than would be the case had the topic dictated a more focused target sample. The general issue of why some of the recipients choose to respond and others did not is still present, as it is in any survey format.

In these postings, we tried to carefully follow another set of ethical considerations, namely, those which by convention constitute good taste for online communication. For example, we did not post the announcement to groups that would likely not be interested, we identified it clearly as a survey solicitation in the subject line, we kept the invitation to participate short, did not repeat solicitations, and otherwise tried to behave in a manner consistent with good "netiquette" (Rinaldi, 1998).

SAMPLE CHARACTERISTICS

Out of 2123 useable respondents (March 1996 through December 1998, scanned for duplicate records and other problems), roughly half were 25 years of age or younger, but about 20% were 40 years or older. Importantly, only 54.5% were male, lower than might have been projected given popular stereotypes re gender differences in computer use. (For purposes of discussion, here and in the following, results will be described as "significant" when they are associated with $p < .05$ or less.) As Figure 1 shows, this gender distribution was true across ages, with a nonsignificant χ^2 for Age × Gender, $\chi^2(12) = 9.49$. The most common education level was "some college," but education level ranged from about 28% with "completed high school" to about 20% with a Masters degree or beyond, and the Education × Gender χ^2 was nonsignificant, $\chi^2(7) = 4.39$.

The average reported income level was the \$30,000–45,000 category, but income ranged up to the low six figures and included a number of respondents below \$15,000 and did not show a significant χ^2 for Income × Gender, $\chi^2(8) = 11.77$. The respondents were largely from North America, some 76% being from the United States or Canada, with about 10% from Europe. The Region × Gender χ^2 was significant, $\chi^2(5) = 25.38$, $p < .001$, as men out-

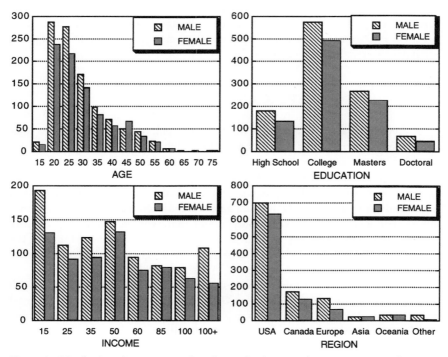

Figure 1   Distribution of survey respondents by gender for age, education, income, and regional categories (y-axis is number of respondents).

numbered women in the three most populous regions and not elsewhere, there being a floor effect in the latter regions.

These demographics compare well to the ongoing Georgia Tech (GVU, 1998) surveys of online users and to other surveys about WWW usage (e.g., EuroMarketing, 1998; InfoQuest, 1998; Klopfenstein, 1998; NUA, 1998). That is, the sample we obtained is not just "freshman male college students in engineering" as popular media stereotypes of computer users might have us fear. Nor is it the profile of the typical introductory psychology class, or even the university freshman class. Perhaps most notably, it is far more gender balanced than most stereotypes allow, in fact more gender balanced than introductory psychology classes. Of course, we must also remember that in striving to achieve a sample that is more representative of the real world than a freshman introductory psychology class, the result is heterogeneity—variability associated with relaxed control in sampling (e.g., greater age range, greater income range, geographic and presumably cultural variation, etc.). Perhaps one can see this in two ways, either as the price one pays in lost control for going off campus or as the reward, but we prefer the latter perspective. There also are problems associated with having a large sample, such as small differences becoming statistically significant though lacking clear practical importance. However, being unaccustomed to an abundance of data, we have to carry on and make the best of this problem.

REPLICATED RESULTS

Another way to check the validity of the online sample is to show that some well-known results from conventional laboratory research were also obtained here; if so, then that would increase confidence in accepting the more novel results here. In the case of test anxiety research there are a number of *marker patterns* that can be used, and these are thoroughly documented in a meta-analysis by Hembree (1988) and a new treatise on test anxiety by Zeidner (1998). For example, it is commonly found that women report significantly higher levels of test anxiety than men, and that was the case here for both the worry subscale, $t(1981) = 5.60$ ($M = 13.3$ vs. 12.1), and the emotionality subscale, $t(1981) = 8.64$ ($M = 16.8$ vs. 14.6).

It is also generally found that test anxiety is negatively correlated with global performance measures such as GPA, and that was found here for total test anxiety, $r(1823) = -.26$. This negative correlation is also usually greater for the worry subscale than for the emotionality subscale, and that was the case here, $r(1823) = -.34$ and $-.18$, respectively. Granted that these are not large effects in some respects, but in fact the same correlations in more controlled experiments are typically modest as well. In other words, the correlations are consistently in the direction of poorer performance with higher test anxiety, but the magnitude of the relationship is never large enough to indicate that test anxiety is the *only* thing affecting performance. Nonetheless, most researchers are satisfied with the reality of the relationship, and most students would prefer to minimize the handicap.

Therefore, although there can always be some question about a sample's validity, several common test anxiety marker effects were present here. These replicated marker effects thus seem to lend some credibility to the interpretation of relationships that are examined for the first time here. In addition to the replicated test anxiety results, an item analysis and factor analysis of the self-efficacy scale results here proved to be highly similar to those for the many preexisting datasets using the self-efficacy scale (e.g., Schwarzer & Jerusalem, 1995), and these data have been reported in more detail elsewhere (Schwarzer, Mueller, & Greenglass, 1999). Thus these replications add to the accumulating evidence (e.g., Pasveer & Ellard, 1998; Smith & Leigh, 1997; and chapters in this volume) that online samples yield results that mirror those found in more controlled settings. Granted, continuing to monitor the issue of how results derived from conventional formats compare to online results seems prudent, but it begins to appear that such concerns may have been overstated in terms of many areas of inquiry.

In sum then, insofar as these online data overlap with well-known effects for both test anxiety and self-efficacy, we can proceed with some confidence to examining the newer patterns of interest here. Designing some such marker patterns into one's survey seems a prudent and useful strategy for any online survey. Marker patterns may lack something in statistical elegance or finality in the interpretation of cause–effect relationships, but confirming old truths in a novel context is still comforting when trying to assess the legitimacy of newer findings.

NEWER RESULTS

EFFICACY

Table 1 presents some basic patterns, a correlation matrix for the test anxiety subscales, self-efficacy, and the demographic variables. Although we have a large number of degrees of freedom here, most of these relationships do seem plausible and thus perhaps they are not merely statistical artifacts. Efficacy, as might have been expected, was negatively correlated with both test anxiety subscales, $r(1974) = -.35$, and positively correlated with grades, $r(1813) = .19$. Efficacy was negatively correlated with self-reported extraver-

Table 1

Correlations between Anxiety, Efficacy, and Demographic Variables

	Emotion	Efficacy	Hand.	Extrav.	Age	Educ.	GPA	Income	Gender
Worry	.76*	−.35*	−.01	.01	−.05	−.14*	−.34*	−.08*	.13*
Emotion		−.36*	.01	.03	−.04	−.05*	−.18*	−.08*	.19*
Competence			−.01	−.14*	.03	.08*	.19*	.18*	−.13*
Handedness				.04	.03	.03	.02	−.02	.02
Extravert					−.06*	−.10*	.03	−.01	−.02
Age						.49*	.07*	.22*	.02
Education							.18*	.06	.01
GPA								.11*	.10*
Income									−.01

*$p < .05$.

sion; that is, extraverts reported higher efficacy, $r(1993) = -.14$ (but because extraversion did not correlate with income or GPA perhaps that is simply a positive attitude as opposed to achievement feedback). The relationship is quite small, but efficacy was positively correlated with level of education; that is, higher education went with higher self-efficacy, $r(1980) = .08$, but efficacy was not correlated with age. Efficacy was significantly lower for women than for men, $t(1969) = 5.72$ ($M = 28.5$ vs. 29.8).

TEST ANXIETY

In addition to the gender differences for test anxiety, and the common GPA deficit for high test anxiety, anxiety was significantly negatively correlated with education level for the worry subscale, $r(1982) = -.14$, and even for emotionality, $r(1982) = -.05$. The inverse correlation of anxiety with education level may mean that with further education one becomes less threatened by evaluation. For example, over time in college, students may learn better coping skills to cope with their test anxiety, and perhaps experienced students also develop better skills for dealing with exams, a test-wiseness effect. Alternatively, or additionally, the anxiety–education correlation may also mean that high test-anxious students progressively drop out at each higher education level. If that is true, then what we see at the postsecondary levels is a more restricted range of test anxiety, missing much of the extreme upper portion of the dimension. This anxiety–education correlation is not a large effect, but it fits readily with theoretical conceptions of test anxiety based on laboratory research.

In the final analysis, higher levels of worry were associated with lower income, $r(1665) = -.08$, and this anxiety–income relationship also was found for emotionality, $r(1665) = -.08$. These are both small effects, but nonetheless plausible.

COMPUTER USE

Our initial motivation was to determine whether there were any benefits to self-efficacy or test anxiety from learning to use computers. Although this is an easy question to formulate in the abstract, there are many specific manifestations with some bearing on the answer. One historically important question is how LOGO instruction may affect measures of efficacy, anxiety, and performance. As noted previously, Papert (1980) argued that LOGO instruction would defuse mathematics anxiety. We do not have data here on mathematics performance per se, so instead we deal with a more tenuous relationship, namely the sense in which a benefit from LOGO might be more general than mathematics confidence and more delayed or enduring in impact than a grade in an immediate mathematics course.

There are a couple of ways to examine this question. One involves a comparison of efficacy scores for those with and without *any* LOGO experience (ignoring how the expertise was acquired), as shown in Figure 2. The other requires a closer examination of the *type* of LOGO instruction within the subset of respondents who have had LOGO expertise, as shown in Figure 3.

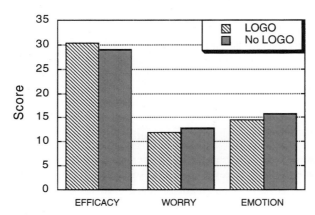

Figure 2   Test anxiety and efficacy for respondents who either had or did not have a course in LOGO programming ($n = 337$ vs. 1786).

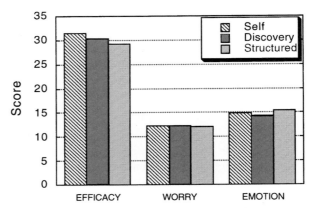

Figure 3 Test anxiety and efficacy by LOGO instruction method (only for the 337 respondents who had a LOGO course).

LOGO per se

Respondents with LOGO experiences of any kind ($n = 337$) reported significantly higher generalized efficacy scores than respondents lacking any LOGO experience, $t(1991) = 4.41$ ($M = 30.4$ and 28.9; $SD = 5.16$ and 5.22). Remember, this outcome reflects an assessment far removed in time from the actual course, not just a short-term end-of-course evaluation. Furthermore, it is not just how a computer experience diminishes computer or mathematics anxiety (or increases computer efficacy), instead this is apparently a broader increment in efficacy that persists over a long period of time.

There was a difference for the worry subscale of test anxiety, in that those with past LOGO experiences reported significantly less worry, $t(1991) = 2.92$ ($M = 11.9$ vs. 12.8; $SD = 4.39$ and 5.07), and likewise they reported lower emotionality, $t(1991) = 3.82$ ($M = 14.4$ vs. 15.8; $SD = 5.10$ and 6.03). However, there was no difference for GPA or income due to the presence or absence of LOGO experience, $t < 1$.

LOGO Method

For those who reported LOGO expertise, the instructional method was classified as either discovery ($n = 111$), structured ($n = 179$), or self-taught ($n = 120$), and these three categories were used as the basis for a one-way analysis of variance. There was a significant difference for generalized *efficacy*, $F(2, 407) = 6.76$, as efficacy was lower for the structured group ($M = 29.3$; $SD = 5.61$) than for either discovery or self-taught, the latter two not being significantly different (M = 30.4 and 31.5, respectively; SD = 5.01 and 4.87). Efficacy being higher with self-instruction seems consistent with the idea that self-instruction avoids the "failure" connotation of error, as does the discovery procedure.

LOGO instruction method did not lead to significant differences for either the worry component of test anxiety, $F < 1$, or the emotionality component, $F = 1.21$. Method of instruction likewise failed to show an effect with GPA, $F = 1.11$. There was a significant effect for instruction method in terms of income, $F(2, 340) = 3.37$, as income was lower for the respondents who had structured LOGO training than for either discovery or self-taught LOGO, the latter two not differing.

Self-Taught versus Course Format

Some of the same expectations can be extended to any other computer experiences obtained in a self-taught as opposed to a structured course format. One of our survey items asked subjects how they had acquired most of their expertise: self-taught or through courses (cf. Figure 4). Reported efficacy was not different for self-taught (n = 983) versus course-based (n = 126) backgrounds, $t(1115) = 1.58$ (M = 29.4 vs. 28.6, respectively). However, self-taught respondents reported significantly less worry, $t(1115) = 2.24$ (M = 12.6 vs. 13.6), and less emotionality, $t(1115) = 2.26$ (M = 15.4 vs. 16.6). There was no significant difference for income, $t < 1$, but self-taught respondents did report higher GPAs, $t(1016) = 2.16$. Self-taught respondents did rate themselves as more introverted (i.e., work alone) than respondents who said they had more often taken courses, $t(1115) = 4.52$ (M = 6.2 vs. 5.3).

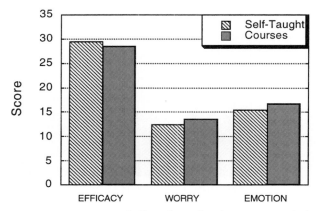

Figure 4   Test anxiety and efficacy by preferred instruction method.

BASIC Course

Respondents could similarly be classified as either having or not having expertise in BASIC programming. BASIC is a common programming language, but not one with a specific rationale associated with it such as that which Papert (1980) provided for LOGO. Nonetheless it offers a way to assess the generality of the LOGO findings in regard to associations with self-efficacy: Does LOGO experience have some unique benefit, or is the enhancement of efficacy also associated with learning to program in BASIC? If BASIC also has a comparable effect, then the decision to distance this project from the legacy of the LOGO literature would seem justified.

As Figure 5 shows, those with expertise in BASIC ($n = 781$) showed significantly higher generalized efficacy scores than those respondents who did not ($n = 1233$), $t(1991) = 3.70$ ($M = 29.8$ and 28.9; $SD = 5.10$ and 5.30). There also was a difference for the worry subscale of test anxiety, in that those with BASIC experiences reported less worry, $t(1991) = 2.44$ ($M = 12.3$ vs. 12.9; $SD = 4.66$ and 5.16), and likewise they reported lower emotionality, $t(1991) = 2.99$ ($M = 15.1$ vs. 15.9; $SD = 5.54$ and 6.11). However, there was no difference for GPA or income due to BASIC experiences, $t < 1$.

CONCLUSIONS

This has been a working paper for some time, but at this point some conclusions seem in order with regard to the substantive questions and also

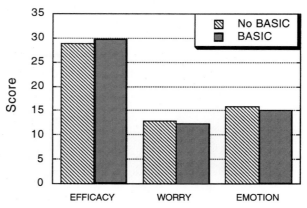

Figure 5 Test anxiety and efficacy for respondents who either had or did not have a course in BASIC programming.

with regard to the value of the Web-based format for addressing these questions.

It seems clear that there is some evidence consistent with the general hypothesis. Specifically, it appears (Figures 2 and 3) that discovery and self-taught LOGO experiences were associated with subsequent higher generalized efficacy—not just efficacy in the domain of computing or mathematics, and simultaneously lower test anxiety. However, the efficacy increment was not associated with higher achievement, at least as assessed here in terms of GPA (nor as perhaps assessed to a lesser extent by income).

It was of interest to determine whether this pattern of benefits was found for other programming languages. The results of the omnibus "self-taught" analysis (Figure 4) above are supportive of the idea that the benefits are not confined to LOGO experiences. Furthermore, the BASIC course results (Figure 5) are likewise consistent with the idea that a variety of computer experiences may be associated with higher efficacy and lower test anxiety. In sum, there seems to be nothing specific to LOGO; rather the result is a more general phenomenon as we argued at the outset.

So we can tentatively conclude that there are apparently some positive benefits associated with computer experiences, especially if those experiences do not involve formal courses. However, there are the usual cause–effect concerns associated with survey data. That is, although there may be correlations between computer experiences and self-reported efficacy (and anxiety), it cannot be rigorously claimed that the computer experiences directly caused the changes. It is a possibility though, so we cannot simply dismiss the possibility because of the correlational nature of these data any more than we can accept it.

Converging data from other investigations will help resolve the concern with causation. Such data could and should come from any number of inquiries, but a couple of illustrations should clarify how, in general, one could proceed to tease apart correlation and causation here. For example, one could now consider a situation where children are assigned to either a computer project or other projects, such as reading literature, writing essays, or second language learning, in each case half with the self-instruction or problem-driven format and half with a comprehensive syllabus-driven format. By taking measures of efficacy (anxiety) before and after these sessions, one could determine the extent to which computer experiences do or do not uniquely produce (cause) self-efficacy, among other things. Alternatively, one could arrange a psychology class where projects involve using computers and online communication, such as turning in assignments as Web pages, with a corresponding class where the work is not at all related to computers. After administering a preliminary self-efficacy assessment, students could then be given a choice as to which section to enroll in, and then performance through the semester would be monitored. If high-efficacy students opt into the computer-based section more readily than the conventional noncomputer format, that would seem to suggest more correlation than causation perhaps, though historical experiences with computing would have to be examined as well.

There is also the question of the limited magnitude of the patterns observed here; that is, perhaps the apparent patterns here are merely being driven by the large sample size. Practically speaking, by comparison, even in laboratory experiments the magnitude of the anxiety–performance relationship is modest, though quite repeatable (cf. Hembree, 1988; Zeidner, 1998). Presumably the smaller effects are obtained because the constructs in question are multiply determined. That is, even though self-directed computer experiences may be one factor that enhances efficacy, no doubt there are many other factors which contribute to increased self-efficacy, and likewise for the factors which reduce test anxiety. Further, no doubt there are factors other than efficacy and anxiety which contribute to better performance. Thus it is reasonable that any one component might show a limited effect no matter how valid or repeatable. Again, converging data will help resolve this concern.

Nonetheless, at this time we feel that the online procedure has proven to be of value in this case. At this point, we are reasonably satisfied with the results and with the methodology of a Web survey. One question is whether the particular question we examined here could have been assessed as well, or better, using more conventional data collection procedures. It does not seem likely that a more definitive answer would have emerged with either a direct intervention in a classroom or a longitudinal design, as those approaches substitute other limitations of their own, as noted earlier. For example, an intervention to teach computers to some students in a specific school would produce a result limited geographically, pedagogically, and in other respects. Methodologies involve trade-offs, and our interest here, as noted at the outset, was exploratory rather than theory testing, assessing the utility of the online data collection format at least as much as the computers and efficacy question itself. With a more heterogeneous sample than otherwise readily achievable, we have data consistent with the idea that self-directed computer experiences may yield enhanced self-efficacy and reduced test anxiety, perhaps because the psychological significance of an error had been changed.

Is our satisfaction with online research simply a unique circumstance produced by the mating of a computer-based data collection format with a computer-related topic? To the contrary, we do not think the suitability of the format is limited to just computer-related content. For one thing, the other efforts reported in this volume show the applicability of the online format to other, noncomputer topics. Furthermore, we have become sufficiently attracted to this form of data collection that we have begun other online research, where the topic does not involve computer-related content. One of these projects considers the extent to which the state of knowledge in the neurosciences can be applied to classroom educational practice. The answer to this is somewhat different when seen from the perspective of neuroscientists as opposed to the way educators understand the state of neuropsychology's findings on cognition (McCrea & Mueller, 1997). In this case, we are using the Web to minimize costs and enhance the reach of the sampling demographics, and there is no computer-related content. Another project uses the online format to extend the reach in participant recruiting in a study of attribution in brain-injury cases compared to other traumatic injuries (Logan, 1998). In this case, the number of such participants in any given geographical region is somewhat limited, but the online format allows participation from across the country. Another online project has used the Web format to examine the pattern of technology adoption among university faculty members (Jacobsen, 1997). In this case, the pattern of responses was examined for those who responded online versus those who would only complete a paper-and-pencil version, among other comparisons. All in all, we think the results of these various projects vindicate the time we spend at the keyboard!

REFERENCES

Adams, S. (1996). *The Dilbert principle*. New York: Harper.

Baron, J. (1998). Using Web questionnaires for judgment and decision making research [WWW document]. Available URL: http://www.sas.upenn.edu/~baron

EuroMarketing. (1998). Global Internet statistics (by language) [WWW document]. Available URL: http://www.euromktg.com/globstats

Georgia Technological University. (1998). GVU Center's WWW user surveys [WWW document]. Available URL: http://www.cc.gatech.edu/gvu/user_surveys/

Gibbs, W. W. (1997, July). Taking computers to task. *Scientific American*, 82–89.

Hembree, R. (1988). Correlates, causes, effects, and treatment of test anxiety. *Review of Educational Research, 58*, 47–77.

Hodapp, V., & Benson, J. (1997). The multidimensionality of test anxiety: A test of different models. *Anxiety, Stress, and Coping, 10*(3), 219–244.

InfoQuest. (1998). Internet surveys and statistics [WWW document]. Available URL: http://www.teleport.com/~tbchad/stats1.html

Jacobsen, D. M. (1997). Teaching and learning with technology [WWW document]. Available URL: http://www.acs.ucalgary.ca/~dmjacobs/phd

Klopfenstein, B. (1998). Links to WWW user research [WWW document]. Available URL: http://www.bgsu.edu/departments/tcom/users.html

Landauer, T. (1995). *The trouble with computers: Usefulness, usability, and productivity*. Cambridge: MIT Press.

Littlefield, J., Delclos, V. R., Lever, S., Clayton, K. N., Bransford, J. D., & Franks, J. J. (1988). Learning LOGO: Method of teaching, transfer of general skills, and attitudes toward school and computers. In R. E. Mayer (Ed.), *Teaching and learning computer programming: Multiple research perspectives*. Hillsdale, NJ: Erlbaum.

Logan, M. (1998). A comparative analysis of causal attribution [WWW document]. Available URL: http://www.acs.ucalgary.ca/~mclogan/start.html

McCrea, S. M., & Mueller, J. H. (1997). Neuroscience and education [WWW document]. Available URL: http://www.acs.ucalgary.ca/~mueller/neuro.html

Mueller, J. H. (1997). Human participants ethics issues [WWW document]. Available URL: http://www.psych.ucalgary.ca/CourseNotes/PSYC413/Study/Tools/ethics/online.html

Mueller, J. H., Jacobsen, D. M., & Schwarzer, R. (1996). Test anxiety and computer experience [WWW document]. Available URL: http://www.acs.ucalgary.ca/~mueller/tai-consent.html

Norman, D. A. (1988). *The design of everyday things*. New York: Basic Books.

Norman, D. A. (1993). *Things that make us smart*. Reading, MA: Addison-Wesley.

NUA. (1998). Internet surveys [WWW document]. Available URL: http://www.nua.ie/surveys/index.cgi

Papert, S. (1980). *Mindstorms: Children, computers and powerful ideas*. New York: Basic Books.

Pasveer, K., & Ellard, J. (1998). The making of a personality inventory: Help from the WWW. *Behavior Research Methods, Instruments, & Computers, 30*, 309–313.

Rinaldi, A. (1998). Netiquette [WWW document]. Available URL: http://www.fau.edu/rinaldi/netiquette.html

Schmidt, W. C. (1997). World-Wide Web survey research: Potential problems, and solutions. *Behavior Research Methods, Instruments, & Computers, 29*(2), 274–279.

Schwarzer, R., & Jerusalem, M. (1995). Generalized Self-Efficacy Scale. In J. Weinman, S. Wright, & M. Johnston (Eds.), *Measures in health psychology: A user's portfolio. Causal and control beliefs* (pp. 35–37). Windsor, UK: NFER-NELSON.

Schwarzer, R., Mueller, J., & Greenglass, E. (1999). Assessment of perceived self-efficacy on the Internet: Data collection in cyberspace. *Anxiety, Stress, and Coping, 12*, 145–161.

Smith, M. A., & Leigh, B. (1997). Virtual subjects: Using the Internet as an alternative source of subjects and research environment. *Behavior Research Methods, Instruments, & Computers, 29*, 496–505.

Spielberger, C. D. (1980). *Preliminary professional manual for the Test Anxiety Inventory*. Palo Alto, CA: Consulting Psychologists Press.

Tapscott, D. (1998). *Growing up digital*. New York: McGraw-Hill.

Zeidner, M. (1998). *Test anxiety: The state of the art*. New York: Plenum.

SECTION III

Computer Techniques for Internet Experimentation

CHAPTER 9

PsychExps: An Online Psychology Laboratory

Kenneth O. McGraw
Department of Psychology
University of Mississippi
University, Mississippi 38677

Mark D. Tew
Department of Electrical Engineering
University of Mississippi
University, Mississippi 38677

John E. Williams
Department of Psychology
University of Mississippi
University, Mississippi 38677

PSYCHEXPS: AN ONLINE PSYCHOLOGY LABORATORY

The interactivity afforded by programs that can be run over the Internet has led to a wealth of online activities, including banking, gaming, catalog shopping, and auctions. Cognitive and social psychology experiments have been added to this list through the appearance of sites that exploit Web technology to give users control over the screen events that are used to elicit their responses. Such sites take experimentation on the Web beyond forms-based data collection to true interaction. In this chapter we discuss the rationale for PsychExps (http://www.olemiss.edu/PsychExps), our particular entry into the world of interactive sites. Included with the rationale is an overview of the technology we have adopted and some of our plans for future development.

RATIONALE

Laboratory courses in which students learn to design experiments, collect and analyze data, and then report findings are considered a fundamental

Psychological Experiments on the Internet

part of the psychology curriculum at nearly every undergraduate institution. According to a survey we conducted, 92% of departments offer such a course and 90% make degrees contingent on students taking such a course (Williams & McGraw, 1999). In addition, most departments have independent research opportunities that students can complete for credit. The introduction of inexpensive computers capable of running programmed experiments revolutionized these traditional laboratory experiences in the years after 1977, the year in which Apple II's were introduced, to the point that there was a sudden, widespread need to establish computer labs for student use. As funds became available, departments purchased computers and laboratory software packages from developers such as CONDUIT, Life Science Associates, or Psychology Software Tools, Inc., and then proudly declared the opening of their computerized undergraduate labs.

The problem with this approach is that funding for equipment and software is aperiodic, whereas hardware and software developments are on a perpetual upward trajectory. Keeping up with the curve seems to be a problem for every department that has established student labs, and for most, the best they are able to do is to occasionally brush against the curve in those years when one-time money becomes available.

One solution to the problem is to reduce the need for departments to be financially responsible for the hardware and software used in their laboratories. Internet communications make this possible. With psychology experiments delivered over the Internet, the software to run experiments exists on the server, not the client computer, so students can run their laboratory exercises from any Internet-connected computer: their own, the library's, or any computer that meets the hardware requirements and is equipped with a Web player.

Among the obvious advantages of Web-based experiments is that they free students from having to come to a fixed site at a fixed time to perform their lab activities. In addition to convenience, ease of access makes it easier to recruit participants, and data collection can be performed in parallel from multiple sites. Web-based experiments make it possible to fit more data gathering into a fixed time period, and perhaps most important, having a single Web-based implementation of an experiment allows data to be pooled across research sites and across time. With data pooling, the types of questions addressed in laboratory work can be answered using large data sets in place of the typical small ones.

Because data collection is often the single longest phase of any research project, the efficient collection of large data sets makes it possible for students conducting independent research to complete their research in a single 15-week semester, as required for many independent research courses. Also, it makes it possible for laboratory students to have data sets large enough to study phenomena with small effect sizes or ones that must be addressed in between-subjects designs. In conventional labs, lab exercises focus on phenomena with especially large effects that can be replicated reliably in small data sets using within-subject designs, because the typical lab class is small (15–20 students) and the only research participants are the students themselves. The possibility of large data sets will have the effect of expanding the library of laboratory experiments in ways that will be interesting to students and potentially valuable to science.

From an instructor's point of view, there are other advantages to Web-based experiments. One is that the instructor does not have to acquire and maintain equipment for classes. Another is availability of free software upgrades, which is a consequence of the fact that, as Web-based experiments become more common, they will become better and better in the same way that Web pages have become better and better. Web pages began with static text and a few graphics but now often include sound, animation, and interactivity.

One factor that will drive the regular improvement of Web-based experiments is that programmers can write to the highest standard, not the lowest. They can do so based on the relatively safe assumption that students will have access to current-capability computers somewhere on campus to use for data collection. If the experiments could only be conducted on dedicated computers purchased and maintained by departments, this assumption seldom would be true. Thus instructors can require experiments employing the latest technology in voice recognition or sound without waiting on their own department to equip its student computers with these features.

From an institutional perspective, the major argument for Web-based labs is cost reduction. Departments that augment undergraduate laboratory experiences with Web-based experiments will have a reduced need to dedicate computers for student use in their own departments. Their ultimate savings in hardware, maintenance, space, and security costs could be considerable.

Realizing the potential advantages inherent in Web-based experiments, we obtained funding from the Department of Education's Fund for the Improvement of Post-Secondary Education (FIPSE) program and from the University of Mississippi to develop PsychExps as a site for conducting social and cognitive psychology experiments. The first year of our three-year project (1997–2000) was spent in designing the site and developing it to the point that it could serve as a fully functioning laboratory to augment existing computer laboratory facilities in undergraduate departments. To that end we developed a set of 10 experiments drawn partly from the laboratory canon (e.g., Mueller–Lyer, Poggendorff, and Mental Rotation) and partly from our own interests (e.g., a lateralized Stroop experiment, a study of illusory line motion, and a false recognition experiment that uses facial photographs as stimuli).

To function as a lab, one must provide data. We do that by displaying user data on the user's screen at the completion of experiments and, more important, by writing a data record that is appended to a cumulative data file on our campus UNIX Web server. For purposes of confidentiality, research participant names are replaced by randomly generated codes in the publicly available data. A separate file that identifies users by name and code is protected, with access restricted to researchers who have registered to collect data at the site.

The publicly available data set is an archive of all those who have elected to send their data to PsychExps. Professors (or others) can download whatever portion of the data file they want (typically the data generated by their own students) and then, depending on their instructional goals, analyze the data themselves or distribute the data to students for analysis. For those who want one-click processing, we offer a set of Microsoft Excel macros that import and organize data from a downloaded PsychExps data file. We chose Excel because it is a cross-platform spreadsheet that is part of the Microsoft Office suite that often comes with new PCs. Using our one-click approach yields an Excel workbook with one page per student and one page of summary statistics for the class, as illustrated in Figure 1.

THE TECHNOLOGY

THE AUTHORING TOOL

The experiments currently available at PsychExps were developed using Macromedia's Authorware, a multimedia authoring tool. As an authoring tool, Authorware rivals experiment generator software such as MEL (http://www.pstnet.com/melpro/melpro.htm), PsyScope (http://psyscope.psy.cmu.edu/), ERTS (http://ourworld.compuserve.com/homepages/berisoft/), and, most recently, E-Prime (http://www.pstnet.com/e-prime/e-prime.htm) but, unlike these packages, it was not developed with psychology experiments in mind. The primary Authorware audience has been corporations wanting to build Web and CD-ROM-delivered training programs and tests. Nonetheless, Authorware's generic functions are easily adapted to the needs of psychologists who want to present multimedia stimulus events with precise control over timing, permit users to interact with screen objects, and measure users' responses with accuracy on the order of milliseconds.

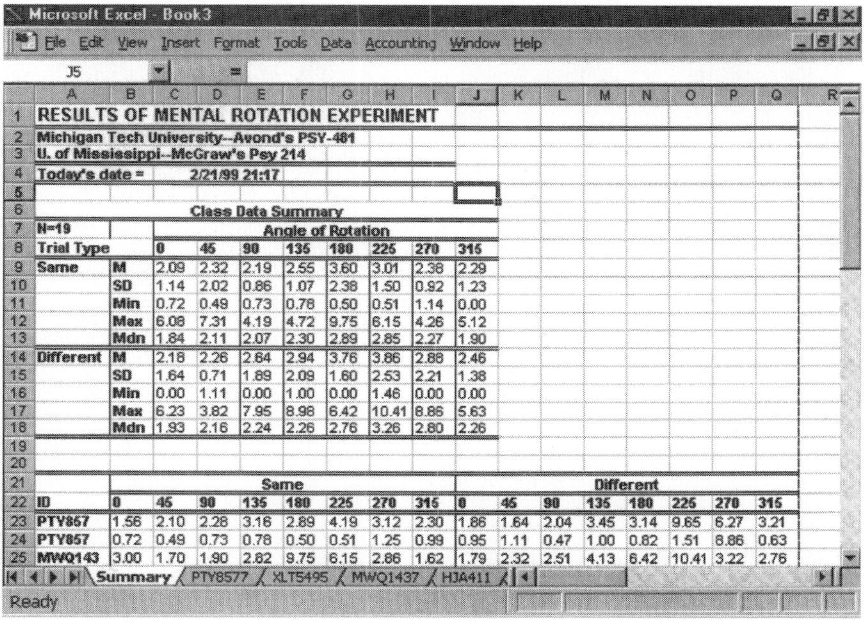

Microsoft Excel - Book3

RESULTS OF MENTAL ROTATION EXPERIMENT

Michigan Tech University--Avond's PSY-481

U. of Mississippi--McGraw's Psy 214

Today's date = 2/21/99 21:17

Class Data Summary

N=19		Angle of Rotation							
Trial Type		0	45	90	135	180	225	270	315
Same	M	2.09	2.32	2.19	2.55	3.60	3.01	2.38	2.29
	SD	1.14	2.02	0.86	1.07	2.38	1.50	0.92	1.23
	Min	0.72	0.49	0.73	0.78	0.50	0.51	1.14	0.00
	Max	6.08	7.31	4.19	4.72	9.75	6.15	4.26	5.12
	Mdn	1.84	2.11	2.07	2.30	2.89	2.85	2.27	1.90
Different	M	2.18	2.26	2.64	2.94	3.76	3.86	2.88	2.46
	SD	1.64	0.71	1.89	2.09	1.60	2.53	2.21	1.38
	Min	0.00	1.11	0.00	1.00	0.00	1.46	0.00	0.00
	Max	6.23	3.82	7.95	8.98	6.42	10.41	8.86	5.63
	Mdn	1.93	2.16	2.24	2.26	2.76	3.26	2.80	2.26

	Same								Different							
ID	0	45	90	135	180	225	270	315	0	45	90	135	180	225	270	315
PTY857	1.56	2.10	2.28	3.16	2.89	4.19	3.12	2.30	1.86	1.64	2.04	3.45	3.14	9.65	6.27	3.21
PTY857	0.72	0.49	0.73	0.78	0.50	0.51	1.25	0.99	0.95	1.11	0.47	1.00	0.82	1.51	8.86	0.63
MWQ143	3.00	1.70	1.90	2.82	9.75	6.15	2.86	1.62	1.79	2.32	2.51	4.13	6.42	10.41	3.22	2.76

Summary / PTY8577 / XLT5495 / MWQ1437 / HJA411

Ready

Figure 1 Excel macros that we offer for analyzing data at PsychExps produce workbooks that include individual data sheets and data summary sheets: (a) sample of data summary for a mental rotation experiment; (b) sample of an individual data sheet.

The graphical interface used in Authorware consists of icons that developers drag onto a flow line. "Display" icons define the text, colors, and images that appear on the screen; "Wait" icons perform functions such as the timing of displays; "Calculation" icons provide a programming language that includes a large number of built-in functions and variables. Other icons provide functions such as branching, decision making, animation, and sound; "map" icons are used to encapsulate the functional icons thus providing convenient divisions of a piece.

Figure 2, which is taken from our line motion experiment, gives an example of what a developer sees when working with an Authorware program. The Level 1 flow line (top left window in the figure) shows the template in which the line motion experiment is pasted. It consists almost entirely of map icons that are labeled to show the major segments of the piece. Clicking on the map icon labeled "Line Motion Experiment" opens it up to reveal a

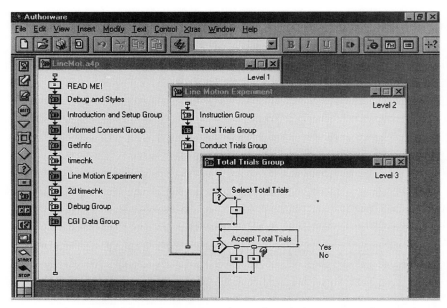

Figure 2   Three levels of the Authorware piece that conducts the line motion study at PsychExps illustrate that building an Authorware piece is similar to creating a flowchart. Levels 1 and 2 in this figure show the overall organization of the piece. Level 3 shows icons that perform interactions with participants in the experiment.

Level 2 structure (top right window in the figure) consisting of three map icons—one for instructions, one for setting the total trials, and one for conducting the trials. Opening up the Conduct Trials icon reveals two interactions (lower right window in the figure) that are used to allow participants to set the number of trials they want to conduct. The first interaction (arrow icon with a question mark) creates a text entry box where participants enter the number of trials; the second creates a two-button interaction where participants click "Yes" to accept the number of trials they have entered or "No" to recycle and choose again.

Even this brief illustration of the structure of an Authorware piece is sufficient to show the contrast between an Authorware piece and the lines of code needed in conventional programs. The labeled icon structure used by Authorware, allows even a novice to get some sense of what is happening and where. The same is not true for conventional programs in which line after line of code controls events. Labeled icons and maps encourage modular programming, and icons are easily structured to be reusable.

While Authorware's icon and flow line programming model offer an inviting interface that encourages modular programming, Authorware is otherwise similar to programming languages for creating stand-alone experiments to be run locally on a lab computer. In particular, an Authorware program can be delivered as a `*.exe` file that is executable on any machine (as long as the free run time player is either available or packaged with the `*.exe` file). The primary advantage of Authorware, therefore, is that programs can be packaged for Web delivery. The technology that makes this possible was first known as Afterburner and Shockwave, though more recently Macromedia refers simply to a Web packager and Web player (Macromedia, 1997, p. 249; `http://www.macromedia.com/support/authorware/attain/how/web/`).

Web-packaged Authorware programs are streamed in segments to client computers. Computers that have the Web player (aka Shockwave) can interpret and execute the segments, and the packaged segments execute locally, an important feature when precise timing is critical.

For Web delivery of experiments, Authorware has no competition among experiment generator packages, but it does have competition from other applications packages that support multimedia interactivity. Java is one (Gosling, Joy, & Steele, 1997). Macromedia's Director (Goddard, 1999) is another. Others are Roger Wagner Publishing, Inc.'s HyperStudio and Microsoft's PowerPoint. We chose Authorware from this set because it combines accessibility with a great deal of programming power. In Authorware, novices can quickly learn to swap icons and change the content of displays. With little or no programming skill, therefore, a novice can make meaningful changes to existing programs.

The desire to have PsychExps evolve into a site controlled by a wide community of developers contributed to the choice of Authorware. Java is a free development tool with the functionality of low-level languages, but we believe it is not as easy for programming novices to learn as Authorware. Had we chosen Java as the tool for developing PsychExps, the site is more likely to have remained in the hands of a few psychologists willing to spend the time needed to become facile with the Java language. Essentially the same would have been true with Director, which requires expertise in Lingo, Director's programming language.

On the other hand, had we chosen HyperStudio or PowerPoint as our development tool, there would have been severe limitations on the types of experiments that could be used at PsychExps. PowerPoint does not permit user control of screen objects, precise display of screen events, precise timing of responses, and it offers no way to create randomized ordering of stimuli and trials. These functions may be available in HyperStudio to some extent, but would require using its programming language, HyperLogo. In brief, then, we believe that Authorware is the development environment of choice among current commercial packages, first for the Web deliverability of products and second for its combination of accessibility and functionality.

How to Generate Experiments

To participate in the communal development of experiments at Psych-Exps, users must first have a copy of Authorware. In spring 1999 a typical reseller price was $370 for an electronic documentation edition and $741 for a full version (academic pricing). This is roughly equivalent in price to the experiment generator software that has become popular in many laboratories. We are offering workshops for psychology instructors who want to participate in the development of PsychExps. Workshop participants receive free copies of Authorware, thanks to the FIPSE grant and generous support from Macromedia.

The experiments currently at PsychExps were developed using both Authorware 4.0 and Authorware 5.0 Attain. Unlike 4.0, which came in both Mac and PC versions, 5.0 authoring requires a PC. The packaged programs will run on either the Mac or PC platform, so that student users and others will not be affected by this change. Authorware developers accustomed to using Macs are affected, however.

To integrate the diverse efforts of those who wish to contribute experiments to PsychExps, we have developed a model Authorware program or template into which developers can paste new experiments. This template allows developers to produce novel experiments that look and function like the others at PsychExps. To do so, authors open color-coded icons to make changes in variable values and names. A single map icon that contains the flow line for the new experiment is inserted into the template. This portion of the piece, called "New experiment," contains the screens unique to the new experiment, measures the dependent variable, and writes the data to a variable named Answer. Using this template, novel experiments can be generated in a day or two by anyone who has reasonable facility with Authorware.

As we move to Authorware 5.0, new programs and adaptations of old ones should become easier through use of what Macromedia calls *Knowledge objects*. These function like the "wizards" included in many commercial programs for tasks such as data analysis, newsletter creation, or writing wills. We will be developing wizards to make it even easier for novices to modify our existing experiments. In addition, we will develop knowledge objects that permit the rapid programming of experiments that follow established paradigms for measuring reaction time, signal detection, and discrimination.

HOW TO DELIVER THE EXPERIMENT ON THE WEB

When an experiment has been developed and tested in the authoring environment, there are two "packaging" steps that prepare the experiment for Web delivery. The first step is to package the experiment as a *.a4r file, which is a noneditable Authorware file. This step is essentially a "Save As" function that is performed directly from the Authorware File menu. The next step in Web preparation is to "shock" the *.4r file. Currently this is done using the Authorware 5 Web Packager. Formerly this step required a freely distributed program called Afterburner. In either case, packaging at this stage divides the *.a4r file into segments (denoted by *.aas extensions) that are delivered sequentially during program execution. Delivery is controlled by a "map file" (*.aam) that the browser accesses via an HTML file with an "embed" tag (see Table 1).

The most important choice during packaging for Web delivery is the segment size. Larger segments result in a longer initial wait time before the experiment begins. Smaller segments result in a shorter initial wait time. The trade-off comes during program execution. Shorter, more frequently streamed segments risk creating delays during execution that would not occur for larger segments which stream in the background while the current segment is being executed. Authors are generally advised to play with different segment sizes to determine what segment size works best. Segment sizes that produce uninter-

Table 1

Use of the Embed Tag in an HTML Page

```
〈html〉
〈head〉
〈title〉PsychExps experiment〈/title〉
〈/head〉
〈body〉
〈center〉
〈embed SRC="psychexps_demo.aam" WIDTH="532"
    HEIGHT="384" WINDOW="onTop"〉
〈/center〉
〈/body〉
〈/html〉
```

rupted event flows for machines with ample RAM and high-speed Internet connections may produce stutters when running on less well equipped machines.

Once the *.aas segments, the *.aam file, and the HTML file are placed at a URL, any browser with the Authorware Web Player can execute the experiment. The Authorware Web Player plug-in resides on the user's computer and basically provides the capability of a run-time player via the user's browser.

DOES WEB DELIVERY AFFECT DATA QUALITY?

When authors first consider putting an experiment on the Web, they wonder whether they will be sacrificing the integrity of their stimulus displays and measurements by doing so. We have begun an experimental plan to gather what we hope will be definitive data on this issue, but at present we have a few observations. Based on them, we believe that Web delivery does not affect the integrity of experiments. A major reason is that once all segment downloads are complete, measurements are limited only by the inherent capabilities of the computer and of Authorware. From the point of view of research participants, therefore, aside from waiting for segment downloads, Web-delivered Authorware experiments should be indistinguishable from those conducted locally using an executable *.exe Authorware file.

We do caution, however, that when timing in an experiment is important, authors should package experiments using a segment size larger than the file size of the packaged file. This will result in a single segment and a single download, which eliminates background streaming of segments while the experiment is in progress. This prevents timed screen displays and reaction-time measurements from being affected by untimely downloads that introduce error additional to inherent machine error. On the research participant side, it is helpful to close all other programs before executing an experiment for which timing is critical—but this is true, of course, regardless of the source of the program code and regardless whether the program is resident or Web-delivered.

Our belief that the timing accuracy of experiments at PsychExps is determined solely by the research participant's machine is supported by timing consistency tests we routinely conduct for all experiments that require tachistoscopic displays or measure reaction time. A consistency test consists of a set of 30 trials in which we read the system clock before and after a delay interval programmed to last for 250, 500, or 1000 milliseconds. One such test is conducted just prior to the experiment and one just after. In these tests, the modal system clock difference on Pentium machines running Windows 95 differs from the target values by from 0 to 2 milliseconds depending on the processor speed, with a few rare spikes that range from 10 to 100 milliseconds. We believe that these spikes reflect clock cycles "stolen" by the operating system, but they do not appear to pose a threat to the integrity of data as revealed by an examination of the actual data we have gathered at PsychExps.

In our word recognition study, for example, words are displayed to the left or right of a fixation point for durations that begin at 90 milliseconds and increment in steps of 10 milliseconds until the word is successfully identified. Data from 176 students from 11 different campuses in fall 1998 and spring 1999 showed that 124 of the 176 subjects showed the expected right visual field advantage in word recognition, as measured using the conventional measure—number correct on first presentation (e.g., Bryden & Rainey, 1963) —or our own novel measure of mean recognition time, which for these data yielded mean values of 123 milliseconds on the left and 113 milliseconds on the right. These results obtained from users on a diverse array of machines running in diverse environments are completely consistent with the results one would expect from comparable laboratory-based measurements (see Banich, 1997, pp. 99–102, for a review).

The same is true for our Stroop experiment. The major effect in this experiment is that noncongruent word–color pairings produce longer response times than congruent word–color pairings (see McLeod, 1991). The 14 classes that conducted this experiment in fall 1998 and spring 1999 all obtained this effect. Collectively the classes contained 220 students. Their mean response time to identify colors on congruent trials was 0.85 seconds and on noncongruent trials, 0.97 seconds. This trend for faster congruent trial responses was present in 176 of the 220 individual data records. Whatever the accuracy achieved in our online experiments, therefore, it is certainly good enough to detect the effects the current experiments are designed to detect.

To Trust or Not to Trust

An issue that arises during Web delivery of experiments is that of "trust/not trust." In trusting mode, a Web-launched program has the ability to read and write to the research participant's hard disk; in nontrusting mode, these capabilities are blocked. When the program is packaged for Web delivery a presentation of a "trust/not trust" dialogue box is the default if the experiment contains any operations that are prohibited in nontrusting mode. Before execution of the experiment, the participant is presented with a dialogue box asking if he or she chooses to trust the site and the participant's response dictates whether or not the functions are allowed. If participants choose to not trust a program that includes prohibited functions or if the "trust/not trust" dialogue box is bypassed, the participant's computer may lock up when a prohibited function is encountered—but the participant's data and hard disk remain protected.

To be nonthreatening to our research participants, we have developed PsychExps so that all experiments run in the nontrusting mode. There are constraints imposed by this decision. For example, nontrusting mode precludes the use of external objects such as movies, because they must be downloaded to the participant's hard disk. Another consequence is that the products of third-party developers who market "extras" for Authorware cannot be used, because these would require trusting mode. Finally, an experiment that begins in nontrusting mode cannot GoTo another Web page that embeds an experiment that requires trusting mode, because the original decision to "not trust" is retained. Although all of the experiments at PsychExps currently use nontrusting mode, trusting may eventually be required for some experiments.

DATA TRANSFER

During the conduct of an experiment, we store data in the volatile memory of the research participant's computer using a generic list variable named "Answer." The framework for doing this is one of the features built into the template we offer to developers. Once data collection is complete, participants have an option to submit their data to the archive.

To append data to our archives and use nontrusting mode, we have adopted the strategy of using a CGI script. This requires formatting the data for processing by the script (no embedded spaces or tabs, etc.), a task that is handled by the template, and it requires accessing the URL where the script resides. Formerly we performed this task by reading an external file that was the script, but in Authorware versions 4.03 and later, Macromedia incorporated a PostURL function. Because this function allows us to stay in Authorware after effecting the data transfer and because it overcomes a 2000-character limit on the data transferred using ReadExtFile, it is the current method of choice.

Once accessed, the CGI script reads and processes the data. For PsychExps, the first datum is the text format data file to which this data set should be appended so that a single script can be used to process data from every experiment.

FUTURE PLANS FOR PSYCHEXPS

While we continue to develop experiments to add to the library of experiments at PsychExps, we are soliciting others to join us in developing the site. The ultimate vision is for a site that is enriched and maintained through the efforts of a large community of educators who want to use PsychExps in their classes and to participate in its development by authoring experiments that can be used at the site. We hope to establish group responsibility for the site in the same sense that there is group responsibility for journals. Journals are continuously relevant and informative because they are sustained by a community of readers, editors, and reviewers who each have a stake in the journal's success. We want PsychExps to be similar in its dependence on a community of stakeholders. This goal comes from our belief that any site that depends on just a few contributors will be limited in scope, short on imagination, and—sooner or later—stale. For long-term viability, the site must be a community effort.

Through workshops we hope to establish an initial community of developers that can expand over time. We are seeking people from all sectors of the site-user community, which we understand to extend from high schools and junior colleges to major research institutions. In 1999, the workshop participants included people with varying degrees of computer and programming expertise. We chose this diverse group to help test the proposition that Authorware is a tool that even novices can use to some degree but that does not impose limits on the imaginations of experienced programmers.

To function as a laboratory on which psychology classes depend, data management is a critical issue. PsychExps needs to provide custom data sets filtered from the archive according to researchers' needs. For example, instructors might want only the data collected by their students in the current semester or they might want cumulative data for the past three semesters. They might also want to either include or exclude data on the gender and hand preference of research participants. For these reasons, the text files used in the early stages of PsychExps are no longer adequate and a database is needed. The current plan is to develop an Access database using Active Server Page technology on our own NT server. In the interim, the database resides at the University of Mississippi's UNIX server where data filtering by date and class can be performed. These filtering functions can also be applied to downloaded data using the Excel macros we provide.

Although the Excel macros allow even novices to make use of the data accumulated at PsychExps, not everyone has Excel; and of those who do, not everyone knows how to use it. Ultimately, to be a site that effectively serves most data collection needs, PsychExps will implement dynamic, online data extraction and processing. Not only will this better meet instructors' needs, but this database connectivity will make our experiments more informative to research participants by giving immediate feedback regarding individual performance. For example, at the end of an experiment a participant could be told, "Your reaction times for congruent trials were at the 71st percentile among the 240 users in the database" or "Your data are interesting in that you were faster to recognize the words on the left than the right. Only 15% of the 240 users so far show this pattern."

In addition to making data extraction and processing easier, we also plan to make experiments easier to generate. The knowledge objects introduced in Authorware 5 provide the tool that will make this possible. At present, to modify existing programs, authors have to open icons to change text and settings. A knowledge object opens the possibility of querying authors and using the responses to modify the experiment. Indeed, this very exciting development further strengthens our conviction that using a regularly up-graded commercial product as the development tool for PsychExps is a good strategy. Although the product is not free (like Java), we have found that the cost thus far has been quite reasonable relative to the power of the tool. We are now using our third version of Authorware, and each upgrade has added features, functions, and variables that we have found to be substantial im-provements. Another benefit is that commercial products such as Authorware are likely to pay considerable attention to backward compatibility. Java 1.2, on the other hand, was so different from 1.0 and 1.1 that code had to be rewritten (Francis, Neath, & Surprenant, chap. 11, this volume).

BECOMING INVOLVED WITH PSYCHEXPS

Those who want to use experiments at PsychExps for data collection need to be added to the registered user list by sending a request to pe@olemiss.edu or by filling out an online form at http://psychexps.olemiss.edu/InstrOnly_Page/usersform.htm. The "affiliation" (e.g., Rhodes College—Wetzel's Psy 212) is added to the list of registered users, a text file that is read from the server at the start of the experiment. Students click on their affiliation to create an entry for a data field that is used when data are filtered. Registered users will be automatically added to our listserver, while others may subscribe to the PsychExps listserver by sending the message "subscribe pe" to majordomo@listserv.olemiss.edu. The listserver is a place for posting questions and sharing ideas and is used to notify site users of proposed and scheduled changes.

Those who want to participate in program development are encouraged to contact us at pe@olemiss.edu address or at any of the personal e-mail addresses given at PsychExps. Although workshops for the summer of 1999 are past, we will also hold workshops in the summer of 2000. Workshop partici-pants are expected to modify an existing experiment or to create a new experiment to expand the offerings at PsychExps.

Summary

PsychExps is an online undergraduate laboratory that is currently available for use. Experiments can be conducted and data collected, just as in traditional labs that use experiment packages or other software for conducting experiments in which students participate as subjects. In spring 1999, there were 10 experiments at the site. The number of experiments will grow rapidly as the community of developers who wish to enrich the site through their own contributions expands.

REFERENCES

Banich, M. T. (1997). *Neuropsychology: The neural bases of mental function.* Boston: Houghton Mifflin.

Bryden, M., & Rainey, C. (1963). Left–right differences in tachistoscopic recognition. *Journal of Experimental Psychology, 66,* 568–571.

Cohen, J. D., MacWhinney, B., Flatt, M., & Provost, J. (1993). PsyScope: A new graphic interactive environment for designing psychology experiments. *Behavioral Research Methods, Instruments, & Computers, 25*(2), 257–271.

Goddard, J. (1999). Staging the world with Macromedia Director. *PC World On-line* [Online serial]. Available URL: http:// www.pcworld.com

Gosling, J., Joy, B., & Steele, G. (1997). *The JAVA language specification.* Reading, MA: Addison-Wesley.

Macromedia. (1997). *Authorware 5 Attain: Using Authorware Attain.* San Francisco: Macromedia, Inc.

McLeod, C.M. (1991). Half a century of research on the Stroop effect: An integrative review. *Psychological Bulletin, 109,* 163–204.

Williams, J. E., & McGraw, K. O. (1999). Undergraduate labs and computers: The case for PsychExps. Manuscript submitted for publication. *Behavior Research Methods, Instruments, & Computers, 31*(2), 287–291.

CHAPTER 10

Techniques for Creating and Using Web Questionnaires in Research and Teaching

Jonathan Baron*
Department of Psychology
University of Pennsylvania
Philadelphia, Pennsylvania 19104

Michael Siepmann
University of Pennsylvania
Philadelphia, Pennsylvania 19104

INTRODUCTION

In this chapter, we describe techniques and procedures we have used for putting questionnaires on the Web, with particular emphasis on the technical details. Before moving to the Web, we used pencil-and-paper questionnaires. Subjects came to a room that was open at certain hours, and they were paid on the spot for completing questionnaires. Almost all the subjects were students. We have been doing studies on the Web for almost two years as of this writing and have completed over 130 studies in that time, each typically involving collection of data from about 50 subjects over a period of a few weeks. We monitor the results as they come in and frequently redesign studies that subjects seem to misunderstand. The first author keeps a list of subjects, which now contains over 700, each of whom has completed an average of about 9 studies. All of our research is now done on the Web, except research with collaborators who use other methods. The topics include utility elicitation for cost-effectiveness analysis in medicine, moral judgments, judgments of fair allocation of resources, risk, and subjective estimates of bias in probabilistic beliefs. Our questionnaires are available on the Web at http://www.psych.upenn.edu/ ~ baron / qs.html.

Jonathan Baron's Web page is at http://www.sas.upenn.edu/~jbaron/; e-mail at baron@psych.upenn.edu.

Psychological Experiments on the Internet

The use of the Web for research is a topic of some recent interest. The NetLab Workshop (National Science Foundation, 1997) recommended encouragement of just this sort of effort. One interesting feature of the Web is that it encourages altruism. That is, people are willing to put in a little bit of work to put something on the Web, without remuneration, but knowing that millions of people—the numbers growing by the minute—will have access to it. This was a feature of the Internet even in the days before Web browsers, but browsers and search engines have made things easier to find. A great deal of Web content may be freely copied and reused.

Much of experimental psychology involves presenting subjects with visual or auditory information and asking them to respond manually. Almost any study of this type can be done on the Web. Once an experiment is available on the Web, others can be invited to copy it and modify it for their own use, although this has not happened much so far. The first author's general experimental procedure (which is continuing to evolve) is to randomize the stimuli separately for each subject. Each session contains 20–100 judgments, depending on their difficulty, and pay ranges from \$1 to \$6, again, depending on the difficulty and time required. In some cases, he presents all the stimuli in one condition before all the stimuli in another condition, and the stimuli are randomized within each condition. Typically, each item is presented separately, in such a way that the subject cannot back up. One current study provides practice items, which teach the subject how to make matching judgments by alternating between numbers that are too high and too low. All designs are within-subject, and the order of major conditions is usually either randomized or counterbalanced. Some advantages we have found Web questionnaires to have over paper ones are:

- The subjects are more varied, and special efforts can be made to solicit particular groups of subjects. Diversity on the Internet increases each year, as more people use the Web.
- It is easier to make sure that subjects answer all the questions, give answers in the appropriate range, and meet minimal conditions on ordering.
- Interactive questioning can be programmed so that it can be described clearly and replicated. In this regard, the method is similar to computer assisted telephone interviewing, but it is much less expensive. Included here are error checking, challenges to past responses, and use of practice trials with feedback about them.
- Some forms of "cheating," such as completing the same study twice, are more difficult than when subjects are paid cash on the spot in a lab, because duplicates can be detected before payment is sent. In our

research, subjects must provide their name and address (and, for Americans, their social security number) to be paid.

- Although random sampling of a population is impossible, as it is in other methods based on convenience samples, the sample is more varied than those that use solely students. Typically, now, most of our respondents are not students, and most are female, despite fears that the Web is male dominated. About 10% are not from the United States, an additional source of variety. Also, we can tell whether any studies are frequently begun and not completed, which could cause a sampling problem, by inspecting access logs on the Web server computer. So far, this has not been a problem. Most are completed once begun.

- Costs of data entry, supervision of subjects, space for completing questionnaires, paper, printing, and paper storage are eliminated. As a result, the same research can be much less expensive.

- The time between planning a study and analyzing data can be reduced considerably, both because more subjects can complete a questionnaire per day (because the Web "lab" is open all hours and can accommodate an unlimited number of subjects) and because the data entry phase is eliminated.

The biggest disadvantage is that, as in other research of this sort, some subjects give little thought to the questions. Error checking can discourage such subjects. (It is annoying to be told repeatedly that your responses are inappropriate.) Even without such checking, we have found the number of nonsensical answers to be lower than before we started using the Web.

DO PEOPLE GIVE DIFFERENT RESPONSES ON WEB AND PAPER QUESTIONNAIRES?

In our own research in the field of judgment and decision making, we have several times used both Web and paper questionnaires as part of the same series of experiments. In most cases, we used Web and paper for different experiments in the same series of experiments. We got the same kinds of effects but could not do any direct comparisons of the magnitude of these effects. Our subjects for paper questionnaires were recruited either from undergraduate courses or from a laboratory that was open during specified hours, in which subjects could complete questionnaires for pay. The laboratory was advertised on the University of Pennsylvania campus and most subjects were students. Our subjects for Web questionnaires were recruited initially by posting notices to Usenet newsgroups relevant to the studies being done (such as `sci.environment` and `sci.psychology`). Other Web subjects came from a nearby college, which required students in introductory psychology to participate in an experiment and counted our studies as meeting the requirement. As word of our Web studies spread, several people put links to our site in their Web pages, and others discovered our site through search engines. In a couple of cases we have asked people to put links to our site on their Web pages.

A study by Baron, Hershey, and Kunreuther (1998) allowed direct comparisons of Web and paper questionnaire responses to very similar questionnaires. Of interest here is their Experiment 2, which compared a Web questionnaire completed by 49 subjects with a paper questionnaire completed by 42 residents of West Philadelphia in the context of a face-to-face interview. The purpose of this study was to look at the determinants of the desire to reduce risks. For each of 32 different risks, such as "cancer from pesticides" or "bacterial infections from drinking water," subjects answered several questions. The main question was about priority for action. It asked: "If you had more money to spend, which of these risks would you spend it on? Circle the priority you would give to each risk: Hi = high, Med = medium, Lo = low, No = no money at all." There were no significant differences between Web and interview subjects in any variables, with one exception. On the Web, the difference between the judged probability of the risk for the average American and for the subject was greater (in the direction of lower for the subject) than on paper.

Closer examination of the questionnaires suggested a reason for this. In the paper version, each risk had its own row, and each question had its own column. The "average American" and "subject" answer columns were side by side. Thus, subjects found it easy to give the same answer to both questions, and many did so. On the Web page, the two answer columns were presented sequentially rather than side by side, and the subject first answered the questions about average risk for all 32 items, and then the questions about the subject's own risk. This suggests that using the Web can affect results indirectly if it affects the form of presentation. (Presenting answer columns side by side on the Web is possible, as explained later, but requires more complex techniques than presenting them sequentially.) Using the Web also makes it more difficult to hold the form of presentation constant across subjects. For example, many browsers allow users to ignore the colors specified in a Web page and choose their own color scheme. Thus, a questionnaire which on paper would be in black ink on white paper for everyone, could potentially be in green "ink" on orange "paper" for one subject, in pink on blue for another, and so on. Different computers have different screen sizes and resolutions, so it can be important to test one's questionnaires at different resolutions and try to make them as similar as possible on a 640-by-480-pixel display, for example, as on a 1280-by-1024-pixel display. (Lynx, one of the earliest browsers, has a purely text-based interface which is so different from the interfaces of graphical browsers that it would probably be best either to have all subjects use Lynx to complete questionnaires specifically designed for Lynx, or to have no subjects use Lynx.)

USING WEB QUESTIONNAIRES IN TEACHING

Web questionnaires make it much easier to have students collect and analyze data, as a teaching exercise. The first author has used Web questionnaires in a research experience course on value measurement and decision analysis, and in his undergraduate course on thinking and decision making. Students learn about the topic both by filling out the questionnaires and by analyzing the data they collectively produce, which are made available to them on the Web in a Systat (SPSS Inc., Chicago, IL) file after everyone has completed the questionnaire. They also learn about the possibility of doing research on the Web.

Some of the exercises concern utility elicitation. Students find "conjoint analysis" particularly interesting, and Web forms using JavaScript (discussed later) are ideal for this method. The questionnaire involves rating a series of objects (e.g., cars) described one by one. The objects vary in a few attributes, such as price, safety, and repair record, with a few levels of each. The idea is to analyze the ratings of the objects to infer the utilities of the attributes. A statistics program such as Systat is used to derive an equation that predicts the ratings from the levels of the attributes. The equation assumes (a) that the ratings of the objects are monotonically related to the utilities of the objects, (b) that the utility of each object is an equally weighted linear combination of the utilities of the object's attributes, and (c) that the utility of an attribute is a function of its level on its dimension.

Examples of programs are available in the course syllabi in the first author's Web page, http://www.sas.upenn.edu/~jbaron, but those programs are constantly changing. A brief introduction to conjoint analysis in Systat is available at http://www.psych.upenn.edu/systat/ CJTEST.SYC and, for analysis across subjects, at http://www. psych.upenn.edu/systat/conjoint.htm.

MAKING WEB QUESTIONNAIRES

Below we discuss techniques for making Web pages using (a) HTML only, (b) HTML and JavaScript, and (c) HTML, JavaScript, and Java (briefly).

Hypertext markup language is the original language of Web pages on the World Wide Web. There are many good references to HTML on the Web itself. We will assume that the reader is familiar with them. (See `http://www.psych.upenn.edu/cattell/manual.html` for a list of these.) JavaScript is a programming language that is built into all the major browsers: Netscape, Internet Explorer, and Opera. (The version of JavaScript in Opera 3.5 does not work for the methods described here. Version 4 of Opera is expected soon.) A JavaScript program or "script," written as part of a Web page, is downloaded along with the rest of the page and is executed by the browser. Most browsers can also run Java programs. Java is a much more powerful language. The second author has used it in one questionnaire, and we discuss it briefly later.

Before we discuss JavaScript in more detail, we should mention that many of our comments are of the form, "it is good to . . . ." JavaScript is a wonderful idea, but it is not consistently implemented across different browsers, or even sometimes across the same browser on different operating systems. It "should" work if you merely follow the rules, but does not always do so. It will work most of the time if you follow the advice we give. There may be additional tricks that we have not learned yet, and we do get occasional complaints about things not working. Flanagan's (1997) book is very helpful not only in explaining the rules but also in explaining some of the tricks.

Part of the problem with JavaScript is that the politics of commercial competition have led to different versions of the language. For example, if you want to write for both Microsoft Internet Explorer and Netscape Navigator you have to resort to a lowest common denominator. Each company has added commands in an effort to persuade people to use their browser and to encourage the development of Web pages compatible with their own but not their competitor's browser. Moreover, these commands appear in later versions but not earlier ones. It is possible to have multiple versions of Netscape Navigator installed on a single computer, allowing one to test one's questionnaire on each of them. Unfortunately it is not possible, at least on the Windows 95 operating system, to have both versions 3 and 4 of Microsoft Internet Explorer installed simultaneously. However, we have been told that this is possible on operating systems other than Windows. Clearly, the wider the variety of operating systems and browsers you have access to, the more thoroughly you can test your questionnaire. However, even if you have the ability to test on many combinations, it may not be worth the time and effort. If a questionnaire works in an older browser like Netscape 3, for example, the chances are good that it will work on most other browsers commonly used today. It may be most efficient to test on Netscape 3 and a version of Internet Explorer, and then find out if problems are occurring on other browsers or operating systems by asking subjects to e-mail you if they encounter problems.

All of the first author's questionnaires work on Netscape 3 and above, and so far he has encountered no browser-specific problems. An alternative approach, discussed by Flanagan (1997), is to have the questionnaire detect which browser the subject is using and then use its capabilities. This complicates programming considerably, and making a questionnaire differ visibly depending on the browser used is typically a bad idea in a research context. However, this approach could be used in ways that do not visibly affect the questionnaire. For example, data about mouse movements could be collected from the subset of subjects using more sophisticated browsers, while keeping the questionnaire usable by, and externally identical for, subjects with less sophisticated browsers.

MAKING WEB QUESTIONNAIRES USING HTML

SIMPLE QUESTIONNAIRES

The simplest sort of questionnaire uses a form, and everything else in this chapter builds on this basic idea. The HTML ⟨form⟩ tag that begins a form can include the name of a "server-side" program that does something with the data entered into the form when the subject submits it, typically by clicking a "Submit" button. (A "server-side" program is one which runs on the server computer on which the Web page resides rather than on the client computer on which the Web page is being viewed.) The following, for example, names a program called mailform:

```
⟨form method = POST action
         = "/cgi-bin/mailform?baron@psych.upenn.edu"⟩
```

Our mailform program (which was written by M.-J. Dominus of the University of Pennsylvania) sends the data in an e-mail message to the address after the question mark, in the form of name–value pairs, such as q5 = 45, where q5 is the name of a form element and 45 is the value assigned to it. Typically, the name is something you make up for the question item (e.g., q5 for Question 5) and the value is the subject's answer to that question. Mailform sorts the name–value pairs by name and puts each pair on a separate line.

Mailform is written in Perl (Wall, Christiansen, & Schwartz, 1996), but many languages can be used for such programs. Schmidt (1997) discusses server-side programs more complex than mailform which can accomplish much of what we use "client-side" JavaScript to accomplish (see later in this chapter). However, server-side programs must be carefully written in order not to make the server vulnerable to break-ins, so it is best to consult your local system administrator for advice about which program to use. For the same reason, client-side JavaScript is probably a better choice when writing your own programs.

It is also possible to put a Web server on a dedicated desktop computer connected to the Internet. Servers are available free from `http://www.apache.org` for most platforms. If the computer is on your institution's network, however, this approach is still subject to policies of your institution concerning security and privacy.

If you do not have access to a Web server on which you can run a suitable server-side program such as mailform, you could try a ⟨form⟩ tag like the following:

```
⟨form method = post

      action = "mailto:siepmann@psych.upenn.edu"

      enctype = "text/plain"⟩
```

In Netscape browsers configured to send e-mail, and perhaps in other browsers, this will result in the browser sending you the data as an e-mail message from the subject (or whoever the browser is set up to send e-mail from) with name–value pairs like those sent by our mailform program. However, a major problem with this method is that whether subjects' responses reach you is determined by details of the subject's browser and how it is set up. If this method is your only option, you should probably require subjects to complete a test form to check whether their browser can actually get data to you. They should be warned not to spend time filling out your real questionaire until you have e-mailed them to confirm you received their test form data. Otherwise, you could be faced with large numbers of e-mails saying "Did you get my data? When will I be paid?" from subjects whose data never reached you.

The form ends with a ⟨/form⟩ tag. In between the beginning and end tags are text, images, and anything else that can go in a Web page. Critically, though, certain other elements are recognized in this context. One is a hidden input tag, such as ⟨input type = "hidden" name = "_qnaire" value = "medu16b"⟩. This does not appear on the Web page, but results in the name–value pair _qnaire = medu16b appearing in the e-mail sent by the mailform program, to identify which questionnaire the data are from. Putting an underscore at the beginning of the name causes it to be listed at the top of the e-mail, before any names that start with a letter, to make it easy to find.

A very useful element is for inputting text, for example, ⟨input type="text" name="q5" size=10 maxlength=20⟩. This presents an input box 10 characters wide that allows an answer of up to 20 characters. If the subject types more than 10 characters, the text window scrolls to the left to accommodate this. We give complete examples including text inputs later.

Buttons are useful in conjunction with JavaScript, which we discuss later. They do something when the subject clicks on them. For example, the following two buttons call a JavaScript function called prac(x,y) which changes a displayed number to change the relative utilities of two options, A and B:

```
⟨input type=button value="A is worse now."
 onClick="prac(0,3);"⟩
⟨input type=button value="B is worse now."
 onClick="prac(1,3);"⟩
```

For example, A might be paralysis of both legs and B might be a specified probability of death. The "value" is displayed on the button and subjects click on whichever button describes how they feel. Each click causes the prac(x,y) function to adjust the probability of death to get closer to the subject's indifference point. The parameters x and y tell the function prac(x,y) which button was pressed and which practice trial is being done, respectively. Subjects stop clicking when they are indifferent between A and B, because then neither button describes how they feel.

Finally, the subject must do something to submit the form. The usual way to do this is to include a submit button immediately before the ⟨/form⟩ element that ends the form, for example:

```
⟨input type=submit

     value="Click here to submit your answers."⟩
```

Other kinds of form elements are radio buttons, checkboxes, lists, and text areas. In some browsers, radio buttons, checkboxes, and lists can only be used with the mouse, and even when they can be used with the keyboard, they are usually better suited to the mouse. It is worth avoiding intermixing large numbers of them with text inputs, because this forces subjects to keep moving back and forth between the keyboard and the mouse. With text inputs, the user can simply type letter keys and then press the Tab key to move from one input field to the next.

Text areas allow several lines of text. If carriage returns are included, the mailform program will not remove them and will spread the data over several lines, like this:

```
comments=I found this
questionnaire
intriguing
```

It is usually undesirable to have carriage returns in a response because each response of each subject should fit in a single cell of a spreadsheet or a single variable in a statistics program. One simple solution is to provide several single-line text inputs instead of a text area. However, text areas may have advantages for open-ended responses because subjects can type and edit their responses freely the same way they do in e-mail or word-processor programs. Later we show how to use JavaScript to get rid of carriage returns in text area responses.

SEPARATE DISPLAY AREAS: FRAMES

It is possible with HTML to divide the browser window into several panels, each called a frame. Each frame can contain a separate HTML document. Frames are useful when you want to have the subject answer several questions about each of several items. In the Baron et al. (1998) study mentioned earlier, subjects were presented with a list of 32 risks (ranging from auto accidents to asteroids hitting the earth) and were asked several questions about each. Each question required a scale. For example, the probability questions used the following scale:

4A. What is the lifetime risk of *the average American family*, for each of the risks listed? Answer with a letter, except for L (less than 1 in 100,000); in that case, write in a decimal or fraction. When something can happen more than once, we want the probability that it happens *at least once*.

	Probability	Example
A	1 in 1	Certain to happen
B	1 in 3	A 80-year-old dying by 85
C	1 in 10	A 65-year-old dying by 70
D	1 in 30	A 51-year-old dying by 56
E	1 in 100	A 35-year-old dying by 40
F	1 in 300	A 20-year-old dying by 23
G	1 in 1000	A 20-year-old . . . in the next year
H	1 in 3000	. . . in the next 4 months
I	1 in 10,000	. . . in the next 5 weeks
J	1 in 30,000	. . . in the next 2 weeks
K	1 in 100,000	. . . in the next 4 days
L	less	(specify the probability)

The scale for each question appeared in the right frame, while the risks and the input fields appeared in the left frame. This allowed the subject to see the scale easily while answering the questions, and for their previous answers on the left to scroll off the screen without causing the scale on the right to move.

Implementation of two frames requires three documents. One is called a frameset document and defines the frames. Its only visible content is its title. The other two documents are displayed in the frames. Their titles are not shown, so they generally do not need titles.

In the Baron et al. (1998) study, the frameset document for the questionnaire was

```
⟨html⟩
 ⟨head⟩⟨title⟩Questionnaire, prot1⟨/title⟩⟨/head⟩
 ⟨frameset cols="50%, 50%"⟩
  ⟨frame src="prot1ans.htm" name="answers"
   scrolling="yes"⟩
  ⟨frame src="prot1qus.htm" name="questions"
   scrolling="yes"⟩
 ⟨/frameset⟩
⟨/html⟩
```

The `frameset` element specified that each frame was a column taking up half of the screen. The two files `prot1ans.htm` and `prot1qus.htm` were the answer and question documents to be displayed in the left and right frames, respectively. They were separate files in the same directory of the server computer containing the Web page. After each set of risks in the answer document, a link was used to bring the next question into view in the frame on the right. The following example shows only the last of a set of risks:

```
Cancer from food additives ⟨input type=text
  size=10 name=q12⟩
⟨br⟩⟨P⟩⟨br⟩⟨P⟩⟨br⟩
⟨a target=questions href="prot1qus.htm/#ques3"⟩
Click here to see question 3; then respond here:⟨/a⟩
```

The `target=questions` part specifies that clicking on the link should affect the frame on the right, which is named `questions` in the frameset document, rather than the left frame which the link itself is in. The `#ques3` part makes the link point to the top of Question 3, marked with the tag ⟨a name="ques3"⟩ in the question document.

PUTTING ANSWER COLUMNS SIDE BY SIDE

It is easy to put columns of answer spaces so that they display side by side, simply by putting them in two columns in a table. However, pressing the tab key will move the cursor to the next answer space to the right, rather than the next one down. This is fine if subjects are supposed to answer one row at a time, but very undesirable if subjects are supposed to complete one column at a time. It is possible to make pressing the tab key move the cursor down by implementing each column as a separate table, embedded within the main table. The following example has two columns and two rows. The first ⟨TR⟩ starts the top row, which contains headings. The second ⟨TR⟩ starts the second row. The first cell of the second row contains the text of the first item. The second cell spans two rows and contains a table within it. That table has two single-cell rows containing the input boxes for questions A1 and A2. The third cell of the second row is just like the second but contains the input boxes for questions B1 and B2. The last ⟨TR⟩ starts the third row. The first cell of the third row contains the text of the second item. It is the only cell of the third row, because the second and third cells of the second row span two rows, so they intrude into the third row.

```
⟨HTML⟩⟨BODY⟩⟨FORM⟩⟨TABLE⟩⟨!-- THIS IS COLUMN.HTM--⟩
  ⟨TR⟩
    ⟨TD ALIGN=CENTER⟩⟨U⟩Item⟨/U⟩⟨/TD⟩
    ⟨TD ALIGN=CENTER⟩A⟨/TD⟩
    ⟨TD ALIGN=CENTER⟩B⟨/TD⟩⟨/TR⟩
  ⟨TR⟩
    ⟨TD VALIGN=TOP HEIGHT="100"⟩1. An item.⟨/TD⟩
    ⟨TD ROWSPAN="2"⟩
      ⟨TABLE⟩
        ⟨TR⟩
          ⟨TD HEIGHT="100" VALIGN=TOP⟩
            ⟨INPUT type=text size=3 name=A1⟩
            ⟨/TD⟩⟨/TR⟩
        ⟨TR⟩
          ⟨TD HEIGHT="100" VALIGN=TOP⟩
            ⟨INPUT type=text size=3 name=A2⟩
            ⟨/TD⟩⟨/TR⟩⟨/TABLE⟩⟨/TD⟩
    ⟨TD ROWSPAN="2"⟩
      ⟨TABLE⟩
        ⟨TR⟩
          ⟨TD HEIGHT="100" VALIGN=TOP⟩
            ⟨INPUT type=text size=3 name=B1⟩⟨/TD⟩⟨/TR⟩
        ⟨TR⟩
          ⟨TD HEIGHT="100" VALIGN=TOP⟩
```

```
     ⟨INPUT type=text size=3 name=B2⟩
     ⟨/TD⟩⟨/TR⟩⟨/TABLE⟩⟨/TD⟩⟨/TR⟩
⟨TR⟩
   ⟨TD VALIGN=TOP HEIGHT="100"⟩2.Another item.⟨/TD⟩⟨/TR⟩
⟨/TABLE⟩⟨/FORM⟩⟨/BODY⟩⟨/HTML⟩
```

HAVING SUBJECTS ALLOCATE THEMSELVES TO DIFFERENT VERSIONS

It is often desirable to have different subjects complete different versions of a questionnaire, for example, to implement a between-subjects manipulation or to counterbalance the order of questions in a within-subjects design. The simplest way to do this is to have subjects select a version on a basis that approximates random assignment, for example, whether they were born on an odd or even day of the month. This method is often quite adequate, but sometimes it may be undesirable for subjects to be aware that there are multiple versions, and it is harder to think of a simple approximately random basis for allocating subjects to more than two versions. To randomly present different versions without involving subjects in the process requires JavaScript, to which we now turn our attention.

MAKING WEB QUESTIONNAIRES USING JAVASCRIPT AND HTML

TRANSPARENTLY ALLOCATING DIFFERENT SUBJECTS TO DIFFERENT VERSIONS

With JavaScript one can randomly allocate subjects to multiple versions of a questionnaire without having to involve them in the process. The following routine assigns each subject to one of three versions, which differ in the text assigned to the variable text. The variable random0to1 is set to a random number between 0 and 1 using the time in milliseconds, because although JavaScript has a random number function, it does not work on all browsers. The division by 10,000 gets rid of trailing zeros, and the %1 gets the remainder after dividing by 1, which is the fractional part. If you repeatedly reload this example in your browser, you will see the different values of random0to1 displayed. The Math.floor expression turns the fractional number from 0 to 1 into an integer from 1 to 3. Further down, the expression "document.myform._qnaire.value+=version" adds the version number to the hidden input called ⎵qnaire which will appear in the data e-mailed to you, letting you know which version the subject did.

```
⟨html⟩⟨! THIS IS MULTI.HTM-- ⟩
 ⟨head⟩
  ⟨script language="JavaScript"⟩
  var random0to1=((new Date()).getTime()/10000)%1 ;
  var version=Math.floor(3*random0to1)+1 ;
  var text;
  if (version==1)
    text="This is the text of the first version.";
  if (version==2)
    text="This is the text of the second version.";
  if (version==3)
    text="This is the text of the third version.";
  ⟨/script⟩
 ⟨/head⟩
⟨body⟩
 ⟨form name=myform⟩
  ⟨input type=hidden name=⎵qnaire
     value="My questionnaire, version"⟩
  ⟨script language="JavaScript"⟩
  document.myform.⎵qnaire.value += version;
  document.write(text);
  document.write("⟨BR⟩⟨BR⟩(⎵qnaire.value is now:/"");
  document.write(document.myform⎵qnaire.value+"/")");
  document.write("⟨BR⟩(random0to1 is:"+random0to1
    +")");
  ⟨/script⟩
 ⟨/form⟩
 ⟨/body⟩
⟨/html⟩
```

RANDOMIZING QUESTION ORDER SEPARATELY FOR EACH SUBJECT

It is possible to randomize the order of questions separately for each subject, by extending the techniques we have described so far. The questions could be either all displayed at once, as a single questionnaire page, or presented one at a time, on separate pages, which is the approach we will focus on. Putting questions on separate pages makes it impossible or difficult (depending on the browser) for the subject to go back to previous questions. This is important in within-subject designs that test variables that subjects think should not affect their responses. When subjects can easily compare and revise their answers at different levels of a variable they think should not affect their responses, they will tend to give the same answer at all levels, masking the true effect of the variable. (Internet Explorer 4 does allow returning to previous pages that have since been rewritten, although Netscape 3 and 4 do not allow this to be done easily. Prevention of such backing up in Internet Explorer 4 can be done by disallowing responses that would result in revision of recorded data.)

In principle, there are many ways to put items on separate pages. You could, for example, use a separate HTML file for each question. This, however, can make it difficult to make modifications of wording that is repeated in every question. According to Flanagan (1997) it is possible to use JavaScript to keep writing over the main window, but we have not gotten this method to work. We use a third method, involving frames, suggested by Flanagan (1997).

The trick is to use two frames, one invisible. The invisible frame contains a form with only hidden input elements. This is done as follows:

```
⟨frameset rows="100%,*"⟩
⟨frame src=visible.htm name=visible⟩
⟨frame src=hidden.htm name=hidden⟩
⟨/frameset⟩
```

The top row takes 100% of the screen, and the asterisk indicates that the bottom row takes up whatever is left, which is 0%, so it is invisible. The visible frame contains a form with questions and input elements. A JavaScript program in the frameset document transfers the subject's answers from the inputs in the visible frame to the hidden inputs in the hidden frame before rewriting the visible frame with the next page of questions. At the end, the form in the hidden frame is submitted as if it were the only form.

Below are three files making up a skeleton of a JavaScript questionnaire that presents separate items in a random order, one at a time. The frameset document, `program.htm`, contains the JavaScript code to run everything. When the questionnaire is first loaded, `program.htm` sets up some variables it will need and decides on the random order in which it will present the items. After that it does nothing until the subject clicks a button on the introductory page, `visible.htm`, which calls a JavaScript function in `program.htm` called `PresentItem()`. The `PresentItem()` function then overwrites `visible.htm` with the first question page. This question page includes a button which, when clicked, calls a function called `GetResponse()`. The `GetResponse()` function transfers the subject's response from the form on the visible question page to the hidden inputs in the form in `hidden.htm`, and then calls the `PresentItem()` function, which overwrites the current question page with the next question page. This cycle continues until the `PresentItem()` function detects that all the questions have been asked, at which point it overwrites the last question with a page asking the subject for information about himself or herself. The button on this page calls the function GetInfo(), which transfers the subject's information from the form on the visible page to the hidden inputs in the form in hidden.htm, and then submits the hidden form and displays a message thanking the subject.

The following is what the user sees initially, visible.htm. When the user clicks the button, it calls the function PresentItem() in the JavaScript program in program.htm, which is in the visible frame's parent frame—the main browser window. The PresentItem() function will then overwrite this introductory page with the first question.

```
〈html〉〈!-- THIS IS VISIBLE.HTM--〉
 〈body〉
 〈h2〉Title〈/h2〉
 Introductory text.
 〈form〉
  〈input type=button
     value="Click if you are ready to go on."
   onClick="parent.PresentItem();"〉
 〈/form〉
 〈/body〉
〈/html〉
```

The following is the hidden document in which data are stored, hidden.htm. The hidden inputs q01, q02, and q03 will hold the responses to the three questions. There must be one hidden input for each response. Most of the hidden inputs provide places to store responses that have not yet occurred, and are initially set to null values (" "), but two are preset to identify the questionnaire and payment.

```
〈html〉〈!-- THIS IS HIDDEN.HTM--〉
 〈head〉〈/head〉
 〈body〉
  〈form name=hiddenForm method=POST
   action="/cgi-bin/mailform?baron@psych.upenn.edu"〉
   〈input type=hidden name=_qnaire value="skeleton"〉
   〈input type=hidden name=q01  value=""〉
   〈input type=hidden name=q02  value=""〉
   〈input type=hidden name=q03  value=""〉
   〈!-- IMPORTANT TO LEAVE ABOVE INPUTS IN THAT ORDER--〉
   〈input type=hidden name=_payment value="$5"〉
   〈input type=hidden name=_sex  value=""〉
  〈/form〉
 〈/body〉
〈/html〉
```

In JavaScript, form inputs can be referred to by name or number, and program.htm refers to them by number when transferring responses to the hidden form. That means it is very important that the inputs in hidden.htm are in the order that program.htm expects them to be. They are numbered starting from 0, so _qnaire is input number 0, q01 is input number 1, q02 is input number 2, and so on. If, for example, you inserted an input between_qnaire and q01, then program.htm would put the response to question 1 into the new input that you inserted, the response to question 2 into your q01 input, and so on. At best, you would later realize what had happened and be able to reconstruct where each datum was supposed to go. At worst, you would either never find out what had happened or you would not find out until after publishing a paper based on the data.

The following is the frameset document which contains the JavaScript program, program.htm. It contains four functions, Random(max), PresentItem(), GetResponse(), and GetInfo(). The code outside of the four functions is run only once, when the questionnaire is first loaded into the Web browser. It sets up some variables and randomizes the order of the questions, using the Random(max) function. After that, nothing happens until the subject clicks the button on the introductory visible.htm page, which calls PresentItem().

```
<html><!-- THIS IS PROGRAM.HTML>
<head>
 <title>Example of randomizing question order</title>
 <script language="JavaScript">
 // DEFINE SOME VARIABLES THAT EXIST OUTSIDE OF FUNCTIONS
 var itmNum=1; // NUMBER OF CURRENT ITEM
 var nItms=3;// NUMBER OF ITEMS
 var junk; // NEEDED BECAUSE OF A BUG IN NETSCAPE 3
 itm=new Object();  // ARRAY TO HOLD TEXT OF EACH ITEM
 itm[1]="This is the 1st item.";
 itm[2]="This is the 2nd item.";
 itm[3]="This is the 3rd item.";
 now=new Date();
 var seed=now.getTime()%714025;
                  // FOR RANDOM NUMBER GENERATION
 // GENERATE RANDOM NUMBERS SEEDED USING TIME THIS PAGE
 // IS LOADED (THIS WORKS IN MORE BROWSERS THAN
 // Math.random() DOES)
 function Random(max)  {
   seed=((seed*4096+150889)%714025);
   return Math.floor(max*seed/ 714025);
 }
```

```
// THIS RANDOMIZES ORDER OF ITEMS ONCE, WHEN THIS PAGE
// IS LOADED
itmOrder=new Object();
var currentItm, itmToSwap, temporary;
for (currentItm=1; currentItm <=nItms; currentItm++) {
  // FIRST RECORD THE INITIAL 123.. ORDER THEY'RE NUMBERED
  // IN
  itmOrder[currentItm]=currentItm;
}
for (currentItm=1; currentItm<=nItms; currentItm++) {
  // NOW SWAP EACH ITEM WITH A RANDOMLY CHOSEN OTHER ITEM
  itmToSwap=Random(nItms+1-currentItm)+currentItm;
  temporary=itmOrder[itmToSwap];
  itmOrder[itmToSwap]=itmOrder[currentItm];
  itmOrder[currentItm]=temporary;
}


// PRESENT THE ITEM AND THE RESPONSE INPUT AREAS
// (THIS IS FIRST CALLED BY THE BUTTON ON THE INTRODUCTORY
// PAGE, AND AFTER THAT IS CALLED BY THE GetResponse()
// FUNCTION, BELOW)
function PresentItem() {
  if (itmNum <=nItms) {
    // IF THERE ARE MORE ITEMS TO GO, PRESENT THE NEXT ONE
    var itmHTML
        ="<html><body><form name=visibleForm>\n"
        +itm[itmOrder[itmNum]]
        +"<P>This is the question asked after each item."
        +"<input type=text size=8 name=response>\n"
        +"<P><input type=button
            onClick='parent. GetResponse()'"
        +"value='Press TAB, then SPACE, or click'>"
        +"</form></body></html>";
    junk=parent.visible.document.open();
    parent.visible.document.write(itmHTML);
    parent.visible.document.close();
  }
  if (itmNum > nItms) {
    // IF ALL ITEMS HAVE BEEN DONE, ASK FOR INFO ABOUT
    // SUBJECT
    var aboutSubj
        ="<form name=visibleForm>\n"
        +"<P>Are you male (m) or female (f)?<br>"
        +"<input type=text size=3 name=_sex>\n"
```

```
    +"⟨P⟩\n" + "Thanks.\n" + "⟨hr⟩\n"
    +"⟨center⟩⟨input type=button
        value= 'Submit responses.'"
    +"onClick= 'parent.GetInfo() '⟩⟨/center⟩⟨br⟩\n"
    +"⟨/form⟩";
  junk=parent.visible.document.open();
  parent.visible.document.write(aboutSubj);
  parent.visible.document.close();
}
// PUT FOCUS ON FIRST INPUT BOX, SO IT IS READY TO
// ACCEPT TYPING
parent.visible.document.visibleForm.elements[0].focus();
return;
}


// TRANSFER RESPONSES FROM VISIBLE TO HIDDEN FORM AND
// PROCEED TO NEXT ITEM (THIS FUNCTION CALLED BY BUTTON
// THAT FOLLOWS EACH ITEM)
function GetResponse() {
  // STORE ITEM IN ITS PROPER PLACE IN HIDDEN FORM (WHICH
  // HAS NOTHING TO DO WITH ITS RANDOMIZED ORDER OF
  // PRESENTATION)
  parent.hidden.document.hiddenForm.elements[itmOrder[itmNum]].value
    =parent.visible.document.visibleForm.response.value;
  itmNum++;
  PresentItem();
  return;
}


// TRANSFER INFO ABOUT SUBJECT FROM VISIBLE TO HIDDEN FORM
// AND SUBMIT (THIS IS CALLED BY BUTTON SUBJECT CLICKS
// AFTER GIVING THEIR INFO)
function GetInfo() {
  parent.hidden.document.hiddenForm._sex.value
    =parent.visible.document.visibleForm._sex.value;
  // NOW SUBMIT HIDDEN FORM
  parent.hidden.document.hiddenForm.submit();
  // DISPLAY MESSAGE SO SUBJECT WON'T PRESS SUBMIT TWICE
  junk=parent.visible.document.open();
  parent.visible.document.write("⟨html⟩⟨body⟩Thanks." +
    "Your answers" are being submitted.⟨/body⟩⟨/html⟩");
  parent.visible.document.close();
}
```

```
</script>
</head>

<!-- NOW THE FRAMESET THAT SETS UP THE VISIBLE AND
     INVISIBLE FRAMES-->
<frameset rows=100%, *>
 <frame src=visible.htm name=visible>
 <frame src=hidden.htm name=hidden>
</frameset>
</html>
```

The lines that say junk=top.visible.document.open() should in principle be able to say simply top.visible.document.open(), but that does not work in Netscape 3. Adding "junk=" makes it work in Netscape 3. The questionnaire should also work in Internet Explorer 3 or above. It does not work with Netscape 2, though there might be a way to make it work. The problem we found with Netscape 2 was that on the question pages that were written into the visible frame by program.htm (as opposed to being an actual HTML file like visible.htm), the JavaScript code in the button did not do anything.

There are some other points to note about program.htm: (a) It is a very good idea, because it works with more browsers, to name the input(s) on the visible form, as we did (e.g., <input type=text size=8 name= response>), and refer to them by name when transferring responses to the hidden form. (b) On the question pages, you might think you can use "onChange" in a text input field to call the function that advances to the next item, to avoid needing a button. This works in Netscape, but not Internet Explorer. However, there is no need to use the mouse in Netscape 3 and 4 and Internet Explorer 4, because pressing the Tab key and then the Spacebar has the same effect as clicking the button. (c) We had to name the array object itm as we did, rather than name it item, because Internet Explorer 4 did not work if it was named item, although Netscape 3 and 4 did—this highlights the importance of testing on multiple browsers.

ERROR CHECKING

Error checking can be added to the GetResponse() function in program.htm. The following example checks to see whether the response is a number between 1 and 5 and alerts the subject if it is not between 1 and 5 or is not a number. Although our example program.htm asks for only one response per page, it is possible to check more than one response at a time, so the following example is written to be easily adaptable to do so:

```
function GetResponse () {
  response=new Object();
  response[1]=
parseInt(parent.visible.document.visibleForm.response.value);
  // TRIES TO INTERPRET RESPONSE AS AN INTEGER. THE EXAMPLE
  // HAS ONLY ONE RESPONSE, BUT YOU COULD CHECK MORE BY
  // ADDING response[2] ETC.
  error=0; // NO ERRORS FOUND SO FAR
  for (i=1; i <=1; i++) {
    // IF WE HAD MORE THAN ONE RESPONSE, THIS WOULD CHECK
    // THEM ALL
    if (!((response[i] > 0)&&(response[i] < 6))) error=1;
  }
  if (error==1) {
    // IF ERRORS(S): NOTIFY; MAKE INPUT READY FOR NEW
    // RESPONSE; STOP
    alert "Each response must be a number from 1 to 5.");
    parent.visible.document.visibleForm.response.focus();
    return;
  }
  // IF NO ERRORS: PROCEED...
  // STORE ITEM IN ITS PROPER PLACE IN HIDDEN FORM (WHICH HAS
  // NOTHING TO DO WITH ITS RANDOMIZED ORDER OF PRESENTATION)
  parent.hidden.document.hiddenForm.elements[itmOrder[itmNum]].value
      =parent.visible.document.visibleForm.
  response.value ;
  itmNum++;
  PresentItem();
  return;
}
```

As another example, if you wanted to test whether a response contained one of the letters u, v, or y, you could take out the parseInt() part, and replace the line if (!((response[i]>0)&&(response[i]<6))) error=1; " in the above example with

```
if( (response[i].indexOf("u")== -1)
   && (response[i].indexOf("v")== -1)
   && (response[i].indexOf("y") == -1)) error=1;
```

indexOf() is called a property of the object response[i]. It returns the position of "u" in the string response[i], or − 1 if "u" is absent. The preceding expression tests whether all three of "u", "v", and "y" are absent and sets the error variable to 1 if so. You would also, of course, want to alter the alert message to something like "You must respond with u, v, or y".

More generally, you can define very complex conditions for giving alerts. You can also store subjects' answers for use in later questions. We will not give examples of these, because, at that point, it is just JavaScript programming. The general rules of programming apply; the more complex the program, the more likely it will have errors.

REMOVING UNWANTED CHARACTER CODES
FROM TEXT RESPONSES

As we noted earlier, text area responses may include carriage returns, which would prevent these responses from fitting into a single spreadsheet cell. Tab characters can also get into responses somehow and can be undesirable for similar reasons. The following demonstrates using JavaScript to replace carriage returns and tabs with text:

```
〈html〉〈!-- THIS IS REMOVE.HTM--〉
〈head〉
 〈script language="JavaScript"〉
  function PerformSubstitution(before) {
   var after="";
   for (var position=0; position<before.length;
       position++){
    if (before.charAt(position)= '\r')
       {after+="[ENTER]"; position+=2;}
    if (before.charAt(position)== '\t')
       {after+="[TAB]"; position++;}
    if (position 〈before.length)
       {after+=before.charAt(position);}
   }
   return after;
  }
  function Substitute() {
   window.document.myform.mytext.value
     =PerformSubstitution(window.document.myform.mytext.value);
  }
 〈/script〉
〈/head〉
〈body〉
 〈form name="myform"〉
```

```
⟨textarea name="mytext" rows=5 cols=40 wrap=soft⟩
Type here!⟨/textarea⟩⟨br⟩
⟨input type=button value="Substitute"
    onClick="Substitute();"⟩
  ⟨/form⟩
  ⟨/body⟩
⟨/html⟩
```

The position in the response string is advanced by two after inserting [ENTER] because a carriage return consists of two invisible characters. The wrap=soft in the text area tag means that the computer will wrap text to the next line without inserting a carriage return, as in a word processor. The substitution can be done automatically when the form is submitted. For example, the following button does the substitution and then submits the form. Note that it is a regular button and not a submit button. The submission is handled by calling the JavaScript submit() function directly:

```
⟨input type=button value="Submit"
onClick="Substitute(); window.document.myform.submit();"⟩
```

PROCESS TRACING, ANALOG SCALES, AND TIMING

You can use JavaScript to find out what subjects are looking at. Payne, Bettman, and Johnson (1993) describe some details and many applications of Mouselab, a method of using computers for finding out what people are looking at, which they developed in the 1980s. Mouselab presents a screen with several boxes, each containing a piece of information. The subject moves the mouse over the box and the information is displayed. The program keeps track of the order and timing of box displays.

Here is a simple way to do this. The idea is to use the input element of a form as the box, and a link that does nothing if clicked but causes a stimulus to be displayed in an adjacent text box whenever the mouse is over the link. The following example simply demonstrates the technique. It counts the number of times the stimulus is displayed and the number of milliseconds the stimulus was last viewed:

```
⟨html⟩⟨!-- THIS IS PROCESS.HTM--⟩
⟨head⟩
⟨script language="JavaScript"⟩
var looks=0, now, timer;
function InOut(which) {
```

```
    if (which=='in') {
        now=new Date();
        timer=now.getTime();
        looks+=1;
        document.myForm.counter.value=looks;
        document.myForm.display.value="Hi!";
    }
    if (which=='out') {
        now=new Date();
        timer=now.getTime()- timer;
        document.myForm.display.value="";
        document.myForm.timer.value=timer;
    }
    return;
}
⟨/script⟩
⟨/head⟩
⟨body⟩
 ⟨form name=myForm⟩ 
  ⟨a href="javascript:void(0)" onMouseOver="InOut('in')"
     onMouseOut="InOut('out')"⟩Show:⟨/a⟩ ⟨input type=
     text size=5 name=display⟩ You've looked ⟨input type=
     text size=5 name=counter value="0"⟩ times.
     You last looked for ⟨input type=text size=5
     name=timer⟩ ms.
  ⟨/form⟩
 ⟨/body⟩
⟨/html⟩
```

Some points to note are: (a) this runs in Netscape 2, 3, and 4 and Internet Explorer 4, but in Netscape 2 the onMouseOver event is generated when the mouse is moved *within* the link, resulting in grossly inflated counts; (b) the now variable is unnecessary if one uses timer=(new Date()). getTime(), but that does not work in Netscape 2; (c) if you just put " " rather than "javascript:void(0)" in the link, then if the subject clicks on the link, it will do something like display the index page or directory listing from this file's directory on the server.

Other techniques used in Mouselab include allowing the subject to use the mouse as an analog input, for example, to indicate position along a continuum. This too can be accomplished in JavaScript. (For this idea, we are indebted to the software library and demonstrations at Les Lenert's site, http://prefdev.ucsd.edu/) The idea is to use an image map (an HTML element), with the component images consisting of thin slivers. A JavaScript function reports which sliver the mouse is on. For an example of this technique, see http:// www.psych.upenn.edu / ~ baron / examples / ohp1.htm. This site also contains the image slivers called emptysca.gif and filledsc.gif, which were copied from Lenert's site. The code for the questionnaire contains the routine for controlling the scale. An important trick here is based on the fact that a link tag with an image takes on the dimensions of the image, so the tag can be quite thin, yet the link tag can still contain the usual functions needed to respond to the cursor. Another trick is to use the fact that a URL in a link tag can be a piece of JavaScript code to be executed. Thus, a typical link tag is

```
⟨a href='javascript:top.change(80)'⟩
⟨img src='emptysca.gif'
    border='0'⟩⟨/a⟩
```

Here the function top.change(80) replaces emptysca.gif with filledsc.gif up to the current link, so the scale takes on the color of the latter image.

MAKING WEB QUESTIONNAIRES USING JAVA, JAVASCRIPT, AND HTML

Details of the use of Java applets (Java programs that run in a Web page) are beyond the scope of this chapter. However, the second author has used one for a study involving probability judgment. He wrote an applet that displayed white dots at constantly changing positions on a black rectangle. The subject's task was to judge the probability that when the computer (i.e., the Java applet) randomly chose a point on the rectangle, there would be a white dot there.

To write an applet, you need a Java compiler. You can download one free at http:// java.sun.com/ products. The second author bought Microsoft's Visual J + + for less than $50 (academic price) at our university's computer store. Getting it set up properly was a considerable challenge, but once working it did make the programming process easier. It came with a very helpful introductory book (Davis, 1996).

Once you have written an applet, you can include it in a Web page with an HTML tag such as ⟨APPLET name = "myApplet" code = bel_9_1.class width = 500 height = 200⟩. (Compiled Java programs have the file extension .class) The JavaScript in the Web page can then control the applet by calling its functions. For example, the second author's questionnaire included a command,

```
window.document.myApplet.changeChances(300),
```

which set the probability display to 300 in 100,000.

GETTING DATA FROM WEB
QUESTIONNAIRES INTO USABLE FORM

The mailform program does not return the data in a form usable by any statistics package or spreadsheet. Mailform, and other similar programs we have seen, send an e-mail message with a list of name–value pairs, such as

```
q1 = 1
q2 = yes
q3 = 98
...
```

Statistics packages usually require a list of variables in a fixed order, with a particular character between each datum (e.g., space, comma, or tab), with the variable names listed only on the top line, and with one line per subject. For example,

```
q1 q2 q3 ...
1 yes 98 ...
```

It is possible to use JavaScript to transform the data into a usable form, but we started using Perl scripts for this purpose. The first author's script performs various checks on the data and translates them into a Systat command file that enters the data into Systat. The second author's script translates the data into a tab-delimited text file, which he then transfers into a spreadsheet program. He uses the spreadsheet program for tasks such as checking that nobody has done the study twice and for working with open-ended responses not suited to a statistics program. He then exports the data from the spreadsheet to Systat.

The first author checks to make sure that nobody has done the study twice before converting the data to a usable form. He does this with a one-line Unix script:

```
grep aemail $1 | sort | uniq-c | grep-v "1 aemail" | more.
```

He has saved this text in a file called `echeck` and made the file executable. To use it on a file called `medu16`, for example, he types at the unix prompt: `echeck medu16`. Here is how the script works. The `grep aemail $1` part outputs only the lines of the e-mail file that contain `"aemail,"` the name he uses for the e-mail address that the subject types in. The `| sort` part passes that output to the `sort` command, which sorts the lines. The `| uniq-c` part passes the sorted output to the `uniq-c` command, which outputs the lines with duplicates removed and a count of the number of times the line occurred on the left. The `| grep-v "1 aemail"` part takes that output and filters out all lines where the count is 1. Finally, the `|more` part displays the resulting output one screen at a time so that it does not scroll off the top of the screen. If someone does the study twice and does not enter exactly the same e-mail address both times, they would not be detected by this method. If you do not have a Unix server, you can get all these commands for Windows 95 from `ftp://mirrors.aol.com/pub/cica/pc/win95/sysutil/unix95.zip`.

ADMINISTRATIVE ASPECTS OF USING WEB QUESTIONNAIRES

INFORMED CONSENT

Informed consent has not been a problem. We simply explain the rules to the subjects. They have to read the rules to know what to do (more carefully than they would have to read or listen to a consent form), so doing the questionnaire is equivalent to consenting to do the questionnaire. Here is the first author's current front page. Of course, the details change almost daily.

> **Jonathan Baron's questionnaires**
> **What you can do now**
> Symptoms and quality of life (ass4)
> Pay: $5
> March 25, 1999
> Note: This is also a class assignment for Psychology 153, designed to illustrate methods of utility judgment. (But anyone can do it.)
> **When I expect to have something new**
> Midnight, GMT, Sunday, March 28 (no promises).
> **When payment checks are sent**
> I submitted the last batch of check requests on March 15. I will submit next batch of check requests on April 19.
> **What you should know**
> These questionnaires are part of my research on judgment and decision making. Anyone can complete them. I assume you can read English and give serious answers. They require very careful reading. You can be paid. If you do not wish to

be paid and do not provide the information required, all I will see is the part of your e-mail address to the right of the @ sign.

Please try to keep track of which ones you have done. To help you do this, I send an automated e-mail reply, which goes to the address you give me. It includes the questionnaire code and the usual pay.

Pay: To be paid, you must give your name, address, and social security number (SSN, required by the University) at the end of the questionnaire, and you must answer all the questions seriously. (The money is from research grants from the National Science Foundation and the Penn Cancer Center.)

Personal information: Once you have given me your e-mail address and other information *as part of a fully completed questionnaire* , you do not need to type the other information each time. I have a data base in which you are identified *by your e-mail address*. This means that you must type that address correctly each time, and you must use the same address (unless you tell me you're changing). *Note: This is NOT a secure server, yet. This is extremely unlikely to matter.*

You may, if you wish, send your SSN by e-mail to baron@psych.upenn.edu, by post to J. Baron, Psychology, University of Pennsylvania, 3815 Walnut St., Philadelphia PA 19104-6196, USA, or by phone (on my answering machine) at 215-898-6918. I will then add it to the data base. You must identify youself with your e-mail address.

Nonresidents of the United States: You need not submit a social security number. I will send a check in U.S. dollars.

Time required: The pay is based on an estimate of $1 for 10 minutes of very careful reading and responding by a slow reader. So a questionnaire that pays $3 should take at most 30 minutes to complete, usually much less.

Technical stuff: If the cursor is not in the box where the response goes, click on the box. Most of these studies require JavaScript (not Java). They should work on Netscape 3 (or above) and Internet Explorer 3 (or above). Please report any problem. (There are occasional problems. Sometimes they go away if you close the browser and then start over.) I use no cookies.

PAYING SUBJECTS

The first author's use of the Internet for data collection has advanced gradually. He began by posting short questionnaires to newsgroups and e-mail lists. He has always tried to pay subjects when it is feasible.

At the beginning he paid subjects by entering them in drawings, to reduce the number of payments necessary. He referred to this as a "lottery," and one subject argued that it violated state law in one state. (This subject turned out to win the "lottery" in question.) Our advice: If you use drawings, do not use the word "lottery." It is not a lottery because subjects do not buy tickets and cannot lose money. We feel that drawings are somewhat undesirable, in that they play into a combination of subjects' altruism and misperception of probability, neither of which we want to rely on if we have other options.

The biggest problem (even from the days of paper questionnaires in the lab) has been finding efficient ways to pay subjects. These problems are probably specific to our university and its financial rules, so we will not go into them, except to make one point. Soon, we will have electronic cash (see, for example, http://www.digicash.com). When this becomes widely available, researchers should encourage their respective financial officers to learn to use it. Part of the problem is that financial people are (as they should be) cautious and conservative, reluctant to change anything that works. As a result, many of the methods for handling accounts, sending checks, and so on seem to be carry-overs from the nineteenth century. Although checks are now written by a machine, it took over a year for the first author to convince the university authorities to let him provide an electronic list of recipients and amounts, to avoid the delay (and expense) of retyping the entire list. The good news is that our department's business office recently obtained a copy of Quicken, a computer program that writes checks (Intuit, Menlo Park, CA), and obtained permission from the university to use a separate bank account. The first author now submits a ".qif file," which he produces with a program he wrote in Perl (Wall et al., 1996; he will provide the program on request; Perl is available free from http:// language.perl.com). He sends out checks once per month. (Some foreign subjects cannot cash U.S. checks at reasonable cost, so he sends them cash. He used to send all subjects cash, but it took a lot of time, and he frequently heard that the cash was "lost" in the mail. Checks, he has found, do not get lost in the mail.)

A similar Perl script keeps a database of subjects and makes a list of payments due. The database is organized by the subject's e-mail address. This may not be the best way to do it. Subjects often change addresses or use different aliases of the same address (e.g., baron@psych.upenn.edu and baron@cattell.psych.upenn.edu both work for the first author). Sometimes a husband and wife use the same e-mail address. Most of the time this works, though. Once the subject types an address and social security number, these are entered into the database and need not be retyped for subsequent studies. The database itself is in the form of an Excel .csv (comma separated value) file, which is a text file with a fixed number of fields in each row, separated by commas, with one row per subject. The first field is the e-mail address, then the name, and so on. The database can thus be edited with Excel or with a text editor. The details of the Perl scripts are probably too idiosyncratic to be useful to others. The general point is that it is worthwhile to automate the entire operation, though it is also important to monitor the output, check it in various ways, and make corrections manually when necessary. There is always the possibility that subjects will do something that one's script is not prepared to deal with.

The payment list is printed on paper and also converted into a `.qif` file for writing checks. This file is then submitted to the Quicken program. We include here a note on the format of the `.qif` file, which is difficult to find in the Quicken documentation and may be useful to others:

```
!Type:Bank
^
D01 / 11 / 99
T- 30000
Nprint
PJON BARON
A80 MYSTREET
AMYTOWN PA 19312
AUSA
Mbribe in return for course grade
```

The file is an ASCII text file, beginning with `!Type:Bank`. Each record begins with `^` on a line by itself. The meaning of each line is determined by the first letter. D is the date. T is the amount. (It seems that the minus sign between the T and the amount of the check is helpful, perhaps because a check is a withdrawal from a bank account.) N is the check number, which should be set to `"print"`, which means Quicken will decide on a number when it prints the check. P is the payee, the lines (up to five of them) beginning with A are address fields, and M is the memo to be written on the check. Then the next record begins immediately with `^` on a line (no blank line in between), and so on. The file must have the extension `.qif`. Make backups of all other Quicken files before you try submitting the file to Quicken.

CONCLUSIONS

In our view, Web questionnaires have many major advantages over paper questionnaires and few major disadvantages. The advantages are likely to increase because, for example, a wider and wider range of people will use the Web more and more frequently, the range of stimuli it is feasible to display on the Web will increase, and electronic cash will simplify the payment process and allow anonymous payments. We have discussed a variety of techniques and procedures we have found useful in creating and using judgment and decision making Web questionnaires. We hope others will find these pointers helpful and will build on them.

REFERENCES

Baron, J., Hershey, J. C., & Kunreuther, H. (1998). *Attitudes toward risk reduction.* Unpublished manuscript.

Davis, S. R. (1996). *Learn Java now.* Redmond, WA: Microsoft Press.

Flanagan, D. (1997). *JavaScript: The definitive guide* (2nd ed.). Sebastopol, CA: O'Reilly.

National Science Foundation. (1997). *NetLab workshop report* [Online]. Available URL: http://www.uiowa.edu/~grpproc/netlab.htm

Payne, J. W., Bettman, J. R., & Johnson, E. J. (1993). *The adaptive decision maker.* New York: Cambridge University Press.

Schmidt, W. C. (1997). World-Wide Web survey research: Benefits, potential problems, and solutions. *Behavior Research Methods, Instruments, & Computers, 29*(2), 274–279.

Wall, L., Christiansen, T., & Schwartz, R. L. (1996). *Programming Perl* (2nd ed.). Sebastopol, CA: O'Reilly.

CHAPTER 11

The Cognitive Psychology Online Laboratory

Gregory Francis
Department of Psychological Sciences
Purdue University
West Lafayette, Indiana 47904

Ian Neath
Department of Psychological Sciences
Purdue University
West Lafayette, Indiana 47904

Aimee Surprenant
Department of Psychological Sciences
Purdue University
West Lafayette, Indiana 47904

In this chapter we discuss the development of an online laboratory for use with cognitive psychology courses. By designing programs with the Java programming language, laboratory demonstrations can be run on almost any computer via the World Wide Web. Placing the laboratory assignments on the Web avoids scheduling and equipment problems faced by traditional laboratories. We suggest guidelines for choosing topics to be presented in this format, and we outline the design of two types of demonstrations. Limitations of this approach are also discussed.

THE COGNITIVE PSYCHOLOGY ONLINE LABORATORY

For undergraduate science students some of the most important classes require hands-on experience with the methods and materials of their discipline. In chemistry laboratory sections students explore the chemical properties of substances, in physics laboratory sections students experimentally validate fundamental laws of nature, and in biology laboratory sections students explore animal and human physiology. The laboratory sections of these classes are so important that it is difficult to imagine learning these disciplines without them.

In contrast, psychology courses rarely involve hands-on experience. The few exceptions tend to be for psychobiology courses and courses that emphasize research methods. Although some topics in psychology do not easily lend themselves to a laboratory section, many do. Cognitive psychology is the scientific study of mental processes (e.g., decision making, language, memory, perception, problem solving), and as a field it has gathered a number of key studies that demonstrate important aspects of cognition in a laboratory setting.

An accompanying laboratory experience in cognitive psychology allows students to better appreciate the relationship between, and need for careful control of, experimental variables. Furthermore, given that the majority of experiments in this field are now carried out on computers, a computer-based laboratory allows not only an efficient method of presenting laboratory exercises, but also experience interacting with the environment and equipment used in psychological research.

It is not trivial to introduce a traditional laboratory section into a course. Time, equipment, software, administrative support, and scheduling must be handled effectively if the laboratory experience is to benefit the students without overwhelming the instructor, and the laboratory exercises should not intrude on an already full lecture schedule. One way to satisfy these constraints is to sidestep many of the difficulties of a traditional laboratory section by creating a virtual laboratory on the World Wide Web. With this approach students do the laboratory work at the time and place of their choosing. The instructor need not find times for everyone to work with limited equipment, make certain that software is installed on all machines, or give up lecture time to laboratory work. This is a better approach for the students as well because they progress at their own pace and spend only as much time as is needed to finish laboratory assignments.

A grant proposal was funded by the Multimedia Instructional Development Center at Purdue University to design an online laboratory for cognitive psychology. Development started in spring 1997 and the resulting laboratory was first used in a section of Introduction to Cognitive Psychology at Purdue in the fall of 1997. Before creating any laboratory demonstrations, we carefully considered what types of exercises should exist online. At that time there were a handful of organized Web sites that demonstrated (mostly visual perception) concepts in cognitive psychology. Most of these sites contained nice color pictures of various phenomena, but did not provide a full experiment in which students could participate and measure their performance.

Laboratory assignments should help students better understand significant properties of cognitive psychology. Students sometimes struggle with certain critical concepts (e.g., neural receptive fields or probability), and some of the laboratories are dedicated to helping students understand those concepts. Experimental techniques and results define much of cognitive psychology. It is sometimes the case that a complicated experiment is never fully understood by students, so the results and their significance remain mysteries as well. Therefore, we decided to design laboratory exercises that mimic key experiments in the research literature. Some care needs to be taken when considering what sorts of demonstrations to design for a cognitive psychology laboratory. Some experiments and demonstrations can be effectively presented during a lecture, so there is little need for a complicated multimedia program when a color transparency would accomplish the same thing. On the other hand, many experiments require the user to carefully attend to stimuli and to repeat a task many times. These experiments are not suitable for in-class demonstrations, but students can learn by participating in them. Such experiments would be the ideal venue for an interactive demonstration where the students can proceed on their own, outside of lectures.

Experiments appropriate for this format should also represent seminal findings within the field. Furthermore, the demonstration should produce robust effects in a twofold manner. First, the effect should be easily obtainable by a single subject within a reasonable number of trials. This characteristic insures that students receive immediate feedback on their cognitive abilities as measured by the task. Second, the expected effect should also be robust with respect to the computer equipment that executes it. Because students may participate using a variety of computers, the demonstrations should be certain to work with a minimal configuration that is not at the extreme upper end of computing performance. The preparation should be robust enough to yield the expected outcome, regardless of minor alterations resulting from hardware differences. To summarize, an appropriate topic for this medium of presentation should (1) not be easily demonstrated by other means, (2) represent an important finding in the field, and (3) be robust with respect to variations in both subjects and equipment. Instructors may wish to add other objectives and the demonstrations described here may be applicable to other situations (e.g., between-subjects comparisons). Indeed, we applied a fourth criterion; that the demonstrations would fit into our courses. We have completed implementation of several demonstrations that generally satisfy these criteria and we have several others in development.

Finally, a means of producing the demonstrations needed to be selected. We needed the programs to function across the Internet, to be usable on a variety of machines with variable properties, to be fast enough to present stimuli for various experiments, and to be safe to install on the departmental Web server. After consideration of several options, we decided to use a programming language, Java, developed by Sun Microsystems.

Java is particularly suited for Internet-based programming applications because, unlike many computer languages, it is interpreted. A Java program comprises platform-independent instructions called bytecodes. A Java bytecode interpreter, known as a Java virtual machine (Java VM), can be installed on almost any computer platform. The Java VM then converts the bytecodes into machine code, which can be executed by the computer. The advantage of Java programs is that they can then be run on any machine with an interpreter. Many recent Web browsers have a built-in Java VM. Thus a Java program on the Web (called a Java applet) can be run via the Java VM in the Web browser and subsequently should run on any computer that can run the Web browser. In practice, this is nearly every computer built since 1996, whether PC, Macintosh, or Unix. For the online laboratory, this means that students do not need to install any special hardware or software, the laboratory demonstrations should work right away with their browser.

Java was beneficial for other reasons as well. Java is an object-oriented language. Code is written in "classes," which distinguish between data and methods that act on the data. Classes are somewhat like generic templates (e.g., there is a class for a button), which have distinct data such as the label on the button, its size, and its foreground and background colors. A button class also has distinct methods that, for example, change the label and generate behavior when the button is pressed (it generates an "action" event). An object is an instance of a class, such as an "OK" button or a "CANCEL" button where the programmer specifies the data of the button and incorporates the button into a larger program that knows how to interpret and react to the action event generated by that button. It is fair to say that we are only beginning to grasp the power of object-oriented programming (as we all come from a background of procedural coding), but it is becoming clear that this is a very powerful way to write good computer code.

In particular, the object-oriented approach (when done properly) makes it very easy to reuse computer code. Java comes with a large number of generic classes that can be used or easily modified to fit the needs of the programmer (e.g., text fields, buttons, windows, colors, image handlers for graphics). In addition, programmers develop their own classes that may vary in reusability.

For example, we have a relatively generic class called ReactionTimeExperiment. This class provides a window, means of presenting images, and methods for recording reaction time (via a keypress) to stimulus presentation. This class by itself runs one type of experiment. To create a different reaction time experiment, we *extend* the ReactionTimeExperiment to create a new class (e.g., Sternberg, to create a variation of the well-known Sternberg experiment on search of short-term memory). This new class only needs to include information about what is different from the standard ReactionTimeExperiment (e.g., stimuli, number of trials, correct or incorrect responses), but does not need to be written from scratch because it inherits properties from the ReactionTimeExperiment.

If we later improve the ReactionTimeExperiment, the improvement will automatically become part of the Sternberg class as well, and of any other class we create that extends the ReactionTimeExperiment class (e.g., mental rotation, visual search, brain asymmetry, lexical decision). This modularity makes organizing code and the inevitable changes and upgrades much easier than for other programming languages.

As another example, after completion of a demonstration, a window often appears that plots the user's performance on that experiment. The class that provides this graph is identical for every demonstration and actually consists of two classes: one that builds the window on which the graph appears, and another that builds the graph itself. Throughout the development of the laboratory, the graphing classes have been modified many times. At one point they were modified to allow users to see a textual representation of their data. This involved adding a menu to the frame and code to respond to the menu selection. To incorporate this new ability into all the labs, the window class was simply modified as desired, and the resulting class was copied to the appropriate locations. The original code specific to a demonstration did not need to be modified or recompiled. One of the goals of object-oriented programming is to build classes as general as possible so that it is later easier to make modifications. We are still learning how to take full advantage of this approach, but the benefits, when we succeed, are quite clear to us.

Another benefit of Java is that it can be used to write programs that are restricted to Web browsers (applets) or to write programs that can be run directly on a computer without the Web browser. Nearly all the demonstrations are stand-alone programs that can be run without a Web browser. There is no modification necessary to make these programs run through a Web browser. The advantage to this approach is that the programs can be used in our laboratories for our research interests. Our research laboratories now use Java as a programming language, and many experiments are variations of programs that were first written for the online laboratory.

A final benefit of using Java is that the tools required to develop applications in Java can be easily obtained over the Internet at no cost. Sun Microsystems makes the Java Development Kit readily available from their Web site (http://www.javasoft.com/products/). In addition, numerous online books, tutorials, and documentation can be found on the World Wide Web, at a local bookstore, or in a university library. More information on where to find these resources can be viewed at our Java Resources Web page (http://www.psych.purdue.edu/~coglab/java.html).

LABORATORY DEVELOPMENT

The demonstrations in the online laboratory are established as a World Wide Web site titled the Cognitive Psychology Online Laboratory (CogLab) at http:// www.psych.purdue.edu/ ~ coglab / . This site is administered by the computing facilities of the Department of Psychological Sciences at Purdue University. As of this writing, there are 15 demonstrations, ranging from studies of perception (e.g., apparent motion, visual search) to memory (e.g., false memories, serial position) to neurocognition (e.g., receptive fields, brain asymmetry) to language (e.g., lexical decision). New demonstrations are added intermittently, and the reader is invited to peruse the site to see what is currently available.

Each demonstration is located on its own page on the Web site. The Web page includes background information about why the experiment is important and the role it has played in cognitive psychology. The page then provides specific instructions on how the user should participate in the demonstration. Usually the user clicks on a button to begin the demonstration. This button click opens a window where the stimuli are presented to the user and where all interaction takes place. The experiments were designed to be (nearly) foolproof. We knew that student users would have varied backgrounds and motivations. With that in mind, we tried to insure that a user would have to give an honest effort to participate in a demonstration before they could finish it.

It may be instructive to look at some representative experiments to see what they consist of and how they are designed in Java. The following discussion looks at two experiments with different presentation constraints. The first is a memory experiment that helped define theories of short-term memory. The second is a perceptual experiment that has influenced theories of perception and attention.

BROWN–PETERSON MEMORY TASK

This demonstration replicates the experiments performed by Brown (1958) and Peterson and Peterson (1959) that contributed to a new interpretation of human memory. In the memory task, the participant views a trigram of consonants (e.g., GKT) and then performs an unrelated distracter task (e.g., counting backwards by 3's) for 20 seconds or less.

The experimental data show that the probability of recalling the trigram decreases as the distracter duration increases. This was a counterintuitive finding in the 1950s, when memory loss was thought to be predominately due to interference from related items. Because the distracter task was unrelated to the consonant trigram, there was little reason to expect interference. The conclusion was that there exists a short-term memory (STM) system that holds information for only a few seconds. Without an active rehearsal by the participant, information in STM fades away.

The Java program that underlies this experiment needs to define and present random strings of consonant trigrams, define and present a distracter task for a specified duration, and record user recall of the trigrams after the distracter task. The basic code for defining stimuli is relatively straightforward for someone used to building memory experiments, and Java makes the presentation and gathering of user responses particularly easy.

Figure 1a shows the window where all interactions take place. The right side of the screen consists of a number of buttons with consonant labels and one button labeled "Next trial." Clicking the Next trial button starts a trial, and the computer presents the consonant trigram on the left side of the window. Simultaneously, the Next trial button is grayed out, meaning it cannot be activated again until the current trial is complete. This prevents a user from (accidentally or purposely) pressing the button repeatedly and skipping trials. The trigram is presented for a few seconds and then replaced by the distracter task. This task consists of classifying digits as odd or even (pressing the "o" or "e" key). Each digit is presented for 1 second, and the user must correctly classify the digits for the current trial to count (this prevents users from ignoring the distracter task). The distracter task is presented for 1, 11, or 21 seconds and followed by the recall task.

For recall, the buttons on the right are made active (Figure 1b). The user selects the consonants, in the correct order, that were presented in that trial. The computer automatically scores the responses and keeps track of the user's performance throughout the experiment. The user clicks on the Next trial button when ready to start the next trial and continues until all trials are finished. Throughout the experiment the user can check on how much longer the experiment will take to finish by choosing the "Trials to go" menu option. Selecting this menu reveals the number of trials remaining.

At the end of the experiment a graph automatically appears that plots the number of trigrams (out of 10 possible) correctly recalled as a function of the duration of the distracter task. The typical result is that the number of correctly recalled trigrams decreases as distracter duration increases. Figure 1c shows typical results for this demonstration.

Compared to other programming languages, Java simplifies the design of this program. Consider the complicated user interface needed for the Brown–Peterson program. The program must open a window and make it moveable (since users may need to reread the instructions) and closeable, add a title bar, add a menu, organize buttons on one side, enable and disable those

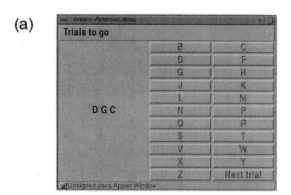

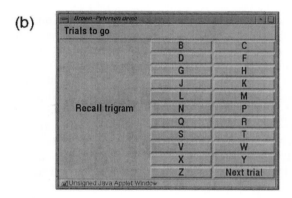

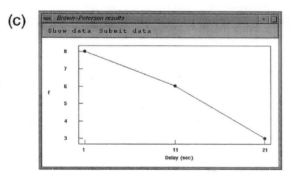

Figure 1 The Brown–Peterson memory demonstration. (a) the experimental window during presentation of a trigram; (b) the experimental window after the distracter task; the user clicks on the buttons to recall the trigram; (c) at the end of the experiment a window plots the user's data. Here the data show that the frequency of recalling a trigram decreases as distracter duration increases.

buttons as appropriate, present timed text on the left side, respond to all button presses, and respond to all keypresses. In most programming languages, this would be a daunting design without the aid of some type of graphical user interface tool. Such tools exist for Java, but we do not use them because the coding can be done easily by hand (the entire program uses 285 lines of code). This is because the Java language already includes reusable code that creates windows, menubars, buttons, and drawing areas, and also includes code that handles many of the procedures necessary to interpret actions from buttons and the keyboard. The programmer simply fills in the details of what is needed, such as the name of the button, the title of the window, and the action to take for different keypresses.

Many of the other CogLab experiments dealing with memory (false memories, memory span, and serial position), look similar to the Brown–Peterson experiment.

PARTIAL REPORT

A second experiment helps to demonstrate another type of demonstration where details of presentation are more important. In the memory experiments presentation time is sometimes controlled, but the necessary resolution of timing is on the order of seconds. In other experiments one needs timing resolution in milliseconds. Java can provide millisecond timing, provided the computer can process information fast enough. A well-known experiment that requires this type of timing resolution is the partial report experiment used by Sperling (1960) to explore properties of perception, attention, and iconic memory. In Sperling's original experiment, the observer saw a three-by-three matrix of random letters on each trial. The letters were flashed for a very short duration (50 milliseconds). After this display turned off, one of three tones sounded, and the observer reported the letters from the row associated with the tone. If the tone was presented directly after offset of the letters, Sperling found that observers were nearly 100% accurate in reporting letters from the indicated row. Because the tone was sounded after the letters disappeared, observers must have focused on the appropriate row as it was stored in some type of sensory store (later called iconic memory) of perceptual information. Moreover, because perfect performance was found regardless of which row was indicated, the sensory store must contain a nearly perfect representation of the total visual percept. This experiment was one of a set that helped define cognitive psychology as a field and demonstrated its ability to identify new properties of cognition (Neisser, 1967).

The CogLab demonstration allows a user to participate in a version of the partial report experiment. Unlike the memory experiments, it is important that the entire screen of the computer be controlled because the iconic memory is quite fragile, and other information on the screen could easily disrupt it. The experiment window fills the entire screen and is devoid of any interfering buttons or text. Instead, all user interactions are handled through the keyboard.

Pressing the space-bar starts a trial. A fixation point appears to require the user to look at the middle of the subsequently presented letter matrix. Two seconds later, a three-by-three letter matrix appears for 150 milliseconds. The matrix disappears and, after a varying duration, an arrow (>) appears to the left of one of the rows to identify the target. (Tones are not used to indicate the target row because many computers in university laboratories do not have sound cards, and if they did, the experiment would probably get students in trouble with others in the same room.) The user then types the letters in the indicated row (guessing if necessary). Pressing the spacebar starts the next trial.

At the end of the experiment a graph appears that plots the percentage of letters correctly reported as a function of the delay between letter matrix offset and arrow indicator onset (in milliseconds). As the delay increases from 0 to 1024 milliseconds, the typical result is that the percentage drops (Figure 2). The shortest nominal delays are 1, 4, and 16 milliseconds, and the jitter in the

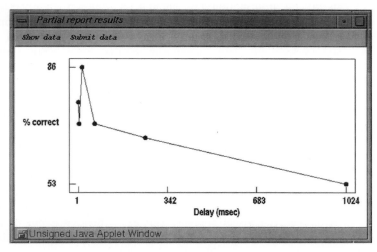

Figure 2 Typical data from the partial report experiment. Except for jitter in the data at very short delays, percentage of letters correctly reported decreases with delay of the indicating arrow.

data at these delays is likely due to limits of the monitor refresh rate (generally 8–16 milliseconds).

Once again, Java makes the creation of this type of experiment relatively easy. Of particular note is the simplicity with which many potential problems can be avoided. For example, each letter matrix is an image, created internally by the program and then presented on the screen. Java includes a variety of methods for creating and presenting images, so this is a relatively easy task. It also insures that each part of the letter matrix is presented simultaneously. Likewise, Java can make calls to the local computer to discover the screen size (in pixels) and resolution (in pixels per inch) of the user's computer monitor. This insures that the stimulus window entirely fills the monitor, but does not extend beyond the monitor edges.

OTHER DEMONSTRATIONS

Some of the other experiments available on CogLab include:

1. *Memory span.* Student's memory span is estimated for a variety of stimuli (letters, numbers, short words, and long words). Memory span is typically around 7 ± 2, but is shorter for long words (e.g., Baddeley, Thomson, & Buchanan, 1975).

2. *Visual search.* Feature and conjunctive searches are given. Reaction times are measured and the student can note that feature searches are unaffected by the number of distracters, while conjunctive searches take longer with more distracters (Treisman, Sykes, & Gelade, 1977).

3. *Serial position effects on memory.* A list of items is presented and the student reports the items in any order. Generally, the first and last items are recalled better than the items in the middle of a list (e.g., Crowder, 1976).

4. *Mental rotation.* Two shapes are presented and the student judges, as quickly as possible, if the two shapes are mirror images or the same. One shape is rotated relative to the other. Reaction time tends to increase with rotation angle (Shepard & Metzler, 1971).

5. *Sternberg memory task.* A set of 1–4 letters is shown and removed; then a target letter is given. The student decides whether the target letter was in the original set. Reaction time tends to increase for larger set sizes. Yes and No reaction times are nearly parallel for increases in set size (Sternberg, 1966).

6. *Attentional blink.* Individual letters are presented in rapid succession. The student notes whenever the stream contains either (or both) of two target letters. Detection of one target letter tends to prevent detection of a second target letter if it quickly follows the first (Weichselgartner & Sperling, 1987).

7. *Receptive fields.* The student draws image patterns to try to stimulate visual cells. The student must design a good stimulus to produce a strong response in a cell and then identify the cell type.

8. *Change detection.* Users read a story where the LeTTErs ArE oF VARioUs CaSEs. As they read, the cases sometimes change randomly. At various times, users are asked to determine if the letters just changed case. The detection of this change is difficult. This finding demonstrates that we only notice change to those parts of the world we are attending (e.g., Rensink, O'Regan, & Clark, 1997).

9. *False memories.* In each trial a sequence of words is presented and the observer is to subsequently classify a set of words as either in the sequence (old) or not in the sequence (new). The sequences are specially designed so that users will tend to report a particular word as part of the sequence, even though it was not presented (Roediger & McDermott, 1995).

10. *Apparent motion.* Presentation of two dots properly separated in space and time leads to a perception of motion between the dots. As the spatial separation between dots increases, the temporal separation also needs to increase (Wertheimer, 1912).

11. *Brain asymmetry.* The left and right hemispheres have different capabilities in split brain patients, and perhaps in normal patients as well. This demonstration measures reaction times to words (classified as present- or past-tense verbs) and shapes (classified by orientation) to the left and right visual fields. Brain asymmetries could be revealed by this experiment.

12. *Lexical decision task.* Reaction time to a target word is faster if the target follows another word semantically related to the target (Meyer & Schvaneveldt, 1971).

13. *Probability demo.* Lotteries are often misunderstood because people fail to understand probability. This demonstration shows the rarity of winning a lottery by simulating daily lottery draws for many years.

In addition to the topics just mentioned there are some other experiments related to visual perception on the Visual Perception Online Laboratory (VisLab) at http://www.psych.purdue.edu/~coglab/VisLab/index.html. We have also started to explore methods that would allow for between-subjects experiments. For example, a notable finding of the Brown–Peterson experiment is that users are nearly always perfect on the first trial, regardless of distracter duration (Keppel & Underwood, 1962). To see if this was true among our students, we modified the Brown–Peterson program so that it caught the first trial and the distracter duration of that trial and sent the information back to the departmental Web server. The information was stored in a file and analyzed later to verify the expected result.

WEB SERVER

There are actually two versions of CogLab, one for students enrolled in our Introduction to Cognitive Psychology courses and one for everybody else. The only difference between the two sites is that on the former we have set up mechanisms to automatically collect additional information from our students. Thus, after completing the Brown–Peterson demonstration, students perform two additional steps. First, they select a "Submit Info" option from the graph that displays the results. This automatically updates a central registry and informs the instructor that the student has completed the assignment. Second, they go to a homework page where several short-answer questions are asked. Using the "Forms" capability of the browsers, they type in their answers and again submit their assignment. This is automatically routed to the appropriate instructor.

The student version of CogLab is housed on a separate machine. Because we use this machine to test changes to the demonstration, it was necessary to have complete access to the system. Until spring 1999, we hosted CogLab on an old IBM PS-ValuePoint, a 486 running at 33 mHz with 16 MB RAM purchased used for $100. The only upgrades necessary were a 5-gigabyte hard drive and an ethernet card (a generic NE2000 clone card that cost $20). The computer runs Linux, a freely available Unix-like operating system (see http:// www.linux.org). The particular version is Red Hat 5.1 (http:// www.redhat.com), which is a complete distribution that includes all necessary networking tools. With the exception of paying $1.99 for the CD, all of the software is freely available at no charge. There is no commercial software used at all.

The Red Hat distribution includes the Apache Web server, which is used by over 50% of all Web sites according to the January 1999 Netcraft survey (http:// www.netcraft.com/ survey /). The program to display the number of unique hits to each page can be found at http:// www.fccc.edu / users / muquit / Count.html. The analysis of the total hits is performed by another free program called Analog (http:// www.statslab.cam.ac.uk/~sret1 / analog /). All of the graphics and text logos are created using a program called The Gimp (the GNU Image Manipulation Program; http:// www.gimp.org).

We use two different methods of collecting responses. The old way is to use a program written in C (Red Hat includes a complete set of C development tools) to process the homework forms. A standard Unix tool, cron, automatically updates this information once a day and delivers it to the appropriate instructor. A newer method, currently in beta testing, is to use Java. Several Java servers run continuously, waiting for connections from the various applets. When a connection is made, the server receives information from the client (either the ID of the student who has completed a task or the results of the first trial of the Brown–Peterson demo) and saves it. We are expanding this server to provide unique user IDs to each student and each class so that the process becomes fully automated. By the end of the spring 1999 semester, we plan to have the server also send to the client the average data collected so far, so that users can compare their data to others.

There are several advantages and disadvantages to this setup. First, there is minimal cost because all of the software is free and performance, even on old computers, is more than satisfactory. Second, because all of the source code to all of the software is freely available, it has been thoroughly tested. Despite the heavy use, the system has never crashed; the longest continuous up-time so far has been 159 days without rebooting. A related benefit is that bug and security fixes are usually available within a day or so of the initial report. Third, administration can be done remotely by any of the people involved in the project. Although we have disabled most methods of connecting for security reasons (for example, telnet sends both user ID and password information over the internet unencrypted), we can still access this site from anywhere in the world using secure shell, which encrypts all communication. Due to U.S. export laws, this software is available from a site in the Netherlands (http: // www.replay.com/).

The main disadvantage is that Linux, like all Unix systems, takes a while to learn. It took one of the members of the project about 3 months to become comfortable with administering a Web site. All of the tools need configuring, which seems a daunting task at first. However, once learned, the tools become very powerful and do exactly what is needed.

CAVEATS

We would be remiss if we failed to present some of the shortcomings of CogLab. While they can be overcome, they should be recognized before anyone attempts a similar project.

First, Java is a work in progress. Sun Microsystems has just recently released version 1.2. Hopefully it does not include as many changes as took place between 1.0 and 1.1. Many of the commands available in Java 1.0 no longer exist (are deprecated) in Java 1.1. While the commands are temporarily supported, they will eventually be phased out. This means that any programs with those calls must eventually be rewritten. At the same time many of the Web browsers do not include the replacement calls for Java 1.1, but do include the old calls for Java 1.0. As a result, we are forced to use the old calls, even though we know it means rewriting code in the future. This is the price one pays for being on the cutting edge of technology.

Second, while Java is touted as a "write-once, run-anywhere" programming language, it often falls short of that goal. We find that some programs do not work in certain Web browsers, on some operating system, for some browser versions, or at all. There is usually nothing we can do about these problems except wait for the creators of Web browsers to work out the bugs in their Java interpreters. In general, we find the programs do work as intended, with exceptions usually being obvious. In fact, the most common failure to run a CogLab demonstration is that the user's Web browser does not have Java enabled. This problem is easily fixed by having the user make a change under the browser's preferences or options menus. To identify this problem we have created a test page (http://www.psych.purdue.edu/~coglab/testpage.html) that indicates whether a Web browser will likely work on the CogLab demonstrations and identifies what needs to be updated if it will not work.

Third, because students complete the laboratories outside of class, they have more trouble than normal when things do not go as planned. We have addressed this problem by establishing office hours in a computer room where we know the programs work properly. With this option available, nearly every student can successfully complete the labs.

Fourth, if one is not used to programming, learning Java will be a challenge. The design of the programs is not, in our experience, something that can be assigned as a semester project to an undergraduate student (or even a graduate student). The learning curve is steep enough that it takes several months before one is proficient enough to write good code. After this training period, however, one can quickly adapt learned skills to new situations to rapidly create new experiments. Moreover, in our experience, what can be accomplished with Java after several months of practice is substantially more than can be done with any other programming language. Individuals interested in starting a project similar to CogLab will find some useful information on CogLab's Java Resources page (http://www.psych.purdue.edu/~coglab/java.html). Included is a program with source code for designing a simple reaction time experiment.

Fifth, there are some types of experiments that cannot be effectively demonstrated outside a controlled laboratory. If visual angle of stimuli must be measured precisely, there is no way to insure that students are sitting the proper distance from the monitor. Similarly, if a few milliseconds of timing make a difference to an experiment, there is no way to be certain that a user's computer is fast enough to properly run the experiment. Likewise, experiments that require intense attention and focus by a subject may not produce the expected results when carried out in a noisy computer room. These limitations are common to any type of Web-based experiment.

Finally, security is an important issue for Web browsers. But for built-in controls, a maliciously written Java program run within a Web browser could destroy a user's operating system or be used to gather sensitive information. To avoid this possibility Web browsers prevent Java programs from reading or writing to the user's computer. This restriction means that experimental data cannot be saved to a file, nor can plots be printed or copied and pasted into another document. This restriction has been a nuisance to students who expect to be able to print out their results. We have two partial solutions to this problem. One is to show students how to take screenshots of the monitor image. This usually creates a bitmap image of the screen or a particular window. This graphic image can be ported to other documents, where it can be printed. The other solution was mentioned earlier. A menu option from the plot window allows users to see a textual presentation of their data. Web browsers do allow text to be copied and pasted from a Java program to another program. This allows the raw data to be put into a spreadsheet, for example, where users can create their own data plots.

SUMMARY

The Cognitive Psychology Online Laboratory is a Java-based Web site that allows users to participate in classical experiments and informative demonstrations of major issues in cognitive psychology. At Purdue University we use CogLab in a variety of courses related to cognitive psychology. Instructors from around the world have also indicated that they use the laboratories for their courses. Students report that they understand experiments better after participating in the lab. Because the laboratory is available on the World Wide Web, it is easily incorporated into psychology classes. Instructors simply tell students the Web address of the site and which laboratories to complete. Students can complete the laboratories at a time and place of their choosing. This is a powerful approach to augmenting traditional courses, and we expect further enhancements.

REFERENCES

Baddeley, A. D., Thomson, N., & Buchanan, M. (1975). Word length and the structure of short-term memory. *Journal of Verbal Learning and Verbal Behavior, 14,* 575–589.
Brown, J. (1958). Some tests of the decay theory of immediate memory. *Quarterly Journal of Experimental Psychology, 10,* 12–21.
Crowder, R. G. (1976). *Principles of learning and memory.* Hillsdale, NJ: Erlbaum.
Keppel, G., & Underwood, B. J. (1962). Proactive inhibition in short-term retention of single items. *Journal of Verbal Learning and Verbal Behavior, 1,* 153–161.

Meyer, D. E., & Schvaneveldt, R. W. (1971). Facilitation in recognizing pairs of words: Evidence of a dependence between retrieval operations. *Journal of Experimental Psychology, 90,* 227–234.

Neisser, U. (1967). *Cognitive psychology.* New York: Appleton-Century-Crofts.

Peterson, L. R., & Peterson, M. J. (1959). Short-term retention of individual verbal items. *Journal of Experimental Psychology, 58,* 193–198.

Rensink, R. A., O'Regan, J. K., & Clark, J. J. (1997). To see or not to see: The need for attention to perceive changes in scenes. *Psychological Science, 8,* 368–373.

Roediger, H. L., III & McDermott, K. B. (1995). Creating false memories: Remembering words not presented in lists. *Journal of Experimental Psychology: Learning, Memory, and Cognition, 21,* 803–814.

Shepard, R. N., & Metzler, J. (1971). Mental rotation of three-dimensional objects. *Science, 225,* 701–703.

Sperling, G. (1960). The information available in brief visual presentations. *Psychological Monographs, 74* (Whole No. 11).

Sternberg, S. (1966). High speed scanning in human memory. *Science, 153,* 652–654.

Treisman, A., Sykes, M., & Gelade, G. (1977). Selective attention and stimulus integration. In S. Dornic (Ed.), *Attention and performance VI* (pp. 333–361). Hillsdale, NJ: Erlbaum.

Weichselgartner, E., & Sperling, G. (1987). Dynamics of automatic and controlled visual-attention. *Science, 238,* 778–780.

Wertheimer, M. (1912). Experimentelle Studien über das Sehen von Bewegung. *Zeitschrift für Psychologie, 61,* 161–265.

CHAPTER 12

The Server Side of Psychology Web Experiments

William C. Schmidt
Department of Psychology
University at Buffalo, The State University of New York
Buffalo, New York 14260

The World-Wide Web (WWW) is quickly becoming a rich tool for the presentation of psychological stimuli and the automated collection and screening of data. The Web offers as close to a unified visual interface for data collection, regardless of a subject's geographical locale or computer operating system, as we have ever had. An important part of Internet-related data collection (and the integrity of the collected data) depends upon the execution of programs on the server side of a Web session. This chapter introduces the reader to the client–server relationship and presents features of the WWW client–server interaction that can afford psychologists with more control in the delivery of experiments on the Web.

THE CLIENT–SERVER RELATIONSHIP

The client–server relationship is presented in Figure 1. A Web client is a computer that runs a Web browser, requests information from a Web server, and displays received information according to a predefined convention (hypertext markup language, or HTML). The client (one of potentially millions of simultaneous users) places a request to the Web server to retrieve an HTML document or to run a program on the server, and the resulting document or the output of the server program is piped across the Internet to be interpreted and displayed on the client computer.

Psychological Experiments on the Internet

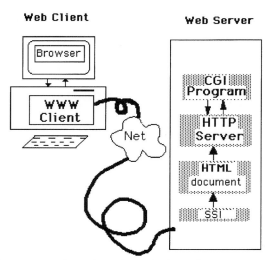

Figure 1 The client–server relationship: The Web client places a request to the server that results in the execution of a CGI (common gateway interface) program, or the retrieval and delivery of an HTML document. The document may include the output of a SSI (server-side include) directive or program.

Although to Web surfers the interaction between the Web server and the browser appears seamless, in reality the two operate as completely independent entities. Because the server is simply a program that sits waiting to fulfill requests, it cannot determine from where or from whom the next request will come, nor without an extensive database and tracking system, can it tell what information the client may have already received. In technical terms, the typical client–server relationship is said to be "stateless" because at no time does the server retain information about the client's current state.

The stateless nature of the client–server interaction presents a real obstacle to creating interactive sessions because some scheme must be enacted to provide the server with information about the client's state. Based on this information the server program can then decide how to update the client's state.

There are two principal approaches to solving this problem. One is to augment the server software and the other approach is to pass information about the client's state with every request for more information. These solutions can be implemented via commercial software additions (i.e., use of Active Server Pages with Microsoft's Web server or server–database software systems that track clients over a protracted period of time) or they can be implemented using freely available software. Commercial schemes may suit researchers, but these solutions require specialized knowledge and software that often will not work under more than one operating system.

This chapter focuses on the approach of passing information about the client's state with each document request. This solution is quite general and does not require database knowledge. Furthermore, discussion is restricted to noncommercial, freely available solutions. What is required is a custom-written program on the server side that interprets information sent by the client and infers the client's state. Based on this inference, the server-side program decides what information is appropriate to send to update the client.

Consider the task of administering a questionnaire that contains skip patterns (different sets of questions are administered depending upon the answers supplied). Figure 2 diagrams the potential interactive sessions that we might want a participant to experience. Suppose that after asking some introductory question we want to present Questions 2–5 if participants answered "yes," and we want to present questions 6–10 if they had answered "no" or "don't know." Furthermore, we want to record the participant's responses to all of these questions in a data file and give back to the participant a summary of the group frequency of "yes," "no," and "don't know" responses to the initial question. To do this requires more than the simple use of static HTML documents because action has to be taken on the server to record the data and to tabulate and present the results. Similarly, if the question presentation is to be automated, then something on the server side will have to make a decision about which questions to present to the participant based on their submitted response to Question 1.

An appropriate solution when side-effects of the request, such as recording data or tabulating and immediately returning cumulative group results, are involved is to use server-side programming. The level of sophistication of such programming has a direct bearing on the level of control that the experimenter can exercise on the interaction with participants.

For the questionnaire example just described, the client would first request a document on the server that contains Question 1. That document would include directions to the client computer that the answer to the question be encoded and sent to a particular program on the server. Alternatively, the client could ask the server to run a program whose output is the HTML containing Question 1 complete with instructions about where submitted data are to be transferred. Once the participant answers Question 1 and clicks on the "Submit" button, the response is encoded according to the common gateway interface (CGI) protocol and transmitted to the server where a program is executed that is capable of extracting information that has been encoded using this protocol. The output of this CGI program is then piped back to the browser, interpreted as HTML, and displayed.

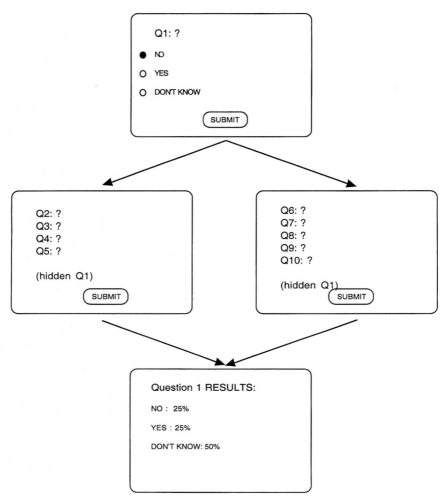

Figure 2 Two potential sessions are outlined, one in which the respondent is shown Questions 2–5 after answering "NO" to Question 1 and a second session in which the respondent is shown Questions 6–10 after responding "YES" or "DON'T KNOW" to Question 1.

In the case of our example, if the participant responded "yes" to Question 1, the CGI program would return Questions 2–5 complete with information about what CGI program to send the data to. Similarly, if the participant responded "no" or "don't know" to Question 1, then the program would respond with the HTML for Questions 6–10. In either case, the results of Question 1 would be encoded in the CGI program's response, but not shown to the participant. The Question 1 results are required to be in the document so that the next time the client contacts the server to submit data, all of the data can be sent. Recall that because the client–server relationship is stateless, the server has no record of this particular client's previous response to Question 1 so it requires all information be sent for it to determine the appropriate response. The CGI program would at this point write the participant's data to disk, add the participant's responses to Question 1 to those of previous respondents, and return summary information to the client to be presented to the participant. Importantly, all of this can be done regardless of the technology that the participant has on the client side. The oldest and simplest browsers are sufficient to allow a user to participate in an experiment. Even nongraphical browsers (i.e., Lynx) can be used for purely text-based experiments.

Based on the preceding example, one could imagine three different CGI programs called at different points in the client–server exchange. One program would simply deliver Question 1 and would direct the results to be submitted to a second program that would be responsible for evaluating the answer to Question 1. Depending upon the data submitted, Program 2 would present the appropriate second set of questions and direct the responses to be sent to a third program responsible for recording the data and computing a frequency breakdown.

Although three such programs would suffice for the example presented, such an approach creates a lot of redundant work and requires the organized modification of several programs independently should it be desirable to change details of the experiment. Instead, it is a common practice to write a single program that can be called multiple times and which will respond appropriately depending upon the context of the call and the information passed to it.

The program logic for such a reentrant program is presented in Figure 3 complete with the contextual information used to determine its response. This program determines where the participant is in the sequence of information exchanges, based on the information presented by the client.

The first time the program is called there are no values passed, so the program returns the first question with a universal resource locator (URL—an address of a document or other resource on the Internet) to itself as the place to direct submitted information.

The second time the program is called there is a submission for Question 1 but not for any other questions. From this information, the program can determine the second set of questions to present. It will also pass back the response to Question 1 hidden from the participant and direct that all submitted information be forwarded to itself.

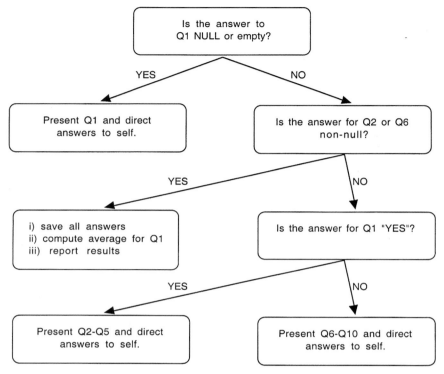

Figure 3 Program logic for a reentrant server-side program capable of implementing the example outlined in the text and diagrammed in Figure 2.

On the third call, data from Question 1 exist, as do data from either Questions 2–5 or Questions 6–10. Even if a participant does not answer any of the questions presented before submitting, there will be values (potentially empty or null) associated with the questions. At this point the program can write the data to disk, update the tabulation of the results, and present the participant with a frequency breakdown.

Every time that the client makes a request the server makes information about that request available to any programs that are executed in the form of "environment variables." Table 1 presents the environment variables that are generally available to server side programs. The precise information associated with these environment variables depends upon the specific client and server being used, as not all client–server combinations support all of the features to which the environment variables pertain. For instance, few of the newer Web clients provide e-mail addresses of the participant, while original Web clients frequently made such information available. Some of these environment variables play a critical role in the capabilities mentioned later in this chapter and will be referred to throughout.

After a discussion of when server side solutions are appropriate, the remainder of the chapter will discuss server side techniques and features of the client–server relationship that can be used to give experimenters more control over the data that they collect. Control over the information delivered and received is foremost in the discussion. Control over information delivery is discussed in the context of server side document preprocessing using server side includes (SSIs). A discussion of online testing and online guided tutorials is also covered. Control over the quality of the data collected is discussed with reference to error checking, security issues, and population sampling. Server side password protection schemes, domain restriction, and the enumeration of participants are discussed as three approaches to better controlling and identifying participants. Finally, several miscellaneous issues are presented, including the use of "cookies" for retaining information across testing sessions, server side program efficiency, and security issues around CGI program execution.

Table 1

Environment Variables Available to CGI and SSI Programs

Variable name	Description
HTTP_REFERER	The URL of referring document or program
HTTP_USER_AGENT	Client identification string
	Often contains browser name, version, and operating system
REMOTE_ADDR	The IP address of the client computer
REMOTE_HOST	If available, the domain name of the client computer
	If unavailable, same as REMOTE_ADDR
SERVER_NAME	The server's domain name
AUTH_TYPE	Password protocol if server supports this feature
REMOTE_USER	Approved username for server password protection
SCRIPT_NAME	Holds virtual path to the script
PATH_INFO	The path to the running script
	May contain additional information beyond SCRIPT_NAME

APPROPRIATENESS OF
SERVER-SIDE SOLUTIONS

Web technology has developed fairly recently and continues to change at a rapid pace. Recent technological advances have brought us a myriad of possible solutions to the problem of the stateless relationship between Web server and client. JavaScript, for instance, aims at reducing the amount of work that the Web server has to do by unloading many tasks to the client computer. Similarly, Java allows the Web client to do more computation and involve the server less and less. (Both JavaScript and Java programs are developed to run on any platform through interpreted code.) Plug-ins also extend a Web browser's capabilities (e.g., through Authorware; see McGraw, Tew, & Williams, chap. 9, this volume), though they often require the user to download and install the correct plug-in for the browser being used and are not always available for every browser, browser version, or operating system.

Ideally JavaScript and Java work similarly on every client. In reality, however, differences exist across operating systems (e.g., between MacOS, Windows, and Solaris), across browser manufacturers (e.g., between Netscape, Microsoft, and Opera) and even across different versions of a browser manufactured by the same company for the same operating system (e.g., between Netscape 3.x and Netscape 4.x for Windows). As a result, not all JavaScript or Java programs will work with all Java- or JavaScript-capable browsers and backward compatibility is not guaranteed (see Francis, Neath, & Surprenant, chap. 11, this volume, and Baron & Siepmann, chap. 10, this volume, for further discussion of incompatibilities across browser platforms).

A survey of average Web users conducted in December 1998 (Georgia Tech's Graphics, Visualization, & Usability Center, 1999) revealed that 43% of users reported that JavaScript and Java incompatibilities were among the biggest problems they encountered while using the Web, and 25% agreed that sites incompatible with multiple browsers constituted a major problem with the Web.

Part of the frustration experienced by such users stems from the fact that not all browsers include Java and JavaScript capabilities. The Georgia Tech survey revealed that 15% of Web users expect to continue the use of a nonstandard Web browser (e.g., non-Netscape or non-Microsoft browsers, hence unlikely to be both Java and JavaScript capable) during 1999. Furthermore, 4% of users reported primarily using a nonstandard browser. Of the users of browsers from the two dominant browser manufacturers, 74% were using version 4.x or above. Hence roughly 29% of all Web users do not have the latest technology installed on their systems and are incapable of displaying Web content that takes advantage of such technology without upgrading.

In contrast to JavaScript, Java, and solutions requiring plug-in extensions, server side programming solutions do not require that the user have anything more than access to the most basic technology. Furthermore, any browser implementing even the earliest hypertext transfer protocol (HTTP 1.0) will work with server side programming solutions. Hence, by playing to the lowest common denominator, server side programming solutions can aim to accommodate the widest possible body of subjects on the Web. Not taking a lowest-common-denominator approach could cause one to alienate users with older technology, without easy access to newer technology, without the skills to upgrade, or special users that rely on simple technology (e.g., Lynx, a simple text-based browser is the primary browser used by the visually impaired because it interfaces easily with text-to-speech converters). Information about who the targeted population of an experiment is should be taken into consideration when determining what level of technology to use when implementing the experiment.

There are many experiments that are not easily implemented by server-side solutions. Clearly anything requiring timing, intensive graphics presentation, or reactivity to user input is not easily accomplished in this manner. These sorts of experiments (described elsewhere in this volume) can be expected to require the latest technology and will demand this of their participants. However, for simple questionnaire and test experiments, server-side program solutions have the fewest browser incompatibilities and will reach the greatest target audience without alienating potential participants.

CONTROL OVER INFORMATION DELIVERY

At this point the reader will have noticed some of the potential benefits of having the data processed on the server side. First, we have been able to control precisely which questions were presented to the participant. This allows experimenters to guide their respondents through a complex survey without letting the respondent see all of the questions or be relied upon to correctly follow directions regarding the skipping of selected items. Second, note that we have been able to selectively return information (the frequency breakdown) to the participant in very little time. This capability allows an experimenter to encourage participation for the sake of contributing to the results (or even for the reward of simply being able to view the results).

Finding out the survey results occurs much faster for the respondent (and for the experimenter) than with conventional paper-and-pencil questionnaires, and it costs no more for the experimenter to distribute the results than it did to collect the data (Schmidt, 1997a). Although the results presented at the time of data submission are not complete, respondents can easily be given a URL which will give them updated results anytime they wish to check. A third benefit of the server-side program is obviously its ability to store data in whatever format is desired. Such a feature removes the burden of data entry on the part of the researcher, and data entry errors that go along with that chore (Schmidt, 1997a). Collected data can be formatted so as to easily be imported into a familiar statistics package.

SERVER - SIDE PREPROCESSING

One technique for presenting dynamic Web pages that is in popular use is to incorporate server-side programming into the delivery in the form of server-side includes (SSI). A SSI is a directive embedded within a static HTML document. When a client makes a request for the HTML document, the Web server parses the document and replaces any SSI directives with the output that is generated as a result of the directive.

Many Web servers have several directives built in that allow the current time, directory listings, or the contents of a file to be inserted into the document that is delivered. Custom programs can also be run, and their output is inserted in the document delivered to the browser. Server-side include programs have access to all of the environment variables associated with CGI programs (see Table 1) as well as several additional variables that are outlined in Table 2. These variables add access to information about the document being requested and time information about the request.

Note that SSIs and SSI programs are different than CGI programs because SSIs do not accept data from the Web client, nor are they directly callable by the Web client. Rather, SSIs are invoked as part of a document request. To the client, there is no discernible difference between the output of a Web page with a SSI in it as opposed to a static document with identical content. SSIs afford the ability to send a customized document to a client based on aspects of the client's configuration (e.g., browser type or version, operating system, referring URL, etc.).

Table 2

Additional Environment Variables Available to SSI Programs

Variable name	Description
DOCUMENT_NAME	The HTML document name
DOCUMENT_URI	The path from server root to this document
DATE_LOCAL	The current date, server's time zone
DATE_GMT	Same as DATE_LOCAL but in Greenwich mean time
LAST_MODIFIED	The last modification date of the requested document

Dynamic Web pages can be created using SSIs through the inclusion of multiple separate components of the final document that is delivered to the client. This is different than what is referred to as dynamic Web pages from JavaScript, Java, or DHTML (which is an extended version of HTML) methods. DHTML, Java, and JavaScript allow Web site designers to use client-side computations to assist in determining what content to show the participant. These latter methods accomplish dynamic Web pages through interpreted code that runs on the client computer. SSIs on the other hand are involved in the dynamic creation of the document that gets delivered to the client all before it is interpreted and presented to the participant.

Because SSIs are expanded on the server side before the browser interprets the document, SSIs can be used to include code to be interpreted. The delivered document may contain HTML, JavaScript, Java, or DHTML. Some of this content may be generated at the time that the request for the Web page is filled by the server. For instance, a very simple example of a SSI is the insertion of the time of a request into the document that is delivered. Such content cannot be known before the page is requested but must be generated at the time of the request. The Web page simply has a SSI directive to the server to insert the current time on the server computer's clock at a certain point in the Web page. When the document is delivered to the participant, the time that the server computer filled the request is presented in place of the SSI directive. In a similar fashion, the output of complex SSI programs can be inserted into the document delivered.

There is no limit to the number of SSI directives that can be in an HTML document, though it should be noted that the inclusion of each one slows the delivery time of the document because the server is required to carry out some processing whenever it encounters such a directive. This time issue is especially important when the SSI requires the execution of a custom program. Start-up time and overhead for running programs can cause delays and place a strain on servers when multiple participants request a document simultaneously. This is likely not to be a major problem for most Web experiments as the number of participants is usually low and not temporally concentrated.

If server load is an issue, experimenters can consider freely available servers or server extensions that have been created that allow more complex embeddings than simple SSIs. Because these servers incorporate SSI functions into the server program, they perform well even when there is a large number of simultaneous requests. Such servers are capable of increasingly sophisticated feats. The PHP/FI server for instance (www.php.net) allows experimenters to program quizzes and tests using static documents. It also allows "webmasters" to create templates that give all of the Web pages of a designated collection a similar stylistic look and feel. An alternative server provided by the ePerl project (www.engelschall.com/sw/eperl/) has a Perl interpreter (Perl is a popular programming language for Web-based projects—www.perl.com) built into the Web server program. An ePerl Web server parses the documents it delivers and executes Perl programs embedded within such documents.

BROWSER COMPATIBILITY ISSUES

Server-side include solutions are ideal for tailoring Web page content to the type of browser that is being used. When the client makes its request for a document, it identifies itself to the server using a string that contains the browser name and version. Server-side programs have access to this information (by checking the HTTP_USER_AGENT environment variable) and can therefore determine at the time of document delivery precisely what sort of content should be returned (i.e., HTML containing JavaScript compatible with Internet Explorer or with Netscape). This variable also identifies the operating system of the client machine and the specific version of the browser. All of this information is of use because, as discussed earlier, Web browsers can treat identical documents differently depending not only on the type of browser (i.e., Netscape Navigator, Internet Explorer, Opera, HotJava, etc.) and the operating system (i.e., Macintosh, Solaris, Windows, DOS, etc.) but also on the specific version of the browser (i.e., 1.0, 2.0, 3.0, etc.).

The author has encountered three specific browser-related problems that could assist experimenters in avoiding difficulties. First, color presentation differences across early browser versions and particularly across platforms regardless of the browser type make it difficult to deliver a uniformly presented document. Second, a problem shared by Netscape Navigator for DOS and Windows, versions 3.01 and earlier is a limit in the number of form items (approximately 100 items consisting of checkboxes, radio button, pop-up menu, or scrolling list items and text input areas can be accommodated) per page that can be displayed (Schmidt, 1997a).

A final error of which the author is aware afflicts Internet Explorer version 3.x (at least under the Windows 95 and NT operating systems) and limits the number of consecutive calls that can be made to a given CGI program using the POST data command (the method used for sending data from a browser to the server). With each call, this version of the browser allocates a large portion of RAM from the operating system. After several such calls the browser freezes or quits because it runs out of available memory. There is no apparent fix for this problem besides limiting the number of pages that a CGI can present.

TESTING AND FEEDBACK

Due to the stateless nature of the client-server relationship, to use conventional Web software technology to implement interactive tests or quizzes and to collect the results, a server-side program is vital. In cases where it is not important to shield correct answers from the participant, an intricately linked set of HTML Web pages could suffice, and JavaScript or Java solutions are possible. If users should not be able to view the correct response, however, then some method must be employed to shield these from prying eyes. Because JavaScript and Java operate on the client side, for such programs to be able to mark a test, they must contain the correct responses. Knowledgeable participants could examine the code sent to their computer to search for the answers. Regardless of such approaches, a server-side program is still required to accept and collate any results.

Server-side programs are capable of scoring or evaluating submitted data, as well as providing feedback based on submitted results. To do this the feedback to be presented and the correct responses against which participant responses are to be evaluated must reside in or be accessible by the server-side program. Such information can either be compiled into the server-side program or exist within a database that the program consults. In either case, the only real restrictions on the type of answers that are acceptable are limited by the algorithms used to evaluate such answers (Schmidt, 1997a, 1997b).

Multiple-choice questions are easily marked because there is a single correct response. Tailored feedback can be presented based on the participant's response. Multiple-response questions, in which several answers may apply and in which some combination of such answers is correct, are also easily marked.

Fill-in-the-blank and open text responses are more difficult to handle because the programmer must anticipate a range of acceptable responses that users may give. In the case of fill-in-the-blank questions, very flexible comparisons are required between the submitted and expected responses to avoid rejections on the part of the marking program due to spelling variations, case of text, aberrant white space, contractions, or colloquialisms. Providing feedback on fill-in-the-blank responses beyond information presented in response to either correct or incorrect responses is challenging. High-frequency errors could be given tailored replies, though the breakdown of such responses is seldom known in advance of the experiment. The marking of open response text is of course quite complicated and would require extremely advanced techniques to do anything creative.

As mentioned previously, server-side programs are capable of marking online tests or quizzes and of providing summary information (Schmidt,

1997b). Implicit within these capabilities is the evaluation of formulae—in the case of test marking, the formula is simply addition. In the case of providing summary information for the entire set of respondents the formula involves the collation and averaging of responses. Different marking schemes or question weighting can be implemented based on the types of question asked or based on predetermined importance. More elaborate formulae can also be implemented and the results logged or displayed.

One potentially interesting capability is to use a participant's responses in a formula and to return feedback to the participant after the completion of the experiment. Such a manipulation can act as a reward for participating in the first place. For instance, an experiment that is collecting data on a topic such as "gender role," "IQ," or "personality type", could compute and classify a participant based on a custom set of responses to some inventory. These derived scores can be logged along with any other data, possibly saving the experimenter from having to compute them later. Furthermore, tailored feedback can be provided to the participant based on an evaluation of the responses.

Several Web products can assist nonprogrammers in carrying out tests on the Web. Survey Assistant (http://survey.psy.buffalo.edu, Schmidt, 1997b) is a service that allows experimenters access to a server with software capable of building CGI programs that carry out testing or surveys. Customized feedback is available for tests, and participant responses can be logged and summarized immediately after submission. No programming experience is necessary. A comprehensive educational package called WebCT (http://homebrew1.cs.ubc.ca/webct) also does testing and provides a complete online course web environment. Finally Authorware by Macromedia (www.macromedia.com) implements testing, though it requires a plug-in and works only on PC and Macintosh computers (see McGraw et al., chap. 9, this volume).

CONTROL OVER DATA INTEGRITY

The main benefits of using server-side programming are flexibility and control over the client–server interaction. Server-side solutions are flexible because they are executable programs designed and implemented to do specifically what the experimenter demands of the situation. Because they are custom programs they allow the experimenter to control the client–server interaction, thereby garnering confidence in the collected data.

Server-side programming can assist experimenters in controlling who has access to participate in their experiments or to determine demographic information about who has participated. Server-side programs can also be used for estimating experiment completion rates, estimating time for completion, and for controlling the acceptability of collected data.

DATA SECURITY ISSUES

The Web is a heterogeneous environment. In theory, any computer on the Internet can communicate with any other computer on the Internet. Anybody who has access to your site can download and examine the source for the HTML pages that you present. They can request anything of your server, though they may not always be allowed access to it. Because CGI programs are simply programs executed in response to URL requests, anybody on the Internet is free to access them. Nothing prevents others from sending data to your CGI program for processing. Hence, nothing prevents others from attempting to foil your survey results (Schmidt, 1997a). For instance, for very simple experiments a new HTML document could be constructed that uses the same variables as your questionnaire, presents the participant with a different set of questions, and sends the data to your CGI for processing.

For the above reasons it may be desirable to have CGI programs that accept data, check the origin of the HTML document that has directed the client's browser to send data. If the client has accessed an unauthorized document that is trying to send data to your CGI to be processed, or if an unauthorized user is attempting to send your CGI bogus data to collect, then it can be detected (for most clients) by examining the HTTP_REFERER variable (see Table 1). This variable contains the URL of the Web page that is referencing the CGI—hence if it is not one that you have approved, then it is possibly bogus. The CGI program should be written such that data originating from form documents delivered by unauthorized Web servers is flagged and only tentatively accepted or included in the results (Schmidt, 1997a).

One consideration of note is that caching proxy servers will store a copy of your Web documents locally so that when proxy server users request your document, the proxy server returns its local copy instead of accessing yours. This means that replies from caching proxy servers will list the proxy server as the referrer rather than your server. Such data are trustworthy.

There is no guaranteed method of determining whether a server is a proxy; however, it is common protocol to include the name proxy in the machine's domain name (e.g. `spider-tk031.proxy.aol.com`). Because it is impossible to know the names of all the proxies before running your experiment, it is best to save the data from unauthorized sources for further scrutiny. When examining such data, if the referrer is not from a trusted host or a proxy server, then it is questionable.

A second data security issue concerns whether the data that a user submits in confidence reaches the experimenter's computer without any intervening interception. The possibility exists that users with high-level access on computers between the participant and the experiment could intercept and examine data packets containing confidential information. Although this is a remote possibility, the use of a secure server that encrypts the information when sending it could ease worries about the security of the data during transmission. Notifying subjects of this possibility while obtaining informed consent should be sufficient for satisfying American Psychological Association guidelines regarding confidentiality of the data collected.

PASSWORD PROTECTION

Many password protection schemes are available for Web experiments. An obvious password protection method is to use the Web server's built-in facility. Most Web servers allow the administrator to protect particular subtrees of the file system hierarchy using a single password that will allow many people to gain access. Anybody knowing the password can access documents. This is ideal for situations in which an experimenter wishes to provide members of a specified sample with a single password but does not need to track which users have logged on individually. This method simply presents a fairly easy way to keep the majority of the world out.

When it is important that the experimenter knows precisely who in a sample has gained access to the experiment, a server-side program can be written to log and keep track of individuals. The experimenter may wish to distribute a personal identification number (PIN) with each URL they supply to the experiment. The PINs can be computer generated and inserted in e-mail messages personalized for each potential participant. The PIN can be a part of the URL itself (i.e., http://myexpt.com/expt1.exe?PIN=4325, in which case the value 4235 is associated with the variable PIN) or it can be supplied separately from the URL and the respondent can be required to input a PIN to gain access to the protected documents. In either case the server-side program can access the PIN and note in a server-side database that the PIN has been used once the experiment is complete and data have been submitted. The server-side program responsible for keeping track of access can either allow PINs to be used multiple times (as with the built-in server protection scheme) or it could expire the participant's PIN from an experimenter-defined list so that subsequent attempts to access the protected information using the same PIN fail. This scheme can be used to ensure that a given participant can only contribute once to the experiment.

The generation of valid PIN numbers can be done using a mathematical scheme that avoids easily guessing valid PINs in the sequence (e.g., only use values that can be factored by large prime numbers), thereby limiting the likelihood that people can easily guess a valid PIN.

Further safeguards can be taken by logging the Internet protocol (IP) number of successful respondents as well as failed requests. The IP number is a set of four integers in the range 0–255 that uniquely identifies the client's computer on the Internet. The IP number of the client is associated with the REMOTE_ADDR environment variable (see Table 1). It is important to note that the IP number does not uniquely identify the participant because multiple participants can use the same computer to access your experiment either at the same time (in the case of a multiuser machine) or at different times (in the case of a single-user machine). By logging the time of access, the IP number, and the PIN used, an experiment administrator can track odd occurrences as they happen and exclude any data collected through suspicious accesses (i.e., data from a client IP that has already contributed successfully but later results in several failed attempts).

PARTICIPANT SOURCE IDENTIFICATION

It is constructive for experimenters to know how their participants accessed the Web site. In a heterogeneous environment such as the Internet, such knowledge can be important because it can yield clues about the participants which will in turn give insight about potential sampling biases, generalizability of the results and what advertising methods worked best at attracting participants. The methods of attracting participants are limited only by one's imagination and determination. Some potential methods for recruiting subjects are through banner advertising on sites that are likely to get traffic which matches the population that you wish to sample, posting URLs at sites that list other popular sites or sites that list new sites, accidental traffic from search engines, the direct e-mailing of potential participants on a topic-related e-mail list, and posting messages on the Internet relay channel or on targeted newsgroups.

When a participant is referred to your site through the Web (i.e., they click on a banner or on a link that brings them to you) the contents of the HTTP_REFERER environment variable (see Table 1) contains the URL of the Web page that the participant was transferred from. Hence the first request to your Web server supplies the URL of the site which referred a participant to your experiment. Subsequent calls to your server will have URLs from your own site as the referrer. All of this information can also be logged by the Web server alone. In the case of participants who arrived as the result of non-Web advertisements, there is no referring Web page information, and the server log has no record of how such participants found the experiment. To circumvent this problem and to give the experimenter a direct account of how a participant was recruited the experimenter can provide identifying information of the source of the participant with the URL that is advertised. Unique identifying information can be included after a question mark at the end of a URL, and this information has no bearing on the server's performance. By identifying each potential source of participants with a different code after the URL, an experimenter can simply examine log files for the frequency of requests associated with those URLs. For instance, if I have advertised my study on gaming in a gaming newsgroup with the URL http://gamestudy.com?id = 1 and have a banner on a gaming Web site linked to the URL http://gamestudy.com?id = 2, I can simply count the number of requests associated with each of these URLs and I know how many participants came from each source.

Although the aforementioned information is stored in the log of the Web server, not all Web server users have access to such logs, and determining precisely what happened from such logs can be difficult. Server-side programs are well situated to keep track of such information in a database that is specially designed for the experiment. The distributed URL could be to a document containing a SSI program that keeps track of the frequency of requests from various potential sources. This can be done by having the SSI access the "id" variable in the case of the gaming example. If the URL does not contain the information in the form of a variable and value pair (i.e., "id = 1") then the program can extract the information by parsing the PATH_INFO environment variable (see Table 1) to examine the extra information that was supplied after the base URL. The same SSI program could be responsible for other tasks as well, such as some of the password protection or PIN schemes outlined previously.

DOMAIN RESTRICTION

In addition to identifying those who select to participate, server-side programs can help restrict participants to smaller groups of individuals based on certain criteria (Schmidt, 1997a). If the circumstances of a particular Web experiment require that only an easily identifiable population on the Internet be allowed to participate, then domain restriction techniques may be of interest. Domain restriction refers to limiting participation to a particular geographically or organizationally defined domain of Internet users. For instance if one wished to limit participation to people from accredited academic institutions in the United States then only participants accessing the experiment from computers whose domain name ended in .edu could be allowed access.

Note that due to the nature of the Internet this method does not actually constrain people geographically, but it does ensure that they have access privileges from a particular geographical locale (i.e., that they are authorized to use a computer at a particular organization). In a similar fashion, respondents could be restricted to being associated with a particular university (i.e., coming from .buffalo.edu to constrain respondents to being from the University at Buffalo). If an experiment targets participants from a particular country, then the country domain endings (such as .ca for Canada or .uk for the United Kingdom) can be used as a criterion for accepting participants. Obviously, combinations of such criteria can apply—hence one could limit the survey to people of the Commonwealth countries.

Domain restriction is accomplished using either SSI or CGI programs to deliver the experiment. These programs would first examine the contents of the REMOTE_HOST environment variable and parse out the suffix. A decision regarding whether or not to allow participation or whether or not to accept or include submitted data in the results could be made on the basis of the suffix. If the REMOTE_HOST cannot be identified, then the IP number of the client's computer will appear in this variable. It should be noted that this method is rather coarse: legitimate members of a target population attempting to access the server from other domains would be rejected. Nonetheless, domain restriction provides an easy way to better control or identify the population that contributes data to a Web research project.

Note that the information supplied by the REMOTE_HOST environment variable gives an alternative way of characterizing the population that the experiment has sampled. As such, this information could supply valuable insight into the results and is worth logging for future reference. An experiment on reading comprehension, for example, may experience peculiar results due to the overrepresentation of respondents from non-English-speaking countries. An experimenter that has logged the host information could then systematically investigate the influence that this subgroup of respondents had on the results.

Domain restriction techniques are limited because Internet domain naming conventions are limited and rather unrestrained. Restriction of participants on many other factors simply relies on trusting them to abide by your requests or requiring that they provide some sort of proof before they are allowed to participate. For instance, restricting a study to persons under 18 years of age relies on the honesty of a potential participant, though further measures such as taking and validating credit card information could be used.

EXPERIMENT COMPLETION RATES

In addition to tracking sources of participants and controlling who can gain access to a Web experiment, server-side programs can also be used to determine experimental completion rates. This refers to the proportion of potential participants that may have started a Web experiment and actually finished as opposed to quitting while only partly finished. This information is important for at least two reasons. First, it is important to know that people can participate. If a large portion of volunteers were unable to complete your experiment, there may be some systematic reason why (i.e., it may have too many questions, or they may have been using the same version of a Web browser which possessed some sort of bug that prevented them from completing your experiment). Insight into such problems may help provide insight into the data (good or bad) or provoke an adjustment of the experiment presentation methods. Second, experiment completion rates allow direct comparison to completion rates for other Web studies and more traditional experimental work.

Experiment completion rates can be tracked using some of the same techniques outlined earlier. When a participant begins the experiment in earnest (i.e., after they have supplied informed consent), they can be counted as having begun the experiment and once they have completed the experiment, and submitted data, the case can be counted as complete. The same SSI and CGI programs discussed previously can implement this sort of capability by modifying the appropriate server-side database.

TIME FOR COMPLETION

Server-side programs are capable of determining and recording the time that a submission is made. This can be used to compute the amount of time that a participant took from start to finish on a given page. As with experiment completion, a SSI program can note the time that a respondent started, and this information can be used in the derivation of the total amount of elapsed time until the final responses are submitted. To do this, a running time total would need to be passed along from one page of the survey to the next, with the amount of time taken to respond to a page to be added at each step. The start time of each page would have to be encoded and passed along as well. For time-limited experiments or tests, submissions beyond the allowable interval can be rejected or ignored, or they can be accepted and flagged for further examination by the experimenter.

ERROR CHECKING

A capability that was not discussed in the introductory example, but that can go even further toward improving the quality of the collected information, is run-time error checking. A server-side program has to accept and record data, so it can also ensure that any and all questions that the experimenter deems necessary to be answered have a response. Any questions for which this is not the case either can be presented a second time or the participant can be informed that they must back up and supply answers before the data are accepted. This can prevent accidentally missed questions and incomplete data sets.

JavaScript provides a good client-side solution to error checking as well. Because JavaScript is simply text, JavaScript routines can be delivered by the same server-side program that presented the original HTML. One benefit of using JavaScript routines for error checking is that it occurs on the client side before the data are passed to the server, resulting in lower processing demands on the server machine and less of a wait for the participant to find out they have made an error. As mentioned earlier, drawbacks of using JavaScript involve an assumption that clients will have adequate technology and browser configurations that take advantage of this language. There is nothing prohibiting the combined use of JavaScript and server-side run-time error checking. Should the user's configuration be incapable of handling the JavaScript solution, then the server-side program will catch any problems.

Even more complex comparisons or requirements of submitted data can made through the use of server-side programming. For instance, the participant can be asked to supply textual input that can be examined before it is accepted or before the participant is allowed to continue. Participants can be screened to ensure that their answers to a particular question are in an acceptable range (i.e., age) or contain acceptably formatted text (i.e., an e-mail address). This capability makes server-side programs ideal for implementing control over participant responses, or even over participant samples. This is precisely one method outlined earlier regarding password protection and PINs.

MULTIPLE SUBMISSION FILTERING

In addition to checking for response omissions, the server-side program can also check for multiple response submissions from the same person. Often duplicate (or repeated) submission of the same information from a client occurs. To ensure that repeated submissions are not included in online summaries of results that may be presented, or even to simply prevent the recording of such information in the data file, the server-side program can filter out redundant submissions at the time they occur. This feature is referred to as multiple submission filtering (Schmidt, 1997a).

In the simplest and most frequently occurring case of duplicate submissions, a participant submits responses then submits them again. A server-side program cannot be guaranteed to receive these two submissions in succession, however, because in the time between the submissions, any number of other data sets could have arrived. Hence the most comprehensive method for filtering duplicate submissions is to search the entire set of collected data for a submission from the same IP number, with the same set of responses. In all likelihood, simply searching and comparing the last half dozen responses will suffice as psychology experiments do not tend to collect data at an overwhelming rate.

Simple comparisons between recent and previously submitted data may not always work because some participants may not only resubmit their data, but resubmit it slightly modified. Unfortunately, it is not good enough solution to simply ignore subsequent submissions from a computer at a particular IP number because (1) it could be the case that two respondents legitimately participated one after the other from the same computer, and (2) many Internet service providers rotate IP numbers dynamically, which means that a computer assigned an IP at one time is not necessarily the same computer using the IP at a later time.

To circumvent these problems, more complex exclusion criteria should be used. For instance, one might set a minimal number of data points that should differ between a previous and the current submission from a client at a particular IP number. This ensures that, at least to foil the server-side program, a user would have to make an extensive effort. An even more elaborate filtering scheme would be to flag duplicate submissions based on the time of submission. If it takes a fixed amount of time to complete the Web experiment, time between duplicate submissions coupled with the amount of duplication in the responses could be used to differentiate attempts to foil the survey from legitimate submissions in cases that are associated with a single IP number. In any case, all duplicate submissions from a given IP number can be flagged for experimenter inspection. If many submissions have been received and the IP is not associated with a multiuser computer, then there is a good chance that they are invalid.

MISCELLANEOUS ISSUES

Two remaining issues will be discussed in this final section. First, it may be desirable to allow participants to complete a Web experiment across several sessions. Two methods for accomplishing this are discussed. Second, server-side performance issues are presented.

FINISHING AN EXPERIMENT STARTED PREVIOUSLY

One capability that is often desirable is to allow people to begin participating in an experiment and to come back to it at a later time to finish. Obviously such experiments are unlikely to be concerned with the overall time that a subject takes, though they could still be concerned about the completion time of individual pages of questions. The capability of bridging multiple sessions is perhaps easiest to provide in situations where each participant is identified beforehand and tracked with a PIN. In this case, the server can save all of the data submitted from the participant and, upon the participant's return and after the PIN has been approved, can present only unfinished aspects of the experimental task. This method is fairly resource intensive because it requires tracking participants and storing partially complete data associated with each PIN. The programming involved in such a venture is likely not to be profitable in all experimental situations, though it will work regardless of the browser being used on the client computer.

An easier method of implementing the ability of participants to continue contributing data to an experiment across sessions can be accomplished using "cookies." The term "cookie" refers to information associated with a given server-side program that is stored on the client's computer. This information can be sent to the server when it is requested and the participant need not do anything to cause this transaction to take place. After each portion of a Web experiment is finished, the server-side program can instruct the client's computer to store a cookie with the participant's responses up to that point encoded within it. When the participant accesses the program again, the cookie can be retrieved, complete with the responses that were made and the server-side program can continue presenting information where it left off on the previous call.

Unfortunately not all browsers support cookies, and participants need to have this feature enabled. Some Web browsers warn when a server is about to send a cookie to the browser and explicitly ask the participant whether to accept the cookie or not, so there is no guarantee that this method will work in all cases. One further caveat with cookies: because the cookie is stored on the client computer and resubmitted to the server at a later time, this feature will only work when the participant accesses the experiment using the same computer system across sessions. Cookies can be set to expire if they have been on a system too long—so limits can be set on how long between sessions a participant can wait before having to complete the experiment from scratch.

SERVER - SIDE PERFORMANCE ISSUES

Although most psychology Web experiments are unlikely to attract enough participants that they would present the problem of overloading a Web server, there are several options available to improve server-side performance. Each time that a server-side program is run it needs to be loaded into memory and initiated. When each client—server interaction relies on running such a program, a slow server response may discourage the most impatient potential participants. In the case of many languages used for server-side programming (such as Perl, Tcl, or Python) the program is a script that is first compiled before being executed by a run-time interpreter. The loading and unloading of such interpreters each time the server-side program executes can be costly if several such programs are starting simultaneously. Although large computer memories improve performance greatly, there are also software solutions.

If Perl (www.perl.com) is the programming language in use on the server-side, the freely available Apache Mod-Perl server can be used. This modified version of the popular Apache (www.apache.org) Web server maintains compiled versions of server-side include and common gateway interface programs in memory, as well as embodying the Perl interpreter. When a server-side program is run, it executes seamlessly rather than requiring expensive run-time overhead. Performance improvements on busy Web sites can be as much as 500% over a server without the Apache Mod-Perl software.

A new method of improving server-side program performance that has recently matured is Java "servlet" technology. Java servlets are precompiled server-side Java programs that integrate seamlessly into Web servers that support them (again, modified versions of the Apache Web server support such technology). As with the Mod-Perl solution described above, Java servlets dispose of overhead associated with the creation of a run-time environment for the server-side program.

PROGRAMMING FOR SPEED AND STABILITY

Server-side programs can be executed frequently, so it is important that they are well written. Heavy processing jobs, such as averaging the results of thousands of subjects' data can be time-consuming. Server-side programs should take measures to accomplish such tasks in a computationally efficient manner. Averaging, for instance, can rely on a separate database containing running totals rather than laboriously recomputing totals. With the addition of new information the program can simply update that database and compute the average from it in a single step rather than requiring one computational step for each piece of subject data. Wherever possible, such short-cut programming techniques should be used to avoid making a participant wait (and possibly leave).

Another server-side issue that needs to be addressed on many operating systems is the problem of file collisions. If two running versions of a program attempt to access a file simultaneously, they are said to collide. Some scheme needs to be worked out so that both programs do not try to modify the same file, otherwise data loss or corruption can occur. The best programming approach to take under these circumstances is to implement file-locking. Under this scenario when the server-side program is about to access a file it locks out other processes from accessing the file. Once it has finished with the file it unlocks it so that other processes can now access it. If the program attempts to access a locked file, either it or the operating system must wait until the file becomes available before it can use the file.

A security threat to server systems running CGI programs concerns the possibility that devious users could hack into the system through poorly written CGI programs. There are two main security holes related to CGI execution. The first security risk occurs when a CGI program executes a program on the server using information supplied as input from a Web client. To guard against this, languages such as Perl (www.perl.com) have the ability to forbid this sort of action. The second sort of CGI security problem occurs when a CGI program is given data that causes it to crash and it exits into a command line shell associated with the Web session. If this occurs, then scrupulous users have the ability to operate other programs on the server.

To guard against a CGI security threat, the Web server can be run as a separate user with minimal permissions. This way, even if hacker gains access, he will have little ability to further jeopardize the system. A second way to guard against a CGI security problem is to ensure that CGI programs are written to take open-ended information from clients. Poor programming that does not check bounds and limits is generally a problem with compiled languages (such as C) that require the programmer to declare limits at compile time but do not ensure that those limits are enforced at the time of execution. Finally, running the CGI programs on a single-user system without a command-line (e.g., MacOS) ensures that even if they should exit, there is no shell for them to exit into.

CONCLUSION

The importance of server-side programming should now be clear. Whenever the server is involved in receiving and recording data or in making decisions based upon participant-submitted responses, server-side programming is required. Server-side programming can be used to improve the quality of data collected, control and identify the participants sampled, and guard against tampering.

If experimenters are to avoid placing technological requirements on potential participants then server-side programming is the only alternative to client-side solutions such as Java and JavaScript. Requiring that potential participants have a computer system and Internet access capable of sustaining features available only in the latest versions of graphical browsers would otherwise limit the selection of potential participants. The use of newer client-side technology in Internet experiments makes a major assumption that participants have the technology appropriately installed and configured (or are willing and capable of installing and configuring their systems in order to participate). Furthermore, such solutions still require server-side programming for data collection. Placing more computations on the server-side allows all people with Web access to participate regardless of technological sophistication. This latter approach plays to the lowest common denominator between client–server technology, thereby allowing the greatest potential for participants to access the experiment.

ACKNOWLEDGMENT

The writing of this paper was supported by NSERC Canada.

REFERENCES

Georgia Tech's Graphics, Visualization, and Usability Center. (1999). *GVU's WWW user surveys* [Online]. Available URL: http://www.cc.gatech.edu/gvu/user_surveys/

Schmidt, W. C. (1997a). World-Wide Web survey research: Benefits, potential problems, and solutions. *Behavior Research Methods, Instruments & Computers, 29*, 274–279.

Schmidt, W. C. (1997b). World-Wide Web survey research made easy with "WWW Survey Assistant." *Behavior Research Methods, Instruments, & Computers, 29*, 303–304.

GLOSSARY OF WEB TERMS

BBS bulletin board system; software on a remote computer, usually accessed by modem, which allows users to download files and read and post messages in asynchronous "conferences."

Caching proxy server a proxy server that keeps copies of Web pages locally so that if it receives a URL request for a page of which it has a copy, it can quickly return the page without having to contact the Internet; caching proxy servers decrease the amount of Web traffic from an ISP and often respond more quickly than fetching the Web page over the Internet.

CGI common gateway interface; protocol by which information is encoded on the user's computer to be sent to the server computer.

CGI script or program common gateway interface program; any program that accepts information in CGI format; common applications for CGI programs are to store user data, process them, and return a dynamic reply.

Chat room similar to an IRC channel, it allows users to "chat" in real time. These are usually conducted via the WWW.

Client any application that is used to request information from a server (i.e., a Web browser, FTP program, custom-written application, etc.); can also refer to the user of the program.

Cookie the server can instruct a cookie-enabled Web browser to store information as a file on the client's computer. This file is called a cookie and is sent by the client to the server with all subsequent requests, even requests made months later. By modifying a cookie's contents, the Web server can save information on the client for future use.

DNS domain naming system or service; domain names are easier to remember but the Internet is really based on IP addresses. DNS converts domain names, such as www.modsoft.com, into IP addresses, such as 207.215.231.99. If one DNS server does not know a particular domain translation, it asks another one, until the correct IP address is returned.

Domain all computers similarly named on the Internet share a common organization referred to as their domain. For instance, all computers ending in .com share a domain.

Flame a hostile or abusive message or response.

Form HTML tag that allows two-way communication between user and Web pages. It supports text boxes, radio buttons, etc. Forms can be used to send information between client and server, and they can also be used to send information from a client to an e-mail address.

FTF face to face; abbreviation used in electronic discussions.

FTP file transfer protocol; method for sending files from one computer to another.

GUI graphical user interface; the interface found in most modern operating systems and applications, in contrast to textual interfaces such as DOS.

HTML hypertext markup language; a tag-based language used to create Web pages. Links put the "hyper" in hypertext.

HTTP hypertext transfer protocol; The protocol used by the WWW to send files between a server computer and the client's browser.

Internet network of computers that exchange files by HTTP, FTP, e-mail, and other protocols.

IP Address internet protocol address; a unique numerical address assigned to each computer or node on the Internet; e.g., 207.215.231.99.

IRC internet relay chat; a network allowing users to "chat" in real-time, in groups known as channels.

ISP internet service provider; a company that provides access to the Internet.

Java programming language supported by most browsers; an object-oriented language that is platform independent and implemented within Web browsers. Java programs can be served to run on Web clients. Java programs are compiled by the author and delivered via the Web, where they are (theoretically) interpreted equally by different browsers on different computer platforms.

JavaScript scripting language, similar to but distinct from Java, usually delivered as source code included in Web pages and interpreted by the browser. JavaScript allows for greater flexibility in the presentation and processing of data on the client computer.

MOO mud, object oriented—a type of MUD.

MUD multiuser domain (or dungeon); classically a text-based fantasy adventure game which many users can play simultaneously, interacting in a "virtual world."

Netiquette net-etiquette; normative online behavior generally accepted by most users as proper.

Newsgroup collection of Usenet articles related to a specific topic (indicated by the name of the newsgroup). Newsgroups are organized in hierarchies and follow set naming conventions, e.g., sci.psychology.research is a group in the "Science" hierarchy dedicated to discussion of psychology research.

Perl practical extraction and report language; a popular, free computer language for implementing CGI programs. PERL is flexible and specializes in the ability to easily manipulate alphanumeric string information.

Proxy server a server situated between a client (e.g., Web browser), and other servers. It intercepts requests to other servers and takes action based on those requests, such as logging the request or contacting the target server itself and relaying the information back to the client.

Server a computer that serves (sends) files to clients, usually by FTP, HTTP, or e-mail.

Spam unsolicited e-mail—essentially, computer junk mail.

SSI server-side include; an HTML directive that instructs the Web server to dynamically substitute information where the directive occurs.

Telnet software protocol for connecting a remote terminal to a host computer.

URL uniform resource locator; global address of files on the Internet. The first part of the address indicates what protocol to use, and the second part specifies the IP address or domain name where the resource is located.

Usenet network of computers (NNTP, or "news" servers) which exchange articles posted to newsgroups.

WWW World Wide Web; a collection of networked computers that exchange files by HTTP.

WYSIWYG what you see is what you get; refers to editors that allow the user to see how the finished document will appear while it is being created.

INDEX